GW00493787

THE COMPLETE
ECHOES FROM THE GNOSIS

by G.R.S.Mead
edited by Stephen Ronan

THE GNOSIS OF THE MIND : THE HYMNS OF HERMES
THE VISION OF ARIDAEUS : THE MYSTERIES OF MITHRA
A MITHRAIC RITUAL : THE HYMN OF THE ROBE OF GLORY
THE HYMN OF JESUS : THE GNOSTIC CRUCIFIXION
THE CHALDEAN ORACLES volumes I & II
THE WEDDING SONG OF WISDOM

All Eleven Volumes of the Original Series
Together with A CONCORDANCE TO THE CHALDEAN ORACLES

CHTHONIOS BOOKS

1987

Originally published in separate volumes
London & Benares 1906 - 1908

First complete edition with additional material
© 1987 CHTHONIOS BOOKS
Additional material © Stephen Ronan 1987

British Library Cataloguing in Publication Data

The complete echoes from the Gnosis.
1. Gnosticism
1. Mead, G.R.S.   II. Ronan, Stephen
299'.932   BT1390

ISBN 0 - 948366 - 06 - 0

CONTENTS

ECHOES FROM THE GNOSIS.

Under this general title it is proposed to publish a series of small volumes, drawn from, or based upon, the mystic, theosophic and gnostic writings of the ancients, so as to make more easily audible for the ever-widening circle of those who love such things, some echoes of the mystic experiences and initiatory lore of their spiritual ancestry. There are many who love the life of the spirit, and who long for the light of gnostic illumination, but who are not sufficiently equipped to study the writings of the ancients at first hand, or to follow the labours of scholars unaided. These little volumes are therefore intended to serve as introduction to the study of the more difficult literature of the subject, and it is hoped that at the same time they may become for some, who have, as yet, not even heard of the Gnosis, stepping-stones to higher things.

G. R. S. M.

THE GNOSIS OF . . . . THE MIND. .

The references in this volume are to the recently-published work—*Thrice Greatest Hermes: Studies in Hellenistic Theosophy and Gnosis. Being a Translation of the Extant Sermons and Fragments of the Trismegistic Literature, with Prolegomena, Commentaries and Notes,* 3 vols. (London, 1906).

THE GNOSIS OF THE MIND.

THE GNOSIS OF THE MIND.

For long I have been spending much of my time in a world of great beauty of thought and purity of feeling, created by the devotion and intelligence of one of the many theosophical fraternities of the ancient world. They called themselves disciples of Thrice-greatest Hermes, and sometimes spoke of their faith as the Religion of the Mind. They were prior to and contemporary with the origins and earliest centuries of Christianity, and they lived in Egypt.

What remains of their scriptures and what can be gleaned of their endeavour has recently been made accessible in the English tongue, in such fashion as I have been able to reproduce their thought and interpret it. The labour of many months is ended; the task of reproduction is accomplished, and the echoes of the Gnosis of Thrice-greatest Hermes are audible across the centuries for English ears in fuller volume than before, and I hope in greater clarity.

It is no small thing—this Gnosis of ten-thousand-times-great Hermes, as Zosimus in an ecstasy of enthusiasm calls Him; for it has as its foundation the Single Love of God, it endeavours to base itself upon the True Philosophy and Pure Science of Nature and of Man, and is indeed one of the fairest forms of the Gnosis of the Ages. It is replete with Wisdom (Theosophia) and Worship (Theosebeia) in harmony—the Religion of the Mind. It is in its beginning Religion, true devotion and piety and worship, based on the right activity and passivity of the Mind, and its end is the Gnosis of things-that-are and the Path of the Good that leads man unto God.

Do I claim too much for the Gnosis of Thrice-greatest Hermes? I do but echo what He teaches in His own words (or rather those of His disciples) turned into English speech. The claim made is for the Gnosis, not for the forms of its expression used by its learners and hearers. All these forms of expression, the many sermons, or sacred discourses, of the disciples of this Way, are but means to lead men towards the Gnosis; they are not the Gnosis itself. True, much that is set forth appears to me to be very beautifully expressed, and I have been delighted with many a thought and phrase that these nameless writers and thinkers of years long ago have handed down to us in the fair Greek tongue; all this however, is as a garment that hides the all-beautiful natural form and glory of the Truth.

What is of importance is that all these Theosophists of the Trismegistic tradition declare with one voice—a sweet voice, that carries with it conviction within, to the true knower in our inmost soul—that there is Gnosis and Certitude, full and inexhaustible, no matter how the doubting mind, opinion, the counterfeit mind, may weave its magic of contrary appearances about us.

Seeing, then, that I have now much in mind of what has been written of this Religion of the Mind, I would set down a few thoughts thereon as they occur to me, an impression or two that the contemplation of the beautiful sermons of the disciples of the Master-Mind has engraved upon my memory.

3

THE GNOSIS OF THE MIND.

And first of all I would say that I regard it as a great privilege to have been permitted by the Gods to be a hander-on in some small way of these fair things; for indeed it is a great privilege and high honour to be allowed in any fashion to forward the preparation for the unveiling of the beauties of the Gnosis in the hearts of one's fellows,—even in so insignificant a way as that of translating and commenting on that which has already been set forth by greater minds in greater beauty centuries ago. The feeling that arises is one of joy and thankfulness that so pleasant a task has been granted by the Providence of God as a respite on the way (to use a phrase of Plotinus'). And so, as in all sacred acts, we begin with praise and thankfulness to God, as Hermes teaches us.

But when is there (the disciple of the Master will interject) an act that is not sacred for one who is a " man " and not a " procession of Fate " ? He who is coming unto himself, who from the unconscious and the dead is beginning to return to consciousness and rise into life, self-consecrates his every act for ever deeper realisation of the mystery of his divine nature; for now no longer is he an embryo within the womb, nourished in all things by the Mother-Soul, but a man-babe new-born, breathing the freer spirit of the greater life, the cosmic airs of the Father-Mind. And so it is that every act and function of the body should be consecrated to the Soul and Mind; the traveller on this Way should pray unceasingly, by devoting his every act unto his God; thinking when eating : As this food nourishes the body, so may the Bread of Wisdom nourish the mind; or when bathing : As this water purifies the body, so may the Water of Life vivify the mind; or when freeing the body of impurities : As these impurities pass from the body, so may the refuse of opinion pass from the mind !

Not, however, that he should think that anything is in itself unclean or common, for all is of the divine substance and of mother-matter; this he already knows in his heart of hearts, but his lower members are not as yet knit together in right harmony; they are as yet awry, not centred in the perfect whole. He as yet sees things from only one point; he has not yet realised that *the* Point is everywhere, and that for every-thing there is a point of view whence it is true and right and beautiful and good. That all-embracing point of view is the one sense, all-sense, the common sense, the sense of the intelligence, in which the sensible and the intelligible are identical and not apart. It is the little mind, the mind in man, the fate-pro-cession, that creates external duality; the Great Mind knows that the without and the within are twain in one, are self-conditioned complements, the one within the other and without the other at one and the same time.

In this Religion of the Mind there is no opposition of the heart and head. It is not a cult of intellect alone, it is not a cult of emotion alone; it is the Path of Devotion and Gnosis inseparably united, the true Sacred Marriage of Soul and Mind, of Life and Light, the ineffable union of God the Mother and God the Father in the Divine Man, the Logos, the Alone-Begotten of the Mystery of Mysteries, the All and One—Ineffability and Effability eternally in simultaneous Act and Passion.

And if you should object to the word Mind as excluding other names of equal

4

THE GNOSIS OF THE MIND.

dignity, know that this also has been spoken of again and again by the disciples of Thrice-greatest Hermes.

He has no name, for He is the One of many names, nay, He is the One of all names, for He is Name itself and all things else, and there is naught that is not He. Nor is He One alone, though He is the One and Only One, for He is All and Nothing, if such a thing as nothing there can be.

But we, because of our ignorance, call Him Mind, for Mind is that which knows, and ignorance seeks ever for its other self, and the other self of ignorance is Gnosis. And seeking Gnosis, whether it love or hate its own false view of what it seeks, ignorance is ever changing into some form of knowing, experiencing some novelty or other as it thinks, not knowing that it is experiencing itself. But Mind is not only that which knows, but also the object of all knowledge; for it knows itself alone, there being nothing else to know but Mind. It self-creates itself to know itself, and to know itself it must first not know itself. Mind thus makes ignorance and Gnosis, but is not either in itself. It is itself the Mystery that makes all mysteries in order that it may be self-initiate in all.

Thus we are taught that Mind, the Great Initiator, is Master of all masterhood, Master of all ignorance as well as knowledge. And so we find the Supreme addressing one of His Beloved Sons, one who has won the mastery of self, as " Soul of my Soul and Mind of My own Mind."

The Religion of the Mind is preeminently one of initiation, of perpetual perfectioning. The vista of possibility opened up to the mind's eye of the neophyte into these sacred rites transcends credibility. One asks oneself again and again : Can this be true ? It seems too good to be true.

But how can it be " too good " (the Master smiles in reply) when the inevitable end of everything is the Perfection of perfection, The Good Itself ?

It cannot be too good, for that which is too good is out of its own self; but with the Good there is neither too little nor too much, it is Perfection.

What then, we feebly ask, is imperfection ? And in the Master-Presence we cannot but reply : It is the doubt "It is too good" that is the imperfection of our nature; we fear it cannot be for us, not knowing that the "little one " who catches some glimpse of the vista, the earnest of the Vision Glorious, sees not something without, but that which is within himself. It is all there potentially, the full Sonship of the Father. It *is* there and here and everywhere, for it is the nature of our very being.

The first glimpse of this Divine possibility is brought to the consciousness of the prepared disciple by the immediate Presence and Glory of the Master, according to the records of the followers of the Religion of the Mind. But who is the Master ? Is He someone without us ; is He some other one ; is He some teacher who sets forth a formal instruction ?

Not so. " This race," that is to say, he who is born in this natural way, " is never taught, but when the time is ripe, its memory is restored by God." It is not therefore some new thing ; it is not the becoming of something or other ; it is a return to the same, we become what we have ever been. The dream is ended and we wake to life.

And so in one of the marvellous

5

THE GNOSIS OF THE MIND.

descriptions of initiation handed on in the Trismegistic sermons, in which the disciple is reborn, or born in Mind, he is all amazed that his "father" and initiator here below should remain there before him just as he ever was in his familiar form, while the efficacious rite is perfected by his means. The "father" of this "son" is the link, the channel of the Gnosis; the true initiation is performed by the Great Initiator, the Mind.

And that this is so may be learned from another sermon, in which a disciple of a higher grade is initiated without any intermediate link; by himself, alone as far as any physical presence of another is concerned, he is embraced by the Great Presence and instructed in the mystery.

The office of the "father" is to bring the "son" to union with himself, so that he may be born out of ignorance into Gnosis, born in Mind, his Highest Self, and so become Son of the Father indeed.

What is most striking in the whole of the tradition of the Mind-doctrine is its impersonal nature. In this it stands out in sharp contrast with the popular Christianity and other saving cults contemporary with it. It is true that the sermons are set forth mostly in the form of instruction of teacher to pupil. We learn to love Hermes and Asclepius and Tat and Ammon, and become friends with all of them in turn; they seem to be living men, with well-marked characters. But they are not historical characters; they are types. There is an Ammon, a Tat, an Asclepius, and a Hermes, in each one of us, and that is why we learn to love them. The "holy four" are in the shrine of our hearts; but transcending all, embracing all, is the Shepherd of all men, the Love

Divine that through the lips of our Hermes teaches us—as Asclepius or Tat or Ammon—as we have ears to hear the words of power, or eyes to see the gnostic splendour of the teaching.

Nay, more than this; such instruction, beautiful and true as it may be, is not the highest teaching of the Mind. They who are born in Mind, are taught by Mind by every act and every thought and every sensation. The Mind eternally instructs the man through body, soul and mind; for now the man begins to know through all of these, for he is changing from the little mind and soul and body that he was to the Great Body and Great Soul and Mind of the Great Man. He no longer seeks a teacher, for all things teach him, or rather the One Teacher teaches him through all. All that there is transforms itself for him into the nature of the Gnosis of the Good.

No longer is he a hearer, but the Hearer; for he has ears on all sides to hear the voice of Nature, Spouse of the Divine, in everything that breathes and all that seems to have no life—the simultaneous winter and summer of the Lord.

No longer is he a seer, but the Seer; for he has eyes on all sides to see the beauty of the whole, and fairest things in things that are most foul.

No longer is he a doer, but the Doer; for all he does is consecrated to the Lord who dedicates Himself to acting in the man.

And so all of his senses and his energies are set on the Great Work of self-initiation in the Mysteries of God; his life becomes illumined by the glory of perpetual perfectioning, and he no longer thinks that he has ever been other than now he is. For memory is ever present with him, and the memory of the Mind is of the

THE GNOSIS OF THE MIND.

nature of eternity, which transcends all time and sees all past and future and all present in the instant that endures for evermore.

And what does the Religion of the Mind teach us of God, the universe and man? It teaches us many things of great solemnity and joyous presage; but one thing especially it seems to teach, and that is the impossibility of human speech to tell the mystery. For every man is but a letter in the language of the Gods; so that all that a man may write, no matter how well stocked his mind may be with systems of the world or of theology, or with the science of the human state, no matter how exactly he may reproduce his thought and trick it forth in fairest human language—all that he can express is but a single letter of his Word. The Words of God are written with the general purposed acts of men, and are not uttered by their individual spoken speech or penned with written words. The Words of God are spoken by the energies of Nature, and are not written on the surfaces of things; the surfaces of things are scribbled over with the false appearances that men project from their unknowing minds.

How then can men describe the universe, except by their inscribing of themselves upon the fields of space? To describe the universe as it is they must become the universe, and then they will describe themselves; and to describe themselves they will be able to discover no better way than that in which the universe gives utterance to itself. It speaks perpetually the Language of the Gods, the Universal Tongue, for it is God for ever giving utterance unto Himself.

The Tongue of the Eternal is the Mind of God. It is by Mind, the Reason of His Self-subsistence, that He perpetually speaks forth all things.

Thus we learn that the Religion of the Mind is pre-eminently the Religion of the Logos, and throughout the whole of our Trismegistic tractates no name comes more frequently before us than the word Logos. For the Logos is the Word of God, not in the sense of a single Word, but the Word in the sense of the Universal Scripture of all worlds and of all men.

And so it is that Hermes is the Scribe of the Gods. Not that Hermes is one of the Gods who is a scribe for the rest, as though they could not write themselves; but Hermes is the Logos of God, and the Words he writes are Gods.

We men are letters of our Word or our God; for man has the glorious destiny before him, nay, the actuality even now in his universal nature, of being a God, a Divine Being, of the nature of Gnosis and Joy and Subsistence. That Word has written itself many times in the world, now one letter and now another; it spells itself in many ways, in sequences of lives of men, and of other lives as well.

And time will be when each and every God-Word, in its own proper turn, will sound forth in all its glory, not letter by letter, but the whole Word simultaneously on earth; and a Christ will be born and all Nature will rejoice, and the world of men will know or be ignorant according to the nature of the times and the manner of the utterance of the Word.

Such are some of the ideas aroused by some of the leading conceptions of the Religion of the Mind, or the Pure Philosophy, or Single Love, as the disciples of Thrice-greatest Hermes called their Theosophy some nineteen centuries ago.

7

THE GNOSIS OF THE MIND.

The most general term, however, by which they named their science and philosophy and religion was Gnosis; it occurs in almost every sermon and excerpt and fragment of their literature which we possess. The doctrine and the discipline of Mind, the Feeder of men and Shepherd of man's soul, are summed up in that fairest word—Gnosis.

Let us then briefly consider the meaning of the name as the followers of this Way understood it. Gnosis is Knowledge; but not discursive knowledge of the nature of the multifarious arts and sciences known in those days or in our own. On this " noise of words," these multifarious knowledges of the appearances of things and vain opinions, the followers of the True Science and Pure Philosophy looked with resignation ; while those of them who were still probationers treated them with even less tolerance, declaring that they left such things to the " Greeks "; for " Egyptians," of course, nothing but Wisdom could suffice.

At any rate this is how one of the less instructed editors of one of the collections of our sermons phrases it. For him Egypt was the Sacred Land and the Egyptians the Chosen Race ; while the Greeks were upstarts and shallow reasoners. The like-natured Jew of the period, on the other hand, called the body " Egypt," while Judæa was the Holy Land, and Palestine the Promised Land, and Israel the Chosen of God ; and so the game went merrily on, as it does even unto this day.

But the real writers of the sermons knew otherwise. Gnosis for them was superior to all distinction of race ; for the Gnostic was precisely he who was reborn, regenerate, into *the* Race, the Race of true Wisdom-lovers, the Kinship

of the Divine Fatherhood. Gnosis for them began with the Knowledge of Man, to be consummated at the end of the perfectioning by the Knowledge of God or Divine Wisdom.

This Knowledge was far other than the knowledge or science of the world. Not, however, that the latter was to be despised ; for all things are true or untrue, according to our point of view. If our standpoint is firmly centred in the True, all things can be read in their true meaning ; whereas if we wander in error, all things, even the truest, become misleading for us.

The Gnosis began, continued and ended in the knowledge of one's self, the reflection of the Knowledge of the One Self, the All Self. So that if we say that Gnosis was other than the science of the world, we do not mean that it excluded anything, but only that it regarded all human arts and sciences as insufficient, incomplete, imperfect.

Indeed it is quite evident on all hands that the writers of the Trismegistic tractates, in setting forth their intuitions of the things-that-are, and in expressing the living ideas that came to birth in their hearts and heads, made use of the philosophy and science and art of their day. It is, in very deed, one of the stories of their endeavour that they did so ; for in so doing they brought the great truths of the inner life into contact with the thought of their age.

There is, however, always a danger in any such attempt ; for in proportion as we involve the great intuitions of the soul and the apocalypses of the mind in the opinions of the day, we make the exposition of the mysteries depart from the nature of scripture and fall into the changing notions of the ephemeral.

8

THE GNOSIS OF THE MIND.

Human science is ever changing; and if we set forth such glimpses of the sure ideas and living verities of the Gnosis as we can obtain, in the ever-changing forms of evolving science, we may, indeed, do much to popularise our glimpse of the mysteries for our own time; but the days that are to come will accuse us of clothing the Beauty of the Truth in rags as compared with the fairer garments of their own improved opinions.

The documents that have been preserved from the *scriptoria* of the Trismegistic tradition are by many hands and the product of many minds. Sometimes they involve themselves so closely with the science of their day that the current opinion of the twentieth century will turn from them with a feeling of contemptuous superiority; on the other hand they not infrequently remain in the paths of clear reason, and offer us an unimpeded view of vistas of the Plain of Truth. But even when they hold most closely to the world-representations and man-knowledges of their own day they are not without interest; for it may be that in their notions of living nature—the very antipodes of our modern day opinions based on the dead surfaces of things—they may have been with regard to some things even nearer the truth than we are ourselves in this so boasted age of grace and enlightenment.

Be this as it may, there are many examples of clean and clear thinking in the *logoi* or sacred sermons, or discourses, or utterances, of the School; and one of the most attractive elements in the whole discipline is the fact that the pupil was encouraged to think and question. Reason was held in high honour; a right use of reason, or rather, let us say, right reason, and not its counterfeit, opinion,

was the most precious instrument of knowledge of man and the cosmos, and the means of self-realisation into that Highest Good which, among many other names of sublime dignity, was known as the Good Mind or Reason (Logos) of God.

The whole theory of attainment was conditioned by the fact that man in body, soul and mind was a world in himself—a little world, it is true, so long as he is content to play the part of a "procession of Fate"; but his Destiny is greater than that Fate, or rather, let us say, his Unknowingness is Fate, his Awareness will be his Destiny. Man is a little world, little in the sense of personal, individual, separate; but a world for all that—a monad. And the destiny of man is that he should become the Monad of monads, or the Mind of God—the Cosmos itself, not only as perceived by the senses as all that is, both that which moves and moves not, which is the Great Body and Great Soul of things; but also as conceived by mind, as that Intelligible Greatness of all greatnesses, the Idea of all ideas, the Mind and Reason of God Himself, His own Self-created Son, Alone-begotten, the Beloved.

On this transcendent fact of facts is founded the whole discipline and method of the Gnosis of the Mind. The Mystery of mysteries is Man or Mind. But this naming of the Mystery should not be understood as excluding Soul and Body. Mind is the Person of persons, the Presence of all presences. Time, space, and causality are conditioned by the Mind. But this Mind, the True Man, is not the mind in bondage to causality, space and time. On the other hand, it is just this mind in bondage, this "procession of Fate," the "servant's

9

THE GNOSIS OF THE MIND.

form," which is the appearance that hides the potentiality of becoming the All, of becoming the Æon, the Presence, —that is, the Subsistence of all things present, at every moment of time, and point of space, and every instant cause-and-effect in the Bosom of Fate. It is true that in the region of opinion, body, soul and mind seem separate and apart; they are held by the man in separation as the fundamental categories of his existence; and truly so, for they are the conditions of *ex*-istence, of standing *out* of Being, that environment of incompleteness—the complement or fulfilment of which is *ec*-stasis, whereby the man goes forth from his limitations to unite himself with Himself, and so reaches that Satisfaction and Fulfilment, which our Gnostics call the Plērōma when set over against the conception of space, and the Æon when set over against the idea of time, and the Good when contrasted with the notion of Fate.

But Being is the Three in One, Mind, Soul and Body—Light, Life and Substance, co-eternal together and co-equal.

It therefore follows that he who would be Gnostic, must not foolishly divorce within himself the mystery of the triple Partners, the Three Powers, or the Divine Triad. For him the object of his endeavour is to consummate the Sacred Marriage within himself, where Three must " marry " to create; that so he may be united to his Greatest Self and become at-one with God. Body, soul, and mind (or spirit, for in this Gnosis spirit is frequently a synonym of mind) must all work together in intimate union for righteousness.

The body of man must be regarded as a holy temple, a shrine of the Divine— the most marvellous House of God that

exists, fairer far than the fairest temple raised with hands. For this natural temple which the Divine has wrought for the indwelling of His beloved sons, is a copy of the Great Image, the Temple of the Universe in which the Son of God, the Man, dwells.

Every atom and every group of atoms, every limb and joint and organ, is laid down according to the Divine Plan; the body is an image of the Great Seal, Heaven-and-Earth, male-female in one.

But how few know or even dream of the possibilities of this living temple of the Divine ! We are sepulchres, tombs of the dead ; for our bodies are half-atrophied, alive only to the things of Death, and dead to the things of Life.

The Gnosis of the Mind thus teaches us to let the Life flow into the dead channels of our corporeal nature, to invoke the Holy Breath of God to enliven the *substance* of our frames, that so the Divine Quickener may first bring to birth in us our divine complement, our other self, our long-lost spouse, and then we may ourselves with ungrudging love and fair wooing of her bring our true selves to birth, so becoming regenerate or reborn,—a trinity of Being, not a unit of vegetative existence, or a duality of man-animal nature, but the Perfect Triangle jewelled with all three sparks of perfected manhood.

It is very evident, then, that if the idea of this Gnosis be carried out logically, the hearer of this Mathesis must strive ever to become a doer of the Word, and so self-realise himself in every portion of his being. The object that he has in view is intensification of his whole nature. He does not parcel out his universe or himself into special compartments, but he strives ever to refund himself into ever

THE GNOSIS OF THE MIND.

more intimate union with himself— meaning by this [his ever-present consciousness; for there is nothing really that he is not.

Indeed it is one of the pleasantest features of the Trismegistic Gnosis, or rather, one may say its chief characteristic, a characteristic which should specially endear it to our present age, that throughout it is eminently reasonable. It is ever encouraging the pupil to think and question and reason ; I do not mean that it encourages criticism for the sake of pedantic carping, or questioning for the sake of idle curiosity, but that it is ever insisting on a right use of the purified reason, and the striving to clarify the mind and soul and body, so that they may become a crystal prism through which the One Ray of the Logos, the All-Brilliancy, as Philo calls it, may shine with unimpeded lustre in clean and clear colours according to the nature of the truth in manifestation.

And here we may attempt to compare, though not with any idea of contrasting to the disparagement of either, the greater simplicity of the Gnosis of the Mind with the dazzling multiplicity and endless immensities of the, perhaps for my readers, more familiar revelations of the Christianised Gnosis. They are two aspects of the same Mystery ; but whereas the former is conditioned by the clear thinking of philosophic reason as set forth pre-eminently in the Logic of Plato, and refuses to sever its contact with the things-that-are " here " as well as " there," the latter soars into such transcendent heights of vision and apocalypsis, that it loses itself in ecstasies which cannot possibly be registered in the waking consciousness.

I, for my part, love to try to follow the seers of the Christian Gnosis, in their soaring and heaven-storming, love to plunge into the depths and greatness of their spiritual intuitions ; yet it cannot but be admitted that this intoxication of the spirit is a great danger for any but the most balanced minds. Indeed, it is highly probable that such unrestrained outpourings of divine frenzy as we meet with in some of the Christian Gnostic Apocalypses, were never intended to be circulated except among those who had already proved themselves self-restrained in the fullest meaning of the term.

The Trismegistic sermons show us that such rapts and visions were also the privilege of " them who are in Gnosis "; but they did not circulate the revelations of such mysteries ; and though they taught the disciple to dare all things in perhaps more daring terms than we find recorded in any other scripture, they again and again force him to bring all to the test of the practical reason, that so the vital substance received from above may be rightly digested by the pure mind and fitly used to nourish the nature below.

But as for us who are hearers of the Gnosis, of Theosophy, wherever it is to be found, it would be unwise to reject any experience of those who have gone before upon the Way. Whether we call it the Gnosis of the Mind with the followers of Thrice-greatest Hermes, or the Gnosis of the Truth as Marcus does, or by many another name given it by the Gnostics of that day, it matters little ; the great fact is that there *is* Gnosis, and that men have touched her sacred robe and been healed of the vices of their souls ; and the mother-vice of the soul is ignorance, as Hermes says. But this ignorance is not ignorance of the arts

THE GNOSIS OF THE MIND.

and sciences and the rest, but ignorance of God; it is the true a-theism, the root-superstition of the human mind and heart,—the illusion that prevents a man realising the oneness of his true self with the Divine.

The dawning of this sacred conviction, the birth of this true faith, is the beginning of Gnosis; it is the Glad Tidings, the Gnosis of Joy, at whose shining Sorrow flees away. This is the Gospel, as Basilides the Gnostic conceived it, the Sun of Righteousness with healing in His wings; that is to say, the Father in the likeness of a dove—the Father of Light brooding over the sacred vessel, or divine chalice, or cup, the awakened spiritual nature of the new-born son.

This is the true baptism, and also the first miracle, as in the Gnosis of the Fourth Gospel, when the water of the watery spheres is turned into the wine of the spirit at the " first marriage."

But perhaps my readers will say: But this is the Christian Gnosis and not the Gnosis of the Mind! My dear friends (if you will permit me, I would reply), there is no Christian Gnosis and and Trismegistic Gnosis; there is but one Gnosis. If that Gnosis was for certain purposes either associated with the name and mystic person of the Great Teacher known as Jesus of Nazareth, or handed on under the typical personality of Great Hermes, it is not for us to keep the two streams apart in heart and head in water-tight compartments. The two traditions mutually interpret and complete one another. They are contemporaneous; they are both part and parcel of the same Economy. Read the fragments of these two forgotten faiths, or rather the fragments of the two manifestations of this forgotten

faith, and you will see for yourselves.

But again, some one may say (as a matter of fact not a few have already said): What do we want with a forgotten faith, fragmentary or otherwise ? We are living in the twentieth century; we do not want to return to the modes of thought of two thousand years ago; we can create a new Gnosis that will interpret the facts of present-day science and philosophy and religion.

I too await the dawn of that New Age; but I doubt that the Gnosis of the New Age will be new. Certainly it will be set forth in new forms, for the forms can be infinite. The Gnosis itself is not conditioned by space and time; it is we who are conditioned by these modes of manifestation. He who is reborn into the Gnosis becomes, as I have heard, the Lord of time and space, and passes from man into the state of Super-man and Christ, or Daimon and God, as a Hermes would have phrased it two thousand years ago, or of Bodhisattva and Buddha, as it was phrased five hundred years before that.

Indeed, if I believe rightly, the very essence of the Gnosis is the faith that man can transcend the limits of the duality that makes him man, and become a consciously divine being. The problem he has to solve is the problem of his day, the transcending of his present limitations. The way to do so is not, I venture to submit, by exalting his present-day knowledge in science or philosophy or religion at the expense of the little he can learn of the imperfect tradition of the religion and philosophy and science of the past, handed on to us by the forgetfulness of a series of ignorant and careless generations. The feeding of our present-day vanity on the husks from

12

THE GNOSIS OF THE MIND.

the feasts of other days is a poor diet for one who would be Gnostic. It is very true that, speaking generally, we do know more of physical observation, analysis and classification, we do know more of the theory of knowledge, and many other things in the domain of the 'lower world of appearances; but do we know more of religion as a living experience than the great souls of the past; do we know more of the Gnosis than the Gnostics of other days? I doubt it.

We are beginning once more to turn our attention in the direction of the Greater Mysteries; the cycles of the Æon are, I believe, once more set in a configuration similar to the mode of the Time-Mind when such illumination is possible for numbers of souls, and not for stray individuals only. But the conditions of receiving that illumination are the same now as they have ever been; and one of the conditions is the power to rise superior to the opinions of the Hour into the Gnosis of the Eternal Æon.

It therefore follows, if I am right in my premises, that the illusion of all illusions which we must strive to transcend is that of the Lord of the Hour; it is just the general opinions and pre-suppositions and prejudices of our own day against which we must be on our watch with greatest vigilance. There are certain forms of knowledge, forms of religion, and forms of philosophy, that dominate every age and every hour; these forms are most potent, for they are alive with the faith of millions; and therefore it follows that it may be we shall find less difficulty, in our endeavour to pierce through the clouds of opinion to the living ideas beyond, if we study forms that are no longer charged with the

passions of mankind,—with that storage of the hopes and fears of incarnated minds, the shock of which few are strong enough to withstand. It may thus be that the forms of the Gnosis of the past may be read more dispassionately and seen through more clearly.

However this may be, it would be manifestly absurd to go back to the past and simply pour ourselves once more into these ancient forms; this would be death and a mental and spiritual "re-incarnation" backwards, so to speak. It is precisely this absurdity which so many literalists attempt in theology, only to find themselves stranded among dead forms with the tide of the spiritual life far out.

On the other hand, there may be some who feel that in what has been said above, the artist and lover of the Beautiful in us risk to be sacrificed entirely to the Philistine. There is such a thing as scripture; there are such things as the best books. *Non refert quam multos sed quam bonos libros legas;* it is not the quantity but the quality of the books we read that is of importance. The Gnosis is enshrined in scripture, in bibles and not in books. And I doubt not that even to-day there are enough bible-lovers, in the wider sense of the word, among us to appreciate the beautiful and permanent in literature.

The Trismegistic sermons have a common language with the writers of the New Testament books, and they also use the language of Plato. They can, therefore, hardly be said to be out of date even as to their form; while as to their content, as far as their main ideas are concerned, I venture to say that they belong to the great books of the world, they are part of the world-scripture.

THE GNOSIS OF THE MIND.

If, then, any would learn of the Gnosis of the Mind, they will not lose anything by reading what the disciples of this form of the Wisdom-Tradition have handed on to us. They may prefer more modern expositions, or they may find some other scripture of the past more suitable to their needs ; but if they are lovers of comparative theosophy, and are persuaded that he who is acquainted with one mode of theosophy only does not know theosophy truly, even as he who is acquainted with one language only knows no language really, they may learn much by comparing the theosophy of the Hermes-Gnostics with the theosophy of the Christian Gnostics, or of the Buddhist or Brahmanical lovers of the Gnosis.

In conclusion, I would add a few quotations touching the Gnosis from the Trismegistic sermons ; for, as Lactantius, the Church Father, tells us of the Holy Scribe who inspired these scriptures :

"He wrote books, indeed many of them, treating of the Gnosis of things divine, in which he asserts the Greatness of the Highest and One and Only God " (iii., 233).

Yes, *He* wrote many books, whether we call Him "Hermes" or by any other of His many names. For as He says in another scripture of that Day of Sunshine, writing of the inner history of the Christ-Mystery, most probably before even there were as yet any Christian scriptures :

"Wherefore, send me, O Father !
Seals in my hands, I will descend ;
Through Æons universal will I make
    a Path ;
Through mysteries all I'll open up
    a Way !
All Forms of Gods will I display ;
The Secrets of the Holy Path I will

hand on,
And call them Gnosis " (i., 192).

Yes, He wrote many books, many sermons and sacred discourses, entitled by many names, one of them called precisely : "An Introduction to the Gnosis of the Nature of All Things" (ii., 68).

Not that there is any precise beginning of the Gnosis or any definite introduction confined to any formal instruction ; it may be presented in infinite modes to the learner and hearer, for it is like unto its Great Original.

And so we read :

"For to the Good there is no other shore ; It hath no bounds ; It is without an end ; and for Itself It is without beginning, too, though unto us It *seemeth* to have one—the Gnosis.

"Therefore to It Gnosis is no beginning ; rather is it that Gnosis doth afford *to us* the first beginning of *Its being known* " (ii., 90).

And so again we find a Jewish mystic, who wrote just prior to the days of Paul, quoting from some scripture of the Gnosis (in all probability from one of the lost sermons of our School) which sets forth the matter in still greater clarity in the striking aphorism :

"The beginning of Perfection is Gnosis of Man ; but Gnosis of God is Perfect Perfection " (i., 178).

Thus Hermes in teaching his beloved son, the seeker, the suppliant and hearer, how to set his feet upon the path of self-realisation, points out the way in the wise and gentle words :

"Seek'st thou for God, thou seekest for the Beautiful. One is the Path that leadeth unto It—Devotion joined with Gnosis " (ii., 114).

And again he sets forth the boundary-

1 4

THE GNOSIS OF THE MIND.

marks of the Way of the Good Commandments in admirable instruction, saying :

"The Seeds of God, 'tis true, are few, but vast and fair and good—virtue and self-control, devotion. Devotion is God-Gnosis; and he who knoweth God, being filled with all good things, thinks godly thoughts and not thoughts like the many think.

"For this cause they who Gnostic are, please not the many, nor the many them. They are thought mad and laughed at; they're hated and despised, and sometimes even put to death. . . .

"But he who is a devotee of God, will bear with all—once he has sensed the Gnosis. For such an one all things, e'en though they be for others bad, are for him good ; deliberately he doth refer them all unto the Gnosis. And, thing most marvellous, 'tis he alone who maketh bad things good " (ii., 131).

The devotee of God is the Gnostic, and "they who are Gnostic " stand in the original as "they who are in Gnosis." It is of more than ordinary interest to compare this simple statement of fact addressed to "those in Gnosis " with the well-known words adapted from some early collection of "Logoi of the Lord " for the comfort of "those in Faith." What the Sayings preserved by the first and third evangelists may have been in their original form, we do not know, though any day the Oxhyrhynchus "rubbish-heaps " may yield us a clue. Some of these "Sayings of the Lord " which in their original form circulated in the inner communities, were, in the highest probability, subsequently adapted to the prophetical mood by a Christian evangelist prior to our first and third synoptists. Thus we find the writer of our First Gospel handing on one of these Sayings as :

"Blessed are ye when they shall revile you and persecute you and shall say all manner of evil against you, lying, for My sake."

Here the "lying " is evidently the gloss of some scrupulous scribe who knew there were some things that could be said against them justly ; whereas the third evangelist keeps closer to his original, writing :

"Blessed are ye when *men* shall hate you, and when they shall separate you forth (from them), and revile you, and cast out your name as evil, for the sake of the Son of *the Man*."

But even so there still seems to be a blend of two traditions before the Saying reached the hands of our third evangelist. The antithesis between "men " and "Son of the Man " is familiar to us in our Trismegistic sermons, and would be understood by all who knew of the "Myth of Man in the Mysteries " (i., 139-198); it is clearly to be distinguished from the "My sake " of the first evangelist. Whereas the separating forth and the casting forth of the name as evil are, I believe, to be understood as expulsion of members from a community and the removal of their names from the list of the brethren.

But to return to the Gnosis. Devotion is God-Gnosis. True Piety is "nothing else than the Gnosis of God "—as Lactantius, quoting Hermes, phrases it in Latin (ii., 243). This piety, however, is something other than pious exercise and the practice of devotional worship ; it leads unto "the complete or all-perfect contemplation," and embraces the "learning of the things-that-are, the contemplating of their nature and the

THE GNOSIS OF THE MIND.

knowing God "; or, in other words, the "being taught the nature of the all and the Supreme Vision" (ii., 264). And that Supreme Vision, if I understand aright, is no rapt into regions beyond the sky, but a Seeing of the Good in everything. For the Master of this Way teaches his disciple concerning the Gnosis of the Good, that is the Gnosis of God, saying :

"For only then wilt thou upon It gaze when thou canst say no word concerning It. For Gnosis of the Good is holy silence and a giving holiday to every sense."

It is the gaining of the "all sense," the "common sense," the "sense of the intelligence."

"For neither can he who perceiveth It, perceive aught else, nor he who gazeth on It, gaze on aught else ; nor hear aught else. . . .

"And shining then all round his mind, It shines through his whole soul, and draws it out of body, transforming all of him to essence.

"For it is possible, my son, that a man's soul should be made like to God, e'en while it still is in a body, if it doth contemplate the Beauty of the Good" (ii., 144).

This is the "deification" or "apotheosis" of a man ; he becomes like unto God, in that he becomes a God. The Beauty of the Good is the Cosmic Order ; and the mode of meditation was that of self-realisation whereby the soul is brought into sympathy with the Cosmic Soul.

nd so speaking of such a soul, of one gnostic in true piety, Hermes writes :

"But on the pious soul the Mind doth mount and guide it to the Gnosis' Light. And such a soul doth never

tire in songs of praise to God and pouring blessing on all men, and doing good in word and deed to all, in imitation of its Sire" (ii., 155).

And so again in the outer preaching, in warning the multitude against the "fierce flood" of ignorance, the missionary of the Gnosis and evangelist of Salvation exhorts them, saying :

"Be then not carried off by the fierce flood, but using the shore-current, ye who can, make for Salvation's port, and, harbouring there, seek ye for one to take you by the hand and lead you unto Gnosis' Gates.

"Where shines clear Light, of every darkness clean, where not a single soul is drunk, but sober all they gaze with their hearts' eyes on Him who willeth to be seen.

"No ear can hear Him, nor can eye see Him, nor tongue speak of Him, but only mind and heart" (ii., 121).

And from this preaching we learn the very interesting fact that there was some great association that the Gnostic evangelist regarded as Salvation's port, a harbour of refuge for many ; but even when safe within the quiet of the discipline that could calm the waves of the fierce flood of passion and ignorance, there was still a further adventure for the soul before the Light of the New Day dawned. A guide who knew the Way to the Gates of the Spiritual Sun must be found, one who was "in Gnosis" and not only "in Faith."

For faith is conditioned upon feeling, upon sense, and not knowledge; as Hermes says :

"But Gnosis is far different from sense. For sense is brought about by that which hath the mastery o'er us, while Gnosis is the end of science, and

THE GNOSIS OF THE MIND.

science is God's gift " (ii., 147).

It is true that a refuge can be found in the Harbour of Salvation by means of Faith ; but Salvation itself is Gnosis.

"This is the sole Salvation for a man—God's Gnosis. This is the Way up to the Mount.

"By Him alone the soul becometh good, not whiles is good, whiles evil, but good out of necessity " (ii., 150).

And again He says :

"The virtue of the soul is Gnosis. For he who knows, he good and pious is, and still while on the earth Divine " (ii., 146).

For in this view of the mystery, in consonance with the teaching of the Buddha, and with Indian theosophy in general, " the soul's vice is ignorance." And so we find Gnosis heading the list of virtues—Gnosis, Joy, Self-control, Continence, Righteousness, Sharing-with-all, Truth ; a septenary consummated in the divine triad of Life, Light and the Good (ii., 246). For Gnosis is that which doth distribute life to all, and light to all, and good to all (ii.; 296). And so the Master, in the spiritual theurgic rite at which he consecrates his beloved son to the holy life, declares :

"Gnosis of God hath come to us, and and when this comes, my son, notknowing is cast out.

"Gnosis of Joy hath come to us, and on its coming, son, sorrow will flee away to them who give it room " (ii., 225).

For it is by this " enformation according to Gnosis " that the man is made like unto the Great Man, the Good Mind or Reason of God. This Gnosis is not only Light and Life, the father-motherhood of God, but also Love. It is this Love of the Gnosis, of that which gives light and life to all, that urges on the disciple ; it is the Breath of God Himself energizing in the heart, inspiring us. It is the Providence or Foresight of God, the Holy Spirit. And so in one of the sacred discourses, called " The Perfect Sermon," we read :

"To them, sunk in fit silence reverently, their souls and minds pendent on Hermes' lips, thus Love Divine began to speak " (iii., 260).

To be Knowers we must be Lovers ; we must have " the Single Love, the Love of wisdom-loving, which consists in Gnosis of Divinity alone—the practice of perpetual contemplation and of holy piety " (ii., 330).

Of such Lovers and such Gnostics we read :

"But they who have received some portion of God's gift, these, son, if we judge by their deeds, have from Death's bonds won their release ; for they embrace in their own mind all things, things on the earth, things in the heaven, and things above the heaven —if they be aught.

"And having raised themselves so far they sight the Good ; and having sighted It, they look upon their sojourn here as a mischance ; and in disdain of all, both things in body and the bodiless, they speed their way unto that One and Only One.

"This is, my son, the Gnosis of the Mind, vision of things Divine ; Godknowledge is it, for the Mind is God's " (ii., 88).

Hard as it may be to leave the " things we have grown used to," the things habitual, it must be done if we are to enter into the Way of the Gnosis. But no new Path is this, no going forth into new lands (though it may have all the

17

THE GNOSIS OF THE MIND.

appearance of being so). The entrance on the Path of the Gnosis is a Going Home; it is a Return—a Turning-Back (a true Repentance of the whole nature). "We must turn ourselves back into the Old, Old Way" (ii., 98).

And for those who will thus "repent," there are promises and words of fair comfort spoken by the Mind Himself in the Gospel of the Gnosis called "The Shepherd of Men":

"I, Mind, Myself am present with holy men and good, the pure and merciful, men who live piously.

"To such my Presence doth become an aid, and straightway they gain Gnosis of all things, and win the Father's love by their pure lives, and give Him thanks, invoking on Him blessings and chanting hymns, intent on Him with ardent love" (ii., 14).

And to the truth of this, testimony is borne by one of those in Gnosis who had heard and had believed and had known, when he writes:

"But I, with thanks and blessings unto the Father of the universal Powers, was freed, full of the Power He had poured into me, and full of what He'd taught me of the nature of the all and of the loftiest vision" (ii., 17).

And so he begins to preach to men "the Beauty of Devotion and of the Gnosis"; for he cannot refrain from uttering the Word, now that he has become a knower, a doer, and not a hearer only. He prays no longer for himself, but that he may be the means whereby the rest of human kind may come to Light and Life, saying:

"Give ear to me who pray that I may ne'er of Gnosis fail, Gnosis which is our common being's nature; and fill me with Thy Power, and with this Grace of Thine, that I may give the Light to those in ignorance of the Race, my brethren and Thy sons" (ii., 20).

With these brief indications of the Gnosis of the Mind, drawn from a wealth of like noble teachings, we bring to an end the first volume of these "Echoes from the Gnosis," in the hope that there may be some who will turn to the fair originals, and "read, mark, learn and inwardly digest them."

1 8

THE HYMNS
OF . . . .
HERMES. .

HYMNS OF HERMES

CONTENTS

The references in this volume are to the recently-published work—*Thrice Greatest Hermes : Studies in Hellenistic Theosophy and Gnosis. Being a Translation of the Extant Sermons and Fragments of the Trismegistic Literature, with Prolegomena, Commentaries and Notes,* 3 vols. (London, 1906).

THE HYMNS OF HERMES.

THE SERVICE OF SONG.

Clement of Alexandria tells us that the whole of the religious philosophy—that is, the wisdom, discipline and multifarious arts and sciences—of the Egyptian priesthood was contained in the Books of Hermes, that is of Thoth. These Books, he informs us further, were classified under forty-two heads and divided into a number of groups according to the various septs or divisions of the priests.

In describing a certain sacred ceremonial—a procession of priests in their various orders—Clement tells us that it was headed by a representative of the order of Singers, who were distinguished by appropriate symbols of music, some of which apparently were carried in the hands and others embroidered on the robes.

These Singers had to make themselves masters of, that is, learn by heart, two of the divisions of the Books of Hermes, namely, those which contained collections of Hymns in Honour of the Gods or of God, and Encomia or Hymns in Praise of the Kings (iii., 222).

Many specimens of similar hymns in praise of the Gods are preserved to us in Egyptian inscriptions and papyri, and some of them are most noble out-pourings of the soul in praise of the majesty and transcendency of the Supreme, in terms that may be not unfavourably compared with similar praise-giving in other great scriptures. But, alas ! the hymn-books of Thoth, to which Clement refers, are lost to us. He may, of course, have been mistaken in so definitely designating them, just as he was indubitably mistaken in thinking that they were collections of hymns composed by a single individual, Hermes.

The grandiose conception of Thoth as the inspirer of all sacred writings and the teacher of all religion and philosophy was Egyptian and not Greek ; and it was but a sorry equivalent that the Greeks could find in their own pantheon when, in the change of God-names, they were forced to " translate " " Thoth " by " Hermes."

Thoth, as the inspirer of all sacred writings and the president of all priestly discipline, was, as Jamblichus tells us, a name which was held by the Egyptians to be " common to all priests "—that is to say, every priest as priest was a Thoth, because he showed forth in his sacred office some characteristic or other of the Great Priest or Master Hierophant among the Gods whose earthly name was Thoth—Teḥuti.

Thoth was thus the Oversoul of all priests ; and when some of the Greeks came to know better what the inner discipline of the true priestly mysteries connoted, they so felt the inadequacy of plain Hermes as a suitable equivalent for the Egyptian name which designated this great ideal, that they qualified " Egyptian Hermes " with the honorific epithet " Thrice-greatest."

It is of the Hymns of this Thrice-greatest Hermes that I shall treat in the present small volume—hymns that were inspired by the still living tradition of what was best in the wisdom of ancient Egypt, as "philosophised" through minds trained in Greek thought, and set forth in the fair speech of golden-tongued Hellas.

But here again, unfortunately, we have no collection of such hymns preserved to us ; and all we can do is to gather up the fragments that remain, scattered through the pages of the Trismegistic literature which have escaped the jealousy of an exclusive bibliolatry.

The main Gospel of the Trismegistic Gnosis is contained in a sacred sermon which bears in Greek the title " Pœmandres." This may perhaps have been

THE HYMNS OF HERMES.

originally the Greek transliteration of an Egyptian name (ii., 50); but from the treatise itself it is manifest that it was understood by the Greek followers of this Gnosis to mean "The Shepherd of Men," or "Man-shepherd." This Shepherd was no man, but Divine Humanity or the Great Man or Mind, the inspirer of all wisdom and hierophant of all spiritual initiations.

This majestic Reality or Essence of Certitude was conceived of as a limitless Presence, or Person, of Light and Life and Goodness, which enwrapped the contemplative mind of the pious worshipper of God or the Good, of the single-hearted lover of the Beautiful, and of the unwearied striver for ,the knowledge of the True.

And so, in His instruction to one who was striving to reach the grade of a true self-conscious Hermes, Pœmandres declares :

" I, Mind, Myself am present with holy men and good, the pure and merciful, men who live piously.

" To such My Presence doth become an aid, and straightway they gain Gnosis of all things, and win the Father's love by their pure lives, and give Him thanks, invoking on Him blessings, and chanting hymns, intent on Him with ardent love " (ii., 14).

And the same instruction is practically repeated in the sermon called " The Key," where we read :

" But on the pious soul the Mind doth mount and guide it to the Gnosis' Light. And such a soul doth never tire in songs of praise to God and pouring blessing on all men, and doing good in word and deed to all, in imitation of its Sire " (ii., 155).

The sole conditions for reaching this consummation, so devoutly to be wished, are here laid down :

The good alone can know the Good; even as one of the invocations to Hermes as the Good Mind, preserved in the Greek Magic Papyri, phrases it :

"Thee I invoke! Come unto me, O Good, Thou altogether good, come to the good!" (i., 86).

The pure alone can know the Pure; and by "Pure" I think Hermes sometimes meant far more than is generally connoted by the term. "Pure" is that which remains in itself, and is neither too much nor too little; it is the equilibrium, the balanced state, the mysterious something that reconciles all opposites, and is their simultaneous source and ending—the Divine Justice.

The merciful alone can know the Merciful, the source of the infinite variety of the Divine Love.

To such the Divine Presence becomes an aid; it is in the field of this " Good Land " alone, in the self-cultivated soil of the spiritual nature—the good and pure and merciful nature—of man, that the Divine Presence can sow the self-conscious seeds of the heavenly Gnosis, so that from this Virgin Womb of Virtue may come to birth the true Man, the child of Freedom, or Right Will, or Good Will.

To others, to those who are still in ignorance of spiritual things, the Divine Presence is also an aid, but unknowingly; for being manifested for them in its reversed mode, by means of the constraints of Fate, the many consider it a hindrance, as indeed it is—a hindrance to their falling into greater ignorance and limitation. The soil must be cleared of tares and ploughed, before it can be sown.

But when man of his own freewill reverses his mode of life, and revolves with the motion of the heavenly spheres instead of spinning against them, the conscious contact with the Divine Presence which is thus effected, stirs the

THE HYMNS OF HERMES.

whole nature to respond; sunlight pours into the true heart of the man from all sides, and his heart answers; it wakes from the dead and begins to speak true words. The Great God gives speech to the heart in the Invisible, even as He does to the dead Osirified; and that unspoken speech is a continual praise-giving of right deeds. There is also a spoken speech, becoming articulate in human words in hymns of praise and thanks to God—the liturgy of a piety that answers to the Divine and is thus responsible.

Indeed this is the basis of all liturgy and cult, even in their crudest forms or reflections—in the dreams of men's sleeping hearts. But the Trismegistic writings are dealing with the self-conscious realization of true Gnostic Passion, where feeling has to be consciously transmuted into knowledge.

The singing of hymns on earth is the reflection of a heavenly mystery. Before the man can really sing in proper tune he must have harmonized his lower nature and transformed it into cosmos or fit order. Hitherto he has been sing-ing out of tune, chaotically—howling, shrieking, crying, cursing, rather than singing articulately, and so offering "rea-sonable oblations" to God.

The articulation of the "members" of his true "body" or "heart" has not yet been completed or perfected; they are still, to use the language of the ancient Egyptian myth, scattered abroad, as it were, by his Typhonic passions; the limbs of his body of life are scattered in his body of death. The Isis of his spiritual nature is still weeping and mourning, gathering them together, await-ing the day of the New Dawn, when the last member, the organ of Gnosis, shall complete the *taxis*, or order, or band of his members, and the New Man shall arise from the dead.

It is only when these "limbs" of his are harmonized and properly articulated that he has an instrument for cosmic

music. It matters not whether the old myth tells us of the fourteen "limbs" of the dead Osiris, or the later instruction speaks of the seven spheres of the creative Harmony that fashion forth the "limbs" of every man, and views them as each energizing in two modes, according as the individual will of man goes with them or against them—it all refers to the same mystery. Man in limitation is two-fold, even as are his physical limbs; man in freedom as cosmicly configured is two in one in all things.

And therefore when this "change of gnostic tendency" is wrought, there is a marvellous transmutation of the whole nature. He abandons his Typhonic passions, the energizings of the nature that has battled with God, in order that what the anonymous writer of that mystic masterpiece *The Dream of Rávan*, so finely calls the "Divine Catastrophe" may be precipitated, and the Titan in him may be the more rapidly destroyed, or rather transmuted into the God.

For though these passions now seem to us to be of the "Devil," and though we look upon them as born of powers that fight against God, they are not really evil; they are the experiences in our nature of the natural energies of the Divine Harmony—that mysterious En-gine of Fate, which is the seven-fold means of manifestation, according to our Trismegistic tradition. For the Divine Harmony is the creative instrument of the Divine Energy, that perpetually produces forms in substance for consciousness, and so gradually perfects a form that shall be capable of imaging forth the Perfect Man.

The natural energies that have been hitherto working through him uncon-sciously, in order that through form self-consciousness may come to birth, are, however, regarded by the neophyte, in the first stages of his gnostic birth, as inimical; they have woven for him garments that have brought experience, but which now seem rags that he would

2 3

THE HYMNS OF HERMES.

ain strip off, in order that he may put on new robes of power and majesty, and so exchange the sackcloth of the slave for the raiment of the King. Though the new garments are from the same yarn and woven by the energies of the same loom, the weaver is now labouring to change the texture and design; he is now joyfully learning gnosticly to follow the plan of the Great Weaver, and so cheerfully unravels the rags of his past imperfections to reweave them into "fine linen" fit for King Osiris.

This gnostic change is in our treatise described by the Great Mind teaching little mind, as following on the stripping off of the vices of the soul, which are said to arise from the downward mode of the energies of the seven spheres of the Harmony of Fate. The subsequent beatification is set forth in the following graphic declaration :

"And then, with all the energizing of the Harmony stript from him, he cometh to that nature which belongs unto the Eighth, and there with those that are hymneth the Father.

"They who are there welcome his coming there with joy; and he, made like to them that sojourn there, doth further hear the Powers who are above the nature that belongs unto the Eighth, singing their songs of praise to God in language of their own.

"And then they, in a band, go to the Father home ; of their own selves they make surrender of themselves to Powers, and thus becoming Powers they are in God. This the good end for those who have gained Gnosis—to be made one with God" (ii., 16).

This is the change of gnostic tendency that is wrought in the nature of one who passes from the stage of ordinary man, which Hermes characterizes as a "procession of Fate," to that true manhood which leads finally to Godship.

The ancient Egyptians divided man into at least nine forms of manifestation, or modes of existence, or spheres of being, or by whatever phrase we choose to name these categories of his natures.

The words "clothed in his proper Power" refer, I believe, to one of these natures of man. Now the *sekhem* is generally translated "power," but we have no description of it whereby we may satisfactorily check the translation ; and so I would suggest that the *khaibit*, though generally translated "shadow" (i., 89), is perhaps the mystery to which our text refers, for "in the teaching of Egypt, around the radiant being [perhaps the *ren* or name], which in its regenerate life could assimilate itself to the glory of the Godhead, was formed the *khaibit*, or luminous atmosphere, consisting of a series of ethereal envelopes, at once shading and diffusing its flaming lustre, as the earth's atmosphere shades and diffuses the solar rays" (i., 76).

This was typified by the linen swathings of the mummy, for "Thoth, the Divine Wisdom, wraps the spirit of the Justified a million times in a garment of fine linen," even as Jesus in a certain sacred act girt himself with a "linen cloth" which Tertullian characterizes as the "proper garment of Osiris" (i., 71). And Plutarch tells us that linen was worn by the priests "on account of the colour which the flax in flower sends forth, resembling the ethereal radiance that surrounds the cosmos" (i., 265).

The same mystery is shown forth in the marvellous passage which describes the transfiguration of Jesus in the Gnostic gospel known as the *Pistis Sophia*, which is of almost pure Egyptian tradition. It is the mystic description of a wonderful metamorphosis or transformation that is wrought in the inner nature of the Master, who has ascended to clothe himself with the Robe of Glory, and who returns to the consciousness of his lower powers, or disciples, clad in his Robe of Power.

THE HYMNS OF HERMES.

"They saw Jesus descending shining exceedingly; there was no measure to the light which surrounded him, for he shone more brightly than when he had ascended into the heavens, so that it is impossible for any in this world to describe the light in which he was. He shot forth rays shining exceedingly; his rays were without measure, nor were his rays of light equal together, but they were of every figure and every type, some being more admirable than the others in infinite manner. And they were all pure light in every part at the same time.

"It was of three degrees, one surpassing the other in infinite manner. The second, which was in the midst, excelled the first which was below it, and the third, the most admirable of all, surpassed the two below it. The first glory was placed below all, like to the light which came upon Jesus before he ascended into the heavens, and was very regular as to its own light " (pp. 7, 8).

This triple glory, I believe, was the " body of light " of the nature of the eighth, ninth and tenth spheres of glory in the scale of the perfect ten. In our text the " clothed in his proper Power " must, I think, be referred to the powers of the seven spheres unified into one, the eighth, which was the vehicle of the pure mind, according to Platonic tradition, based originally, in all probability, on Egyptian tradition. This " vehicle " was " atomic " and not " molecular," to use the terms of present-day science, simple and not compound, same and not other— " very regular as to its own light."

And so when this gnostic change is wrought in the man's inner nature there is an accompanying change effected in the substance of his very " body," and he begins to sing in harmony with the spheres; " with those that are he hymneth the Father."

He now knows the language of nature, and therewith sings praise continually in full consciousness of the joy of life. He sings the song of joy, and so singing hears the joyous songs of the Sons of God who form the first of the choirs invisible. They sing back to him and give him welcome; and what they sing the lover of such things may read in the same *Pistis Sophia* (p. 17), in the Hymn of the Powers " Come unto Us "— when they welcome the returning exile on the Great Day of that name.

But this is not all; for higher still and higher, beyond and yet beyond, are other choirs of Powers of even greater transcendency who sing. As yet, however, the newly born cannot understand or bear, their song, for they sing in a language of their own, there being many tongues of angels and archangels, of daimones and gods in their many grades.

But already the man has begun to realize the freedom of the cosmos; he has begun to feel himself a true cosmopolitan or world-citizen, and to thrill in harmony with the Powers. He experiences an ineffable union that removes all fear, and longs for the consummation of the final Sacred Marriage when he will perform the great sacrifice, and of himself make joyful surrender of all that he has been in separation, to become, by union with Those alone who truly are, all that has ever been and is and will be—and so one with God, the All and One.

It is thus evident that our Hymns of Hermes are in direct contact with a tradition which regarded the spiritual life as a perpetual service of song; and this is quite in keeping with the belief of the Egyptians that man was created for the sole purpose of worshipping the Gods and rendering them pious service. The whole duty of man was thus conceived of as an utterance of " true words " or a continual singing of a song of harmony of thought and word and deed, whereby man grew like unto the Gods, and so at last becoming a God was with the Great God in the "Boat of

THE HYMNS OF HERMES.

the millions of Years," or "Barque of the Æons," in other words, was safe for eternity.

And now we will turn to the four hymns preserved to us in Greek from the hymn-book of this truly sacred liturgy.

The first is appended to the "Pœmandres" treatise, and was evidently intended to give some idea in human terms of the nature of the Praise-giving of the Powers to which reference has just been made. For, as we shall see later on, the less instructed of the community fervently desired to have revealed to them the words of this Song, thinking in their ignorance that it was some hymn resembling those of earth, and not yet understanding that it was the heavenly type of all earth-praising, whether expressed by man or animal, by tree or stone.

The first part of our hymn consists of nine lines, divided by their subjects into three groups, every sentence beginning with " Holy art Thou ! " It is thus in the form of a three-fold " Holy, Holy, Holy ! "—and we may thus, for want of a proper title, call it " A Triple Trisagion."

A TRIPLE TRISAGION.

Holy art Thou, O God, the Universals'
Father.
Holy art Thou, O God, Whose Will per-
fects itself by means of its own Powers.
Holy art Thou, O God, Who willest to be
known and art known by Thine own.
Holy art Thou, Who didst by Word make
to consist the things that are.
Holy art Thou, of Whom All-nature hath
been made an Image.

Holy art Thou, Whose Form Nature hath
never made.
Holy art Thou, more powerful than all
power.
Holy art Thou, transcending all pre-
eminence.
Holy art Thou, Thou better than all
praise.
Accept my reason's offerings pure, from
soul and heart for aye stretched up to Thee,
O Thou unutterable, unspeakable, Whose
Name naught but the Silence can express !
Give ear to me who pray that I may
ne'er of Gnosis fail—Gnosis which is our
common being's nature—and fill me
with Thy Power, and with this Grace of
Thine, that I may give the Light to those
in ignorance of the Race, my Brethren
and Thy Sons !
For this cause I believe, and I bear
witness. I go to Life and Light. Blessed
art Thou, O Father. Thy Man would
holy be as Thou art holy, e'en as Thou
gavest him Thy full authority to be.

" Holy art Thou, O God, the Universals' Father."

God is first praised as the Father of the Universals, that is of the Greatnesses of all things, the Æonic Immensities, or Supreme Mysteries that are plural yet one—the Subsistencies of the Divine Being in the state of pure Divinity.

" Holy art Thou, O God, Whose Will perfects itself by means of its own Powers."

God is next praised as the Power or Potency of all things ; for Will is regarded by our Gnostics as the means by which the Deity reveals Himself unto Himself by the Great Act of perpetual Self-creation of Himself in Himself. " From Thee " are all things—when God is thought of as Divine Fatherhood ; and " Through Thee " are all things—when God is regarded as Divine Motherhood. For this Will is the Divine Love which is the means of Self-perfection, the source of all consummation and satisfaction, of certitude and bliss. The Deity for ever initiates Himself into His own Mysteries.

THE HYMNS OF HERMES.

"Holy art Thou, O God, Who willeth to be known and art known by Thine own."

The Will of God is Gnostic; He wills to be known. The Divine Purpose is consummated in Self-knowledge. God is knowable, but only by "His own," that is by the Divine Sonship, as Basilides, the Christian Gnostic, calls it, or by the Race of the Sons of God, as Philo and our Gnostics and others of the same period phrase it.

The Sonship is a Race, and not an individual, because they of the Sonship have ceased from separation and have made " surrender of themselves to Powers, and thus becoming Powers they are in God." They are one with another, no longer separated one from another and using divided senses and organs ; for they. constitute the Intelligible Word or Reason (Logos) which is also the Intelligible World (Kosmos) or Order of all things.

The next three praise-givings celebrate the same trinity of what, for lack of appropriate terms, we may call Being, Bliss and Intelligence, but now in another mode—the mode of manifestation or enformation in space and time and substance of the Sensible Universe, or Cosmos of forms and species.

The three *hypostases* or *hyparxes* or subsistences of this mode of the Divine self-manifestation are suggested by the terms Word, All-nature and Form. Word is the Vice-regent of Being, because it is this Word or Reason that established the being of all things, the that in them which causes them to be what they are, the essential reason of their being ; All-nature is the ground or substance of their being, the All-receiver or Nurse, as Plato calls her, who nourishes them, the Giver of Bliss, the Ever-becoming which is the Image of Eternity ; while Form is the impression of the Divine Intelligence, the source of all transformation and metamorphosis.

The final trisagion sings the praise of God's transcendency, declaring the powerlessness of human speech adequately to sing the praise of God.

Therefore is it said that the sole fit liturgy, or service of God, is to be found in the offerings of reason alone, the reason or *logos* which is the Divine principle in man, the image of the Image, or Divine Man, the Logos. It is the continual raising of the tension of the whole nature whereby the man is drawn ever closer and closer to God, in the rapt silence of ecstatic contemplation—when alone he goes to the Alone, as Plotinus says. The Name of God can be expressed by Silence alone, for, as we know from the remains of the Christianized Gnosis, this Silence, or Sigē, is the Spouse of God, and it is the Divine Spouse alone who can give full expression to the Divine Son, the Name or Logos of God.

The prayer is for Gnosis, for the realization of the state of Sonship, or the self-consciousness of the common being which the Son has with the Father. This is to be consummated by the fulfilment of the man's whole nature, by the completion of his insufficiency or imperfection (*hysterēma*), whereby he becomes the Fullness or Wholeness (*Plērōma*) the Æon or Eternity. This is to be achieved by the descent of the Great Power upon him, by the Blessing of God's Goodwill, that Charis or Grace or Love, which has been all along his Divine Mother, but which now becomes his Divine Spouse or Complement or Syzygy.

The prayer is not for self but for others, that so the man may become the means of illumination for those still in darkness, who as yet do not know of the Glad Tidings of the Divine Sonship, who are ignorant of the Race of Wisdom, but who nevertheless are, as are all men, brethren of the Christ and sons of God.

And so in this ecstasy of praise, the traveller, as he sings upon the Path of the Divine, feels within him the certitude that he is indeed on the Way of Return,

THE HYMNS OF HERMES.

his face set forward to the True Goal; he is going to Light and Life, the eternal fatherhood and motherhood that are ever united in the Good, the One Desirable, or Divine Father-Mother, two in one and three in one.

Finally as God has been praised throughout in His nature of holiness, that is as most worshipful, meet to be adored, praiseworthy and the object of all wonder, so that which has proceeded from Him, His Man, or the Divine in man, now longs consciously to become of like nature with Him, according to the Purpose and Commandment of the Father Who has destined him for this very end, and bestowed on him power over all things.

It is indeed a fair psalm—this Hymn of Hermes, that is, the praise-giving of some lover of this Gnosis who had, as he expresses it, "reached the Plain of Truth" (i., 19), or come into conscious contact with the reality of his own Divine nature, and so been made a Hermes indeed, capable of interpreting the inner meaning of religion, and of leading souls back from Death to Life—a true psych-agogue. It matters little who wrote it; his body may have been Egyptian or Greek or Syrian, it may have borne this name or that, it may have lived precisely from this year to that, or from some other to some other year, all this is of little consequence except for historians of the bodies of men. What concerns us here more nearly is the outpouring of a soul; we have here a man manifestly pouring forth from the fulness of his heart the profoundest experiences of his inmost life. He is telling us how it is possible for a man to learn to know God by first learning to know himself, and so unfold the flower of his spiritual nature and unwrap the swathings of the immemorial heart of him, that has been mummified and laid in the tomb so many ages of lives that have been living deaths.

And now we may pass to our next hymn. It is found in a beautiful little treatise which bears as title the enunciation of its subject, "Though Unmanifest God is most Manifest," and is a discourse of "father" Hermes to "son" Tat. The subject of this sermon is that mysterious manifestation of the Divine Energy which is now so well known by the Sanskrit term Māyā, so erroneously translated into English as "Illusion"—unless we venture to take this illusion in its root-meaning of Sport and Play; for in its highest sense Māyā is the Sport of the Creative Will, the World-Drama or God in activity.

The Greek equivalent of *maya* is *phantasia*, which, for lack of a single term in English to represent it rightly, I have translated by "thinking-manifest." The Phantasy of God is thus the Power (Shakti in Sanskrit) of perpetual self-manifestation or self-imagining, and is the means whereby all "This" comes into existence from the unmanifest "That"; or as our treatise phrases it:

"He is Himself, both things that are and things that are not. The things that are He hath made manifest, He keepeth things that are not in Himself.

"He is the God beyond all name—He the unmanifest, He the most manifest; He whom the mind alone can contemplate, He visible unto the eyes as well. He is the one of no body, the one of many bodies, nay, rather, He of every body."

"Naught is there which He is not, for all are He, and He is all" (ii., 104).

He is both things that are "here" in our present consciousness, and all that are not in our consciousness, or rather memory—"there" in our eternal nature. He is both the Manifest and Hidden—hidden in the manifest and manifest in the hidden, manifest in all we have been and hidden in all we shall be.

From the things that are not He maketh things that are; and so He may be said to create out of nothing—as far

THE HYMNS OF HERMES.

as we are concerned; indeed He creates out of nothing but Himself.

He is both that which the mind alone can contemplate—that is the Intelligible Universe, or that constituted in His Divine Being which the divided senses cannot perceive—and also all that which the senses, both physical and super-physical, can perceive—the whole Sensible Universe.

He is to be conceived simultaneously from a monotheistic, polytheistic and pantheistic point of view, and from many others—as many points of view indeed, as the mind of man can conceive, not to speak of an infinitude that he cannot ever imagine. He is corporeality and incorporeality in perpetual union. He is in no body, for no body can contain Him, and yet is He in every body and every body is in Him. " Naught is there which He is not, for He is all."

It is indeed difficult to understand why so many in the West so greatly dread the very thought of allowing pantheistic ideas to enter into their conception of God. This fear is in reality over-daring or rash presumption, for they have the hardihood to dare to limit the Divine according to their own petty notions of what they would like God to be, and so they bitterly resent the disturbance of their self-complacency when it is pointed out that He will not fit the miserably narrow cross on which they would fain crucify Him.

What right have we, who in our ignorance are but puny creatures of a day, to exclude God from any one or any thing? But they will reply: It is not God who is excluded; it is we who exclude ourselves from God.

Indeed; try as we may, we cannot do so. This is the impossible, for we cannot exclude ourselves from ourselves. And who are we apart from God? Did we create ourselves? And if we did, then we are God, for self-creation is the prerogative of the Divine alone.

But the pious soul will still object

that God is good alone. Agreed, if you will; but what is Good? Is Good our good only, or the Good of all creatures? And if God is the Good of all creatures, then equally so must He be the Evil of all creatures; for the good of one creature is the evil of another, and the evil of one the good of another—and so the Balance is kept even. It is a limited view to say that God is good alone, and then to define this as meaning some special form of good that we imagine for ourselves, and not that which is really good for all; for it is good that there should be such apparent evil in the universe as pantheism, and that man's notions of apparent good should so far fall short of the reality. The wise man, or rather the man who is striving after Gnosis, is he who can see in the Good and Evil as conceived by man good in every evil, and evil or insufficiency in every good.

But if we say with Hermes that " All are He and He is all," we do not assert that we know what this really means, we only assert that we are in this declaration face to face with the ultimate mystery of all things before which we can only bow the head in reverent silence, for all words here fail.

And so the mystic who wrote these sentences continues his meditation with a magnificent hymn, expressive of the inability of the learner's mind rightly to sing God's praises, which, for lack of a better title, we may call " A Hymn to All-Father God."

A HYMN TO ALL-FATHER GOD.

WHO, *then, may sing Thee praise of Thee, or praise to Thee?*

WHITHER, *again, am I to turn my eyes to sing Thy praise; above, below, within, without?*

There is no way, no place is there about Thee, nor any other thing of things that are.

THE HYMNS OF HERMES.

*All are in Thee ; all are from Thee ;
O Thou Who givest all and takest naught,
for Thou hast all and naught is there
Thou hast not.*

And WHEN, *O Father, shall I hymn
Thee ? For none can seize Thy hour or
time.*

FOR WHAT, *again, shall I sing hymn ?
For things that Thou hast made, or things
Thou hast not ? For things Thou hast
made manifest, or things Thou hast
concealed ?*

HOW, *further, shall I hymn Thee ? As
being of myself ? As having something
of mine own ? As being other ?*

*For that Thou art whatever I may be ;
Thou art whatever I may do ; Thou art
whatever I may speak.*

*For Thou art all, and there is nothing
else which Thou art not.*

*Thou art all that which doth exist, and
Thou art what doth not exist,—Mind when
Thou thinkest, and Father when Thou
makest, and God when Thou dost energize,
and Good and Maker of all things* (ii., 105).

Who is capable of singing God's praises,
when it requires the whole universe of
Being, and the countless universes of all
the beings that are, to sing the praises
of God in any truly adequate manner ?
Who, then, what man, has the understanding wherewith to praise God fitly,
when though in his separated conscious-
ness he knows not who he is, he yet begins to realize that the " who he
really is " must inevitably be God and
no other ? In what manner can the
Divine sing praises of itself as of some
other than itself, when " I " and " Thou "
must essentially be one, and the utterance of praise as of some other one seems
to be a departure from the blessed state
of that Divine intuition.

Is God again to be limited by space
and spatial considerations ? Is there
a " whither " in respect to God ? Certainly there cannot be any special place
where the Divine may be said to be, for
He is in all places, and all places and
spaces are in Him. He cannot be said
to be in the heart more than in any other
organ or limb of the body, for He is in all
things and all things are in Him. Equally
so is there no special direction in which
the eyes of the mind can turn, for He is
to be seen in every direction of thought
in which the mind can proceed ; and if
we say there are evil turnings of the
mind, evil thoughts, he who has experienced this " change of gnostic tendency " will reply that the only evil he
now knows is not to be conscious that
God is in all things, and that with the
dawning of this true self-consciousness
the right side of every thought presents
itself with the wrong side in the joy of
pure thinking.

The idea of the next praise-giving
is perhaps somewhat difficult to follow,
as it appears to be a contradiction in
terms. But in these sublime heights of
human thought all is seeming contradiction and paradox, because it is the
state of reconciliation of all opposites.

It might be said that if God is He
who gives all things, equally so must He
be He who receives all things ; but the
antithesis can be equally well declared
by the thought of all and nothing as by
the idea of giving and receiving, for God
manifestly takes nothing, in that He
has no need of anything, seeing that
He already has all things.

And if God cannot be limited by space,
equally so is it impossible that He can
be conditioned by time. Therefore the
true Gnostic *Te Deum* cannot be sung
at any one time only, but must be sung
eternally ; the man must transform himself into a perpetual song of praise in
every thought and word and deed.

Nor can the Deity be hymned for one
thing, rather than for another, for all
things are equally from God, and he
who would make himself like unto God
should have no preferences, but should
view all things with equal eye, and
embrace them all with equal love.

On account of what, again, as regards
himself in distinction from the world,

shall the Gnostic praise God? Shall he hymn the Divine for the fact of his own self-existence, or because of the powers and faculties and possessions that are his, or because he is other than, presumably, the many who are not in Gnosis? The uselessness of all such distinctions becomes apparent in the doubt that the very asking of such questions awakens, and the devotee of Wisdom brushes them all aside in splendid outburst: "For that Thou art whatever I may be; Thou art whatever I may do; Thou art whatever I may speak." There is no separation in the reality of things. Whatever the man is in this ecstatic state, it is the Being of God in him; whatever the man does, it is the Working of God in him; whatever the man speaks, it is the Word of God in him.

Nay, more than this; to such a consciousness God is in very truth all things both manifest and hidden. God is Mind when we think of Him as thinking, devising and planning; God is Father when we conceive Him as willing and creating and bringing all things into existence; and God is Good when we regard Him as energizing or inworking or breathing in all things to give them Light and Life. He is the Good or End of all things, even as He is the Beginning or Maker of all.

Our next hymn is found in the marvellous initiation ritual which now bears the title "The Secret Sermon on the Mountain," with the sub-heading "Concerning Rebirth and the Promise of Silence," but which might very well be called "The Initiation of Tat."

This Rebirth or Regeneration was, and is, the mystery of the Spiritual Birth or Birth from Above, the object of the greater mysteries, even as in the lesser mysteries, the subject of the instructions

was concerning the Birth from Below, the secret of genesis, or how a man comes into physical birth. The one was the birth or *genesis* into matter, the other the essential birth or *palingenesis*, the means of re-becoming a pure spiritual being.

It is the mystic rite of the "laying on of hands," the rite of invocation by Hermes, the hierophant or father on earth, whereby the Hands of Blessing of the Great Initiator, the Good Mind, are laid upon the head of Tat, the condidate, his son. These Hands of Blessing are no physical hands, but Powers, Rays of the spiritual Sun, even as they are symbolized in the well-known Egyptian frescoes of the Atem-cult. Each Ray is a Gnostic Power, the light and virtue of which drive out the darkness of the soul's vices and prepare the way for transforming the fleshly body into the true ray-like or star-like body of a God— the *augoeides* or *astroeides*, to which we referred under its Egyptian equivalent at the beginning of this little volume.

This mystic rite of Gnostic initiation brings the God in man to birth; he is at first, however, but a baby God, who as yet neither hears nor sees, but only feels. And so when the rite is duly ended, Tat begs as a great privilege to be told the marvellous Song of the Powers of which he has read in his studies, and which his father, Hermes, is said to have heard when he came to the Eighth Sphere or Stage in his ascent of the Holy Mountain or Sacred Stairs.

"I would, O father, hear the praisegiving with hymn which thou dost say thou heardest when thou wert at the Eight."

In answer to Tat's request Hermes replies that it is quite true the Shepherd, the Divine Mind, at his own still higher initiation into the first grade of masterhood, foretold that he should hear this Heaven-Song; and he commends Tat

31

THE HYMNS OF HERMES.

for hastening to "strike his tent" now that he has been made pure. That is to say, the final rite of purification has now been operated in Tat, the powers of the cathartic or purifying virtues have descended upon him, so that he now has the power to "strike his tent," or free himself from the trammels of the body of vice, and so rise from the tomb which has hitherto imprisoned his "daimonic soul," as the Pythian Oracle says of Plotinus.

But, adds Hermes, it is not quite as Tat supposes. There is no one Song of the Powers written in human speech and kept secret ; no MS., no oral tradition, of some physically uttered hymn.

"The Shepherd, Mind of all masterhood, hath not passed on to me more than hath been writ down, for full well did He know that I should of myself be able to learn all, and see all things.

"He left to me the making of fair things. Wherefore the Powers within me, e'en as they are in all, break into song."

The Song can be sung in many modes and many tongues, according to the inspiration of the illumined singer. The man who is reborn becomes a psalmist and a poet, for now is he tuned in harmony with the Great Harmony, and cannot do otherwise than sing God's praises. He becomes a maker of hymns and is no longer a repeater of the hymns of others.

But Tat persists ; his soul is filled with longing to hear some echo of the Great Song. "Father, I wish to hear ; I long to know these things !"

And so Hermes is at last persuaded, and proceeds to give him a model of such praise-giving which he now can use in substitution for the prayers he has previously employed, and which were more suited to one in the state of faith.

Hermes bids Tat calm himself and so await in reverent silence the hearing of the potent theurgic outpouring of the

whole nature of the man in praise of God, which shall open a path throughout all Nature straight to the Divine. This is no ordinary hymn of praise but a theurgic operation or gnostic act. Therefore, Hermes commands :

"Be still, my son ! Hear the praise-giving that keeps the soul in tune, Hymn of Rebirth—a hymn I would not have thought fit so readily to tell, had'st thou not reached the end of all."

Not, of course, the end of all Gnosis, but the end of the probationary path of purification and faith, which is the beginning of the Gnosis. Such hymns were taught only to those who had been made pure ; not to those who were slaves of the world or even to them who were still struggling with their lower vices, but only to those who had got themselves ready and "made the thought in them a stranger to the world-illusion" (ii., 220).

"Wherefore," says Hermes, "this is not taught, but is kept hid in silence."

It is a hymn that must be used ceremonially at sunrise and sunset.

"Thus then, my son, stand in a place uncovered to the sky, facing the west, about the sinking of the setting sun, and make thy worship ; so in like manner, too, when he doth rise, with face unto the east."

And for those who cannot perfect the rite on all planes, let them stand naked, with all the garments of false opinion stripped from them, naked in the midst of High Heaven's clear sphere, facing straight with the Spiritual Sun, or the Eye of Mind that illuminates the Great Sphere of our spiritual nature in the stillness of the purified intelligence.

And so Hermes, before he sings what is called "The Secret Hymnody," once more utters the solemn injunction :

"Now, son, be still !"

THE HYMNS OF HERMES.

THE SECRET HYMNODY.

Let every nature of the world receive the utterance of my hymn !
Open, thou Earth ! Let every bolt of the Abyss be drawn for me ! Stir not, ye Trees !
I am about to hymn creation's Lord, both All and One.
Ye Heavens open, and ye Winds stay still ; and let God's Deathless Sphere receive my word !
For I will sing the praise of Him who founded all ; who fixed the Earth, and hung up Heaven, and gave command that Ocean should afford sweet water to the Earth, to both those parts that are inhabited, and those that are not, for the support and use of every man ; who made the Fire to shine for gods and men for every act.
Let us together all give praise to Him, sublime above the Heavens, of every nature Lord !
'Tis He who is the Eye of Mind ; may He accept the praise of these my Powers !
Ye Powers that are within me, hymn the One and All ; sing with my Will, Powers all that are within me !
O blessed Gnosis, by thee illumined, hymning through thee the Light that mind alone can see, I joy in Joy of Mind.
Sing with me praises, all ye Powers !
Sing praise, my Self-control ; sing thou through me, my Righteousness, the praises of the Righteous ; sing thou, my Sharing-all, the praises of the All ; through me sing, Truth, Truth's praises !
Sing thou, O Good, the Good ! O Life and Light, from us to you our praises flow !
Father, I give Thee thanks, to Thee Thou Energy of all my Powers ; I give Thee thanks, O God, Thou Power of all my Energies.
Thy Reason sings through me Thy praises. Take back through me the All into Thy Reason—my reasonable oblation !
Thus cry the Powers in me. They sing Thy praise, Thou All ; they do Thy Will.
From Thee, Thy Will ; To Thee, the All. Receive from all their reasonable oblation. The All that is in us, O Life,
preserve ; O Light, illumine it ; O God, inspirit it !
It is Thy Mind that plays the Shepherd to Thy Word, O Thou Creator, Bestower of the Spirit upon all.
For Thou art God ; Thy Man thus cries to Thee, through Fire, through Air, through Earth, through Water, and through Spirit, through Thy creatures.
'Tis from Thy Æon I have found Praise-giving ; and in Thy Will, the object of my search, have I found Rest (ii., 230-232).

We can see at once that this is no ordinary hymn, no hymn conceived in the mode of the psalms to which we have been used, but the gnostic outpouring of a man who has begun to realize the nature of his own spiritual dignity and proper place in the universe, based on the tradition of what is best in Egyptian theurgy, or that Divine energizing which sends forth words of command that all nature willingly obeys.

He is about to utter words " that are true," words that from the true go unto the True, without let or hindrance. Every nature will therefore receive such words and hand them on. All elements will hasten to serve the man who is serving God with the lawful liturgy of his whole nature.

The Earth in the midst, the Heaven above, the Abyss beneath, will open all the gates of their secret ways to let the true words of him who is " true of word " pass onwards to the Deathless Sphere of the True God—that is, to the Æon itself wherein the True God dwells, not to some space of Heaven or of Earth or of the Abyss, but to that which transcends them, and is the source, preserver and end of all of them.

Not only the trees of the earth, but also the Trees of Paradise, the Divine Beings that dwell in Æonic Bliss, will rest in reverent silence as the potent praise of

THE HYMNS OF HERMES.

proper reverence passes to the end of all adorations.

The winds of earth will still themselves, and also the Winds of Heaven, the Intelligent Breaths in the inmost chambers of man's Greater Mind.

For the praise-giving is not poured forth to this or that daimon or god, but unto the Lord of All; and they, the Obedient Ones, whose life consists in praising God, cannot but rejoice that the Disobedient One should at last of his own freewill join in the unwearied liturgy of nature.

The hymn is in praise of the One and All, of the One Lord of all creation, who is both the One who creates and the All that is created. It is a hymn sung in harmony with the liturgy, or service of praise, of the four great primal natures, the Cosmic Elements of Earth and Air and Water and Fire—Father Heaven and Mother Earth, Father Fire and Mother Ocean. The man sings *with* them the glory of their common Lord, the Eye of Mind—that is, the Mind, the True Spiritual Sun, whose eyes are the countless suns in space. This True Sun is the True Light, the Light that mind alone can see; the little mind of man, now illumined by the Light of Gnosis, becomes of the nature of the Great Mind, and so a prismatic trinity of Good and Light and Life, through which the All-Brilliancy of the One and All shines forth in a septenary of Powers or Virtues,

These Powers are, with one exception, given in our hymnody in the exact classification in which they stand in the text of the mystic rite, namely: Gnosis, Joy, Self-control, Continence, Righteousness, Sharing-with-all, and Truth—which severally drive out Not-knowing, Sorrow, Intemperance, Desire, Unrighteousness, Avarice and Error. And with the coming of Truth the measure of the Good is filled full, for unto Truth is joined Good and Life and Light.

The nature of the persons of the latter trinity is still further revealed and the transmutability of these hypostases, by praising God as the Energy of all Powers and the Power of all Energies, that is, as Light and Life again, Light the masculine energizer, and Life the feminine nourisher, the father-motherhood of God, the Good, the Logos or Reason of all things.

And so the gnostic psalmist at last resolves his praise-giving into the offering of a reasonable oblation—which, in final analysis, is the Song of the Logos; the Reason, the Son of God, the Alone-begotten, singing through the whole nature of the man and refunding the cosmos which is himself into the source of his Being. It is the consummation of the Great Return; the Will of God is now the sole will of the man.

" *From Thee* Thy Will; *To Thee* the All."

That is, from Thee proceeds Thy Will; Thou art the Source of Thy Will, Thy Desire, Thy Love; and Thy Will is Thy Spouse, through whom are all things, the whole universe, Thy Alone-begotten, whose end also as well as beginning is Thyself, for He is Thyself eternally.

For as another mystic hymn of the period phrases it (i., 146): " *From Thee* is Father and *Through Thee* is Mother " —to which we may add " and *To Thee* is Son."

And so the hymn-singer continues with his " reasonable oblation," the offering of his true self, the *logos* within him, of his angel " that perpetually beholds the Face of the Father,"—praying that his whole cosmos, the whole that there is of him, may be preserved or saved by Life the Mother, illumined or irradiated by Light the Father, and inspirited or inspired or spiritualized by the Great Breath of God that eternally and simultaneously outbreathes and inbreathes.

For the man is now no longer a single " Letter " or a " Procession of Fate," but a true " Name," a free Man, a Word of God, a proper Cosmos, ordered in due and lawful harmony by the conversion of

3 4

THE HYMNS OF HERMES.

self-will into a willing union with God's Will; and of that Word, or God, or Angel, the Shepherd, or Feeder—He who gives the Divine nectar, or spiritual food, by which that Word is nourished —is the Great Mind, or Light, or Illuminator, the twin of the Great Soul, or Saving Life, the Inspirer and Preserver, both of which are bestowed upon us by God the Creator.

The man has now become a Man, a Word, a true Being of Reason, whose energy is expressed in living ideas that can be impressed upon the souls and minds of men, and lived out in a life of example; from an imperfect man he has become a perfect Cosmos or Order, or Harmony, and thus he can make his own purified natures sing together with the great elements and the quintessence of all of them, which is the Spirit or Breath of God, the Atman of Indian theosophy.

For having attained unto this true mode of breathing—breathing and thinking with the Great Life and Great Mind of things—the man is no longer a man but a Man, an Æon, an Eternity, and so rebecoming his own true Self he expresses his natural joy in songs of praise, and finds his rest in the Great Peace, the Motherhood of God. He is born anew, a child Christ; and, as he grows in stature, towards full manhood, so will she, who has hitherto been his mother, refreshed with the eternal youth of the Gods, change from mother into spouse.

The remaining hymn that has been preserved to us in the extant Trismegistic literature is found at the end of " The Perfect Sermon," of which, unfortunately, the Greek original has been lost. We are dependent solely on an Old Latin version, which is frequently unsatisfactory.

This sermon is by far the longest of our extant Trismegistic *logoi*. The introduction informs us that Hermes and Asclepius and Tat and Ammon are gathered together in the *adytum* or holy place. There the three disciples reverently listen to their master, who delivers a long instruction on the Gnosis, with the purpose of perfecting them in the knowledge of spiritual things. The discourse is, therefore, rightly called "The Perfect Sermon," or "The Sermon of Initiation."

Asclepius, Tat and Ammon stand for three types of disciples of the Gnosis, three natures of man. Asclepius is the man of intellect, skilled in the knowledge of the schools, of the arts and sciences of the day. Tat is intuitional rather than intellectual; he is "young" compared with Asclepius; nevertheless it is he who succeeds Hermes as teacher, when Hermes is taken to the Gods, for he has the spiritual nature more strongly developed than Asclepius, so that he can soar to greater heights of illumination. Ammon is the practical man of affairs, the king, the doer, not the scientist or the mystic.

It would, however, be a mistake to keep these types too clearly distinguished in our mind; for mystically all three are in each of us, and the true illumination of our three-fold nature depends upon their proper balance and harmony, upon the brotherly love of the three disciples —James, John and Peter—who must each complete each other, and subordinate themselves to one another, and vie with one another in love of their teacher, the purified mind, or Hermes, through whom alone the instruction of the Great Mind, the Shepherd, can as yet come to them.

And so we find the conditions of right contemplation dramatically set forth in the last sentence of the introduction of the sermon in the words :

" When Ammon, too, had come within the holy place, and when the sacred group of four was now complete with piety and with God's goodly Presence—to them, sunk in fit silence reverently, their souls and minds pendent on Hermes' lips, thus Love Divine began to speak (ii., 309).

3 5

THE HYMNS OF HERMES.

This Love Divine is that same Presence, the Highest Mind, or Shepherd of men, which illumines Hermes, or the higher mind within us, directly; but these immediate living words of power have to be passed on in human words to the three natures of our lower mind, the Asclepius and Tat and Ammon in us, who are the learners and hearers.

After the instruction is ended and they have come forth from the holy place, the narrative tells us that they turned their faces towards the setting sun, before uttering their hymn of praise.

That is to say mystically, the mind ceasing from contemplation, in which the outward energies have been caught up to the heights, or turned within, and stilled by the higher in the intercourse of Love that has been blessed with the Presence of the Divine, these energies, before betaking themselves to their appointed separate tasks, all unite in a hymn of praise, with their eyes still turned to the now apparently departing glory of the setting spiritual Sun.

Hereupon the knower of forms in us, the Asclepius who is wise in the sciences and arts, and ceremonies, proposes to Tat, in whispered words, that they suggest to their father Hermes, that they should say their prayer to God " with added incense and with unguents." This is the suggestion of the mind that still clings to outward forms, the ritualist. But Hermes recalls them to the gnostic nature of their spiritual cult.

" Whom when Thine greatest heard, he grew distressed and said :

" ' Nay, nay, Asclepius ; speak more propitious words ! For this is like to profanation of our sacred rites—when thou dost pray to God, to offer incense and the rest.

" ' For naught is there of which He stands in need, in that He is all things, and all are in Him.

" ' But let us worship, pouring forth our thanks. For this is the best incense in God's sight—when thanks are given to Him by men " (ii., 388).

And so they begin their praise-giving, which for lack of a better title we may call " A Hymn of Grace for Gnosis."

A HYMN OF GRACE FOR GNOSIS.

We give Thee grace, Thou highest and most excellent ! For by Thy Grace we have received the so great Light of Thy own Gnosis.

O holy Name, fit Name to be adored, O Name unique, by which God only must be blest through worship of our Sire,—of Thee who deignest to afford to all a Father's piety, and care, and love, and whatsoever virtue is more sweet than these, endowing us with sense, and reason, and intelligence ; —with sense that we may feel Thee ; with reason that we may track Thee out from the appearances of things ; with means of recognition that we may joy in knowing Thee.

Saved by Thy Power divine, let us rejoice that Thou hast shown Thyself to us in all Thy Fullness. Let us rejoice that Thou hast deigned to consecrate us, still entombed in bodies, to Eternity.

For this is the sole festival of praise worthy of man—to know Thy Majesty.

We know Thee ; yea, by the Single Sense of our intelligence, we have perceived Thy Light supreme,—O Thou True Life of life, O Fecund Womb that giveth birth to every nature !

We have known Thee, O Thou completely filled with the Conception from Thyself of Universal Nature !

We have known Thee, O Thou Eternal Constancy !

For in the whole of this our prayer in worship of Thy Good, this favour only of Thy Goodness do we crave : that Thou wilt keep us constant in our Love-of-knowing-Thee, and let us ne'er be cut off from this kind of Life (ii., 389, 390).

3 6

THE HYMNS OF HERMES.

We give Thee thanks, grace for Grace, goodwill for Thy Goodwill. The Goodwill of God is, as we have already learned, that " He willeth to be known," and the goodwill of man is his " love of knowing God."

The Latin of the next sentence is very obscure, but judging by other passages and by the context, the unique effable Name of God is " Father." The worship of God as Father is true religion, piety and love, since these are the natural expressions of thanks to God, in that it is He who pours out on us the treasures of His piety and care (*religio* in Latin) and love, though indeed all of these words really fall short of expressing this Divine *efficacia*, or power of giving utter satisfaction, of God; for He alone gives without stint, in that He bestows His Fullness upon us.

He endows us with sense and reason and intelligence, the three means of knowing Him : with sense to feel God in all things ; with reason to track out the manifestation of the Divine in all phenomena ; and with intelligence, or spiritual intuition, which is the means of face to face recognition, when objective and subjective blend, and when object and subject blend and there is the complete joy and satisfaction of Self-knowledge.

The Power of God is the Will of God, the Goodwill, whereby He willeth to be known, that is to say, the Purpose of which is Gnosis ; and this brings joy and rejoicing, for it is the manifestation of God to man in all His Fullness, that is to say, the manifestation of the Plērōma, the Intelligible Cosmos, or God in the nature of His Alone-begotten Son.

The " holy four " sing with joy in that they have been made holy, hallowed as priests of the Most High, while still in the tomb of the body ; and so their very bodies have been consecrated as fit temples of the Son of God, the Æon or Eternity.

Therefore the sole festival of praise worthy of man in his divine nature, that is, in his true manhood or union with Great Mind—is to know God's Majesty or Greatness, that is, again, the Æon.

This Knowing, or Gnosis, is achieved by the Single Sense of the intelligence ; not by sense alone, nor by mind alone, but by a means superior to both, in which the twain blend in Gnosis, and so become conscious with a new consciousness, or self-knowledge, of the Light of God, or the Over-mind of all things, and of the Life of God, or the Over-Soul of all things, which latter is graphically described as the " Fecund Womb that giveth birth to every nature."

This is the Gnosis of the Divine as the Plērōma, or Fullness, which is replete with the Conception of universal nature from God Himself.

Finally, God is praised for being known as the Eternal Constancy, Stability, Duration, Unchangeableness, Sameness.

And so this beautiful gnostic thanksgiving or grace ends with the one prayer of those in Gnosis, namely, that He who is Eternal Constancy, or God in His energy of Æonic Sameness, will ever keep them constant in the Pure and Single Love, the Love of knowing God.

What noble hymns are these four, hymns worthy of all that is best in man, and all that is worthiest in the true worshipper of God ! If only we had a psalter of such psalms, as doubtless once existed in this excellent community of servants of God and Gnostic liturgists ! But alas ! while the indifference of time has preserved for us so much of the classical writers that we could not unfrequently well spare, the jealousy of Providence has kept from us the major part of the most beautiful monuments of man's gnostic genius—perchance, however, because the world was not ready to appreciate them.

There is, therefore, nothing to do but to follow again the Way of the Hermeses of the past, and betake ourselves once more to " the making of fair things," for what

THE HYMNS OF HERMES.

man has once achieved he can again accomplish, and, if I am not mistaken in my augury, the times are again becoming ripe for such true poesy.

We have no more Hymns of Hermes wherewith to make glad the hearts of our readers—as we would fain hope they have gladdened them—but we will add another hymn of so like a nature that it might very well have been penned by a Hermes of the Trismegistic faith.

It is " A Song of Praise to the Æon," which is said to have been inscribed on a "secret tablet," by some unknown Brother of a forgotten Order, perhaps one of the Communities of the Æon—the Highest and Supercelestial One—which Philo of Byblos, in the second half of the first century of our era, tells us were in existence in Phœnicia in his day, and doubtless were also existing in Egypt (i., 403). The text is found in the Greek Magic Papyri.

A SONG OF PRAISE
TO THE ÆON.

Hail unto Thee, O Thou All-Comos of ætherial Spirit !

Hail unto Thee, O Spirit, who doth extend from Heaven to Earth, and from the Earth that's in the middle of the orb of Cosmos to the ends of the Abyss !

Hail unto Thee, O Spirit, who doth enter into me, who clingeth unto me or who doth part Thyself from me according to the Will of God in goodness of His heart !

Hail unto Thee, O Thou Beginning and Thou End of Nature naught can move !

Hail unto Thou, Thou Liturgy unweariable of Nature's Elements !

Hail unto Thee, O Thou Illumination of the Solar Beam that shines to serve the world !

Hail unto Thee, Thou Disk of the night-shining Moon, that shines unequally !

Hail, Ye Spirits all of the ætherial Statues of the Gods !

Hail to You all, whom holy Brethren and holy Sisters hail in giving of their praise !

O Spirit, Mighty One, most mighty circling and incomprehensible Configuration of the Cosmos, hail !—celestial, æthereal, inter-æthereal, water-like, earth-like, fire-like, air-like, like unto light, to darkness like, shining as do the Stars—moist, hot, cold Spirit !

I praise Thee, God of gods, who ever doth restore the Cosmos, and who doth store the Depth away upon its Throne of Settlement no eye can see, who fixest Heaven and Earth apart, and coverest the Heaven with Thy golden everlasting wings, and makest firm the Earth on everlasting Thrones !

O Thou who hangest up the Æther in the lofty Height, and scatterest the Air with Thy self-moving Blasts, who mak'st the Water eddy round in circles !

O Thou who raisest up the Fiery Whirl-wind, and makest thunder, lightning, rain, and shakings of the earth, O God of Æons !

Mighty art Thou, Lord God, O Master of the All ! (i., 408, 409).

The Æon is the Invisible Intelligible Cosmos, the All-Cosmos of Æthereal Spirit or Quintessence, as distinguished from the Sensible Cosmos of the four Great Elements, pure Fire and Air and Water and Earth, and not our mixed elements.

The reader has only to compare the opening and closing sentences of " The Secret Hymnody " with the first paragraph of our hymn to see that we are in precisely the same circle of ideas.

Heaven, Earth and the Abyss, the three worlds, through which the Spirit, like Vishnu in the Purāna's, takes "three strides."

It is this Spirit, the Great Breath of Life, that is the out-breath and in-breath of man's manifold existences. When the Spirit breathes out he is born, from death into life, and also from life into death ; for the life of the body is the death of the soul. And when the Spirit inbreathes he becomes dead, dead to things of the body, but alive to the things of the soul.

And all this is " according to the Will of God in goodness of His heart." For the Will of God is the Energy, or Effective Working, of God,—that which transcends all our human ideas of Love—dictated by the goodness of His heart, which ever wills the good of all beings, for the Heart of God is the Good Itself, the Æon.

The Æon is neither Beginning nor End, but both ; for all the Spheres of Being which it energizes, end where they begin, and begin where they end—they dance in eternal revolution, for their " everlasting revelling-place " is in the Vortex of the Ceaseless Liturgy, or Service, of the Elements. The Æon is the Cause of the Magna Vorago, the Mighty Whirlpool of the Universe, for it is the Monad or Supreme Atom of all atoms and all combinations of atoms.

The Æon is the Illumination or Source of Light for all the Lights of Heaven, the Sun and Moon and all the rest of the " Æthereal Statues of the Gods "— the countless suns in space.

The Æon is Spirit, of Light and Life consisting, and so Father-Mother of all Spirits, whose true Bodies are the fiery spheres, the sidereal bodies—ray-like, star-like.

Therefore, the Brethren and Sisters of this community of gnostic servants of God rightly praise all the Gods, for these Gods are the true community of saints or holy ones in Heaven, even as the Brethren and Sisters are endeavouring to become saints on earth, holy as they are holy.

The Æon is the Great Paradigm or One Exemplar of all things, the Eternal Configuration of the Cosmos and all cosmoi, in a septenary of three quint-essential and four essential elements, which are completed by the all-colour, Light, and no-colour, Darkness, into a decad of which Spirit is the beginning and the end, existing in three modes—

reminding us of the Trigunam, or three-fold nature of Prakriti or Nature in Indian theosophy—moist, hot, cold ; black red, white ; Tamas, Rajas and Sattva.

The Great Work of the God of Gods is perpetually to restore the Cosmos, to refresh, to renew it, in its threefold nature of Height and Midst and Depth —the endoderm, mesoderm and ecto-derm, as it were, of the cosmic germ-cell —over which the Spirit broods with its golden everlasting wings, as the Great Bird who perpetually hatches forth the Egg of the Universe.

And from this brooding there ever comes forth into being the perpetual cosmo-genesis of all things ; and, seeing that all beings come forth from the Æon, each and all, in their cosmic nature, are Æons as well, so that the Æon is also God of Æons.

He is the God of millions of years, of millions of months, and millions of days —whether those time-periods be of the earth or of the universe—and so God of all existences, even as He is God of the Eternity of all beings.

And here we must bring our little hymn-book to a close, in the hope that some may be found to sing in response to the Hymns of Heathen Hermes even in this twentieth century of Christian grace ; for perhaps, after all, Hermes and Christ are not in reality such strangers to each other as traditional theological prejudice would have us believe.

39

THE . . . .
VISION . .
OF . . . .
ARIDÆUS. .

THE VISION OF ARIDÆUS

CONTENTS

The text used is that of Bernardakis, published in the Bibliotheca Teubneriana series (Leipzig ; 1891).

THE VISION OF ARIDÆUS.

THE VISION OF ARIDÆUS.

PREAMBLE.

The Story of Aridæus is the most detailed and graphic Vision of Hades preserved to us from classical antiquity, and exceeds in interest even Plato's Story of Ēr and Cicero's Dream of Scipio, not to speak of the less known Visions of Krates and of Zosimus.

It brings to a striking conclusion the instructive treatise of Plutarch, the Greek title of which may be rendered, *On the Delay of the Deity in Punishing the Wicked* or *On the Delay of Divine Justice.*

Plutarch of Chæroneia, in Bœotia, flourished in the last quarter of the first and first quarter of the second century (? 50-120 A.D.). He was one of the most enlightened of the ancients, exceedingly well versed in the details of the religious philosophies and the sciences of his day, and possessed of good critical abilities ; he was also a man of wide religious experience, holding high office at Delphi in the service of Apollo and also in connection with the Dionysiac Rites, and had a profound knowledge of the inner grades of the Osiric Mysteries, and doubtless of other Mystic traditions. He was educated in Athens and Alexandria and lectured at Rome.

Plutarch is one of our most valuable sources of information on the Hellenic and Hellenistic theology, theosophy and mystagogy of the first century, and is therefore indispensable in any comparative study of the Gnosis.

Our philosopher has been variously styled a Platonist, Neo-platonist, Eclectic, Ethicist and Syncretist ; but it is very difficult to label Plutarch precisely, for as Dr. John Oakesmith, in his instructive essay, *The Religion of Plutarch : A Pagan Creed of Apostolic Times* (London ; 1902),

says, he " suggested a frame of mind rather than inculcated a body of dogma." He was in some ways a very good specimen of what we ought to mean to day by the term theosophist. Though there is not a single word in the whole of his voluminous writings to show that he was acquainted with Christianity, it has nevertheless been argued that he must have derived his ethics and monotheistic ideas from Christianity ; and, curiously enough, Dr. Charles Super, in his *Between Heathenism and Christianity* (Chicago ; 1889), selects the very treatise of Plutarch's which contains our Vision (together with Seneca's *Concerning Providence*), to demonstrate the intimate points of contact between the religio-philosophy of the time and the New Religion.

We have, however, shown at length in the Prolegomena to *Thrice Greatest Hermes* that the doctrines of Hellenistic theology, theosophy and gnosis were widespread in the first century, and had in many ways a common language with the books of the New Testament writers ; there is, however, no question of direct plagiarism on either side.

The Vision of Aridæus is of interest in many ways, and doubtless that interest would be increased for us if we could be persuaded with Count Joseph de Maistre, that " it is permissible to believe that Dante took the general idea of his Inferno " from the description of the punishments in our Vision, as de Maistre writes in his translation of the treatise (Paris ; 1856). I must, however, leave that suggestion to Dante scholars, with the remark that it is now proved, especially by the work of Dr. J. E. Sandys, that the Renaissance of classical studies began, long before the capture of Constantinople, in the days of Petrarch and Boccaccio.

Concerning the source and composition of the Vision, and how Plutarch intended us to take it, as many opinions may be held as in the case of the better-known

43

THE VISION OF ARIDÆUS.

Vision of Ēr in Plato. I would, however, myself suggest that the key to the situation is to be found in the following passage of our philosopher-mystagogue :

" When a man dies he goes through the same experiences as those who have their consciousness increased in the Mysteries. Thus in the terms τελευτᾶν ('to die ') and τελεῖσθαι (' to be initiated ') we have an exact correspondence, word to word and fact to fact.

" First of all there are wanderings and wearying journeyings and paths on which we look with suspicion, and that seem to have no end ; then, before the end, every kind of terror, shuddering, trembling, sweating, stupor.

" But at last a marvellous light shines out to meet us, pure spots and fair fields welcome us, with song and dance and the solemnities of sacred sounds and holy sights.

" In which state he who has already perfected himself in all things and received initiation, reaches his full freedom, and passing everywhere at will, receives the crown, and accomplishes his mystery, in communion with the holy and pure; gazing down upon the unpurified multitude of the uninitiated who are still in life, wallowing in the deep mire and mist, and herded together below him, abiding in misery from fear of death and want of faith in the blessedness of the soul-life.

" For you should know that the intercourse and conjunction of the soul with body is contrary to nature." (Plut., *Fragm.* v. 9, ed. Didot).

The further consideration of this suggestion, however, will more conveniently come later, when the reader has become acquainted with the Vision.

The treatise is in the form of a Platonic dialogue. The persons of the dialogue are : Plutarch himself, who is the chief speaker ; Patrocleas, his son-in-law ; Timon, his brother ; and Olympichus, an intimate friend. The scene is the Portico of the Temple of Apollo at Delphi. The tract is addressed to a certain Quintus, who must have been a Roman, but of whom nothing further is known.

In the course of his argument, Plutarch remarks that no punishment is more distressing and makes us more ashamed than to see our children suffering through our misdeeds. And if the soul of an impious law-breaker could after death see his children or friends or family in great adversity because of him and paying the penalty of his misdeeds, no one would ever be able to persuade him, even for the wealth of Zeus, to be unjust or licentious again on his return to earth.

" I could tell you a true story (*logos*) which I lately heard," he continues, " but I'm afraid you would think it a tale (*mythos*) ; I therefore confine myself to probability only."

As, however, the others pressed for the story, Plutarch replied : " Permit me first to finish the argument as to probabilities, and then, if you like, I will set the tale going, if indeed it be a tale."

Plutarch here evidently intends it to be understood that for him the story is *logos* and not *mythos* ; and by *logos* he means as evidently that it is based on " fact " and not " probability."

This is plain from his own words, and is further strengthened by the general use at that date of the word *logos* for a serious narrative, especially a " sacred discourse," or a story of initiation.

It is further of interest to note that Plato at the end of his story of the Vision of Er refers to it as a *mythos*. Can Plutarch have had this in mind, and does he wish to draw a distinction between his " logos " and the famous "myth " of Plato ?

It is more than probable that the myths of Plato had been frequently discussed in the schools, and that there were very various opinions as to how they were to be taken ; the term *myth* had fallen into disrepute among the learned, and Plutarch

THE VISION OF ARIDÆUS.

here as elsewhere uses *logos* as a better description of a narrative connected with the doctrines of initiation.

Plutarch tells us that the hero of his story was a certain Aridæus of Soli, a town on the sea-coast of Asia Minor ; he was an intimate friend of Protogenes of Tarsus (Plut., *On Love*, ii.) who stayed with Plutarch for some time at Delphi. Aridæus related his experiences to Protogenes and other intimate friends ; and so we may suppose that Plutarch first heard the story from Protogenes, and finding it somewhat in keeping with what he himself had been taught, or seen dramatically represented, in one or other of the initiatory-rites through which he had passed, he polished it up and amplified it to suit his purpose.

This Aridæus had lived a notorious life of great profligacy and villainy ; he was a sort of millionaire scoundrel of the period. Report had it that on his sending to ask the Oracle of Amphilochus, at Mallus in Cilicia, whether there was any chance of his living a better life for the rest of his days, he received the reply that he would do better when he was dead. Shortly after, Aridæus had a severe fall, and though he broke no bones, the shock did for him. Three days later, just as they were about to bury him, he recovered consciousness. After this unpleasant experience, Aridæus became an entirely reformed character, of quite exemplary virtue. Such a startling change could not pass unnoticed ; but it was only to a few of his greatest friends that he told what had happened to him during the " three days." The story runs as follows :

THE VISION.

When his consciousness passed out of the body, he experienced from the change the same sort of sensation that a sailor would who had been swept overboard into deep water. Then, coming up a little, he seemed to breathe in every part of him, and to see on every side at once, as though the soul—the " single eye "—had been opened.

Of objects with which he had been previously familiar, he saw none save the stars ; they were, however, of stupendous size and at enormous distances from one another, and poured forth a marvellous radiance of colour and sound, so that the soul riding smoothly in the light, as a ship in calm weather, sailed easily and swiftly in every direction.

Omitting most of the things he saw, he said that the souls of the dead, in passing from below upwards, formed a flame-like bubble from which the air was excluded ; then the bubble quietly broke, and they came forth with men-like forms and well-knit frames. They, however, differed in their movements ; some leaped out with wonderful lightness and darted straight up ; but others kept turning round together in a circle, like spindles, bobbing up and down, with a mixed and confused motion, which recovered its balance only after a long time and with great difficulty.

As to the majority of them, he did not know who they were ; he recognized, however, two or three acquaintances, and tried to join them and enter into conversation. They, however, neither heard him, nor were they themselves. Demented and panic-stricken, avoiding every look and touch, they first turned round and round by themselves ; then, falling in with many in the same condition, they huddled together, drifting about in every direction confusedly, with no object in view, and

THE VISION OF ARIDÆUS.

uttering meaningless shouts, like war-cries, intermingled with wails and screams of fear.

Other souls, however, were to be seen above at the top of the envelope [or surround] shining with joy, frequently approaching one another in friendly inter-course but avoiding the troubled souls below them. They seemed to show their dislike by drawing themselves together into themselves, and their joy and delight by expansion and extension.

In that region, he said, he saw only one soul of a relative, though he was not quite sure about it, for his kinsman had died while he (Aridæus) was still a boy. However, he came up to him and said : "Welcome, Thespesius !" And on his replying in surprise that his name was not Thespesius, but Aridæus, the other remarked :

"It *was* Aridæus, but from henceforth it will be Thespesius [that is, 'Sent by the Gods ']; for indeed thou art not dead, but by the will of the Gods thou art come hither with thy reason about thee, whilst thou hast left the rest of thy soul, as it were an anchor, in the body. And this thou mayest now and hereafter prove to thyself by the fact that the souls of the dead cast no shadow and never close their eyelids."

On hearing this, Thespesius set himself the more to use his rational faculties, and taking a closer look he saw that he had a faint and shadowy outline attached to him, while they [the dead] shone all round and were transparent, though not all in the same way. For some were like the purest full-moon light, emitting one smooth, continuous and even colour ; while others had patches across them or narrow strips. Others again were quite mottled—extraordinary sights—dappled with livid spots, like adders ; and others had faint scratches.

Then Thespesius' kinsman (for there is nothing to prevent our calling souls by persons' names) pointed out everything, telling him that Adrasteia, daughter of Necessity and Zeus, had been set in highest heaven to administer retribution for all offences ; and no sinner was either great enough or small enough to escape her by force or avoid her vigilance.

" There are three kinds of punishment," he continued, " each appropriate to one of the warders and executors [of Adrasteia]. For speedy Punishment (Poinē) deals with those who are chastized at once, in the body and through their bodies, but in somewhat mild fashion, since many offences are passed over as requiring purification only. In the case of those, however, whose moral cure is a more serious business, they are handed over by their conscience (lit. *daimōn*) to Justice (Dīkē) after their decease. And finally, in the case of those who are rejected by Justice as altogether incurable, Fury, (Erinys) the third and most implacable of Adrasteia's ministers, pursues them as they wander and flee, some one way, some another, and pitifully and cruelly undoes them all and thrusts them down into a state of which we can neither speak nor think.

" Of these [three] kinds of correction," he said, " that which is effected by Punishment, while a man is still alive, resembles a method of chastisement in vogue with the Persians, among others, when they strip the clothes and head-dresses off the culprits and scourge the former, while the latter entreat them with tears to stop. In like manner, punishments by means of loss of goods and bodily suffering do not really probe the disease sharply nor reach vice itself, but for the most part touch only the reputations and sensibilities of the culprits.

" Accordingly whenever a man leaves that world for this unpunished and im-pure, Justice grips him by the soul just as he is, naked, unable to put anything on, and so hide and cloak his villainy,

4 6

but every bit of him in full view of every one on all sides.

"And first of all he is shown to his good parents, if such they are, or to his ancestors, as an object of loathing and a disgrace to the family ; whereas if his forebears are bad, he has to look on their punishments and they on his ; and this continues for a long time, until he has exhausted every one of his evil tendencies in pain and toil, which in extent and intensity as much exceed all suffering in the body, as waking consciousness is more vivid than a dream. And the scars and marks of every one of their evil tendencies more or less remain on all of them.

"Observe," he continued, " the colours of the souls of every shade and sort : that greasy brown-grey is the pigment of sordidness and selfishness ; that blood-red inflamed shade is a sign of a savage and venomous nature ; wherever blue-gray is, from such a nature incontinence in pleasure is not easily eradicated ; innate malignity, mingled with envy, causes that livid discoloration in the same way as cuttle-fish eject their sepia.

"Now it is in earth-life that the vice of the soul (being acted upon by the passions and reacting upon the body) produces these discolorations ; while the purification and correction here have for their object the removal of these blemishes, so that the soul may become entirely ray-like (*augoeidēs*) and of uniform colour.

"As long as these colours are present, there are relapses into the passions, accompanied with pulsings and throbbings ; with some souls faint and soon suppressed, but with others vigorously intensified.

"Of these, some by dint of repeated correction at length recover their proper disposition and condition ; others again, by the strength of their intractability and their being nailed down to the love of pleasure, are carried down to the bodies of beasts.

"The former, through weakness of reason and inertia of the contemplative principle, are carried down by the practical element to birth [as men] ; while the latter, lacking an instrument for their unbridled lust, long to unite desires to enjoyment and bring these together by means of [any] body,—for out of body there is only an imperfect shadow and dream of pleasure without fulfilment."

After these explanations he was conducted by his guide at great speed across an immense space, as it seemed, nevertheless easily and directly as though supported by wings of light-rays, until, having arrived at a vast vortex extending downwards, he was abandoned by the power which supported him.

He observed also that the same thing happened to the rest of the souls there ; for checking their flight, like birds, and sinking down, they fluttered round the vortex in a circle, not daring to go straight through it.

Inside it seemed to be decked, like Bacchic Caves, with trees and verdure and every kind of foliage ; while out of it there breathed a soft and gentle air, laden with marvellous sweet scents, making a blend like wine for topers, so that the souls feasting on the perfume were melted with delight in mutual embraces, while the whole place was wrapt in revelry and laughter and the spirit of sport and pleasure.

Thespesius' guide told him that this was the way by which Dionysus ascended to the Gods and afterwards took up Semelē ; it was called the Place of Oblivion (Lēthē).

Therefore he would not suffer Thespesius to stay there, though he wished to do so, but forcibly dragged him away ; explaining how that the rational element of the soul was melted and moistened by pleasure, while the irrational and that which tends to body being thus moistened and made fleshly, awakens the memory of the body, and from this memory comes a yearning and desire which drag down the

THE VISION OF ARIDÆUS.

soul into generation, . . . the soul-being weighed down with moisture.

Then Thespesius, after taking another journey as great as the former one, seemed to see in the distance a huge basin, with streams flowing into it : one whiter than the foam of the sea or snow ; another like the purple which the rainbow sends forth ; while others were tinged with other colours, each at a distance having its own splendour.

But when they came closer, the basin itself (the surroundings disappearing and the colours growing fainter) lost its varied colouring and retained only a white brilliance. And he saw three beings (*daimones*) seated together, forming a triangle one with the other, mixing the streams in definite proportions. Thespesius' soul-guide thereupon informed him that Orpheus had advanced as far as this when he went in search of the soul of his wife, but, through not remembering correctly, had spread an erroneous report that the Oracle at Delphi was shared by Apollo and Night, whereas Apollo had nothing to do with Night.

" But that which you see," he said, " is the common oracle of Night and Selēnē, which eventuates nowhere on the earth in one particular seat, but meanders in every direction manwards in visions and images. It is from this that dreams, after being mixed, as you see, spread abroad a mixture of the simple and true with the complex and fallacious.

" As for the Oracle of Apollo," he continued, " you have not seen it, nor will you be able to do so, for the stern-cable of your soul does not give or slacken further upwards, but drags it down through being made fast to the body."

At the same time his guide brought him closer and tried to show him the light which streamed from the Tripod, as he explained, through the Bosom of Themis and rested upon Parnassus.

But though he longed to see, he could not because of the dazzling nature of the light. As he passed, however, he caught a woman's high voice in rhythmic verse prophesying—among other things apparently the time of his own death.

His genius (*daimōn*) told him that this was the voice of the Sibyl, who sings of things to come as she circles in the face of the Moon. He would therefore have liked to hear more, but was driven in the opposite direction by the Moon's impetus, as in the eddies of a whirlpool. So he heard but little, but that little contained a prophecy about Mount Vesuvius and the destruction of Dicæarcheia by fire, and a scrap about the reigning Emperor, which ran :

" Being good, by sickness will he leave his throne."

After this they turned back to see the punishments. And first of all nothing but distressing and pitiful sights met their eyes ; till suddenly Thespesius, without at all expecting it, came across his own friends, kinsfolk and intimates in torment ; and they in their terrible sufferings and unseemly and painful chastisements lamented and wept aloud to him.

And last of all he looked down upon his own father emerging from some sort of a pit, covered with marks and scars, stretching out his hands to him ; he was no longer allowed to keep silence, but compelled by the authorities to confess that his hands were stained with the blood of some wealthy strangers he had poisoned. On earth he had completely succeeded in escaping detection, but in the after-state all was brought home to him ; for part of his crimes he had already been punished, but for the rest he had still to suffer.

But so great were Thespesius' consternation and terror, that he dared not intercede or entreat for his father. When, however, he would have turned and fled, he could no longer see his gentle and familiar guide, but was thrust forward by

4 8

THE VISION OF ARIDÆUS.

others of terrifying appearance, and as though there were no choice but to go through with the business.

Thus he had to see that the shades of those who were known to be bad and had been punished in earth-life, did not get such a dressing, as they had already done hard labour for their irrational and passionate natures; whereas those who had passed their lives in undetected vice, under cloak and show of virtue, were forced by those who surrounded them, to turn their souls inside out in throes of pain, wriggling in unnatural contortions, just as sea-polyps turn themselves inside out after swallowing the hook.

Some of these they flayed, and peeling off their skins showed them covered with spots and festering sores, owing to the diseased condition of their rational and ruling principle. Others, he said, he saw entwined like snakes, two, three, or more together, malevolently devouring one another in revenge for what they had suffered or done to each other while living.

There were further [three] lakes alongside one another : one of boiling-hot gold ; one of lead, bitterly cold ; another of iron, terribly hard. And there were dæmons on duty, who, just like smiths with tongs, put in and took out the souls of those who suffered from the vice of insatiable greed and avarice.

After they had been made red-hot and transparent by firing them in the gold lake, they thrust them into the lead one and gave them a bath in it; and after they had been frozen there and made as hard as hail, they further transferred them into the lake of iron ; there they became terribly black, and after being smashed up by its hardness and crushed to atoms, they changed their shapes. They were then in this state taken back again to the gold lake, suffering, he said, terrible agonies in their transformations.

But the most pitiable sufferings of all, Thespesius declared, were those of the souls who, when they seemed to have at last got their discharge from Justice, were arrested again. These were the souls of those whose crimes had been visited on their children or descendants.

For whenever one of the latter happened to come up, he fell upon the criminal in a rage, crying out against him and showing him the marks of his sufferings, reproaching him and pursuing after him. And though he tried to get away and hide himself, he could not ; for the chastizers speedily hunted them back to Justice and constrained them all over again, in spite of their pitiful cries for mercy owing to what they already knew of the punishments in store.

And to some of them, he said, many of the souls of their descendants attached themselves, just like bees or bats, crowding thick upon each other, and gibbering in anger at the memory of what they had suffered through them.

Last of all he saw the souls [of this class] who were returning to birth, being forcibly turned into all sorts of beasts, having their shapes changed by the shapers of animals, with blows of curious instruments. In some cases they hammered the whole of their parts together ; in others they twisted them back, and some parts they planed off smooth, and got rid of them entirely, so that they might be fitted to other habits and modes of life.

Among them he saw the soul of Nero in a bad state generally and pierced with red-hot nails. The smiths had in hand for it the form of Pindar's viper, in which it would be conceived and come to life by gnawing itself through its mother. Hereupon, he said, a great light suddenly shone forth, and a voice from the light was heard giving orders to change it into a milder type, and devise a creature that croaks round marshes and lakes ; he had been already punished for his crimes,

THE VISION OF ARIDÆUS.

and now some favour was due to him from the Gods for having freed Greece, the most excellent nation of his subjects and the one dearest to the Gods.

This was as far as Thespesius got in his vision. When, however, he was going to turn back, he had a most terrible fright ; for a woman of amazing form and size seized hold of him, with the words : " Come thou to me so that thou mayest the better remember the details " ; and she was just going to use on him a red-hot stylus, like [encaustic] painters, when another woman stopped her.

Then, as though he were suddenly sucked through a tube by a terribly strong and violent in-breath, he lit in his body, and woke up just as they were on the point of burying him.

COMMENTS.

The consideration of this story of vision opens up so many important questions that the main difficulty is to compress within the limits of this small volume a portion of what might be written. I shall therefore attempt to touch on some of the more general points of interest only.

We first notice that the consciousness of the soul passes from what we may call the plane of " earth " to that of " water " ; and it is probably from this, which seems to be a somewhat general fact of psychic experience, that the glyphs of " water," " sea," " ocean," etc., have been adopted so widely as symbolic of subtle matter.

In this state souls may be said to " sail about," because apparently there is no motion of limbs ; their " astral " vehicle

is conveyed by the current ; they sail about on sound- or light-waves, perceiving no ordinary physical mind-forms, but " stars," certain magnitudes, or perhaps " nodes," where certain greater currents meet. Or, if we must interpret this sublime spectacle in a more physical sense, it may be said to pertain to the region beyond the lower earth-atmosphere where sight is unobscured by that atmosphere.

The " single eye " is a Platonic term.

The " flame-like bubble " vehicling the souls of the dead is a graphic phrase that reminds us admirably of all we have heard of what has been called in modern theosophy the " auric envelope."

But why is the " air " said to be excluded from it ? If it is permissible to lay stress on the point, I would suggest that it is because what is called here " air," in connection with what has been previously called " earth " and " water," is that which brings with it proper self-consciousness. " Fire," " water," and " earth " play together to make the " forms." If the " bubbles " had had " air " in them, they would have been fully developed proper souls, capable of looking at themselves, considering and studying themselves from without personality. The " bubbles " thus pertain to a lower state of development, namely, the " watery spheres."

But I fear that this mode of interpretation may perhaps prove slightly perplexing, and I will therefore not pursue it. It need only be added, to complete the idea for those who choose to follow it up for themselves, that it might be said that every one at death delivers over something, and then reappears in his own true inner form. Those who " darted straight up " to the higher " air," would thus be those who were able to retain with themselves something outside personality.

" Air," in this sense would be outside

THE VISION OF ARIDÆUS.

personality, and we need something within ourselves to correspond, to attract us "up" to these more transcendent states of consciousness.

To keep more closely to our text ; the vision here seems to describe in graphic fashion the difference between souls that are balanced and souls that are unbalanced ; the former pass to a state of calm, if not of equilibrium, and the latter remain in the swirling currents of the lower emotional nature, the currents or streams in the great emotional sea, on the waves of which they drift rather than sail. Its state is determined by whether the soul's consciousness is centred in a properly built formal or completely human mind or in an embryonic or animal-human mind. In Greek terms, these states or habitats are called Elysium and Hades ; or, if we please, the higher and lower Hades or Invisible.

The state of the less developed souls is well depicted by our vision, for numerous seers in our own day agree in stating that many of those who die are either in great fear owing to the soul-paralyzing doctrine of an eternal hell, or are all-distraught at the strange and unexpected nature of their surroundings, being aware of neither where they are nor what is expected of them.

Our seer tried to talk to them, but they avoided him. This is apparently more or less true at all times and in all places under such circumstances ; for Aridæus being still alive, and being under special favour, or "the will of the Gods," had his consciousness out-turned, whilst theirs was in-turned. And in general it may be said that people who are selfish and live with their minds turned inwards, or centred on themselves, will never pay attention when higher intelligencies speak to them. Fear is another characteristic of souls in this state ; they always think external forces are going to injure them. This is presumably because it stops their

own self-meditation, which is their only idea of happiness.

The envelope or surround that contained Elysium and Hades was thought of by the ancients as extending " as far as the moon " ; for they generally thought of the after-death state from a purely objective physical standpoint. The " moon " was thus the physical moon, and the sublunary regions were the earth's atmosphere as far as the moon. Mystically the sublunary are the states " ruled by the Moon," the Mystic Mother who weaves the silver ghosts that dance round all, up to a certain stage in evolution, when the Sun of the true mind shines forth with golden rays.

With regard to souls in the higher portions of the surround, the Elysian state *proper* or higher heaven-world, the unselfish outward-looking characteristic of mind always brings joy, radiant joy, which in its fairest modes may well be thought to go forth so as to benefit all the world. There should always be a large capacity for such joy in any soul that is really and truly thus turned outward and is growing fast. Such souls expand to show joy; this expansion connotes at the same time, adhering and clinging to the beloved object. The two expand till they embrace and interpenetrate ; for love interpenetrates.

The change of name from Aridæus to Thespesius is to be noted. Change of name is found in almost all initiatory rites, and corresponds to an inner change of power. In the mystery-language of the Greeks, the epopt may be said to meet with the psychopomp ; the soul meets with a more ancient kinsman belonging to the family of its higher self.

The soul of Aridæus was still attached to the body by a link, which when translated into terms of physical vision appeared as a cord. This has been very frequently seen by seers ; it corresponds

THE VISION OF ARIDÆUS.

with the umbilical cord of the child. There is apparently a corresponding connection between any two vehicles of man's consciousness ; but whereas on the physical plane it is a cord, on other planes it would be better, perhaps, to think of it as a super-physical (magnetic, psychic, mental, etc.) connection.

Aridæus is next told to notice that the souls of the dead never close their eyelids. And it has been remarked by many that "ghosts" and apparitions of the dead never do so. The natural closing of the eyes is normally conditioned in our world by alternations of light and darkness, depending on the revolution of the earth ; but in the subtle state of matter, where the solid earth does not intervene to shut out the sunlight, the realm of the " astral light," there are no alternations of light and darkness.

It is said that the Gods never close their eyes, and there is also an apocryphal legend that tells us the same of Jesus.

The "shadow," again, which Aridæus throws owing to his still being alive and not one of the dead, is presumably some portion of subtle physical matter which clouds his psychic envelope, in that he was still "anchored" to his body, by means of what we may call a psycho-physical magnetic current.

Mystically it may be said that while the physical external sun casts a shadow, when we are our own Sun, we do not cast a shadow.

Again mystically it may be said that it is the mind in man which casts shadow and gives position relative to the inward Sun.

The "dead," again in this connection, may also mean those who have retired right out of the physical and mental form and are struggling in either the lower or higher soul-state.

It is said that there are states of subtle matter analogous to the solid, liquid and gaseous states of the physical, synthesized by a fourth, the etheric ; or again, the earthy, watery, airy, fiery states, synthesized by the fifth, or quintessence, according to the immemorial scheme of the four elements ; or again of seven, perhaps by a duplication of the first category.

After death, it is said, the soul, or rather the psychic envelope, passes through corresponding stages, gradually shedding off the denser phases and becoming more and more ethereal. This subtle matter and all of its phases are luminiferous, and with this in mind it is easy to follow the idea of the light-colours playing over and through the soul-envelope, and to understand how they are of different radiance according to the phase of substance which is dominant in this subtle envelope.

The majority of humans, it is said, spend most of their after-death existence in such conditions. But it would seem that the intermediary state and the heaven-state are conditioned by modes of motion rather than by form. I can well believe that we do not die in order to live in another kind of a prison-house of a subtle body of form, but rather that we die to experience the exact opposite of what we experience on earth, to be turned as it were "inside out," to revivify ourselves, to live in a state where form is ever interchangeable and power or life is the law or rule or guiding principle.

Most people, if we can believe our text is based upon a foundation of true vision, are carried about on the psychic streams ; those who have built themselves a formal mind preserve their balance, and sail about in the sea very happily ; those whose mentality is only slightly developed and have no right tendencies, wobble about, so to speak, and get somewhat giddy, we may suppose.

More advanced souls who have built themselves what is called a "formless" mind, enter the spiritual state. We cannot, I believe, get there without a "formless" mind, for we must have some

THE VISION OF ARIDÆUS.

mind there for experience ; for it is by mind that the psychic is changed to the spiritual state. It is mind in its widest sense that mystically alters for the individual the direction of the ceaseless ever-flowing psychic into the self-centralization and all-directions of the spiritual. Perhaps some may object to this use of the term " psychic " and " spiritual," but I am using them here in their Gnostic meanings.

The term " formless mind " is obscure. It represents the Sanskrit *arūpa*, and I here mean by it the power of mind deduced from its forms.

This mind would spiritually cast no " shadow " ; it would give its possessor the capacity of seeing round himself, so to say, observing that which was other than himself, for the fundamental principle of mind is to observe that which is not oneself.

Those among the " dead " who possess it, it is easy to believe, can converse and learn and come back (according to the doctrine of re-incarnation) far wiser than those who spend their time encased in selfishness and unable to respond to " external " contacts, except those that happen exactly to match their own, when of course they can hardly be said to be " external." If they are in unison there is not much to be learned.

We have next an exposition of the Kārmic Powers at work in the world.

First, there is the Unmanifest ; then the Manifested or Creative Logos, Zeus, in his mode of self-limitation, that is to say, with his counterpart, spouse, power, or syzygy, Necessity.

The daughter of Zeus and Necessity is Adrasteia, the Inevitable (She-from-whom - none - can - escape, literally), the Kārmic Law.

Servants to her are the three great Powers, Punishment (or Retribution), Justice and Fury (or Vengeance).

Thus there are seven great Kārmic Powers in all. This may be said to be the hierarchy of the justice-side of the Logos ; the hierarchy of the mercy-side is another, and yet, perchance, the same.

Punishment has Earth assigned to her as her field of operation ; to Justice is assigned the realm of Hades. Mystically this Justice may be well thought of as the pure light of conscience, so beautifully named the Virgin of Light, the Judge, in Magian, Gnostic and Manichæan tradition. The Virgin of Light is, I believe, that pure state which gives birth to really unbiassed understanding. It may be said to be man's higher unbiassed impersonal mind shining into his lower mind. The idea of Justice,-Purity and Virginity are here all intimately connected.

Vengeance, the third of Adrasteia's ministers, thrusts the incorrigible down " into a state of which we can neither speak nor think," says our seer's guide ; for such speech or thought, presumably, would bring its pictures up before the sight of the " single eye." This is evidently the state which the Greeks called Tartarus (*Tar-Tar*), doubtless a loan-word from some other, and perhaps more ancient, tongue ; a " double " possessed of a mystic root-meaning for those skilled in the most primitive of all languages, which the Greeks called *onoma-topoiēsis*. It corresponds, though very imperfectly, with the Avichi of the Brahmans and Buddhists. The word *a-vichi* is said to mean " wave-less." In its extreme sense it is the final state into which the irredeemably evil in spiritual wickedness are thrust, until the end of a world-period. It is called waveless, presumably, because it is a state of complete isolation, and is referred to frequently in the *Pistis Sophia*, a Christian Gnostic document with an Egyptian background.

The torments of this Tartarus are set forth graphically later on in our text. With regard to the corrections in Hades, or the Invisible, I would suggest that the inner side of the matter (whatever the outward appearance may be to the seer) is that we live over again all our evil and

THE VISION OF ARIDÆUS.

good deeds, but now with knowledge and understanding.

Realization makes us understand the justice of punishment and reward. We go through the whole thing ourselves, working it out in immediate experience. The light of our own higher consciousness casts our imperfections into deeper shadow. Our thoughts and emotions become objective to us, and the problems are worked out in very convincing dramatic incidents of a most intimate nature, supplied by the kaleidoscopic memory of the pictures of past deeds.

We are stripped naked to ourselves, and hence, to the world of our consciousness; we have no shell in which to hide, we can no longer deceive. This stripping naked is an indispensable condition of progress, and this is why we must be utterly honest with ourselves. We thus may be said in "trampling on the garment of shame" to lose all shame. "Naked we go to the Naked"—that is, to the Pure.

It is next to be remembered that in all folk-conceptions of after-death states, and the relation of the living to the dead, the blood-bond is *the* bond. This is, I think, at the bottom of all ancestor-worship. It is the idea of the group-soul, tribe and family. The root-contact is along the line of blood; that is, the kinship of the animal-human soul. Aridæus thus naturally meets with his "ancestors."

The scheme of the "colours of the souls" most probably pertained to the mystery-doctrine or esoteric teaching which was at that date spread so widely in the Hellenistic world. Thus, referring to Jacob's dream of the white, and spotted, and ring-straked, and speckled kine, Philo of Alexandria tells us that this must be taken as an allegory of souls. The first class of souls, he says, is "white."

"The meaning is that when the soul receives the Divine Seed [of the Logos], the first-born births are spotlessly white,

like unto the light of utmost purity, to radiance of the greatest brilliance, as though it were the shadowless ray of the sun's beams from a cloudless sky at noon." (*De Som.*, i. 35.)

I might also suggest an analogy from the markings of bird's eggs; the thought-birds that issue from such soul-eggs being of different classes.

I need hardly add for most of my readers, that the colours of the souls and their meanings given in our text agree very closely with the scheme of colours published in a number of modern theosophical works.

In connection with these colours and the purification of souls, Plutarch gives us an interesting piece of information concerning the philosophy and psychology of the doctrine of metempsychosis as held in his day, when he writes:

"The former souls through weakness of reason, and inertia of the contemplative principle are carried down by the practical element to birth as men; while the latter, lacking an instrument for their unbridled lust, long to unite desires to enjoyment and bring them together by means of any body,—for out of body there is for such souls only an imperfect shadow and dream of pleasure, without fulfilment."

The contemplative and practical elements of the soul may be usefully compared with the qualities or modes (*guṇa's*) of nature which the Indian philosophers characterize respectively as "pure" (*sāttvika*—the symbolical colour of which is "white"), and "passionate" (*rājasa*—colour "red")—though indeed it is very difficult to find English equivalents for the root-meanings of these Sanskrit terms.

According to Proclus the contemplative (or theoretic) and the practical are the higher and lower tendencies of the rational principle (*logos*).

5 4

THE VISION OF ARIDÆUS.

The term " theoretic " has nothing to do with the modern meaning of the word, but is derived from *theoría*, which signifies direct sight or eye-to-eye knowledge—gnosis.

Macrobius tells us further that the former is " ruled by Saturn " and the latter by " Jupiter." According to the mythology, or rather theology, of the Greeks, Kronos (Saturn) was father of Zeus (Jupiter). Zeus may here be said to be the fabricative power and Kronos the emanative power of the Logos.

Porphyry, in his Introduction to the philosophy of Plotinus, tells us that the contemplative or theoretic life has three grades of virtues, the highest of which is the ideal or paradigmatic, pertaining to the spiritual (formless) mind alone. These are the Uranic powers latent in man ; Uranus being father of Kronos. They transcend the rest of the soul-powers, just as the type or paradigm transcends the image ; for the spiritual mind contacts at one and the same time all the essences which are the types of lower things.

The most intractable class of souls are centred in the animal nature ; they are dominated by that mode (*guṇa*), which the Indian philosophers call " dark " (*tāmasa*—colour " black "), and the description of their most characteristic tendency is corroborated by many seers to-day.

When this mode is in the ascendant, then, and only then, it is said, is retrogression into the " nature of an animal " possible ; such a soul allies itself with the irrational. The theory of " re-incarnation into animals " is treated at some length in my volumes on Thrice-greatest Hermes, and it is only necessary here, in order to safeguard the philosophical view of the matter, to quote from Proclus :

" But the true reason asserts that though the human soul may be degraded to brutes, it is only to brutes that possess the life suited to such purpose, while the degraded soul is *as it were* vehicled in this *life* [not body], and *bound to it sympathetically.*"

Our story next introduces us to a change of scene, a vision of the Descent into Genesis, the Vortex that carries the souls down to physical birth.

What the meaning of the Bacchic Caves may be I am not able precisely to say. One commentator tells us that there were in Naxos, and on Parnassus, and elsewhere, caves dedicated to Bacchus, " *i.e.*, to mirth and jollity " ; and that " the mouths of these caves were of course decked with all of verdure and bloom that could make them charming and attractive." This may be so ; but I am more inclined to think that Plutarch, who was an initiated Dionysian, is comparing the vision with the scenic setting of the mystery-rites.

However this may be, others have described something very similar concerning this mystery and that of the Basin later on, as the following picture of what the writer calls " The Mart of Souls " (see *Theosoph. Rev.*, Mar., 1905) may testify.

" He looked down, and behold a whirlpool swirled and swept unceasingly before him, the brim of which was stained as though with dyes. Above his head hung a mighty upturned chalice, from whose lip drained a measure as of honey ; and it seemed to the man that drop by drop fell into the swirl of the pool, and laid itself along the brim. . . .

" The man saw the thin pale flame-shapes gather round the margin of the pool. Behind them crept strange mists and pallid shadows, shapeless, yet holding potential forms ; forms of ripples, of waves, of the strange clouds that lie about the sky at sunset, of all things unearthly, yet which mimic earth. And the shapeless shadows, too, crept down to the lip of the pool. As they reached the edge where the dyed waters leapt, flame and shadow fused and melted into one, and

5 5

THE VISION OF ARIDÆUS.

stood a moment fully formed upon the brink. And the man saw through and through each soul as it stood in its winding sheet of mist. Behind, beyond and through the colours of the vesture, running from the honeyed chalice and the dyed waves, up through the shadows round the separate white flames, the man saw past and future linked in the present; the individual life manifest from that which is called its beginning to that which men call the end. So that to him for the moment, as to each soul, all hearts were opened, and from him no secrets were hid. And he saw this knowledge burning in the flame of each.

" Then the shadow-flames circled round the pool as though in a mystic dance, and the sound of them as they drifted by was as the music of a spell. Deeper hues swept from the brim of the pool to the edges of the shadows, and thicker and ever thicker fell the drops of honey from the chalice over them. The shadows took shape and colour before the man, standing for a moment men like himself, and yet unlike. For they stood as men may stand on Judgment Day, victim and priest, judge and sinner, one and the same, each himself, yet each but part of the rest, judging the earth in himself, and himself in the earth. Then the colours thickened, each hue losing its poignant individuality, merging each in each. And as the colours blurred, so grew the forms more dense. And as the density increased, so did each shadow—erstwhile vast—diminish, drawing to its centre, till it seemed to the man that he looked but on a swarm of bees circling round the rims of one gigantic honey pool. The dyed brim seemed to throw out flowers, great petalled blossoms of amber and orange and scarlet and sapphire, reaching from edge to edge of the whirling water. There was the taste and taint of honey in the air."

But to return to the text of our vision; if this mystery be the " way down,"

equally is it the " way up." It was " the way by which Dionysus ascended to the Gods." Here again, I think, Plutarch refers to a mystery-myth into which he was initiated. Generally, it may be said to refer to the " greater mysteries "—those of " regeneration," the " way up," while the " lesser mysteries," those of " generation," pertain to the " way down."

The young Bacchus, the Iacchos of the Mysteries, after his own ascent, took up his mother to the Gods—the assumption. Semelē, in giving birth to Bacchus, the son of Zeus (the creative power of the Logos), is said to have been killed, and subsequently restored by her son to life among the Gods, under a changed name. Mystically, the soul is said to " die " in giving birth to itself on this plane. The " child " thus born may in its turn, in the case of one truly regenerate, become the saviour of its " mother," and raise her from the " dead " to spiritual life among the immortals.

In Christian Gnostic tradition this was shown forth at great length in the Sophia-mythus or Wisdom-myth. The Christ rescues and raises the fallen and dead Sophia or soul.

Speaking of this Vortex, which is also called Cratēr (Mixing-bowl) or Basin, Macrobius writes :

" Plato speaks of this in the *Phædo* and says that the soul is dragged back into body, hurried down by a new intoxication, desiring to taste a fresh draught of the overflow of matter ; whereby it is weighed down and brought back to earth. The astral Crater of Dionysus is a symbol of this mystery ; and this is what the ancients called the River of Lēthē."

I have treated of these matters at length in the volumes already referred to. It is necessary, however, to remind ourselves that all these mystery-terms may be taken in a number of senses. I have here attempted to suggest only the

5 6

THE VISION OF ARIDÆUS.

meaning which seems most suited to the text. The River of Lēthē, or Place of Oblivion, separates all states and planes from one another. Happy he who can remember and cross it safely whenever and wherever it meets him.

The scene again changes, and the vision is that of the " way up " of the seer, the same mystery as before, but from another point of view. For if there is a Plain of Forgetfulness, there is also a Plain of Truth, of which the scene in our vision is a reflection. For Plutarch elsewhere, speaking of the Great Triangle of the Universe, writes :

" The Area of the Triangle is the Common Hearth of all, and is called the Plain of Truth, in which the *logoi* and ideas and paradigms of all things which have been, and which shall be, lie immutable ; and the Æon (or Eternity) being round them, Time flows down upon the world like a stream. And the sight and contemplation of these things are possible for the souls of men only once in 10,000 years, should they have lived a virtuous life."

That is to say, I believe, following the tradition of the Pythagoreans, 10 x 10 x 10 x 10,—the completion or perfection (10) of all the possibilities of the Square (4) of matter, as contrasted with the Triangle (3) of spirit.

Plutarch continues (in this I think speaking of what he knew or had been taught) :

" And the highest of our initiations here below is only the dream of that true vision and initiation ; and the discourses [*sci.*, delivered in the mysteries] have been carefully devised to awaken the memory of the sublime things above, or else are to no purpose."

But to return to our text and the lunar reflection of this eternal Sun-land ; the

statement that Orpheus had advanced "as far as this " only, must, I think, be taken as an indication of *jalousie de métier*. Plutarch was high priest of Apollo at Delphi and had doubtless a bone of contention to pick either with his Orphic contemporaries or with the Orphic tradition, which had perhaps belittled the Delphic Oracle.

However this may be, this Crater is declared to be the Oracle of Selēnē, the Moon. That is to say, it pertained to all sublunary dreams and visions—" a mixture of the simple and true with the complex and fallacious."

Beyond this Aridæus could not see, for thereafter began the true Light-world, glimpses of which are so marvellously pourtrayed in Gnostic tradition. Aridæus was still bound to the body, and had not yet been made pure, or freed himself from the " world-illusion," as the Hermesmystics called it.

The Light of the Spiritual Sun streamed from the Supernal Tripod, or Triangle, of the Plain of Truth, through the Bosom of Themis.

Themis is fabled to have been the daughter of Uranus and Gē, of Heaven and Earth, the primæval cosmic pair, or syzygy. Themis is Order, Truth, Equity. The tradition of the Delphians was that their Oracle was first possessed by Gē, then by Themis (whom antiquity regarded as a very ancient prophetic divinity), and finally by Apollo. Parnassus was their Holy Mount. The whole symbolism, therefore, agrees with many another mystic tradition, in which the Mount of Contemplation must be ascended before the Sunrise can be seen.

But this was not for Aridæus as yet ; he could not see, he could only hear—the voice of the Sibyl. Legend supposed that the so-called face of the moon was that of the Sibyl gazing down upon the earth and singing its fate and that of its dwellers as she circled round.

The " prophecies " we must, I suppose,

57

THE VISION OF ARIDÆUS.

take as we take those of the Jewish Sibyllines; that is, as after the event. The famous eruption of Vesuvius took place in 79 A.D., and this event is said to have been foretold in the Roman Sibylline Books. Dicæarcheia was one of the towns destroyed, afterwards called Puteoli, the modern Puzzuoli.

As Vespasian died of disease and was not assassinated, as were so many of the Emperors, also in 79 A.D., we may perhaps have here an indication of a date terminus of our story, or of the writing of the treatise of Plutarch, if that is of any importance.

The scene next changes to a gruesome vision of the inferno, where it is to be noted that his terror deprived the seer of the presence of his "gentle and familiar guide," and immersed him in all the horrors of the infernal living picture-gallery.

The idea of being turned "inside-out" in the after-state is graphically compared with the sea-polyps or scolopendra, a fish that was supposed by the ancients to have the power occasionally of throwing out its intestines. When caught by a hook it was fabled to eject its entrails, remove the hook and then take them in again—an excellent "Philologic" romance, that does not, however, seem to have come down to the mediæval Bestiaries. When used of the soul it suggests that the "inner" became as the "outer," and the "outer" as the "inner." That is to say, in earth-life the modes of passion are ever changing, while the external form remains the same; whereas in this state of soul-life, the ruling modes of passion are more constant and the external forms are ever changing. In other words, the passions may be said to objectivize themselves, in that they immediately work out or clothe themselves in appropriate forms.

We next come to the "lakes" of the

inferno, there being three of them, the root-number of the tradition in which our vision has its setting. The "lakes" and the alchemical processes suggest that the background of the whole picture had its original in Egypt.

The scene appears to depict symbolically the preparation of degenerate souls prior to their being vehicled in the "life of an animal." From the standpoint of mystic psychology this concerns the "configuration" of the passional nature, or that nature which man shares with the animal, and may be said to be connected with types of mind that may be classified by parallels drawn from the types of animals, the lords of which are the "sacred animals."

The allusion to Nero is, of course, topical and again affords an indication of date.

What "Pindar's viper," or a "Pindaric viper" may mean is hard to say. It is most natural to suppose that we have here reference to some famous comparison of the great poet's, and that the ode which contained it is now lost.

It refers, of course, to Nero's guilt of matricide; while the "creature that croaks" is a humorous allusion to the Emperor's vanity and his appearing in the theatre as a singer. It is, however, not true that Nero freed Greece; he freed the province of Achæia only from taxes.

Who the "woman of amazing form and size" may be, I cannot divine, unless she be Memory, the counterpart of the Scribe of the Gods. Encaustic painters, as they were called, burnt in the colours with a heated rod or stylus.

Aridæus returned to his body by way of a "vortex," even as he went forth in the manner of a "bubble."

In conclusion I would suggest that the story of the experiences of Aridæus is either a literary subterfuge for describing

THE VISION OF ARIDÆUS.

part of the instruction in certain mysteries, or the vision, in popular story-form, was considered so true a description of what was thought to be the nature of the invisible world and the after-death conditions of the soul, that it required little alteration to make it useful for that purpose.

It is further interesting to notice that one of the characters in Plato's Vision of Er is called Ardiæus, while in Plutarch the main personage is called Aridæus. The transposition of a single letter is so slight as to make the names practically identical, and the subject matter is so similar that one is inclined to think there must be some connection between these two famous visions. Moreover Aridæus is said to have been a native of Soli in Cilicia, just as Er is said to have been a Pamphylian ; the tradition of both stories would then seem to have been derived from Asia Minor, and the origin of them may be hidden in the syncretism of that land—where West and East were for ever meeting.

Our story would thus seem to be intended to give the reader an idea of the impression made on the mind of one whom Plutarch would have us consider one of the uninitiated, by the Vision of Hades, or of the Invisible World, " as far as the moon." Sopatēr of Apamea also tells us the story of a young man who had seen the mysteries in a dream and had to be initiated afterwards.

We are told that Aridæus returned to his body before undergoing some process whereby he might " the better remember the details." What he remembered, therefore, is confused, clothed in the language and symbols of the mythologic recitals with which he was acquainted. Had Aridæus been really initiated, he would probably not have been represented as requiring a guide, and would have remembered everything clearly without the cloaking of images reflected from physical forms, and of scenery created by the recitals of popular religion, or the dramatic setting of formal mystery-rites.

5 9

THE . . .
MYSTERIES
OF . . .
MITHRA. .

THE MYSTERIES OF MITHRA

CONTENTS

BIBLIOGRAPHY.

CUMONT (F.), Art. "Mithras." Roscher's *Lexikon d. griech. u. röm Mythologie*, II. ii. 3027-3071 (Leipzig, 1894-1897).

CUMONT (F.), *Textes et Monuments figurés relatifs aux Mystères de Mithra*, 2 vols. (Bruxelles, 1896-1899).

The Conclusion of Cumont's Introduction has been translated into English by T. J. McCormack (Chicago, 1903).

THE MYSTERIES OF MITHRA.

THE MYSTERIES OF MITHRA.

PREAMBLE.

This brief outline of the comparatively meagre information we possess on what at one time was the most widely spread mystery-institution in the Roman empire, is introductory to the following small volume which will deal with the only Mithriac Ritual known to us.

In dealing with this exceedingly instructive Ritual I found that the limits of one booklet would not suffice for an adequate introduction ; and without this, I fear, many readers will not be in a position to appreciate the Ritual at its just value.

For, in spite of the wealth of epigraphic and monumentary material now in our hands, the texts of the ancient writers which treat of the religion of Mithra, are, with rare exceptions, provokingly deficient in information on the doctrines and inner meanings of these famous Mysteries ; and, therefore, a Ritual that unfolds to us the nature of the chief secret to which the lower grades of the mystery-rites conducted the brethren, is of the utmost value. It articulates, clothes with flesh, and puts life into what have been hitherto for the most part the dry bones of a skeleton.

And this, too, in spite of the splendid labours of the Belgian Hellenist Franz Cumont, who has done all that scholarship can do to make accessible to us every scrap of information on the subject that industry can discover.

The two sumptuous quarto volumes of Cumont's *Textes et Monuments figurés relatifs aux Mystères de Mithra* will long remain the most authoritative work on the subject ; and the unstinted thanks of all who are interested in this fascinating study are due to Cumont for the admirable presentation of the labours which

have occupied upwards of ten years of his life.

The second volume, which is embellished with no less than 493 figures and nine heliogravures, contains a reproduction of (i.) the literary texts—Oriental, Greek and Latin ; (ii.) the inscriptions or epigraphic texts ; and (iii.) the figured monuments and bas-reliefs ; while the first volume, which contains fourteen additional figures and a map, is devoted partly to a critical introduction, in which this heterogeneous and puzzling mass of information is skilfully analyzed, and partly to the conclusions that may be drawn from the evidence.

Cumont has endeavoured rigorously to exclude any appearance of subjectivity from his judgments, and claims to have founded his conclusions on purely objective data. But when we remember that the secrets of the Mithriaca have been most strictly guarded by all the faithful, and that not even a single Church Father has been able to boast that he is in possession of their jealously guarded rites and doctrines, it will be seen that the elements of subjectivity and speculation must enter largely into the conclusions of even so rigid an objectivist as Cumont, at any rate as far as the rites and doctrines are concerned.

Again, it is the habit of most of those who follow the German school, in spite of the excellence of its methodology, to rest content when they have traced the elements of the main doctrines and features of a tradition to elements of a similar nature of an earlier date. If what are called " sources " and " prototypes " can be indicated, it is almost tacitly assumed that there is an end of the matter.

It is true that this is all the rigid adherents to pure objectivity can accomplish ; but in the domain of religion it is with every day becoming clearer that many doctrines which have been hitherto held to be direct physical derivatives from prior doctrines, have arisen independently

THE MYSTERIES OF MITHRA.

owing to the natural evolution of the human soul and mind; that is to say, their source is subjective and not objective. The human soul has needs which it seeks to satisfy; and in all climes and times of similar stages of culture, similar means of satisfaction have been devised. And this simply because man is man.

The history of the evolution of the tradition of the Mithra-religion in Hither Asia, and of its continued development when it spread like wild-fire through the length and breadth of the Roman empire, in the first four centuries of our era, is an instructive study; but the main interest for many of us is the inner nature of the religion itself.

This, however, is a subject of extreme difficulty, as we have seen, owing to the jealousy and secrecy with which its tenets were guarded. In spite of more than 400 inscriptions, in spite of our upwards of 500 sculptures and bas-reliefs, we are unable to reconstruct the doctrines.

It is as though the living tradition and written records of Christianity had dis-appeared from the world for fifteen hundred years, and there remained to us only a few hundred monuments and the ruins of some three-score churches. What could we glean from these of the doctrines of the faith? How, from such meagre remains, could we reconstruct the story of the God, the saving doctrines, the rituals, the liturgies?

Nevertheless the fragments of informa-tion which can be gleaned from all this *débris* are of immense importance for the comparative history of religion, and throw light on many problems.

The Mithraism that spread over the Roman world in the first four centuries of our era, though it was the strongest, was not the only stream from the same source that reached the Western world.

Post-exilic Judaism was strongly tinged with Mazdaism, in the form of Pharisæism. Though it is strongly disputed by some,

the Pharisees (Gk. Pharisaioi, Aram. Peri-shaya, Heb. Perushim) may have even owed their name to those whose doctrines they had partially absorbed; and Pera-shim may thus spell Persi in Hebrew transliteration, even as Pārsī does in India to-day;

But not only were the Pharisees, who gradually became the national party among the Jews, imbued with Mazdæan ideas, but many schools of a mystic and gnostic nature arose in Syria and Arabia who were more or less adherents of the Magian traditions, or influenced by Magian doctrines. Such schools formed one of the links bètween Jewish and Semitic Gnosticism on the one hand, and the Christianized Gnosis on the other.

It is to be remarked that Simon, whom the Church Fathers regarded as the earliest Gnostic heretic in Christendom, was surnamed the Magian, and that *The Great Announcement*, which was the prin-cipal document of the Simonian tradition, is filled with Magian doctrine.

Moreover the names of the Æons in a number of Christianized Gnostic systems, are those of ethical abstractions, pre-cisely as are the names of the Amshas-pands in the Avesta.

And not only are there distinct traces of this influence in some of the Christian Gnostic documents preserved to us, as for instance in the system underlying the Coptic Gnostic works contained in the Askew and Bruce Codices; but also we have many indications of a large literature derived from the doctrines of Zoroaster, and his Mazdayasnian successors, and directly attributed to him by the Greek writers.

This literature was in circulation among certain Christian Gnostic circles, and is also directly referred to by Porphyry, in his *Life of Plotinus*, when giving a list of the Gnostics against whom his master wrote one of the books of his famous *Enneads*.

Moreover the beautiful Syriac " Hymn of the Soul," which I have called elsewhere

THE MYSTERIES OF MITHRA.

" The Hymn of the Robe of Glory," and which is almost certainly the work of the Christian Gnostic Bardaisan (Bardesanes), is thought by some to be based almost entirely on Magian doctrines. It may, therefore, contain valuable material for unveiling part of the inner secrets of Magianism, and, therefore, help us better to understand the innermost doctrines of the Mithriaca ; and I hope to treat of it later in another small volume.

Though it is true that the religion of the conquering Achæmenidæ—the line of Cyrus, Darius, Xerxes, and the rest— did not have any effect on Hellas proper, it is highly probable that it did strongly affect the Hellenic cities of Asia Minor. Setting aside the statement that Pythagoras sojourned for years with the Magi at Babylon, and was initiated into their mysteries, it is for me almost indubitable that Heraclitus of Ephesus (c. 524-475 B.C.) was strongly imbued with Magian ideas ; and not only was the influence of Heraclitus on subsequent Greek thought immense, but he was regarded by some Christian Gnostics and also by the Trismegistic tradition as one truly inspired by the Logos, and as therefore speaking true " logoi."

The conquest of Egypt, in the sixth century, by the Persian arms, moreover, cannot have failed to have made known to some extent the tenets of the Mazdæan faith in that land of lovers of religion, and to have awakened the curiosity of those learned in the mysteries of that land of wisdom in the allied teachings of the Magian priests.

Again, the conquest of the East by Alexander brought Greece into close contact with all the lands into which Magianism had directly spread itself, and this contact would aid in the diffusion of a knowledge of general Mazdæan tenets among the learned. Moreover, when Alexandria became the intellectual centre of the Grecian world, this interest in Magianism increased ; and we learn that one of the librarians of the famous

Brychion, Hermippus, the pupil of Callimachus, not only wrote a work in several books About the Magi, but, if we can believe Pliny, he catalogued the works of Zoroaster in the possession of the great Library, and found that they added up to the amazing total of 2,000,000 lines.

But Magianism did not reach Alexandria in its original form ; it was already combined with many Chaldæan elements.

The " Books of the Chaldæans " also were well known at Alexandria ; for Zosimus, the Pœmandrist, referring to the traditions of the Chaldæans, Parthians, Medes, and Hebrews, says that they were to be found "in the book-collections of the Ptolemies, which they stored away in every temple, and especially in the Serapeum."

The Serapeum was the second great building in which the world-famed Library was kept, when the rolls had grown too numerous for the Brychion.

Not only then were these Books in circulation in the original tongues in Syria, Palestine and Arabia, especially among the numerous mystic and gnostic communities, but also in Egypt. Zosimus, moreover, further informs us that they were translated into Greek and Egyptian.

It was on such translations, we must suppose, that the famous Greek poem known as The Chaldæan Oracles (and also as the Oracles of Zoroaster) was based. This was certainly in circulation in the second century, and may have existed earlier even in its present form.

When further we remember that, from the time of Porphyry onwards, the Later Platonic School esteemed these Oracles highly, and that at the same time Porphyry was intimately acquainted with the Mithriac Mysteries, and that the leading philosophers of the School were almost all Initiates of these Mysteries, we are not without hope of recovering the general drift of the main doctrines, on lines other than those Cumont has followed. But consideration of this side of the subject

THE MYSTERIES OF MITHRA.

must be postponed until I come to deal with this poem itself in a subsequent volume.

All this shows that before the direct immigration of the Mithriac Mysteries (as known to us from the monuments) into the Roman empire, Magian doctrines had already strongly influenced Hellenistic religious thought.

As, however, we have already indicated, it is not to be supposed that the Magian doctrines of which we are speaking were of pure Iranian derivation. Magianism was already a blend. Irrespective of divisions and reforms within its own originally purely Aryan tradition, it had, from the days of Cyrus onwards, absorbed many elements from the astral lore and theurgic practices of the complex of Semitic religious traditions that formed the cults of Babylon. As so often happens in the world's history, the conquerors in war were subsequently conquered by peaceful means.

This stream of Magianism came direct from Babylon *via* Syria to Hellenistic Greece. The stream which we know later on as the Mysteries of Mithras, came by another way; it matured first of all especially in Armenia, Pontus, and Cappadocia (that is, Eastern Asia Minor), doubtless absorbing there some fresh elements from the indigenous cults, and eventually passed by way of the sea and military routes into the Roman empire.

Nevertheless the Mithriac tradition, in spite of its absorption and adoption of foreign elements, clung tenaciously to its ancestral myths and rites and doctrines, as constituting the real esotericism of its cultus ; within them alone, it claimed, was to be discovered the *secretum secretorum* of its Mysteries.

The tradition of the Mithriaca, therefore, is of interest not only to students of the history of the influence of Oriental faiths on the culture and religion of the West, but should also be of value to the Pārsīs, and to all students of the Zend and Pahlavi books, who generally hold that the Avestan tradition is indubitably in the main stream of direct Mazdæan descent ; and that therefore the accounts of the Western classical writers are to be rejected when they do not agree with these documents.

On the other hand, it is a most remarkable fact that the Mithriac traditions possess features that more closely resemble the beliefs and practices of the Great Kings of the Achæmenid line, than do the Zend and still later Persian writings. Indeed no less an authority than Darmsteter has argued that Avestan Mazdaism was a later development, and as it were a systematized reform of Zoroastrian Magianism effected during the period of the Sassanid dynasty (226-628 A.D.). With this view Cumont agrees, and maintains that the Mithriac traditions preserve more of the earliest features of the original Iranian faith than do the Zend writings.

ORIGINS AND DEVELOPMENT.

In the Magusæan tradition, that is the tradition of the Magians of Asia Minor, Mithra is all-important ; in Avestan theology, the latest development of the great Zoroastrian reformation, Mithra holds but a subordinate place among the *yazatas*, or celestial deities, created by Ahura-Mazda.

It is, however, quite evident both from the oldest Vaidic hymns and the oldest traditions preserved in the Avestan documents, that in the beginning the God whom the Hymns call Mithra was one of the highest deities of a pantheon which was in prehistoric ages the common property of the forefathers of both the Iranian and Hindu Aryan races.

It is true that in the Zend books the ancient grandeur of the God is attested

THE MYSTERIES OF MITHRA.

only by incidental allusions; but His attributes are such as to place Him on almost an equality with the Supreme.

In earliest days Mithra was God of Light, and was invoked together with Heaven (Zd. Ahura, Sk. Varuna).

In the Avesta, Mithra is Lord of the Heavenly Light, and therefore of the heavenly lights. He is the Light, and not the Sun; the Sun is His Chariot, or rather His Charioteer. He is "ever awake, ever on watch." He is neither sun nor moon nor stars; but with His "thousand ears and His ten thousand eyes" watches over the world. He hears all, sees all; no one can deceive Him. And so by a natural transition He is God of truth and loyalty; He is invoked in taking oaths, and guarantees all contracts and punishes all who violate their bond and plighted word.

And if He is Light, He is also Heat, and Life—the Vaidic Kāma, the Orphic Erōs. He fecundates all Nature. Mithra is "the Lord of wide pastures"; 'tis He who makes them bring forth. "He giveth increase; He giveth abundance; He giveth herds; He giveth progeny and life." He poureth forth the waters, and causeth the plants to grow; He bestoweth on His worshippers health of body, wealth and well-dowered offspring.

In fact He is precisely what the worshippers of Osiris, and the followers of the Trismegistic tradition, and other Hellenistic cults, called Agathodaimōn or the Good Spirit, the Benefactor.

And not only does He bestow material benefits, but He also gives the good things of the soul—peace of heart, wisdom, and glory; He makes concord among the brethren who worship Him.

As God of Light He is the relentless foe of the Darkness and all its creatures—all suffering, sterility, vice and impurity. Against the forces of evil Mithra "sleeplessly on watch protects the creation of Mazda." He is the Leader of the hosts of Heaven against the hosts of the

Abyss, and in all probability the prototype of Michael.

And in general it may be said that the picture which the Zend and Pahlavi books give us of this ancient Aryan divinity is similar to the portrait with which the Vaidic hymns present us, though in the latter case with less clear detail.

But though the Zend Gāthas allow us to catch clear glimpses of the physiognomy of the Light-God, the Zoroastrian system, in continuing His cult, reduced the ancient grandiose conception of the God to somewhat meagre proportions, owing to the exigencies of the Avestan theology which placed Him among the *yazatas.*

Nevertheless every now and again the high rank of Mithra forces itself to the front in spite of all theological suppression, and we find Him several times joined with Ahura in one and the same invocation; the two forming a pair. Again it is said that though Ahura created Mithra as He created all things, nevertheless He made Him as great as Himself.

Mithra is a *yazata,* but at the same time He is the greatest of all *yazatas.* "Ahura-Mazda hath established Him to guard the whole world of life, and to watch over it." It is by means of this Mediator, the Ever-victorious Warrior, that the Supreme Being destroys the demons (the *daevos* or *devs*) and causes the Spirit of Evil himself to tremble. The main outline of the Magian system which Plutarch hands on to us at the end of the first century, agrees with this, as also does the ancient tradition placed at the beginning of the later Pahlavi *Bundahish.*

This suggests that the fundamental religious conception of the subjects of the Achæmenid kings was simpler than the more complex and refined Zoroastrian theology. It presents us with a Supreme Deity throned above the stars in the Empyrean, reigning in eternal serenity

6 7

THE MYSTERIES OF MITHRA.

and peace. Below Him stands an Active God, His Delegate, Mithra, Chief of the celestial armies in this perpetual struggle against the hosts of the Spirit of Darkness, who from the Abyss below the earth sends forth his *devas* to war on the " good creation " of Mazda.

From the inscriptions we know that the Great Kings (the Achæmenids) invoked Mithra alongside of Ahura-Mazda, and gave him special worship as their Protector. It was He who bestowed upon them the power of success, or the presence or glory, called Hvarenō, which can also be translated as " aureole." This Grace and Good Fortune of Mithra was a guarantee of perpetual victory. The epithet " most glorious," signifying the power of bestowing this Hvarenō, was given to Ahura-Mazda and Mithra alone. Mithra in one of the Yashts is spoken of as He " who goeth through all the regions dispensing glory ; . . . He goeth dispensing sovereignty and increasing victory."

The supremacy of Mithra is also shown by the enormous number of names of kings, princes and nobles containing the name of the God, and this not only in later days, but also in the earliest times.

The conquering kings of Persia established their religion wherever they carried their victorious arms. Especially at Babylon, which became the winter-residence of the Great Kings, was the Magian cult established in great splendour.

The Persian arms had laid low the temporal power that had previously reigned over the cities of the Chaldæi, and the priests of the conquerors, the Magi, were established in the highest place as the representatives of the religion of the Court. But the Iranian religion was not strong enough to resist the fascination of the ancient faith of the conquered that reached back, as it were, to the night of time, and preserved a science of the heavens that far surpassed the knowledge of the followers of Mazda. So strong was this influence

that centuries later in Rome it was believed that the native land of Mithra lay on the banks of the Euphrates.

If we are unable to say that in Mesopotamia the religion of the Magi was entirely transformed, we can assert that it absorbed so many new elements that it assumed an entirely new form.

Of its spread eastwards we know little, though the astronomer Ptolemy assures us that Mithra was worshipped everywhere in all the lands from Assyria to India.

Babylon, however, was only the first stage in the propaganda of Mazdaism westwards, and also in its absorption of new elements. Under the Great Kings it spread rapidly into Armenia, Cappadocia, Pontus, Galatia, and Phrygia ; and in these countries too we must believe it absorbed new elements from the ancient cults of these lands, and from the mystery-rites that handed on the inner instruction and preserved the secrets of the outer forms of worship.

In the great confusion that followed the downfall of the Persian empire, all political and religious barriers were broken down. Already to some extent Ionian philosophy had, in a few instances, felt the influence of general Magian ideas ; but now in the train of the conquering arms of Greece, the influence of Greek civilization in its turn made itself felt on the Orient, and the Iranian princes and priests submitted to its charm.

The contact of all the religions of the " Orient " and of all the philosophies of Greece produced the most unexpected combinations. It was probably in the years following the Conquest of Alexander that the Magian priests departed from the reserve that they had hitherto maintained as far as Greece was concerned ; for that reserve had been already broken down entirely with regard to the Chaldæan science, and doubtless to a large extent in the intercourse of the Magusæi with the initiatory cults of the more

THE MYSTERIES OF MITHRA.

immediate countries north and west of Babylon.

Then it was that Mithraism blended with itself Grecian elements, and doubtless began to translate into Greek some of its rituals and liturgies, replacing the native names of its pantheon with what equivalents or approximations it could find in the names of the Olympian deities.

As Cumont writes, "it is certainly during the period of the moral and religious fermentation promoted by the Macedonian conquest, that Mithraicism received its more or less definitive form" —that is to say, the form in which it spread in the Roman empire.

This "synonomy," or translation of names, though perhaps necessary if the doctrines of Mithra were destined to spread widely in the West, was from a mystic or spiritual point of view unfortunate. For the vague personifications conceived by the Oriental imagination in no long time borrowed the precise forms with which Greek art had clothed the Olympian gods.

Perhaps the Iranian deities had never previously been represented under a human form; if there had been images, they were probably similar to the "monstrous" or symbolic creations of the East, and of the same order as the awe-inspiring figure of the Æon which was still preserved in its original lineaments in the Mithræa.

And in the spread of the Mithraica westwards, not only did art aid in softening what to those trained in Greek culture would appear to be the rudeness of these ancient Mysteries, but philosophy also was called in to help in the task; or rather the priests of the Invincible One, Nabarze, declared that in the best of philosophy were also to be found the secrets of their own sacred traditions.

The school whose tenets lent itself most easily to this purpose was that which later became the most popular of all among the cultured of the Roman world, the School of the Porch. When the cult of Mithra reached the upper classes of Roman society, after its first irruption among the soldiery and slaves, it was the adherents of the Stoic School who were most successful in finding in the dogmas and myths of the Magian tradition traces of an ancient wisdom consonant with their own ideas.

And in this connection it is of interest to repeat that the philosophy of Heraclitus had already strongly influenced the disciples of Zeno, the founder of the Wisdom of the Stoa, and that Heraclitus, who passed his life at Ephesus in the last quarter of the VIth and first quarter of the Vth century B.C., was almost indubitably indebted to Persian influence for his leading doctrines of the Ever-living Fire, of the transmutation of the Elements, of Struggle or Strife, and some other features of his remarkable system.

The analysis, therefore, of the compost of the Mithriac doctrines as propagandised in the Roman empire, presents us, as it were, with a series of stratifications. The deepest deposit belongs to the faith of ancient Iran ; on this foundation of pure Mazdaism was deposited a thick layer of Semitic doctrines from the ancient religions of Babylon ; and on this again a shallower sediment of the cults of Asia Minor.

In this fertile soil, Cumont says, a luxuriant growth of Hellenic ideas sprang up and largely concealed from view its original nature. But if it is true that Mithraism in its contact with the West clothed its outermost form in Greek dress and with Greek art, it is equally true that it owed nothing of an essential nature to Hellenic notions. Its inner mystery-teachings were independent of Hellas ; and any attempt to interpret these teachings from the standpoint of purely Hellenic ideas is doomed to failure.

Such was the composite faith—though hardly a Hellenized Parsism, as Cumont calls it—which flourished in the Alexandrine period in Armenia, Pontus and

6 9

THE MYSTERIES OF MITHRA.

Cappadocia ; and had Mithridates Eupator of Pontus realized his dreams of conquest, it would doubtless have become the religion of a vast Asiatic empire.

It was probably on the downfall of Mithradates that the *débris* of the Pontic armies and fleets spread the knowledge of the Iranian Mysteries among the sea-kings of Cilicia. Under the protection of Mithra these hardy adventurers pillaged without fear the most sacred sanctuaries of Greece and Italy ; and so for the first time, it is said, the Latin world heard the name of the Conquering God (Per. Nabarze, the Courageous, Gk. Anikētos, Lat. Invictus, the Unconquered) who was soon to receive the homage of the armies and navies of Rome, and finally of its emperors.

DIFFUSION IN THE ROMAN EMPIRE.

It would be out of place in this short sketch to touch on anything but the main features of the diffusion of the Mithriaca in the Roman empire. The admirable account of Cumont, in the second chapter of his Conclusion, is practically exhaustive of the subject, and shows in detail, and with the aid of an excellent map, how the religion of the Victorious God spread into the most remote regions of the West, from the time that the Roman arms under Pompey, in the second quarter of the first century B.C., began seriously to undertake the conquest of the nearer East.

It was in Cilicia that Pompey's legionaries were first initiated into these Mysteries.

It is not surprising that the religion of Mithra should have found favour with the soldiery ; for the cult of Victory was essentially a cult of warriors. Mithra was a warrior and a God of warriors ; He was not only General of the celestial militia in the Good Fight, but also Protector of all brave deeds and chivalrous adventures.

It is a somewhat remarkable fact that the Magian influence in its earlier southwestern diffusion, *via* Syria, Palestine and Egypt, seems to have been exclusively welcomed by strict ceremonialists like the Pharisees, or by mystic and ascetic communities of gnostic tendencies, or by circles of the learned at Alexandria ; whereas in its direct spread westwards, it at first contacted a totally different stratum of society. It was welcomed at first almost exclusively by the common soldiery, and also by the slaves or those who had been freed from the state of servitude. The first propaganda of this second stream of Magianism thus followed the lines of the great military and trade routes.

The legions were being continually moved from station to station ; corps raised in the East were, in accordance with the Imperial policy, despatched to the most distant provinces of the West ; and the veterans on gaining their discharge either settled in the districts where they had last been stationed, or returned home, and so spread a knowledge of Mithra among their neighbours.

Much of the trade in the great marts and factories was in the hands of Syrians and Levantines, whose chief commodity was the traffic of human flesh. The slaves brought from Asia Minor helped largely to spread the cult of Mithra among their fellows, and as many of them eventually held positions of responsibility in the management of the huge properties of the Roman nobles, they gradually succeeded in interesting their masters in their religion.

The above facts show very clearly

THE MYSTERIES OF MITHRA.

that there were two distinct forms of Magianism that influenced the West; the one a doctrine better suited to priests and the learned, the other a teaching more adapted for warriors and the illiterate.

If we might so put it, one was of a Brahmaṇa form, the other of a Kshattriya nature. The south-western stream seems to have been a form of Zoroastrian priestly Mazdaism; the direct western stream shows itself originally as a cult of kings and warriors, who exalted Mithra almost to equality with Ahura-Mazda.

The flood of Mithraism flowed with ever-increasing strength westward during the first and second centuries. It ascended the great rivers; and on the banks of the Danube, the Rhone, and the Rhine, it established its temples in great numbers. It penetrated to the North of Britain, to Spain, to the borders of the Sahara. Gradually it was established in all the great cities and trade centres, until with the third century we find it practically the dominant cult of the Empire, under the protection of the Imperial lords of Rome, whose claims to divine kingship were strongly supported by the tenets of a faith which attributed the power and victory of kings to the direct Favour and Glory of the God of Victory.

By this time, however, we have strong reason to suppose that the two streams of Magianism were, at any rate in some of the circles of the learned, flowing together. At any rate we see that in the case of Porphyry, at the end of the third century, this philosopher was not only learned in all that pertained to Mithra, but was also deeply versed in the Hellenized Mago-Chaldæan Oracles; and that from this time onwards the members of the Later Platonic school were mostly initiated into Mithraism and also great lovers of these Oracles.

Much has been written on the struggle between Later Platonism and Christianity for the possession of the Western world.

This Platonism was not a direct renascence of the older Platonism, but derived immediately from Alexandrian Hellenism. This Alexandrian Hellenism already consisted in a philosophizing of Oriental ideas—and among these ideas we must include a tincture of Magian tenets.

There is, therefore, little surprise that the most mystical school of Greek philosophy should have allied itself closely with the Mysteries of Mithra; and in so doing it supplemented its too aristocratic doctrines with ancillary tenets that had already found favour among the masses of the poor, the rude, and the unlettered.

But even so, neither Mithraism alone nor Neo-Platonism combined with it was destined to become the Faith of the West. It is true that in the years just prior to Constantine, the religion of Mithra seemed almost to have triumphed. But it was not to be; Christianity ascended the throne of the Cæsars, and Christianity became Cæsarized.

The daring effort of the Emperor Julian (A.D. 360-363) to re-establish the ancient order of things, or rather to save the ancient order by purifying it, and so winning the world to a loftier cult of the Gods, interpreted by philosophy and the mystery-teaching, collapsed; and with it passed the Gods from the Græco-Roman world.

Mithraism gradually faded out; or concealed itself in cognate Manichæism, which long survived as a harbour of refuge for the shipwrecked Gnostics and Mystics of the ancient world and early Middle Age.

Indeed the doctrine of Mani seems to have been in no small measure a third outpouring, so to speak, of Magianism. This outpouring blended itself intimately with the doctrines of the Christ-mystery, and even perhaps with Buddhism, and handed on a Gnosis that may ere long be better appreciated. For no less than 800 fragments of Manichæan MSS., in an ancient Persian dialect, have recently

7 1

THE MYSTERIES OF MITHRA.

been discovered at Turfan in Chinese Turkestan, and are now at Berlin awaiting publication. As these are the only direct documents we possess of the religion of Mani—the rest of our information being derived from hostile sources—it is highly probable that we shall at last learn the true secret of its success, even as the Ritual we shall treat in our next volume, will enable us to see in some measure why Mithra exercised such sway over the hearts of His worshippers.

A certain form of Christianity conquered; that is to say, of all the various forms of faith in the West in those early years, Christianity in a certain form proved the most suited for the souls and minds of the coming nations. That form survived which was the fittest to survive for the instruction of the young nations which were gradually to develop into the ruling nations of the West. But that which withdrew did not die; it returned whence it came. It is there as it ever has been to reappear in other forms according to the birth, and growth and death of nations, and according to the coming and going of souls.

When souls are born who are not content with the forms of faith handed on by the ancestors of their bodies, their longing for what they consider new forms more suited to their needs, does but bring into manifestation once more the same Wisdom that instructed their spiritual forebears. We are to-day at an epoch when many such souls are in incarnation, and the interest in the doctrines of the Ancient Wisdom is accordingly increasing on all sides.

The religion of Mithra was one of the many forms of the Christ-mystery ; and the mystery of the Christ is the mystery of man's perfectioning and final apotheosis. A comparative study of christology, in this its widest sense, and in all its manifold aspects, in the great religions that have disappeared or are still existing, is of the utmost value ; and it is from this standpoint mainly that we are interested in the nature of the great secret of the Mithriaca.

The secret of regeneration, of being born anew, or spiritually, or from above —in brief, the divinizing of man, was the last word of the Mithra-rites ; all else is introductory or ancillary.

This secret was the one secret of all the great mystery-rites and mystery-arts. It was the secret of the Gnosis in all its forms, contemplative or operative. We are, therefore, not surprised to learn that even as early as the end of the fourth century we find Zosimus, a disciple of the Trismegistic lore, and an alchemist, in a treatise " On Asbestos "—that is to say, presumably, on that pure body of man that can remain in the Fire without being consumed—writing as follows in mystic fashion :

" And if thou dry it in the sun thou shalt possess the mystery that no man can impart, in which no one of all the wisdom-lovers hath ventured to initiate in words ; but only by the sanction of themselves [that is, the sanction of their own divinity] have they imparted its initiation. For this they have called in the scriptures the chief of all mysteries : The Stone that is no stone, the unknowable known unto all, the that which hath no honour yet is of greatest honour, the that which none can give but God alone. But I will sing its praise, the that which none can give but God alone, the one (material) thing in all our operations which is superior to all that is material. This is the remedy which doth contain all power—the Mithriac Mystery."

THE MYSTERIES OF MITHRA.

In this short sketch it is only possible to dwell on one or two of the most striking passages from the classical writers. Dion Chrysostom (c. 50-120 A.D.) was born at Prusa in Bithynia, travelled extensively in Asia Minor, and was very familiar with the Magian cult; in all probability he was himself an initiate of the Mithriaca. In one of his Orations, Dion hands on to us a very instructive mystery-myth which was chanted by the Magi in one of their sacred hymns.

They sang of the Supreme, as the Perfect and Primal Charioteer of the Most Perfect Vehicle—more admirable and ancient far than the chariot of the sun which all can see. This Perfect Vehicle was the Cosmic Car drawn by the four Great Elements. It was the All-perfect Sphere of the Æon, or Eternity; that is to say, of Boundless Time, who was also regarded by the Magi as Infinite Space. He is the Zervan Akarana, Eternity without Bounds, who in this tradition of Magianism transcended Ahura-Mazda Himself.

The Four Elements are the Steeds of the Great Chariot of all things. The course of the first Winged Horse is beyond the limits of heaven itself. This Steed transcends the rest in beauty, greatness and speed, and shines with purest brilliance. Its resplendent coat is dappled o'er with sparks of flame, the stars and planets and the moon. Such is the Steed of Fire.

The second Horse is Air. Its colour is black; the side turned towards its shining mate is bright with light, but that in shade is dark. In nature it is mild, and more obedient to the rein; it is less strong than Fire and slower in its course.

The third is Water, slower still than Air; while Earth, the fourth of this great Cosmic Team, turns on itself, champing its adamantine bit. Round it its fellow Steeds circle as round a post. And this continues for long ages, during which the Cosmic Team work steadily together in peace and friendship.

But after many ages, at a certain time, the mighty Breath of the first Steed, as though in passion, pours from on high and makes the others hot, and most of all the last. And finally the fiery Breath sets the Earth Horse's mane ablaze. In the suffering of this cosmic passion the Earth causes such distress to its neighbour Steed and so disturbs its course, that exhausted by its struggles it inundates the Earth with floods of sweat.

This all happens at certain great periods of time when the Charioteer either reins in His Steeds or urges them on with the whip, as need may be to keep the world-course that His Will marks out.

But at the end of the world's age a still stranger mystery is wrought. A Divine Contest takes place among the Steeds; their natures are transformed, and their substances pass over to the mightiest of the Four. It is as though a sculptor had modelled four figures in wax, and melted them down again, and remade them into one form.

The One Element becomes omnipotent, and finally in its triumph is identified with the Charioteer Himself.

It is easy to see in this great myth, the periods of partial world-destruction by fire and water; and finally the re-absorption of all things in the Ever-living Element, now rebecome the One Element, the Single Body of all things.

To the Church Father Origen, writing some seventy-five years afterwards, we owe an important quotation from the *True Word* of the philosopher Celsus, who composed his criticism of Christianity about 175 A.D.

THE MYSTERIES OF MITHRA.

Origen, after telling us that Celsus is treating of the way of souls down and up through the planetary spheres, continues with a *verbatim* quotation as follows (vi., 22):

" These things are symbolically set forth by the Wisdom of the Persians and the Initiation of Mithra which is practised among them. In the latter there is a certain symbolic representation of the two circuits in the heaven—both of the regular circuit and of that which is assigned to the irregular spheres—and of the passage of the soul through them.

" This symbolic representation is as follows : A ladder with seven gates, and at its top an eighth gate.

" The first of the gates is of lead, the second of tin, the third of copper, the fourth of iron, the fifth of alloy, the sixth of silver, and the seventh of gold.

" The first they assign as Saturn's, indicating by lead the slowness of the star ; the second as that of Venus, setting in correspondence with her the brightness and softness of tin ; the third of Jupiter, for it has a copper basis and is hard ; the fourth as Mercury's, for both Mercury and iron are patient of work of every kind—the one transacts all business, the other is wrought with much labour ; the fifth as that of Mars, for it is irregular from its mixture and variegated ; the sixth as the Moon's, the silver one ; and the seventh as the Sun's, the golden—in imitation of their colours."

Origen then tells us that Celsus gives further reasons for this arrangement, based on the symbolism of the names, and adds " musical reasons " as set forth in the " theology of the Persians."

This is the only description we have of the famous Mithriac Climax or Ladder, and it must be confessed that it leaves much to be desired. Whatever be the correct attribution of the metals to the " planets," and whatever may be the correct key to the alchemical or astrological secrets involved in it, it may be of interest to remark that this scheme was adopted as a means of theurgical yoga.

Mirrors of different metals were placed on the walls of an octagonal chamber, and in the centre was a couch, the legs of which were insulated. On this lay the seeker, and gazed into the mirror before him ; in it he was supposed to see visions of invisible things, and develop in himself the senses of the soul.

My old friend and instructor had one of these chambers built shortly before her passing away, but it was never furnished, and so the experiment was not made. But recently a young friend of mine who had never heard of this, has had a dream-experience of a similar chamber, in which he seemed to have been once lying in Egypt. The couch on which he lay was a lion-couch.

The Church Fathers, however, seem to have had but the meagrest information on the Mithriaca.

Justin Martyr (*c.* 150 A.D.) says that the evil demons in the Mysteries of Mithra aped the Christian Eucharist ; for there was an offering of bread and of a cup of water with certain explanatory sacred formulæ.

Tertullian in his exhortation *On the Crown*, written about 210 A.D., also accuses the Devil of aping some of the divine teachings in order to put the Christians to shame ; and he instances certain of the Mithriac practices as follows (*c.* xv.) :

" Blush, ye Fellow-soldiers of Christ, who need not be condemned by Him, but by any Soldier of Mithra.

" For when this Soldier is initiated in the Cave—in the Camp of Darkness as may well be said—and a crown is offered him at the sword's point—as though it were a mimicry of martyrdom—and then placed on his head, he is bidden to put up his hand and change it from his head to, it may be, his shoulder, declaring that Mithra is his Crown.

" And henceforth he never allows a

74

crown [or wreath] to be put on him; and this he has as a mark whereby to prove himself, if on any occasion he should be tried concerning his mystery; immediately he is recognised as a Soldier of Mithra, if he cast down the crown, and declare that his Crown is his God." Again in his treatise *On Prescription against Heretics* (c. xl.), Tertullian returns to the same convenient theory that the Devil by his wiles has perverted the truth, and "emulously mimics even the precise particulars of the divine sacraments by the mysteries of idols. "He too baptizes some—of course his own believers and faithful; he promises the remission of sins by a bath. If I still remember rightly, Mithra there [that is in the Cave] signs his Soldiers on their foreheads, celebrates also the offering of bread, introduces an image of the resurrection, and purchases for himself a crown at the sword's point. "What are we to say also of his appointing for his chief priest a single marriage only. He, too, has his virgins; he, too, has his celibates."

Augustine, at the end of the fourth century, in boasting that the Christian faith publishes and uncovers all the secret mysteries invented by the evil demons, instances the Mithriaca in the passage: "But what kind of a play is that which is played for them in the Cave with veiled eyes? For they have their eyes veiled lest they should shudder at the disgraceful dishonour to which they are put. Some like birds flap their wings imitating the cry of ravens; others again roar like lions; while others with hands bound with the entrails of fowls are made to leap over trenches filled with water, and then some one comes and severs the bond, and calls himself their liberator." This apparently typified the effort of the soul, bound with the bonds of the passions, to overleap the watery regions, and gain the other shore, where the saviour severs the bonds with the sword of knowledge.

Lastly, Jerome, about the same date, in endeavouring to prove to a lady correspondent called Læta (Letter cvii.), that it is never too late to be converted, instances a certain patrician named Gracchus, "who had repudiated the Cave of Mithra and all the monstrous figures used in the initiations of the Raven, Griffin, Soldier, Lion, Persian, Sun-courser, and Father."

So much for the Fathers; as for the Philosophers, the one who tells us most about the Mysteries is Porphyry (c. 234-304 A.D.). His information is of importance not only owing to the reasons we have given above, but also because he was a careful student of a large literature on the subject which has since disappeared.

In his *Cave of the Nymphs*, an allegorical, philosophical and mystical interpretation of a famous passage in Homer, he tells us that the Ancients very properly symbolized the world by a cave, and then continues (c. vi.):

"Thus also the Persians, in their mystery-rites which give instruction on the path of souls in their descent to earth and the way out and up of their return, initiate the candidate (*mystēs*) in what they call the Cave.

"For, according to Eubulus, Zoroaster was the first who consecrated, in the mountains near Persia, a [certain] brilliantly coloured natural cave, with springs in it, in honour of Mithra, the Creator and Father of all things. This cave represented for him an image of the world which Mithra had made, and its regular stratification symbolized the cosmic elements and zones.

"After this Zoroaster, the practice was established among the rest [of the Magi] also of using grottoes or caves, either natural or artificially excavated, for the handing on of the mysteries."

In the Leontica or Lion-grade of the Mithriaca there was a honey-rite. To

THE MYSTERIES OF MITHRA.

this Porphyry refers when he writes (c. xv.):

" The theologers have used 'honey' in many different symbolic ways owing to its being a same deduced from many powers, [and especially] because it has both a purifying and preservative virtue ; for by honey many things are preserved from decay, and with honey long open wounds are purified. Moreover it is sweet to taste, and collected from 'flowers' by 'bees' who happen to be 'ox-born.' [These are evidently all mystery-terms.] " When, therefore, they pour into the hands of those who are receiving the Leontic initiation, honey for washing instead of water, they bid them keep their hands pure from everything that causes pain or harm, or brings defilement ; just as when the purifying medium is fire, they bring the candidate appropriate means of washing, declining water as inimical to fire.

" Moreover it is with honey too they purify their tongues from every sin.

" Further, when they bring honey to the Persian [that is, to the candidate who is being initiated in this grade, in the rites called Persica], as to the 'Keeper of the Fruits,' they symbolically signify the power of keeping [or preserving]."

The use of honey in the Leontica is corroborated by the engraved figure of a lion with a bee in its mouth. Nor is it easy in this connection, when we remember the bas-reliefs of the heroic deeds of Mithra, and the similar cycles of exploits of solar heroes, such as Nimrod, Gilgamesh and Hercules, to refrain from quoting the famous riddle put to Samson : " What is sweeter than honey ? What is stronger than a lion ? "

I also remember the mystic experience of a friend, who in a symbolic vision was chased by a great bee, and when in fear was told to let it suck his honey ; after which a lion was sent to protect him, and he was told that he was being taught the veiling of the mystery. But to return to our text.

Porphyry then goes on to say that some think that honey further typifies the celestial nectar and ambrosia, and also the pleasure which draws souls down into generation. Then is the soul moistened and becomes watery ; it is sucked down into the watery spheres within the great Cup or Cratēr of Generation ; and so a crater or bowl is placed near Mithra to signify this.

" The Ancients moreover used to call the priestesses of Mother Earth (Dēmētēr) Bees, in that they were initiates of the Terrene Goddess, and the Maid (Korē) herself Bee-like. They also called the Moon the Bee, as Lady of Generation ; and especially because [with the Magians] the Moon in exaltation is the Bull, and Bees are Ox-born—that is, souls coming into birth are Ox-born—and the 'God who steals the Bull' [Mithra] occultly signifies generation."

Further on Porphyry tells us that there are two entrances to the Cave ; namely, the zodiacal Crab by which souls descend, and the Goat by which they ascend. By the northern gate the souls descend as men, by the southern they ascend to become gods. The northern regions and the southern are thus apportioned to souls descending into generation and then separating themselves from it (c. xx.).

" Hence they assigned to Mithra His proper seat upon the equinoctial circle." Thus astrologically interpreted, he may be said to bear the sword of the Ram, which is a martial sign, and to be borne upon the Bull, which is under the rule of Venus. And Mithra as well as the Bull is the Demiurge, or Creator, and Lord of generation.

One side of the Magian Mysteries, therefore, dealt with the descent of souls into generation, and the other with the ascent of souls and their freedom from the necessity of rebirth—that is, with their becoming gods. And this agrees with the nature of the Lesser and Greater Rites of all the great Mystery-institutions.

THE MYSTERIES OF MITHRA.

In his famous treatise *On Abstinence*, Porphyry further gives us a hint that the signs of the zodiac and the rest were but a veil to still more recondite secrets, in the following interesting passage (iv., 16) :

"Among the Persians those who are wise concerning divinity and are servants of God, are called Magi ; for this is the meaning of Magus in their native tongue. This race was considered so great and august among the Persians, that [King] Darius, son of Hystaspes, in addition to the rest of his titles, had engraved upon his tomb the fact that he had also been Master of the Magic [Mysteries].

"The Magi were divided into three castes, as Eubulus, who wrote the history of Mithra in many books, informs us. The first and most highly trained of them neither eat nor kill anything possessed of soul, but adhere to the ancient rule of abstinence from animals. The second [? the warriors] use flesh, but do not slay tame creatures. While the third [though they eat domesticated animals] do not use all of them as do the rest of the people.

"For the chief doctrine of all of them is that of metempsychosis. And this they also seem to make clear in the Mysteries of Mithra ; for they are accustomed to indicate us [that is the grade or nature to which we belong] by means of animal forms, thus mystically symbolizing the nature which we have in common with the animals.

"Thus they call the initiates who take part in the actual rites Lions . . ., and those who serve [or the subordinates] Ravens. In the case of the Fathers moreover [the same symbolism is used], for they are called Eagles and Hawks.

"[These are the distinguishing marks of the three great grades] ; in addition, he who receives the initiations in the Lion-grade is dressed in many animal-forms.

"And Pallas, in his books about Mithra, when giving the *rationale* of this, says that the general opinion would carry it right up into the zodiacal circle, whereas the true and correct reply declares that it has to do with the mystery of human souls which, they say, are clothed in bodies of every kind."

The above passages contain the most important scraps of information we can glean from the Greek and Latin texts. Owing to their fragmentary nature it is, of course, impossible to recover anything but a few scattered outlines of what must have been a very complex tradition.

There was in the East an elaborate public cult as well as an esoteric side of Mithraism ; in the West there was nothing that can be called a public cult in any precise form, and no doubt, also, the mystery-rites were considerably modified to suit Greek and Roman ideas—at any rate in the exterior degrees of the general inner rites. Moreover, as they were introduced by the rough soldiery, these preliminary degrees retained or even exaggerated the rude features of the tradition ; and it was only in the hands of the philosophers and the cultured that the inner rites contacted the deeper truths and intimate experiences which they were devised to veil and guard.

We will next turn to the evidence of the monuments.

THE MYSTERIES OF MITHRA.

FROM THE MONUMENTS.

It is, of course, generally assumed that where there is any doubt between the evidence of the texts and the testimony of the monuments, the latter must decide the question. If, however, we should apply the same test to, say, Christianity, or to any other great religion in imagined similar circumstances, we see at once that the monuments would by no means be the more important witnesses; indeed they would be frequently very misleading. What, for instance, could we make out of the Stations of the Cross, if we possessed no single word of the Gospel story? What, from the naïve mediæval figured representations of the Creator, could we divine concerning the true attributes of the Supreme?

Of all the sculptured figures discovered in the ruins of the Mithræa, the most extraordinary, and even awe-inspiring, is the symbolic statue of the mysterious Æon, transcending gods and men. He is the Everliving One, the Lord of Light and Life—the Autozoon, He that gives life to Himself, and is the Source and Ender of all lives. He is Zervan Akarana, Boundless Time, and also Infinite Space, the Ingenerable and Ineffable, the Pantheos.

The rest of the Mithriac sculptures are disguised by the genius of Greek art, which in beautifying the originals and humanizing the symbolic creations of Oriental imagination deprived them of their mysterious nature. The Æon alone remained intractable to the ingenuity of Hellenic iconography.

This mysterious figure is that of a "monster" as it is called; or rather it typifies the source or prototype of all ensouled forms including that of man.

The body is that of a man, and is frequently covered with the signs of the zodiac.

The feet are sometimes human, sometimes animal, sometimes they end in the coils of a serpent.

In all cases there is a huge serpent coiled round the body of the Æon, generally in seven coils; and the head of the serpent lies on, or curves over, the head of the statue, and in one case bends round into the Æon's mouth.

The head of the figure is that of a lion thickly maned.

From the shoulders spring two wings upwards, and below these two wings hang down. These are sometimes decorated with symbols of the four seasons.

On the breast is the sacred bolt of power, and in either hand a key, while the right holds a sceptre or rod as well.

This startling image generally stood on the celestial sphere; occasionally other symbols were added to the pedestal—such as the serpent-rod of Hermes, the cock of Asclepius, the tongs and hammer of the Fire-god, Hephæstus, and the pine cone. All these symbols are connected with the creative power.

The Æon therefore typified the power of all things and of all gods. The Æon was Lord of the whole Celestial Sphere, and of the Four Great Elements. The serpent symbolized earth; the head of it entering the mouth is paralleled by a number of monuments on which the serpent drinks from a crater or water-vessel; the wings symbolize air; and the lion-head with its shaggy mane typifies fire and light.

The keys are the keys of life and death, of light and darkness, of all the opposites. The bolt and sceptre are the emblems of supreme power.

But the Æon was not only a symbol of the cosmogonical power of the creator. The promise that was gradually revealed to the initiate was that he might not only see the Æon in all His glorious actuality, but finally become the Æon. There was not only instruction as to the

THE MYSTERIES OF MITHRA.

way down, but also precise doctrine as to the way up.

Man was destined to become the Æon by making his own body cosmic as was the Body of the Æon. There was a Perfect Body in man hidden in the imperfection of his partial frame. The serpentine power and all the other powers were to come to birth in him when the time appointed by the Æon should be fulfilled.

Of the rest of the monuments the chief was the group of the Bull-slaying Mithra. In every Cave this formed the chief object, and it was placed in the apse of the subterranean temple like a modern reredos.

Within a sculptured frame representing a natural cave, the ever-young God, with averted face, as though in sorrow, plunges his short sword, or broad sacrificial knife, into the heart of the Bull, grasping its nostrils with the left hand, and with his left knee upon the back of the kneeling beast.

Mithra is clad in trowsers and a single robe girdled round the centre, and with a mantle flying in the wind, as though it were the wings of an eagle settling on its prey. This mantle or cloak is generally covered with constellations. On his head is a Phrygian cap.

The blood that flows from the wound of the Bull is sometimes represented by bearded ears of corn, and frequently the tuft of hair at the end of the Bull's tail is also composed of similar wheat-ears.

A dog, the symbol of instinct and watchfulness, laps the blood ; while below the smitten beast is a serpent and a cratēr, or water-vessel, and a scorpion seizes the generative parts of the Bull.

On either side are two smaller figures, almost duplicates of Mithra ; one holds a torch upwards, the other a torch reversed. These dadophors or torch-bearers represent the powers of life and death, of waking and waning, of spring and autumn, of ascent and descent. They are also the symbols of the two

great powers, represented, in Alchemical and Rosicrucian tradition, by the right hand raised with finger pointing upwards, and the left down with finger pointing downwards—accompanied by the mystic utterances Coagula and Solve ; Collect and Disperse, Fix and Volatilize.

This famous artistic group was based on an Attic original by an artist of Pergamum in the second century B.C. The original was a bas-relief which ornamented the balustrade of the temple of Athena-Nikē on the Acropolis—the well-known figure of Victory sacrificing a bull.

But the group of the Tauroctonous Mithra was significant of greater things.

According to the Avestan tradition the first living creature created by Ahura-Mazda was a Bull. The Spirit of Opposition, Ahriman, oppressed it with every ill and finally compassed its death ; but, marvellous to tell, from its body sprang up the whole vegetable kingdom.

In the Mithriac tradition, in which we find scarcely any reference to Ahriman, the mystery is otherwise explained. It is the Vice-regent of the Supreme who accomplished the primal sacrifice. This is depicted admirably by the artists who delineated the look of regret and remorse on the face of the God, sacrificing His own most prolific creation that greater benefits might be showered upon the barren earth.

The wheat-ears typify vegetation on the one hand and also the spermatic power of the creative life on the other. Moreover the *Bundahish* tells us precisely that when the Primal Bull was slain, all the different species of plants sprang from the different parts of its body, and especially from its spinal marrow.

But this was not all. If there were mysteries of generation, cosmic and human, there were also mysteries of regeneration. There was a christology and soteriology as well as a cosmology.

We know from our texts that the ancient Persians believed in a resurrection of the dead, and the Mazdæan books

THE MYSTERIES OF MITHRA.

prophesy that at the last day the Saviour Saoshyañt will slay a Bull, and from its fat mingled with the juice of the white Haoma (the Indian Soma, replaced in the West by Wine) will prepare a Draught of Immortality for all men.

But the highest initiates of Mithra knew that the last day was for every man when the Æon gave command ; and that Mithra as Creator was ever slaying the Cosmic Bull, and Mithra as Saviour was ever slaying the Bull of Generation in the presence of His true worshippers. The Draught of Immortality was ever ready for him who had made himself ready.

But the Tauroctonous group though the central one, was not the only scene depicted on the Mithriac reredos.

Besides various symbolical representations connected with the sun, moon and planets, etc., there are two series of tableaux which specially invite our attention. It is, of course, somewhat rash, in the absence of all confirmatory texts, to hazard a suggestion of anything but the main purport of these two series of scenes.

The first consists of six scenes ; the second of ten. The first is apparently a history of cosmogenesis ; the second is clearly a pictorial memorial of the exploits of Mithra.

I. THE COSMOLOGIC TABLEAUX.

1. The first tableau consists of a full face, surrounded by a thick encircling which appears to be divided into eight parts. This is evidently the primordial deity ; in its solitariness doubtless the Æon, but taken in connection with the next scene it is Heaven.

2. For the second tableau represents a woman, with the upper part of her body naked, reclining on the earth ; her left hand touches a basket of fruits, her right is raised above her head. Near her is the figure of a man, visible only as far as his waist, who supports a great sphere on his head. This Atlas is clearly Heaven

and the recumbent figure Earth — the primordial pair.

3. Then follows a male figure half recumbent on the rocks ; a similar figure sometimes appears with water flowing at his feet. This is clearly Ocean ; and the Avestan tradition has preserved the ancient saying : " All was created from water." Did Thales, then, derive his leading dogma from Iranian mythology ?

4. Next comes a group of three female figures in long robes. They are the triple Fortune or Fate, who was regarded in Persia as the daughter of Heaven and Earth. All the above related to the night of time, during the reign of Zervan.

5. For the next scene depicts Zervan (Kronos) handing over to Mazda (Zeus) the sovereignty of the world.

6. Finally, we have a scene which depicts Ahura brandishing his thunderbolt and hurling down from heaven the rebellious giants.

II. THE HEROIC TABLEAUX.

1. The first scene represents the birth of the God from a rock. This stone was called the Generative Rock. Frequently this rock is surrounded by a serpent raising its head towards the child, whose body is naked, and only half out of the stone. On his ringlets he wears a Phrygian cap, and carries in the right hand a knife and in the left a torch.

The cosmogonic interpretation connects this birth from the rock with the birth of light from the firmament which was regarded as solid in Iranian tradition, while the solar interpretation would refer it to the rising of the sun from behind the mountains. But let us come to something nearer home. Our tableau seems to represent a greater mystery— the birth of what may be called the first spark or again the first outpouring of life on earth.

If we may elaborate somewhat the mystery of that which sleeps in the

THE MYSTERIES OF MITHRA.

mineral, wakes in the animal, and is perfected in man, it might be said that the first light-spark, or life-stream, according as we regard it in its masculine or feminine potency, is passive or sleeps in the mineral and is active or wakes in the vegetable.

The second spark, or the intensification or power of the first, sleeps in the animal and wakes in man; while the third is the mystery of what Basilides would call the third "sonship," which is that of Christhood.

2. It is, therefore, of interest to remark that next to the tableau of Mithra Petrogenēs comes a scene in which there is a great tree with leafy branches extending to the top of the picture. Before it is standing a young man, quite naked, except for his Phrygian cap. He is cutting from the tree a branch covered with leaves and fruit. The spark becomes active in the vegetable kingdom on earth; it plants there a branch from the tree of life.

Often in this same scene is seen a figure clothed in an oriental tunic half issuing from the leafage of the tree, while another figure blows or breathes straight in his face. This is evidently a different incident in the cycle of experience, and the two scenes were sometimes depicted apart. It seems clearly to represent the passage from the vegetable to the animal kingdom, and the inbreathing of the second spark, the breath of lives, the animal soul. The naked first spark is half clothed by the second.

3. The next tableau represents a young man clad in an Asiatic costume and wearing a Phrygian cap, the usual full clothing of Mithra. He holds in his hand a bow and shoots an arrow at a lofty rock. Where the arrow hits the rock there cascades forth a spring of water. A kneeling figure catches the stream in the palms of his hands and drinks of the water greedily.

This seems to represent the coming to birth of the generative power, and

animal nature in man. It may even hide an ancient mystery tradition that man was born before the animals on earth, and through his greedy delight in the passion nature of the watery planes, he produced the animal world as known on earth. However this may be, the symbolism seems to suggest that the water is the stream of genesis and that man is absorbed in its delights. There is as yet no war in his members; he is the natural primitive animal man.

4. With the next tableau the order changes, and the Bull is brought upon the scene.

First of all we have two representations which are closely connected, and are always found together when they occur on the same monument, though one of them sometimes is found alone. A kind of wherry which appears to float upon the waters, bears on it, either standing or lying down, the mythic Bull.

Alongside of this scene, is another consisting of a little gabled house from which the Bull is ready to leap. One of the monuments gives us the reason of this leaping forth. Two persons, of whom one is indubitably Mithra, seem to be applying torches to the roof and door of this byre.

This seems to suggest the descent and the rousing into activity of the animal generative power under the fervent heat of the divine impulse.

5. We next come to a series of scenes variously depicted, but all connected with the contest of Mithra with the Bull.

First the sacred animal is seen browsing quietly in a meadow, or raising its head as though to listen.

Then Mithra comes on the scene. Sometimes he is seen carrying the Bull on his shoulders, like the Good Shepherd with the lamb, or Hermes Criophorus with the kid; he turns his head as though he feared pursuit.

Sometimes he walks alongside of the beast, holding its horns; again he mounts astride upon it and rides it quietly,

8 1

THE MYSTERIES OF MITHRA.

guiding it with one hand by means of its nostrils.

In another scene the Bull starts off in a wild gallop; Mithra with his arms round its neck lies flat along its back as though all but swept off by its rush; sometimes he has fallen and only just saves himself by clinging desperately to its horns.

At last, however, the fierce animal is conquered; the God takes it by its two hind feet over his shoulders, and drags it off, with its front hoofs trailing on the ground. He thus carries it to the cave where he is finally to slay it.

Whatever other interpretations there may be of this most famous exploit of the God, it seems very clear that it chiefly signified the conquest of the irrational nature by the reason, and the final reversal of the latter,—the beginning of the ascent, the true "repentance," or "conversion."

But to me it seems to indicate as well certain processes of mystic physiology or psycho-physiology. What I have called a spark (following a certain gnostic nomenclature) is really a power or substance hidden in every atom of the body, and is only graphically spoken of as one spark or atom.

These scenes in which Mithra grasps the horns of the Bull, seem to signify the marriage of what might be called an atom of the mental nature with an atom of the passional nature. There is struggle, there is conquest, and finally there is death prior to resurrection.

The passional nature is converted, led back by the initiate into the cave in the depth of his own substance, there to be slain—"the lamb slain from the foundation of the world"—and from its blood will spring up the plants and trees of life, and it will give corn with which to feed the hungry with the bread of life.

6. The next group depicts Mithra holding in his right hand above his head the shoulder of a calf; kneeling before him is a young man naked, or in a simple chlamys, raising his hands in sign of supplication. With this must be taken a similar scene in which Mithra apparently lays aside the object in his right hand, and with his left places on the suppliant's head a radiant crown; while again in another scene he lays his left hand on the head of the sword at his waist, and the crown lies on the ground between them.

The shoulder of the calf is, in celestial imagery, the symbol of the seven stars of the constellation of the Bear which were supposed to turn the great sphere. These are the Lords of the Pole, and Mithra is their Lord. The seven jewels, representing the seven simple senses of the celestial or spiritual body, are now ordered in the initiate's heaven and he is crowned with the Sun.

7. The next scene represents a compact or bond of brotherhood between Mithra and the Sun. Perhaps this represents the grade of the Heliodromos, or Suncourser, as I have translated it above in the passage from Jerome; of the man whose course is now as the course of the stars in high heaven.

8. Whether or not this scene is here in the right order, it is impossible to say. It represents what is apparently Mithra's Hunting. The God is mounted on a horse in full gallop; his cloak flies in the wind behind him and he shoots his arrows, while an attendant follows with a quiver of darts.

This seems to suggest the activity of the perfect man, mounted on the white steed of purified passion, and directing his powers against the forces of evil; the attendant is perhaps the Sun, who supplies him with his arrows.

9. The next tableau depicts a feast. Mithra and the Sun are seated on a cushioned couch with a table before them on which are loaves, quartered by a cross, and they hold goblets in their hands. Surrounding them, and serving them apparently, are symbolic representations of the initiates of various

degrees—such as the Raven, Persian, Soldier and Lion—and below the latter are some of the sacred animals, notably the Bull ; indeed, from one of the greater monuments it seems as though the Bull's back formed the table of this final Banquet or Agapē.

This feast perhaps pertained to the Master-grade alone ; it could only be partaken by the Fathers.

10. The last scene depicts the Departure of Mithra, in the Chariot of the Sun, towards the Region of the West, represented by the figure of Ocean. It is the *consummatum est ;* He goes unto His own.

One is well aware that these mythic scenes can be interpreted in many other ways, according to the number of times there may be power to turn the key. One is also well aware how hazardous is the present undertaking in the absence of all documents. But as there is confidence that all the great Mystery-traditions set forth chiefly the Mystery of Man, I have ventured to suggest the above interpretation from what I have gleaned of other similar traditions and a comparative study of the Gnosis.

From this brief sketch I have been compelled to omit a thousand points of interest and a thousand puzzles of scholarship. But as there has been no intention of writing an elaborate treatise, but only the object of getting as much of interest as one could into these few pages, as introductory to the more definite subject of the Ritual which Dieterich has rescued from the chaos of the famous Greek Magic Papyrus of Paris, I must now break off, and reserve what else there may be to say for the next small volume.

A . . . .
MITHRIAC
RITUAL. .

A MITHRIAC RITUAL.

CONTENTS

Text : Dieterich (A.), *Eine Mithrasliturgie* (Leipzig, 1903).

A MITHRIAC RITUAL.

PREAMBLE.

The last little volume gave the reader a brief outline of what is known of the cult of Mithra and the spread of the Mithriac Mysteries in the Western world. We have now to deal with a Mithriac Ritual of the most instructive and intensely interesting character, which introduces us to the innermost rite of the carefully guarded secrets of the Mithriaca.

This Ritual is all the more precious in that our knowledge of the Liturgies of the ancient Pagan cults of the West is of the scantiest nature. A few fragments only remain, mostly in the form of hymns; whereas the Ritual before us is complete, and the only complete one so far discovered. Dieterich calls it a Liturgy; but a Liturgy is a service in which several take part, whereas it is plain that our Ritual was a secret and solemn inner rite for one person only.

The credit of unearthing it from the obscurity in which it was buried, and of conclusively demonstrating its parentage, is due to Dieterich; for though Cumont in his great work quotes several passages from the unrevised text, he does so only to reject it as a genuine Mithriac document.

It is dug out of the chaos of the great Paris Magic Papyrus 574 (*Supplément grec de la Bibliothèque nationale*), the date of which is fixed with every probability as the earliest years of the fourth century A.D. The original text of the Ritual has, however, been plainly worked over by a school of Egyptian magicians, who inserted most of the now unintelligible words and names (ἄσημα ὀνόματα, *nomina barbara, nomina arcana*), and vowel-combinations and permutations (*voces*

mysticæ), of their theurgic language, which were known in Egypt as "words of power."

The subject is naturally one of the most obscure that is known to scholarship, and so far no one has thrown any real light on it. That, however, there was once in Egypt and Chaldæa a science of this "nature language," or "tongue of the gods," which subsequently passed into the superstition of a purely mechanical tradition, is highly probable; and one means towards a recovery of the understanding of its nature is a study of the still living tradition of *mantra-vidyā*, or the science of *mantrāḥ*, or mystic utterances and invocations, in India of to-day.

When these evidently later insertions are removed, there still remains a certain number of *nomina arcana* and *mysticæ voces* which cannot be removed without doing violence to the text. It, therefore, follows that these stand as part of the Ritual. Did they, however, form part of the *original* Ritual? The original Ritual must have contained, one would have imagined, Persian names. But the distinguished scholar Bartholomae, whom Dieterich has called in to his assistance, declares that nothing Persian can be made out of them without violent changes of the letters. But why, it might be asked, should not the original Persian Ritual have contained *nomina arcana* taken over from Chaldæa? However this may be, our Greek Ritual evidently contained certain names and words "of power," before it reached the hands of the Egyptian magical school who inserted the majority of the māntric formulæ in our present text.

The latter are, of course, entirely eliminated from the translation, while the former are marked by obeli.

On the whole the most likely supposition is that we have before us (when the latter insertions are removed) a Ritual translated or paraphrased into Greek, and adapted for use in Egypt,

A MITHRIAC RITUAL.

and that, too, for picked members of the most esoteric circles. For our Ritual is not for the initiation of a neophyte of the lower grades, but for a candidate who is to self-initiate himself in the solitary mystery of apotheosis, whereby he became a true " Father " of the inmost rites, one possessing face to face knowledge and gnosis.

Dieterich thinks that this Greek ritual was first made in Egypt about 100-150 A.D., and was used in the Mysteries until 200 A.D. It was then that it got into the hands of the magical school, and was included, together with many other pieces, some of them similarly treated, in a collection which was copied on the papyrus which we now possess, about 300 A.D.

It is exceedingly probable, therefore, that we have in this Ritual of initiation certain theurgic practices of Egyptian tradition combined with the traditional Mithriac invocations done into Greek.

As to the chanting of the vowels, it is of interest to learn from Demetrius, *On Interpretation*, c. 71 (p. 20 Raderm.), that :

" In Egypt the priests hymn the Gods by means of the seven vowels, chanting them in order ; instead of the pipe and lute the musical chanting of these letters is heard. So that if you were to take away this accompaniment you would simply remove the whole melody and music of the utterance (*logos*)."

The statement of Nicomachus of Gerasa, the " musician " and mystic (second century A.D.), is still clearer ; for he not only tells us about the vowels and consonants, but also of certain other " unarticulated " sounds which were used by the theurgists, and which are directed to be used in the rubrics of our Ritual. In speaking of the vowels or " sounding letters "—each of the seven spheres being said to give forth a different vowel or nature-tone—Nicomachus (c. 6) informs us that these root-sounds in nature are combined with certain material elements, as they are in spoken speech with the consonants ; but " just as the soul with the body, and music with the lyrestrings, the one produces living creatures and the other musical modes and tunes, so do those root-sounds give birth to certain energic and initiatory powers of divine operations. It is because of this that whenever theurgists are awestruck in any such operation, they make invocation symbolically by means of ' hissings ' and ' poppings ' and unarticulated and discordant sounds."

The exact translation of the Greek terms, συριγμὸς and ποππυσμός, is somewhat of a difficulty. The first denotes a shrill piping sound or hissing, the Latin *stridor*. It is used of such different sounds as the rattling of ropes, the trumpeting of elephants and a singing in the ears. The second is used of a clicking or clucking with the lips and tongue, and of the whistling, cheeping, chirruping, warbling or trilling of birds. It is used of the smack of a loud kiss and also of the cry " hush." Both Aristophanes and Pliny tell us that it was used as a protection against, or rather a reverent greeting of, lightning ; and the latter adds that this was a universal custom.

The English " pop " perhaps represents the idea of the Greek most nearly. In the Ritual, however, I have rendered it by " puff " as it is connected with breath.

It is evident that we have here to do with certain nature-sounds, which have disappeared from articulate speech, except in some primitive languages such as the " clicking " of the Zulus. It pertains to the art of *onomatopoiïa* or *onomatopoïēsis*, or the forming of words expressive of natural sounds. The root-idea seems to be that in mystic operations designed to bring man in touch with the hidden powers of nature, the language of nature must be employed.

As we have said, the Ritual before us is not of the nature of a church or temple service ; on the contrary, it contains directions for a solitary sacrament, in which the whole effort of the celebrant

A MITHRIAC RITUAL.

is to stir into activity, and bring into conscious operation, his own hidden nature or the root-substance of his being. It is a *yoga*-rite (*unio mystica*), or act for union, in which the physical breath, the etheric currents, and the psychic auræ, or life-breaths, or *prāṇa's*, work together with the inbreathing of the Great Breath, or Holy Spirit, or Ātmic Energy.

It should therefore prove of very great interest to many who have of late heard much concerning *yoga*, both in its higher contemplative modes, and also in its modes of deep and psychic breathing (*haṭha-yoga*) ; for it may be news to many that in the ancient West, especially in Egypt, there was a high art of this selfsame *yoga* which has been developed so elaborately in India.

We will now give a translation of the Ritual and then proceed to comment on it. The prayers and utterances are printed in italics, and the rubrics or instructions in Roman type.

THE RITUAL.

I.

[THE FATHER'S PRAYER.]

O Providence, O Fortune, bestow on me Thy Grace—imparting these the Mysteries a Father only may hand on, and that, too, to a Son alone—his Immortality—[a Son] initiate, worthy of this our Craft, with which Sun Mithras, the Great God, commanded me to be endowed by His Arch-angel ; so that I, Eagle [as I am, by mine own self] alone, may soar to Heaven, and contemplate all things.

II.

THE INVOCATORY
UTTERANCE (LOGOS).

1. *O Primal Origin of my origination ; Thou Primal Substance of my substance ;*

First Breath of breath, the breath that is in me ; First Fire, God-given for the Blending of the blendings in me, [First Fire] of fire in me ; First Water of [my] water, the water in me ; Primal Earth-essence of the earthy essence in me ; Thou Perfect Body of me—N. N., son of N. N. (fem.)—fashioned by Honoured Arm and Incorruptible Right Hand, in World that's lightless, yet radiant with Light, [in World] that's soulless, yet filled full of Soul !

2. *If, verily, it may seem good to you, translate me, now held by my lower nature, unto the Generation that is free from Death ; in order that, beyond the insistent Need that presses on me, I may have Vision of the Deathless Source, by virtue of the Deathless Spirit, by virtue of the Deathless Water, by virtue of the [Deathless] Solid, and [by virtue of] the [Deathless] Air ; in order that I may become re-born in Mind ; in order that I may become initiate, and that the Holy Breath may breathe in me ; in order that I may admire the Holy Fire ; that I may see the Deep of the [New] Dawn, the Water that doth cause [the Soul] to thrill ; and that the Life-bestowing Æther which surrounds [all things] may give me Hearing.*

3. *For I am to behold to-day with Deathless Eyes—I, mortal, born of mortal womb, but [now] made better by the Might of Mighty Power, yea, by the Incorruptible Right Hand—[I am to see to-day] by virtue of the Deathless Spirit the Deathless Æon, the Master of the Diadems of Fire—I with pure purities [now] purified, the human soul-power of me subsisting for a little while in purity ; which [power] I shall again receive transmitted unto me beyond the insistent Bitterness that presses on me, Necessity whose debts can never go unpaid—I, N. N., son of N. N. (fem.)—according to the Ordinance of God that naught can ever change.*

4. *For that it is beyond my reach that, born beneath the sway of Death, I should [unaided] soar into the Height, together with the golden sparklings of the Brilliancy that knows no Death.*

A MITHRIAC RITUAL.

5. *Stay still, O nature doomed to perish,* [*nature*] *of men subject to Death! And straightway let me pass beyond the Need implacable that presses on me; for that I am His Son; I breathe; I am!*

III.

[THE FIRST INSTRUCTION.]

1. Take from the [Sun-]rays breath, inhaling thrice [as deeply] as thou canst; and thou shalt see thyself being raised aloft, and soaring towards the Height, so that thou seem'st to be in midst of Air.

2. Thou shalt hear naught, nor man nor beast; nor, shalt thou see aught of the sights upon the earth, in that same hour; but all things thou shalt see will be immortal.

3. For thou shalt see, in that same day and hour, the Disposition of the Gods—the Ruling Gods ascending heavenwards, the other ones descending.

And through his Disk—the God's, my Father's—there shall be seen the Way-of-going of the Gods accessible to sight.

4. And in like fashion also [shall be seen] the Pipe, as it is called, whence comes the Wind in service [for the day].

For thou shalt see as though it were a Pipe depending from His Disk; and toward the regions Westward, as though it were an infinite East Wind. But if the other Wind, toward the regions of the East, should be in service, in the like fashion shalt thou see, toward the regions of that [side,] the converse of the sight.

5. And thou shalt see the Gods gazing intently on thee and bearing down upon thee.

Then straightway lay thy dexter finger on thy lips and say:

IV.

[THE FIRST UTTERANCE.]

O Silence! Silence! Silence!

The Symbol of the Living God beyond Decay.

Protect me, Silence! †!

Next " hiss " forth long : $\bar{S}$! $\bar{S}$!

Then " puff " saying : † !

And thereon shalt thou see the Gods gazing benignly on thee, and no longer bearing down upon thee, but proceeding on the proper order of their doings.

V.

[THE SECOND INSTRUCTION.]

When, then, thou see'st the Upper Cosmos clean and clear, with no one of the Gods (or Angels) bearing down on thee, expect to hear a mighty thunderclap so as to startle thee. Then say again :

VI.

THE [SECOND] UTTERANCE (LOGOS).

1. *O Silence! Silence!* *I am a Star, whose Course is as your Course, shining anew from out the Depth* †.

Upon thy saying this, straightway His Disk will start expanding.

2. And after thou hast said the second utterance—to wit, twice *Silence* and the rest—" hiss " twice, and " puff " twice ; and straightway shalt thou see a mighty host of stars, five-pointed, emerging from His Disk, and filling all the Air.

3. Then say again :

O Silence! Silence!

And when His Disk is opened [fully] out, thou shalt behold an infinite Encircling and Doors of Fire fast closed. Straightway set going then the utterance that follows, closing thy eyes :

A MITHRIAC RITUAL.

VII.

THE THIRD
UTTERANCE (LOGOS).

1. *Hear me, give ear to me*—N. N.,
son of N. N. (fem.)—*O Lord, who with
Thy Breath hast closed the Fiery Bars of
Heaven ; Twin-bodied ; Ruler of the
Fire ; Creator of the Light ; O Holder
of the Keys ; Inbreather of the Fire ;
Fire-hearted One, whose Breath gives
Light ; Thou who dost joy in Fire ; Beau-
teous of Light ; O Lord of Light, whose
Body is of Fire ; Light-giver [and] Fire-
sower ; Fire-loosener, whose Life is in
the Light ; Fire-whirler, who sett'st the
Light in motion ; Thou Thunder-rouser ;
O Thou Light-glory, Light-increaser ;
Controller of the Light Empyrean ; O
Thou Star-tamer !*

2. *Oh ! Open unto me ! For on account
of this, the bitter and implacable Necessity
that presses on me, I do invoke Thy
Deathless Names, innate with Life, most
worshipful, that have not yet descended
unto mortal nature, nor have been made
articulate by human tongue, or cry or
tone of man :*

*Ēeō · oēeō · iōō · oē · ēeō · ēeō · oēeō ·
iōō · oēĕe · ŏĕe · ŏoē · iĕ · ēō · oŏ · oĕ · ieō ·
oē · ŏoē · ieōoē · ieeō · eē · iō · oē · ioē ·
ōēō · eoē · oeō · ōiē · ōiēeō · oi · iii · ĕoē ·
ōuē · ēō · oĕe · eōēia · aēaeēa · ēeeē · eeē ·
eeē · ieō · ēeō · oēeeoē · ēeō · euō · oē · eiō ·
ēō · ōē · ōē · ōē · ee · ooouiōē !*

3. Utter all these with Fire and Spirit
once unto the end ; and then begin
again a second time, until thou hast
completed [all] the Seven Immortal Gods
of Cosmos.

When thou hast uttered them, thunders
and crashings shalt thou hear in the
Surround, and feel thyself a-shake with
every crash.

Then once more utter *Silence !* [and]
the utterance [following it].

4. Thereon open thy eyes ; and thou
shalt see the Doors thrown open, and the
Cosmos of the Gods that is within the
Doors ; so that for joy and rapture of
the sight thy Spirit runs to meet it, and
soars up.

Therefore, hold thyself steady, and,
gazing steadily into thyself, draw breath
from the Divine.

When, then, thy Soul shall be restored, say :

VIII.

[THE FOURTH UTTERANCE.]

1. *Draw nigh, O Lord !*

Upon this utterance His Rays shall
be turned on thee, and thou shalt be in
midst of them.

2. When, then, thou hast done this,
thou shalt behold a God, in flower of
age, of fairest beauty, [and] with Locks
of Flame, in a white Tunic and a scarlet
Mantle, wearing a Crown of Fire.

Straightway salute Him with the Salutation of the Fire :

IX.

[THE FIFTH UTTERANCE.]

1. *Hail Lord ! O Thou of mighty
Power ; O King of mighty Sway ; Greatest
of Gods ; O Sun ; Thou Lord of Heaven
and Earth ; O God of Gods ! Strong is
Thy Breath ; strong is Thy Might !*

*O Lord, if it seem good to Thee, make
Thou announcement of me unto God
Most-high, who hath begotten and created
Thee !*

2. *For that a man*—I, N.N., son of
N.N. (fem.), *born of the mortal womb*
of N.N. (fem.), *and of spermatic ichōr,
yea, of this* [ichōr], *which at Thy Hands
to-day hath undergone the transmutation
of re-birth*—, *one, from so many tens of
thousands, transformed to immortality in
this same hour, by God's good-pleasure,
of God transcendent Good*—, [*a man, I
say,*] *presumes to worship Thee, and
supplicates with whatsoever power a mortal
hath.*

A MITHRIAC RITUAL.

3. Upon this utterance He shall come to the Pole, and thou shalt see Him moving round as on a path.

Then gaze intently, and send forth a prolonged "bellowing," like to a horn-note, expelling the whole breath, with pressure on the ribs, and kiss the amulets, and say first to that upon the right :

X.

[THE SIXTH UTTERANCE.]

Protect me ! † *!*

When thou hast uttered this, thou shalt behold the Doors thrown open, and, issuing from the Depth, Seven Virgins, in byssus-robes, with serpent-faces, and golden sceptres in their hands. These are they who are the so-called Heaven's Fortunes (*Tychai*).

When thou dost see these things, make salutation thus :

XI.

[THE SEVENTH UTTERANCE.]

1. *Hail Heaven's Seven Fortunes, Virgins august and good, ye sacred ones who live and eat with* † *! Ye holiest Protectors of the Four Supports !*

Hail thou, the First, † *!*
Hail thou, the Second, † *!*
Hail thou, the Third, † *!*
Hail thou, the Fourth, † *!*
Hail thou, the Fifth, † *!*
Hail thou, the Sixth, † *!*
Hail thou, the Seventh, † *!*

2. There come forth others, too—Seven Gods, with faces of black bulls, in linen loin-cloths, with seven golden fillets on their heads. These are the so-called Heaven's Pole-lords.

And in like fashion unto each of them thou must make salutation with his special name.

XII.

[THE EIGHTH UTTERANCE.]

1. *Hail Guardians of the Pivot, ye sacred sturdy Youths, who all, at once, revolve the spinning Axis of Heaven's Circle, ye who let loose the thunder and the lightning, and earthquake-shocks and thunder-bolts upon the hosts of impious folk, but [who bestow] on me, who pious am and worshipper of God, good-health, and soundness of my frame in every part, and proper stretch of hearing and of sight, and calm, in the now present good-hours of this day, O mighty Ruling Lords and Gods of me !*

Hail thou, the First, † *!*
Hail thou, the Second, † *!*
Hail thou, the Third, † *!*
Hail thou, the Fourth, † *!*
Hail thou, the Fifth, † *!*
Hail thou, the Sixth, † *!*
Hail thou, the Seventh, † *!*

2. Now when they [all] are present in their order, here and there, gaze in the Air intently, and thou shalt see lightnings down-flashing, and lights a-quiver, and the earth a-shake ; and [then] a God descending, [a God] transcending vast, of radiant Presence, with golden Locks, in flower of age, [clad] in a Robe of brightness, with Crown of gold [upon His Head], and Garments [on His Legs], holding in His Right Hand the golden Shoulder of the Calf.

This latter is the Bear that moves the Heaven[-dome], and changes its direction, now up now down, according to the hour.

Then shalt thou see lightnings leap from His Eyes and from His Body stars.

3. Straightway send forth a "bellowing" prolonged, with belly-pressure, to start thy senses going all together—prolonged unto the very end, kissing again the amulets and saying :

9 2

A MITHRIAC RITUAL.

XIII.

[THE NINTH UTTERANCE.]

†, [O Lord] of me—N. N.—abide with me, within my Soul ! Oh ! leave me not ! For † bids thee [remain].

And gaze intently on the God, with " bellowing " prolonged, and thus salute Him :

XIV.

[THE TENTH UTTERANCE.]

Hail Lord, Thou Master of the Water ! Hail, Founder of the Earth ! Hail, Prince of Breath !

O Lord, being born again, I pass away in being made Great, and, having been made Great, I die.

Being born from out the state of birth-and-death that giveth birth to [mortal] lives, I now, set free, pass to the state transcending birth, as Thou hast established it, according as Thou hast ordained and made the Mystery.

COMMENTS.

First we have the Prayer of the Father, who invites the Presence or Glory (Hvarenō as it is called in ancient Persian) of *his* Father, the Great Father of all Fathers, or Supreme Initiator, Mithra the Invincible, to be favourable both to himself and also to his beloved Son who is deemed worthy of having the final secrets imparted to him, so that he in his turn may become a Father.

The highest initiates of the Mithriaca (as of many other mystery-associations of the time) were called the Fathers. They were also called Eagles, and doubt-less in Egypt also Hawks, for they had to be born anew as Horus. The sacra-ment is the mystery of the Birth of Horus in one of its variants ; the rite is that of *Athanasía* or Immortality, of *Apothéōsis* or Deification or Birth as a God.

The initiates of the next lower grade were called Sons of the Fathers. The tie between them, however, was far stronger than that of human father and child, for it was a spiritual bond ; they were their true God-fathers. And these God-fathers of the Mysteries were the true Sons of *their* Father, Mithra Himself, Father of all fatherhood, Master of all masterhood.

This Son has already passed through a long probation and been found worthy of receiving the secret instructions of the Great Act. This Great Act is the Birth of Power, and it is called in the text *Dynamis*, which I have translated Craft. It was a Craft in its highest sense, for it was of the nature of Creative Power.

The Greek *mystérion*, in the sense of an initiatory act, that is to say, an operation which started (*initiare*) new powers in a man, was, since the time of Tertullian, translated in the language of the Western Church by *sacramentum*, and Dieterich (p. 93) thinks that *dynamis* is a synonym of *sacramentum*. And this particular Dynamis or Craft is a synonym of the Great Work of the Alchemists, as we saw from a quotation from Zosimus in our last volume (p. 72.).

Initiation, however, does not mean consummation. An initiation is the start-ing of things going ; it lies with the can-didate entirely to make the initiation valid, to seal up the link so to speak. Without this, information will all be vague ; there will be retained only vague memories, hints and suspicions.

I am inclined to think that in " Sun Mithra " we have the gloss of an ignorant copyist. Mithra was not the Sun, either in the Iranian religion or in the Mithriac Mysteries ; as He is clearly also not the Sun in the rubrics of our Ritual. On the contrary, the Sun is rather the Archangel of Mithra, the Light, and is thus for us the chief mind-power of the Mind of all masterhood.

A MITHRIAC RITUAL.

Speaking in a still more mystical fashion, a Father, as a master, may be said to be one who can stud his own heaven, or great surround, or buddhic substance, with his own stars, or mind-powers. Such a one is capable of being an Initiator into Great Things, or cosmic mysteries. He is capable of projecting his immortality, or super-human power, or ātmic radiance.

Thus an Eagle is one capable of rising into the true Air and looking straight at his own Sun. Such a one does not have to see God reflected in Nature as ordinary man does; he is capable of grasping or understanding the Divine without form. Heaven for such a consciousness is the Great Surround in which all "things"—the things-that-are—are studded as Stars; or to put it otherwise, where every part or portion is a whole or wholeness (to use Platonic terms); they are all "one with another," as Plotinus has it.

II.

We now come to the Ritual proper, and to the first solemn utterance (*logos*) or invocation. The Theurgist invokes his "perfect" or cosmic body, from the depths of his own substance. This is the mystic "enformation according to substance," which is set forth in cosmic terms in the Sophia-mythus or Wisdom-saga of the Christianized Gnosis (*F.F.F.*, 2nd ed., pp. 335, ff.).

General Gnostic tradition teaches that it is by the definite use of all the organs of the body that perfected man is brought into contact with the Great Cosmos, for in a very definite way the body when perfected is a microcosm. We have thus to think of every part of the body possessing sense capable of conveying to consciousness things of an outside and inside world.

1. This great sensitivity is brought about by a transmutation in substance, a rearrangement of atoms so to speak.

The Theurgist, or Operator of the Divine Work, evokes from the depths of his own being his own primal substance or root-plasm, the One Element, differentiated according to the modes of the four cosmic elements—the elements of his mortal body being all permutations of the Earth-element alone; namely, fiery earth, airy earth, watery earth, earthy earth. This Great Four is the Tetraktys of the Pythagoreans—the "Fourfold Root of Everflowing Nature"—in one of its aspects.

It will be noticed that that which brings about this "Blending of the blendings" in him is Fire. This is it which makes him not only of the blending or temperament called man, but also is the means whereby his blending can be transmuted. Five is "God-given," and the chief instrument of the Divine Creator in His fashioning of this fundamental body, the One Body of the man that can be transformed into any shape.

It is probable that the "Honoured Arm and Incorruptible Right Hand" is not purely a figure of speech, but belongs to a precise symbolism. I am somewhat tempted to connect this "Arm" with the "Shoulder of the Calf" (which comes later on in the Ritual), typifying the seven "pole-lords," the servants of the Pivot on which all things turn. It is He who makes the spheres revolve, and turns all things upon the cosmic lathe, or potter's-wheel.

This "fashioning" of substance, is not the splitting up of matter into geometrical forms, but far more fundamental, and is therefore done in a world that is prior to differentiated light and life as we know it.

"N. N., son of N.N. (fem.)" signify that here must be inserted the names of the candidate and of his mother. The mention of the name of his mother and not father is remarkable. No women were admitted unto the Mithriaca; the women were initiated into the associated Mysteries of the Magna Mater, or Great Mother.

A MITHRIAC RITUAL.

2. He now prays to the great powers of his Single Body, his Wholeness, his Cosmic Vesture, his Sun-barque, his Pegasus, to translate him from Death to Life, from appearance to reality, from Darkness to Light. The bonds of the prisoner are at last to be freed ; the " knot " of personality in the " heart " (as the Upaniṣhads phrase it) is to be unloosed ; the man is no longer to be a " Procession of Fate," but is to set his foot upon the Spheres of Fate, and make them the Wheels of his Chariot, free in Air.

Fate, Insistent Need, Necessity, Death, is what a Buddhist or a Brāhman ordinarily means by Karma. Elsewhere in the Ritual it is called " bitter." It is the Bitterness, which constricts, which presses on one, the power of gravity, of condensation.

And here we may note a phrase from a mystic cosmogony of the early centuries : " Through the Bitterness of God, there appeared Mind . . . that restrains the heart, and was called Hermes."

Also compare the Hymn at the end of the J. source of the Naassene Document, where speaking of the wandering " deer," the human soul, it says :
" Far from Thy Breath away she wanders !
She seeks to flee the bitter Chaos,
And knows not how she shall escape."
And again, from a document of the Christianized Sethian Gnosis :
" He (the Light-spark) was a Ray from Above, from that Perfect Light, overpowered in the sinuous and awesome and bitter and blood-stained Water."
And yet again for one of the Orations of the Emperor Julian, who was both initiate into our Mysteries and also knew the Hellenized Mago-Chaldæan Oracles :
" The Oracles of the Gods declare that through purification not only our soul but also our bodies are judged worthy of being greatly helped and preserved, for it is said in them : ' The mortal vesture of bitter matter is preserved.' "

(For references see index of *T.G.H.*). This is just what the utterance of our Candidate tells us (c. 3) ; not only is he judged worthy in other respects, but he has made the human " soul-power " or soul-plasm in him to " subsist for a little while in purity." He has " created a nucleus "; he is " with pure purities now purified." And this purity enables him to contact the pure and unmixed elements. We must have something in us of a similar nature before we can become conscious of the things-that-are. For as the verse of Empedocles has it :
" By earth we Earth perceive; by water, Water ;
By æther, godly Æther ; and by fire, the unseen Fire."
It is thus he is to be " reborn in Mind," by means of the Great Breath of Life and Light—terms which occur over and over again in the mystical Trismegistic sermons. This and this only is the true Initiation.

Thus will he see the Great Mysteries in their true nature : the Holy Fire ; the Deep of the New Dawn and the Water of Life ; the All-surrounding Æther that will give him cosmic hearing, when his Single Body becomes all-ear.

As the Initiate in the Trismegistic " Virgin of the World " treatise says (c. 4):
" But when the Sun did rise for me, and with all-seeing eyes I gazed upon the hidden mysteries of that New Dawn."

The Deep of the New Dawn is the real substance of true Mind ; and Dawn suggests the rising of the Sun or Ātman above the horizon of the lower mind, so that you begin to see into the depths of Mind.

The Holy Breath breathing in the man is the first stirring of his true Airbody. That is to say, the substance of the Single Body becomes as it were sponge-like, so that the cosmic Air can inter-penetrate it ; the man has within himself a link between himself and Greater Air, a new Airy sense or " centre," which is also a great circumference.

A MITHRIAC RITUAL.

We can only understand, enjoy or really grasp a thing if we possess a fraction of it already; it is only thus we can experience. Even to get ideas about a thing (which is other than experiencing) it is necessary at least to possess within normal consciousness something to correspond to the conception that is being shown us.

3. " Deathless eyes " ; the eye is symbolical of mind, and the deathless mind is the higher mind. Compare the great verse of Manilius (iv. 905) :

" He stands alone upright ; and, Victor, Sends forth his starry eyes unto the Stars."

The " Might of Mighty Power " is the Power of Ātman, whereby the man is to behold the Deathless Æon, Eternity, the Lord of time and space, and Supreme Creator, the Master of the Diadems of Fire. These Diadems of Fire are foreshadowings of the ordered constellations that will be ranged round the man's Heaven, his Great Surround or Envelope. They are Fiery, all Fires and Flames, Rays and Brilliance, creative powers like archangels.

The beginning of this Greatness is already within him " subsisting in purity"; that is perhaps in a state of tranquillity or equilibrium, not conceiving any form.

4. " The golden sparklings of the Brilliancy that knows no Death " is a beautiful phrase. It is always difficult to say precisely what these mystic phenomena may denote, for they can be regarded from so many. points of view ; but keeping within the range of interpretation we have chosen, the phrase may be said to suggest that the man has already attained to a stage when he can, to a limited extent, at any rate, project his " fiery current " and watch it fly forth as myriad sparks of Brilliancy, and thus light up and make apparent to himself his own world-body. But he cannot follow with that part of consciousness which brings with it full sensation. We may watch and know a great deal about a thing, but we do not really master it, till we fully experience it and thus make it become us.

5. The body is now reduced to absolute quietude before the mystic breathing is begun. No longer is the man to breathe as a mortal ; he is to take into his inmost self deep draughts from the Divine Air. He is to breathe as a Son of God.

Compare with this the following utterance from a Ritual of the Gnostic Heracleonitæ :

" I, the Son from the Father, the Father Pre-existing, but the Son in present existence, came to behold all things—things both other than my own and of my own ; yet things not altogether other than my own, but of Achamōth (Wisdom), the Mother who is female, and made them for herself. But I derive my Race from the Pre-existing, and I am going back unto my own whence I have come." (See my *World-Mystery*, 2nd ed., p. 60).

III.

1. We now come to the first instruction or practical directions.

Now in the Great Work there is what may be termed a projection and an establishing. What are called the " fires " of the body are definitely used to project consciousness forth into the greater Air. Fire is thus used for the first projection forth ; but the fire is the man's Life-fire, and in projecting it he uses his own bodily organs, for within the physical body lie dormant all the necessary organs for contacting the cosmos.

To this side of the mystery our Ritual does not refer ; it deals with the use of Breath and for similar purposes. Breath is as it were a spouse of the Fire which has already been projected. That is to say, the Ritual is intended only for those who have already made themselves ready ; they must be " worthy of this our Craft."

Fire has to do with what we may call the " Spark "-side of things, the masculine

A MITHRIAC RITUAL.

creative fire. After the implanting of each " Light-spark," as the Christian Gnosis phrases it, there is what may be called a feminine descent, or a further " clothing " and freeing of the imprisoned " Spark," for this clothing is a " robe of power."

Thus one " Spark," and we have the mineral kingdom ; this clothed upon by the feminine descent or life-outpouring gives birth to the vegetable kingdom. Two " Sparks " bring into existence the animal kingdom ; and this multiplied by the feminine descent gives birth to man. Beyond this there is a third " Sonship " of Fire, and a third descent of the Great Breath—the Ātmic mystery.

Breath is in a sense the reverse of Fire. The one dries the substance, the other causes the drying to cease and establishes the buddhic plasm with a certain definite capacity for holding together ; it is no longer watery.

It is to be noted that the Theurgist has to keep touch with his physical body all the time ; he goes forth, yet he remains—it is the mystery of emanation.

The operation is to be effected in sun-light. The man breathes into his body that which dwells within every ray of sun-light ; by means of this " breath " he gets into touch with the soul of each ray. After thus breathing in a special way as deeply as possible three times, he begins to feel himself get light (in weight). This feeling is said to be experienced at the back of the head. The man then feels himself as it were rising in the air.

2. He then begins to see a different order of things, which are in our Ritual set forth symbolically according to the tradition of the school. These appearances will differ according to the mind-content of the man.

3. Whatever be the forms, the ascending and descending Gods are in any case the man's own soul-powers forth and in.

The Vision would seem to be the casting of the shadow of himself,—of his inmost body, and the ordering of it according to the scheme of the cosmos in his mind,—on to the mirror of true cosmic substance.

The next sentence seems to suggest that after he has projected his Fire forth, which is the first initiation of himself into his own world-substance, he begins to see his own Disk. It is the Father's Disk ; that is to say, from one point of view, it is the field of consciousness of his Great Person, or Higher Self, who is the father of the little person or mortal personality. But although the Higher Self is our Father, and in a sense we are born from him, we have mystically down here to " create " our own Great Person if we would have any conscious relationship with him.

The " Way-of-going of the Gods " suggests that there now opens up before his sight some plan or scheme of things, of all the many soul-powers.

4. The true interpretation of symbols depends upon the capacity of the learner to make them alive, and to see them from as many points of view as possible. All true symbols should first of all be made solid, then made interpenetrable, then made alive, in-breathing and out-breathing.

The natural breathing through one nostril for two hours, succeeded by a breathing through the other for a similar period, is a well ascertained fact, and a common-place in treatises on *hatha yoga*. This, however, is but a reflection of a great law, which is set forth symbolically in our text. Mystically the Pipe is the central " tube " of life, whether we regard the great body as a great atom in-breathing and out-breathing, or each small atom as of a similar nature, the whole system been polarised by the relation of these " tubes " or " pipes " to one another. It is through this Pipe that the true cosmic currents of Fire, Air, Water, and Earth can pass without killing the man. As they pass through this Pipe the man who is initiated,

A MITHRIAC RITUAL.

becomes possessed of the power of which-ever cosmic element is playing through him. This Pipe is also a Pole or Axis or Pivot, and is connected with his Great Person or Higher Self.

In a very extended interpretation of the symbols, " East " would signify the Cosmic Power playing forth towards birth, and " West " the return journey back to the Greatness.

5. This seems to indicate the watching of the man's own universe of gods or soul-powers—the powers of his Higher Self, and also, from another point of view, perhaps the essence, so to speak, of such of his past lives as are worthy of immortality ; as he watches them, they gaze intently on him and draw near.

The " laying the dexter finger on the lips " reminds us of the well-known figure of Harpocrates, the symbol of silence. Harpocrates (Ḥeru-p-khart), Horus the Younger or the Child, sym-bolized the young man-god, or super-man ; he was a form of the Rising Sun, of which the Egyptians distinguished seven aspects.

IV.

The visions that now present them-selves to the inner eye of the initiate are of so sublime a nature that he cannot hold himself steady, but is shaken, or " moved wholly," as the Christian Mystery Ritual has it (*Hymn of Jesus*, p. 140), and the appearances are conse-quently blurred and appear inimical.

These and similar visions of initiation are referred to by classical writers variously as : figures or schemas, the technical term for the appearances of the Gods ; blessed apparitions and beatific visions ; mystic sights and wonders ; what is most beautiful to see in the world ; holy appearances ; sacred shows ; ineffable and divine apparitions. (See my " Notes on the Eleusinian Mysteries," *Theo. Rev.*, xxii, 156, note).

Tranquillity and equilibrium, and with them the restored benignity of the appear-ances, are obtained by the solemn invoca-tion of Silence (Sigē), the Supernal Mother of all things, and Spouse of the Divine.

While the lower nature of the man would utter this as an invocation, the higher would issue it as a command,—a powerful utterance, or word of power,—to stop what appear as hurricanes, so to speak, to one who is experiencing such new forces for the first time.

When a man first becomes conscious in his world-body things are naturally somewhat tumultuous, and this *mantra* is used to protect himself, so to speak, from his own gods, or world-powers, and it brings down the power of his own Great Person who dwells in silence.

As the Heathen commentator of the Naassene Document says :

" This same Man the Phrygians also call Papa ; for He calmed all things which, prior to His own manifestation, were in disorderly and inharmonious movement.

" For the name Papa is the Sounding-of-all-things-together in Heaven and on Earth, and beneath the Earth, saying : ' Calm, Calm ' the discord of the cosmos." (*T. G. H.*, i., 172).

But the greater disturbance takes place in the physical body ; and as it is abso-lutely essential that this should be kept steady, so that the link of memory be not broken, physical means are resorted to in order to restore its equilibrium.

I have hesitated long before adopting the translations of " hiss " and " puff " for the Greek terms. I feel fairly sure about the " hiss," for the sibilant s's are added ; but the precise meaning of the second word escapes me. It would seem to mean that in the one case the breath is expelled continuously, and in the other there is an expulsion of breath that is broken by a series of short " puffs " ; it may be what has been called the " cleansing breath " in yoga-breathing.

98

A MITHRIAC RITUAL.

Curiously enough a friend of mine who has passed through some mystic experiences of a somewhat similar nature, was given as a *mantra* what sounded like the English phrase "Cheer up!" But this was to be pronounced in a special way, *Cheeeeee*—which is very similar to " hissing forth long " ; then a very distinctly rolled *r*, with a very distinct explosion for the *up*—which is not so far from the " pop " in *poppysmos*.

With regard to such sounds it may be of interest to remind the reader of the otherwise strange expression in the *Book of the Coming-forth by Day*, the " hissing " and " clucking " of the " Great Cackler "—the Great Bird or Mother who hatches forth the eggs of men.

Having regained his attention and with it a clean and clear field of vision, a deeper " shaking " than that of sight takes place, which he hears as a roar as of thunder. The substance of his world-body is being moved by the very root-sounds of nature

VI.

1. Again he utters " Silence ! " This he follows with the great declaration : " I am a Star "—an Æon. With this compare the utterance of the Orphic initiate :

" Child am I of Earth and Starry Heaven ; nay, my Race is Heaven's [alone] ! "

These words are from a portion of an ancient Orphic Ritual, on a gold tablet, which had been rolled up and placed in a hexagonal cylinder, hanging from a gold chain. It was found in a grave at Petelia, in Southern Italy, and is now in the British Museum. Gold Ornament Room (Table-Case H.).

" Shining anew from out the Depth " seems to mean that in his resurrection he rises out of the Watery Spheres, the Great Ocean of Change and Becoming, and shines forth as a Sun, an Æon, an Eternity.

The Disk is the Inner Door, that leads to the True Heaven. And so we find Zosimus, the Pœmandrist, writing :

" But Hermes and Zoroaster have said the Race of Wisdom-lovers is superior to Fate [the Watery Realms], by their neither rejoicing in her favours—for they have mastered pleasures—nor by their being struck down by her ills,—for ever living at the Inner Door." (*T.G.H.*, iii. 274).

Again the early Jewish Commentator in the Naassene Document writes :

" This is the Entrance, and this is the Gate, which Jacob saw, when he journeyed into Mesopotamia."

This a later Christian Gnostic commentator explains as the " passing from childhood to puberty and manhood "— the time of the first initiation of a candidate for the Egyptian priesthood. And the Jewish mystic continues :

" And Mesopotamia is the Stream of Great Ocean flowing from the Middle of the Perfect Man." (*T.G.H.*, i. 171.).

This was the Gate of the Lesser Mysteries ; but when the Pagan Mystic speaks of the Greater Mysteries, our Jewish Gnostic continues :

" This Mystery is the Gate of Heaven, and this is the House of God, where the Good God dwells alone ; into which House no impure man shall come. But it is kept under watch for the Spiritual alone ; where when they come, they must cast away their garments, and all become bridegrooms, obtaining their true manhood through the Virginal Spirit.

" For this is the Virgin big with child, conceiving and bearing a Son—a blessed Æon of Æons." (*T.G.H.*, i. 181.).

The man now so to speak begins to enter into himself. The Disk seems to expand and the myriad hosts of heaven in angelic form seem to people all space ; until he again becomes confused at the marvels of the heavenly panorama, the

A MITHRIAC RITUAL.

celestial bioscope of his own nature. He therefore stops the vision with another utterance of "Silence."

3. He thus finds himself in his own Great Sphere, which he no longer sees as an objective Disk, but which has now become himself or the field of his consciousness. There is an Infinite Encircling and yet again Doors of Fire, "fast closed."

He is now substantially at one with his Great Person or Higher Self, and these Doors of Creative Fire will, when they are opened, introduce him to his Fellow-Greatnesses. Though the Candidate has risen into his own Great Body he is not yet in direct touch with the Cosmos, any more than a baby is in touch with the physical world the moment he is born, though he has the necessary vehicle.

The Candidate is now born into his cosmic vehicle ; he has the powers of his world-sphere properly ordered, but his senses *forth* into the cosmos are closed.

He must now close his eyes. That is to say, he must not be too interested in his new world-body ; he must close his eyes to it, and try to go forth again, and use the mighty sphere as a vehicle only, as a "single eye" in the world of the Gods.

VII.

1. Thereon follows a magnificent invocation to the Æon, his own Ātman, who is all opposites, male-female and the rest. The Breath is the feminine power of Ātman which has bestowed on him his world-body, has closed him in and given him a Great Surround, a true Air-body. The praise of the might of the Æon should be compared with the description of the symbolical image of the Æon given in out last small volume (pp. 78 ff.).

2. I have retained this specimen of magical chanting to give the reader some idea of one mode of theurgic language. The vowels are all open flowing sounds, are all feminine ; there are no consonants

or masculine arrestings to cut these great waves of sound up into forms. The sounds can interpenetrate each other and stir the deepest substance.

The throat is opened and the breath is allowed to come forth in different "shapes" — "shapes," not forms ; "shapes" may be said to be more fundamental than forms. The breath must be sent forth without contacting any organs, so to speak, without being cut up by the tongue or lips or teeth, just shaped by the shape of the throat, root-sounds, so to say.

The Candidate is trying to get outside or beyond his own Great Person (though indeed he moves not), and so link himself on with other Great Personæ. You can only get out of yourself, it is said, by attaching yourself to someone else.

3. Perhaps the sevenfold utterance means that the utterance has to be chanted or intoned in seven keys.

The root-sounds on the physical plane, issuing from the depths of the body, but without contact with the organs of articulate speech, sympathetically induce changes which are, so to speak, the way-forth out of the man's world-surround. The inner spiritual power, or Fire, goes forth at first unconsciously without Breath ; so there must be chanting if consciousness is to accompany the man, and he would still keep hold of his physical body.

These root-sounds play upon the great surround, and then the man begins to hear real cosmic sounds, such as a Voice that roars with a roar of thunder all round the sphere ; yet though it utters one sound only it means all the world to the fortunate hearer. It means whatever he may choose to turn his attention to, and can teach him anything he may desire ; for it is Intelligence. This Voice causes his whole world-body to tremble.

4. The spiritual Doors are thus again thrown open. He has, as it were, shattered his world-body, or risen above it, to use it and not dwell within it.

1 0 0

A MITHRIAC RITUAL.

The Beatific Vision bursts upon him. His true Spirit or Consciousness runs out of his sphere, through the energizing of Ātman, and goes forth to meet Cosmic Consciousness.

He has now to retain his individuality no longer by means of any body or surround, but by steady attention, by gazing at the Spark of his Divinity. Thus he becomes a conscious Spiritual Atom in God, and he draws Breath or a new mode of Consciousness from the Divine, beyond even his own Great Person or Higher Self.

VIII.

1. He now receives consciously the Third Spark, his Highest Self.

The invocation " Draw nigh, O Lord " reminds us of perhaps the most magnificent passage in Plotinus which describes the secret of his ecstasy.

" Let there, then, be in the soul some semblance of a sphere of light transparent, having all things in it, whether moving or still, and some of them moving and others still.

" And, holding this sphere in the mind, conceive in thyself another sphere, removing from it all idea of mass ; take from it also the idea of space, and the phantom of matter in thy mind ; and do not try to image another sphere merely less in mass than the former.

" Then invoking God who hath made that true sphere, of which thou holdest the phantom in thy mind, pray that He may come.

" And may He come with His own cosmos, with all the Gods therein—He being one and all, and each one all, united into one, yet different in their powers, and yet, in that one power of multitude, all one." (*T.G.H.*, i. 252.).

IX.

Thus His Rays are turned upon the man, and a new Golden Splendour becomes his, or he becomes it, or is magnified into the Greatness. He has thus a new link with the Divine ; he is in the midst of this Splendour or Flame which wraps itself round him—that is to say, his great sphere—like a serpent in seven coils, as in the symbolic image of the Æon ; it is no longer only potential in him, but actual.

The description in the text is a symbolic portrayal of what we have previously referred to as the Third Spark—or Christ, the Serpent of Wisdom.

X.

1. The man thus prays to be brought unto the Father by this the true Son and the Spirit of the Sun.

It seems to mean that a great change has now been consummated, and that the lesser differentiated ātmic " sparks," which he has previously seen unordered or potential in his nature, as atoms of spiritual essence, that this potential spirit, or these atoms of spirit, have by the Presence of the Glory and the Flame united into a true living five-fold Star ; he has risen upon ātmic spirituality into being a Spirit. The five-fold is of the nature of Mind.

3. " Upon this utterance He shall come to the Pole." However this may be taken astrologically, or according to the schema of the theurgical astronomy of the adyta of those days, the Pole for the true mystic can only mean the man's own Pole, that is his Great Person, or Higher Self, that which in his lower cosmos " has stood, stands and will stand "—his individuality. From the point of view of substance and of symbolic vision, this can be equated with the Heaven-Pole, the Pivot " on which all doth turn." But in this subjective-objective vision the truth is reversed. The God does not really move round on a path ; it is He who is the True One " who stands." It is the æonic, or the " starry " body of the man, the *augoeides*

or *astroeides*, that turns on this Pivot as on an axis, in a course that is now as the course of his fellow Stars.

3. In order to keep pace with the power of the Great Experience through which the Epopt is passing, a new and deeper mode of breath is to be practised physically, so that the link with the physical body may be retained. But this mode of breath is perhaps rather etheric than physical ; it is not exactly a physical alteration which could be detected outwardly, for ordinary breathing may go on all the time.

Nor do I think it necessary in connection with this " bellowing," to refer to the sacred instrument called the " bull-roarer "—used in the mystery-cults of certain primitive peoples, in New Mexico, Australia, New Zealand and Africa, to summon the " God " or announce his coming, and upon which no woman may look and live. I need only remark that it evidently typifies an instrument of virile power.

In yoga,—and our Ritual before all else is a yoga-rite,—the " bellowing " must be connected with the " power of the bull," or creative power, the use of which for spiritual operations constituted the greatest secret of the Mithriaca.

In the *prāṇayāma* (or restraint of the breath) practices in yoga, the internal " bellowing " would connote the result of drawing the deepest breath possible and causing it to vibrate or throb or roar, and so press on, or set going, certain centres. These centres are the " amulets " proper ; but in ceremonial magic physical phylacteries were used, and placed on the corresponding external centres.

The " bellowing " is in Greek the utterance of the sound " *moo* "—and this is in some sort an inversion of the sacred syllable *oṁ*.

XI.

This operation if successfully accomplished will open out the consciousness still further. The imagery and symbolism are doubtless derived from Egyptian tradition, superimposed on Chaldæan astral doctrine.

It is to be noticed that the Seven Virgins are called : " Ye holiest Protectors of the Four Supports." With this compare the Mystic Ritual of the Baptism of the Water of Life in the *Book of the Great Logos*, where the Master and Saviour (Aberamenthō) utters the following prayer, prefixed with an invocation in the mystery-tongue, interspersed with triple Amens :

" Hear Me, My Father, Father of all fatherhood, Boundless Light, Who art in the Treasure of Light ! May the Supporters come, who serve the Seven Virgins of Light who preside over the Baptism of Life ! May they come and baptize My disciples with the Water of Life of the Seven Virgins of Light, and wash away their sins and purify their iniquities, and number them among the heirs of the Kingdom of Light !" (*F.F.F.*, 2nd ed., 525.).

And Proclus (*In Tim.*, ii. 137 B ; Schneid. 323), with regard to Phanēs— whom he calls the " All-perfect Living One," and characterizes as the Paradigmatic or Intelligible Cause, that is the Logos—tells us that the Theologist (*sci.* Orpheus) sings of Him as alone " bearing the glorious seed of the Gods," implanted by the Hidden Deity. And from Phanēs is derived the secondary ordering of the Gods, as supports of the primary. Thus the true Heaven and the true Earth proceed as an intelligible unity—Father-Mother. And She, the true Heavenly Mother, " She in her turn gave birth to the extended [primal] Heaven and Earth "—that is, extended in space. And then Kronos unites with Rhea ; at the third birth, this Earth, the Mother, brought forth again :

" Seven Virgins fair, bright-eyed and pure, and Seven kingly and down-covered Youths."

It is to be noticed that this vision presents itself after the Doors are thrown

102

open for the third time; that is after the third great change of consciousness on the return journey.

It is also to be noticed that the Virgins carry the gold in their hands and the Youths wear it on their heads. They are the children of the Mother-side of things and the progeny of the Lord of the Pole, Kronos or the Æon, the Great Individuality or Person.

The spouse of Kronos is Rhea. This Mother-substance is in a chaotic or ever-flowing condition (Rhea, from *rhein*, to flow), that is flowing in all directions at once. But when the Third Spark embraces the world-body of the man, his mother-substance becomes differentiated into seven pure elements—seven instead of four, as has previously been the case—that is, with powers of contact with the seven planes of cosmos. The Virgins seem to symbolize the substantial side of things, while the black-faced Youths are poles or pivots, in their turn, cords, supports, or radii. The black faces seem to symbolize powers turned from the Sun, and going forth on their own account, independent, intelligent.

The One Substance, or Mother-octave, or Ogdoad, has now become seven spheres, all revolving independently, yet in perfect order. The man's Body has been made a perfect correspondence with the Great Cosmos. True cosmic instinct is thus bestowed upon him at this rebirth.

When the Mother-octave is spoken of, it connotes the relationship between the man's world-body and the Great Elements or Cosmos; when the Son-octave is referred to, it indicates how this same world-sphere is linked up with the man's true Person; while the Father-octave suggests that this same world-octave is linked on to a still vaster mystery. And yet it is all one mystery.

In the case of normal man the linking up is with Four and not with Eight or Seven.

XII.

The supreme moment arrives when the man is to meet with Mithra, the Great Initiator, face to face, and gaze upon His Mystery with cosmic senses, the whole of him one sense, and all senses in one.

XIV.

Then is it that the Lord of Fire, or Risen Great Person, the man at-oned with his Higher Self, become now Lord and Ruler, or King, is Master of Water, Earth and Breath. He is Master of Water or all manifestation; Lord of Earth, or all his personalities; and King of Breath or all vehicles of consciousness.

It is magnificent, sublime, stupendous. Is it all an empty dream; or may it be a glorious reality?

And if there be those who are deterred from accepting the under-meaning, because of the symbolism which arose out of physical conceptions of the universe which modern science has outgrown, may we venture to suggest that to the deeper mystic consciousness, a heliocentric or a geocentric theory of phenomena is a matter of indifference; both are equally far from the reality, no matter how superior the one may be to the other for purposes of intellectual training.

One has doubtless been over-bold in some of the above speculations; but after many years of study of the contemporary literature of the Gnosis and the Mysteries, of Theosophy and Theurgy, many things which at first appeared utterly irreconcilable seem somehow now to fall together; ideas unite, symbolism becomes more plastic.

It would, of course, be impossible in so small a compass as this little volume to set forth all the thoughts which so rapidly flash through the mind in meditating on this Ritual, and the many passages that could be quoted in illustration of the many points of mystic interest that have been touched upon. That would require a long and learned treatise, and this is not the purpose of these booklets.

I have, therefore, simply attempted to set forth the impression that this remarkable Ritual has made upon myself, in the hope that some of my readers may recognise a fellow-feeling in themselves ; and that some day they may be able to say with the Victor made victorious by the Invincible One :

" Being born from out the state of birth-and-death that giveth birth to mortal lives, I now, set free, pass to the state transcending birth, as Thou hast stablished it, according as Thou hast ordained and made the Mystery."

THE . . .
HYMN OF .
THE ROBE .
OF GLORY.

THE HYMN OF THE ROBE OF GLORY.

CONTENTS.

BIBLIOGRAPHY.

Wright (W.), *Apocryphal Acts of the Apostles* (London, 1871), ii. 238-245.

Nöldecke (T.), Rev. of Wright, *Zeitschrift der deutschen morgenländischen Gesellschaft* (1871), pp. 670—679.

Macke (K.), "Syrische Lieder gnostischen Ursprungs. Eine Studie über die apocryphen syrischen Thomasacten," *Theologische Quartalschrift* (Tübingen, 1874), pp. 24—70.

Lipsius (R. A.), *Die apocryphen Apostelgeschichten u. Apostellegenden* (Brunswick, 1883, 1884), i. pp. 292—300 ; ii. pt. ii. p. 422.

Bevan (A. A.), *The Hymn of the Soul—Texts and Studies* (Cambridge, 1897), vol. v., no. 3.

Hilgenfeld (A.), Rev. of Bevan, *Berliner philologische Wochenschrift* (Berlin, 1898), xviii., no. 13, pp. 389—395.

Burkitt (F. C.), *The Hymn of Bardaisan*. Printed at the Press of the Guild of Handicraft, Essex House (London, 1899) ; 300 copies only printed.

Bonnet (M.), *Actes de Saint Thomas, Apôtre. Le Poème de l' Âme*. Version grecque remaniée par Nicétas de Thessalonique. Extrait des *Analecta Bollandiana* (Bruxelles, 1901), tome xx. pp. 159—164.

Bonnet (M.), *Acta Apostolorum Apocrypha* (edd. Lipsius et Bonnet), vol. ii., pt. ii. (Leipzig, 1903), pp. xxii., 219 ff.

Hoffman (G.), "Zwei Hymnen der Thomasakten," *Zeitschrift für die neutestamentliche Wissenschaft* (Giessen, 1903), vol. iv. pp. 273—294.

Preuschen (E.), *Zwei gnostische Hymnen* (Giessen, 1904).

Burkitt (F. C.), Rev. of Preuschen, *Theologisch Tijdschrift* (Amsterdam), May, 1905, pp. 270—282.

F. = Mead (G. R. S.), *Fragments of a Faith Forgotten* (2nd. ed., London, 1906).

H. = Mead (G. R. S.), *Thrice Greatest Hermes* (London, 1906).

THE HYMN OF THE
ROBE OF GLORY.

THE HYMN OF THE
ROBE OF GLORY.

PREAMBLE.

The original title of this beautiful
Gnostic Poem has been lost, and it is now
generally referred to as *The Hymn of the
Soul*. Preuschen, however, calls it *The
Song of Deliverance (Das Lied von der
Erlösung)* ; while in my *Fragments* (1900)
I ventured to name it *The Hymn of the
Robe of Glory*. I here, also, prefer to
retain this title, as it seems the more
appropriate.

The original text of the Poem is in Old
Syriac, in lines of twelve syllables with a
cæsura, and so in couplets, for the
most part of six syllables. A text
of a Greek version has recently been
discovered by Bonnet at Rome (C. Valli-
cellanus B. 35) and published in his text
of *The Acts of Thomas* (1903). It is
partly literal, partly paraphrastic, with
occasional doublets and omissions of whole
lines. In addition there is a summary in
Greek by a certain Nicetas, Archbishop of
Thessalonica, who flourished prior to the
XIth century (the date of the MS. in which
his abridgment is found), but who is
otherwise unknown. This seems to be
based on another Greek version.

The copy of the original Syriac text
is found in a single MS. only (Brit.
Mus. Add. 14645), which contains a collection of Lives of Saints, and bears the
precise date 936 A.D. Our Poem is found
in the text of the Syriac translation from
the Greek of *The Acts of Judas Thomas
the Apostle;* it has, however, evidently
nothing to do with the original Greek
text of these Acts, and its style and
contents are quite foreign to the rest of
the matter. It is manifestly an independent document incorporated by the
Syrian redactor, who introduces it in the
usual naïve fashion of such compilations.
Judas Thomas on his travels in India
is cast into prison. There he offers up
a prayer. On its conclusion we read :
" And when he had prayed and sat
down, Judas began to chant this hymn :
The Hymn of Judas Thomas the Apostle
in the Country of the Indians."

After the Poem comes the subscription :
" The Hymn of Judas Thomas the
Apostle, which he spake in prison, is
ended."

This literary phenomenon is precisely
similar to that presented by *The Hymn
of Jesus* (Vol. V.), to the introduction of
which the reader is referred for a brief
consideration of the nature of the Gnostic
Acts.

Our Hymn is indubitably Gnostic ; but
of what school or tradition ? Learned
opinion is preponderatingly in favour of
attributing it to the Syrian Gnostic
Bardaiṣān (Gk. Bardēsánēs—154—122
A.D.), or, less precisely, to some Bardes-
anist poet. (For Bardesanes, see *F.* pp.
392-414).

This is borne out by the text of the
Poem itself, in which the mention of the
Parthians (38a) as the ruling race is
decidedly in favour of its having been
written prior to the overthrow of the
Parthian dynasty in 224 A.D.

There are also other indications pointing to Bardaiṣān as the poet ; not only
are some of the leading doctrines pecu-
liarly those of this distinguished teacher,
as has been pointed out by Bevan and
Preuschen, but also, as I have ventured
to suggest, there is a certain personal
note in the Poem.

Bardaiṣān's parents were rich and
noble ; and their young son not only received the best education in manners
and learning procurable, but he was
brought up at the court of Edessa with
crown prince, who afterwards succeeded
to the throne as one of the Abgars. Not
only so, but Bardaiṣān subsequently

109

THE HYMN OF THE
ROBE OF GLORY.

converted his friend and patron to Gnostic
Christianity, and induced him to make
it the state-religion ; so that our Gnostic
must have the credit indirectly of establishing the first Christian State.

The description of the trade-route
from Parthia to Egypt and of the adventures of the hero in Egypt, moreover,
has led me to ask whether a real piece
of personal biography may not have been
woven into the Poem. May there not
be in it a lost page from the occult life
of Bardaiṣān himself ?

Filled with longing to penetrate the
mysteries of the Gnosis, he joins a caravan
to Egypt, and arrives at Alexandria.
There he meets with a fellow-countryman
on the same quest as himself, who gives
him some useful hints about the many
corrupt and charlatanesque schools of
pseudo-gnosis that thrived in that centre
of intellectual curiosity and religious
enthusiasm. He, however, in spite of
these warnings, seems to have fallen into
the hands of the unscrupulous, and so,
for a time, forgets his true spiritual quest,
in the by-ways, perchance, of lower
psychism and magic. Only after this
bitter experience does he obtain the
instruction he longs for, by initiation
into the spiritual Gnosis of the inner
circles of, it may have been, the Valentinian tradition.

Of course this speculation is put forward with all hesitation ; but it is neither
impossible, nor improbable.

In any case, it is the least important
element, and need not detain us except
as being a possible source of the local
colouring matter. The Hymn itself is
a truly poetic inspiration, and deals
with far higher mysteries and experiences. But before we can venture to
suggest an interpretation, the reader
must be made acquainted with the Poem
itself in a version based on a minute comparison of all the existing translations.

THE HYMN.

I.

*When, a quite little child, I was dwelling
In the House of my Father's Kingdom,*

*And in the wealth and the glories
Of my Up-bringers I was delighting,*

*From the East, our Home, my Parents
Forth-sent me with journey-provision.*

*Indeed from the wealth of our Treasure,
They bound up for me a load.*

*Large was it, yet was it so light
That all alone I could bear it.*

II.

*Gold from the Land of Gīlān,
Silver from Ganzāk the Great,*

*Chalcedonies of India,
Iris-hued [Opals ?] from Kūshān.*

*They girt me with Adamant [also]
That hath power to cut even iron.*

*My Glorious Robe they took off me
Which in their love they had wrought me,*

*And my Purple Mantle [also]
Which was woven to match with my stature.*

III.

*And with me They [then] made a compact ;
In my heart wrote it, not to forget it :*

" *If thou goest down into Egypt,
And thence thou bring'st the one Pearl—*

" *[The Pearl] that lies in the Sea,
Hard by the loud-breathing Serpent,—*

" *[Then] shalt Thou put on thy Robe
And thy Mantle that goeth upon it,*

110

THE HYMN OF THE ROBE OF GLORY.

" And with thy Brother, Our Second,
Shalt thou be Heir in our Kingdom."

IV.

I left the East and went down
With two Couriers [with me] ;

For the way was hard and dangerous,
For I was young to tread it.

I traversed the borders of Maishān,
The mart of the Eastern merchants,

And I reached the Land of Bābel,
And entered the walls of Sarbūg.

Down further I went into Egypt ;
And from me parted my escorts.

V.

Straightway I went to the Serpent ;
Near to his lodging I settled,

To take away my Pearl
While he should sleep and should slumber.

Lone was I there, yea, all lonely ;
To my fellow-lodgers a stranger.

However I saw there a noble,
From out of the Dawn-land my kinsman,

A young man fair and well favoured,
Son of Grandees ; he came and he joined me.

VI.

I made him my chosen companion,
A comrade, for sharing my wares with.

He warned me against the Egyptians,
'Gainst mixing with the unclean ones.

For I had clothed me as they were,
That they might not guess I had come

From afar to take off the Pearl,
And so rouse the Serpent against me.

VII.

But from some occasion or other
They learned I was not of their country.

With their wiles they made my acquaintance ;
Yea, they gave me their victuals to eat.

I forgot that I was a King's son,
And became a slave to their king.

I forgot all concerning the Pearl
For which my Parents had sent me ;

And from the weight of their victuals
I sank down into a deep sleep.

VIII.

All this that now was befalling,
My Parents perceived and were anxious.

It was then proclaimed in our Kingdom,
That all should speed to our Gate—

Kings and Chieftains of Parthia,
And of the East all the Princes.

And this is the counsel they came to :
I should not be left down in Egypt.

And for me they wrote out a Letter ;
And to it each Noble his Name set :

IX.

" From Us—King of Kings, thy Father,
And thy Mother, Queen of the Dawn-land,

" And from Our Second, thy Brother —
To thee, Son, down in Egypt,
Our Greeting !

" Up and arise from thy sleep,
Give ear to the words of Our Letter !

" Remember that thou art a King's son ;
See whom thou hast served in thy slavedom.

111

THE HYMN OF THE
ROBE OF GLORY.

" *Bethink thyself of the Pearl*
For which thou didst journey to Egypt.

X.

" *Remember thy Glorious Robe,*
Thy Splendid Mantle remember,

" *To put on and wear as adornment,*
When thy Name may be read in
the Book of the Heroes,

" *And with Our Successor, thy Brother,*
Thou mayest be Heir in Our Kingdom."

My Letter was [surely] a Letter
The King had sealed up with His
Right Hand,

'Gainst the Children of Bābel, the wicked,
The tyrannical Daimons of Sarbūg.

XI.

It flew in the form of the Eagle,
Of all the winged tribes the king-bird ;

It flew and alighted beside me,
And turned into speech altogether.

At its voice and the sound of its winging,
I waked and arose from my deep sleep.

Unto me I took it and kissed it ;
I loosed its seal and I read it.

E'en as it stood in my heart writ,
The words of my Letter were written.

XII.

I remembered that I was a King's son,
And my rank did long for its nature.

I bethought me again of the Pearl,
For which I was sent down to Egypt.

And I began [then] to charm him,
The terrible loud-breathing Serpent.

I lulled him to sleep and to slumber,
Chanting o'er him the Name of my Father,

The Name of our Second, [my Brother],
And [Name] of my Mother, the East-
Queen.

XIII.

And [thereon] I snatched up the Pearl,
And turned to the House of my Father.

Their filthy and unclean garments
I stripped off and left in their country.

To the way that I came I betook me,
To the Light of our Home, to the Dawn-land.

On the road I found [there] before me
My Letter that had aroused me—

As with its voice it had roused me,
So now with its light it did lead me —

XIV.

On fabric of silk, in letters of red [?],
With shining appearance before me [?],

Encouraging me with its guidance,
With its love it was drawing me onward.

I went forth ; through Sarbūg I passed ;
I left Bābel-land on my left hand ;

And I reached unto Maishān the Great,
The meeting-place of the merchants,

That lieth hard by the Sea-shore.

XV.

My Glorious Robe that I'd stripped off,
And my Mantle with which it was covered,

Down from the Heights of Hyrcānia,
Thither my Parents did send me,

THE HYMN OF THE
ROBE OF GLORY.

By the hands of their Treasure-dispensers
Who trustworthy were with it trusted.

Without my recalling its fashion,—
In the House of my Father my childhood
*   had left it,—*

At once, as soon as I saw it,
The Glory looked like my own self.

XVI.

I saw it all in all of me,
And saw me all in [all of] it,—

That we were twain in distinction,
And yet again one in one likeness.

I saw, too, the Treasurers also,
Who unto me had down-brought it,

Were twain [and yet] of one likeness;
For one Sign of the King was upon them —

Who through them restored me the Glory,
The Pledge of my Kingship [?].

XVII.

The Glorious Robe all-bespangled
With sparkling splendour of colours:

With Gold and also with Beryls,
Chalcedonies, iris-hued [Opals ?],

With Sards of varying colours.
To match its grandeur [?], moreover,
*   it had been completed :*

With adamantine jewels
All of its seams were off-fastened.

[Moreover] the King of Kings' Image
Was depicted entirely all o'er it ;

And as with Sapphires above
Was it wrought in a motley of colour.

XVIII.

I saw that moreover all o'er it
The motions of Gnosis abounding ;

I saw it further was making
Ready as though for to speak.

I heard the sound of its Music
Which it whispered as it descended [?]:

"Behold him the active in deeds !
*   For whom I was reared with my Father ;*

"I too have felt in myself
*   How that with his works waxed my stature."*

XIX.

And [now] with its Kingly motions
Was it pouring itself out towards me,

And made haste in the hands of its Givers,
That I might [take and] receive it.

And me, too, my love urged forward
To run for to meet it, to take it.

And I stretched myself forth to receive it ;
With its beauty of colour I decked me,

And my Mantle of sparkling colours
I wrapped entirely all o'er me.

XX.

I clothed me therewith, and ascended
To the Gate of Greeting and Homage.

I bowed my head and did homage
To the Glory of Him who had sent it,

Whose commands I [now] had accomplished,
And who had, too, done what He'd promised.

[And there] at the Gate of His House-sons
I mingled myself with His Princes ;

113

THE HYMN OF THE
ROBE OF GLORY.

For He had received me with gladness,
And I was with Him in His Kingdom ;

XXI.

To whom the whole of His Servants
With sweet-sounding voices sing praises.

* * * * *

He had promised that with him to the Court
Of the King of Kings I should speed,

And taking with me my Pearl
Should with him be seen by our King.

COMMENTS.

THE PEARL.

Both Hoffmann and Preuschen are of opinion that the Poem is a free elaboration of the chief element in the very briefly recorded Parable of the Pearl which the first Evangelist alone has preserved (*Matt.* xiii. 45, 46) :

"Again the Kingdom [or Kingship] of the Heavens is like unto a merchantman seeking fine pearls ; and when he found a pearl of great price, he went and sold all he had and bought it."

This seems hardly sufficient in itself to account for the genesis of our Poem. Certainly for the Gnostics, if the Pearl meant the Kingdom of Heaven in the sense of the Gnosis, it also meant something more definite and intimate, and in all probability the tradition of the mystic meaning went back to pre-Christian days.

Thus the pre-Christian Hellenistic initiate who was the first commentator of the Naassene Document, quotes a mystery-saying of the Phrygians— ? from the Mysteries of the Great Mother—as follows :

"If ye have eaten dead things and made living ones, what will ye make if ye eat living things ? "

On this the Jewish commentator, who was in high probability a contemporary of Philo of Alexandria—let us say about the first quarter of the first century— writes :

"And by 'living things' they mean *logoi* and minds and men—the 'pearls' of the Inexpressible Man cast into the plasm below."

Those *logoi*, or "words" or "reasons" —that is spiritual minds or true "men" —are the "angels" who perpetually behold the Face of the Father, that is live in the Divine Presence. The Inexpressible Man is the Transcendent Logos, and the *logoi* are His sons. In brief the Pearl is the " Higher Self."

Later on, in the same Document, the Christian Gnostic writer, who further comments on the interpretation of the Jewish exegete, adds :

" That is what He saith :

" ' Cast not the holy thing to the dogs nor the pearls to the swine.' "

And on this finally the Church Father Hippolytus remarks :

" For they say that the work of swine is the intercourse of man with woman." (*H.* i. 175).

It is to be noted that in the *Chaldæan Oracles* (p 207) " dogs " are a technical term for a certain class of " daimones " ; so also " swine " may for the Gnostics have designated another class.

In any case we get the equation, pearl =*logos ;* that is, the "light-spark," the ray of the Logos, the Christ-nature in man. And so also in *The Acts of John*

THE HYMN OF THE
ROBE OF GLORY.

we read the following, in a hymn of praise put into the mouth of John, at the sacred feast prior to his departure from the body. It is addressed to the Christ, and the sentence that concerns us runs :
" We glorify the Resurrection shown unto us through Thee ; we glorify Thy Seed, Word (*Logos*), Grace, Faith, Salt, True Pearl ineffable." (*F*. p. 440).

It is thus evident that the Pearl is in some way the mystery hidden in man, and, indeed, buried in the body. For "Egypt" is the body.

EGYPT.

Thus in the same invaluable Naassene Document, the Jewish commentator, quoting from some still more ancient commentary, writes :
" This is what is written :
" 'I have said, Ye are Gods and all Sons of the Highest '—if ye hasten to flee from Egypt and get you beyond the Red Sea into the Desert."

And to this he himself adds in further explanation :
" That is, from the Intercourse Below to the Jerusalem Above who is the Mother of the Living."

And then he resumes his quotation from presumably some old Jewish Gnostic commentary :
" But if ye turn back into Egypt— (that is, to the Intercourse Below)—' Ye shall die like men.' "

And on this he again remarks :
" For all the Generation (*Genesis*) Below is subject to Death, but the [Birth] begotten Above is superior to Death."

And, speaking of the Great Ocean of Genesis, he continues :
" This is the Great Jordan, which, flowing downwards and preventing the Sons of Israel from going forth out of Egypt, or the Intercourse Below, was turned back by Jesus [LXX. for Joshua] and made to flow upwards."

After "Egypt" the Church Father Hippolytus interjects the gloss :

" For Egypt is the body, according to them." (*H*. i. 163, 164).

All of this Gnostic allegorizing is, in high probability, to be assigned to pre-Christian Chassid and allied (*e.g.* Therapeut) circles, similar to those which developed the ethical teaching of *The Testaments of the Twelve Patriarchs*, which Prof. Charles has, in his just published text and translation,'so brilliantly conjectured to have been written about 109—106 B.C. This ethic, he contends, influenced very strongly the writers of the New Testament documents, and anticipated some of the most characteristic Sayings of Jesus.

How the symbolism of Egypt, the Red Sea, the Desert, and the Promised Land, was developed by these Mystics may be seen from what Hippolytus (*Ref.* vi. 16) summarizes of the system of the Peratæ or Transcendalists, who were contemporaries of the Naassenes.

The Gnostic treatise that the Church Father had before him, was treating of the Great Water or Ocean of Genesis that moistens the soul and plunges it into the Region of Death, according to the word of Heraclitus :
" For to souls water becomes death."

The Peratic writer continues :
" This Death overtakes the Egyptians in the Red Sea together with their chariots [*sci.* vehicles]. Now all who are ignorant [*sci.* are without the Gnosis] are Egyptians."

Hippolytus then summarizes as follows :
" And this, they say, is the Going-forth out of Egypt—out of the body. For they consider that the body is a little Egypt, and that they cross over [or transcend— hence their name Peratæ] the Red Sea (that is, the Water of Destruction, which is Kronos [that is, Time]), and reach a state beyond the Red Sea (that is, Generation), and enter the Desert (that is, reach a state free from Generation), where there are all together the Gods of Destruction and the God of Salvation."

And the Peratic writer adds :
" Now the Gods of Destruction are the

115

THE HYMN OF THE
ROBE OF GLORY.

Stars [that is, the Fate-spheres] which bring upon sentient beings the necessity of changeable Generation [*Genesis*, the Brāhmanical and Buddhist *Saṁsāra*].

"These Moses called the Serpents of the Desert who bite and destroy those who imagine they have crossed the Red Sea.

"To the Sons of Israel, therefore, who were being bitten in the Desert, Moses revealed the True Serpent [*sci.* of Wisdom], the Perfect One ; and they who believed on Him, were not bitten in the Desert (that is, by the Powers).

"No one, therefore, is thus able to save and deliver those who come forth from the Land of Egypt (that is, from the body and from the world), save only the Perfect Serpent, Him who is full of [all] fulnesses.

"He who centres his hopes upon Him, is not destroyed by the Serpents of the Desert (that is, by the Gods of Generation)."

It is thus evident that for these mystical allegorists Egypt stood for both the body and also the hylic or gross-material realms, and that the use goes back along the Naassene-Ophite trace to pre-Christian Jewish Gnostic circles. It is, therefore, unnecessary to bring forward later passages from Clement of Alexandria and Origen in confirmation of the use.

THE PARABLE OF THE PRODIGAL.

That our Poem is simply an elaboration or embellishment (*Ausschmückung*—Preuschen, p. 66) of the briefly-recorded Parable of the Pearl, as has been supposed, is a very insufficient hypothesis to account for its genesis. Even if we were so inelastic as to imagine that it must necessarily have its point of departure in canonical scripture, we might more appropriately surmise that it is rather an elaboration of the beautiful Parable of the Prodigal, which is recorded by the third Evangelist alone (*Lk.* xv. 11-32).

That, however, it is something far other than a mere embellishment even of this beautiful Parable, must be evident to the most casual reader. There is originality in it, and its resemblances may, with far greater probability, be referred to knowledge of the inner facts that both Parable and Poem set forth, rather than to any slavish following of the canonical text. Still it is well to remark the resemblances :

The Father and the two Sons, of whom the younger goes forth ; the dividing up of the substance (οὐσία) or living (βίος) ; the far country ; the joining himself to a citizen of that country—the reverse in the Poem ; the eating the food of swine—the symbol of generation ; the calling to remembrance of the Father's household ; the return ; the running of the Father to meet him, as he speeds to meet the Father, and the kissing of him ; the putting on of the robe.

It is, however, evident that the whole matter is treated from another standpoint; it is far more intimate and reveals a fuller insight into the spiritual mysteries.

In the Parable there is no mention of the Divine Mother, the Queen of the East ; and this is in keeping with later Rabbinical exclusion of the Divine Feminine. But in the circles of the Mystics the Holy Spirit was regarded as feminine, the Spouse of Divinity, and in the Wisdom-literature Wisdom herself.

As in the other great traditions, so also in pre-Christian Jewish Gnostic circles, the natural Trinity was a fundamental of their symbolism, and so also in many a system of the Christianized Gnosis.

The origin of the Dual Sonship, however, must, in one direction at any rate, be sought for along that very obscure line of descent that is called Ophite (Naassene), and which has its roots in the pre-Christian Gnosis and the widespread Myth of Man (see *H.* i. 139-198).

THE DUAL SONSHIP.

A faint trace of this is preserved for us in a system which the polemical *Refutation* (I. xxx) of Irenæus associates

THE HYMN OF THE ROBE OF GLORY.

with the Ophite tradition, but which Theodoret (*Hær. Fab.* I. xiv.) ascribes to the Sethians. Unfortunately the original Greek text of Irenæus is here lost, and we have to be content with the barbarous Old-Latin translation ; in addition the Church Father is very hostile and contemptuous, and at no great pains to understand the objects of his detestation. Such as it is, however, we will set it down :

" But others again give forth portentous utterances : that there dwells in the Power of the Depth a certain Primal Light, blessed, indestructible, boundless ; this is the Father of all and is called the First Man.

" They declare further that His Thought proceeding from Him, is the Son of Him who sends forth [His Thought] ; and that this Thought is Son of Man, the Second Man.

" That below these again is the Holy Spirit ; and below this Highest Spirit, the [Primal] Elements were separated forth—Water, Darkness, Abyss, Chaos ; and on these was borne the Spirit, whom they call the First Woman.

" Subsequently, they assert, the First Man together with His Son, delighting in the Beauty of the Spirit, that is the Woman, and filling Her with Light, begat from Her Incorruptible Light, the Third Man, whom they call the Christ, Son of the First and the Second Man and of the Holy Spirit, the First Woman."

Here we have clearly set forth the idea of the Dual Sonship—though from a different point of view from that of our Poem—and of Man, Son of Man, a term that occurs frequently in the Gospels, and which so far scholarship refuses to explain gnostically, preferring to lose itself in the philological labyrinth of a quite unsatisfactory Aramaic Bar-Nāshā.

That the ruling idea of the Dual Sonship was widespread in Gnostic circles, both non-Christian and Christianized, may be seen from the following parallels,

though where we are to seek the prototype of it—whether along some single line of Babylonian, Chaldæan, Magian, Syrian or Egyptian mystagogy, or as a common possession of Chaldæa and Egypt —is hard to say.

1. In the Mago-Chaldæan system underlying the early Simonian document *The Great Announcement* (see *The Gnostic Crucifixion*, pp. 163) :

The Power of the Depth = { The Great Power, Incomprehensible Silence. }

The First Man = { The Father, Mind of the Universals. }

Man Son of Man = } Great Thought.

The First Woman, Holy Spirit or Breath = } The Middle Distance, Incomprehensible Air.

The Christ = { He who has stood, stands, and will stand. }

2. In the system underlying the Chaldæan Oracles, a Greek mystery-poem of the first century in which Mago-Chaldæan material is " philosophized ":

The Power of the Depth = { God-nurturing Silence. }

The First Man = { The Father, Mind, Fire. }

Man Son of Man, The Second Man } = { Mind of Mind, The Second Mind. }

The First Woman } = The Great Mother.

The Christ = { The Æon (as Monad, Atom, Light-spark, Symbol). }

3 Again in the system underlying the oldest extant treatise of the Trismegistic literature, " The Pœmandres " or " Man-Shepherd " (*H.* ii. 3 ff.) :

The Power of the Depth = { The Silence before the Voice. }

117

THE HYMN OF THE ROBE OF GLORY.

The First Man = All-Father Mind.

Man Son of { Formative Mind,
Man = { The Second Mind.

The First
Woman = } Nature.

The Christ = { Man, Brother of the
{ Formative Mind.

There is thus little doubt that in Gnostic circles, both pre-Christian and Christian, there was a clear tradition of Two Sons, one who remained, and one who went forth; and the one who went forth or returned was the Christ. Our Poem is therefore a Song of the Christ-Mystery.

"Thy Brother, Our Second," or Next-in-rank, is the Supernal Man, Son of Man; and the Christ, because of His Descent, and His winning of the Pearl of Self-consciousness in manifestation, is exalted to equality with the Supernal Son, or even to still higher rank; yet are they both one.

THE ROBE OF GLORY.

It is to be noted that there are two Vestures: the Robe of Glory and the Purple Mantle.

Now in the canonical scriptures *John* xix. 24 (*cf. Matth.* xxvii. 35, *Mk.* xv. 24, *Lk.* xxiii. 24, all of which look back to *Psalm* xx. 18) reads:

"They parted my Garments among them;

"And for my Vesture they cast lots."

The fourth Gospel (xix. 23) distinguishes the "Garments" and the "Vesture," adding that the "Coat" (*chitōn*) "was without seam, woven from the top throughout."

Now the chitōn, or *tunica*, was an under-garment, and was generally worn under a woollen cloak, or mantle (*chlamys*, or *toga*) during the day.

The writer of the fourth Gospel was a Mystic, and doubtless meant to convey an under-meaning to those who had "ears to hear."

As the "Garments" were divided into four among the "four soldiers," can it be that he intended to convey the idea of a Cloak of the four elements, and a Vesture of the one element, or quintessence, the complement of the four? At any rate this would be in keeping with the mystery-teaching concerning the "perfect body" or "body of resurrection," as may be seen from the *Mithriac Ritual.*

Whether or not he had any such intention, and whether or not he had further the same ground-ideas in mind as those set forth by the Gnostic poet in our beautiful Hymn, must be left to the opinion of the reader according to his knowledge or ignorance.

The difference between the under-garment and mantle may be seen in many a Mithriac monument; while in the *Mithriac Ritual* we read (p. 91):

"Thou shalt behold a God. . . in a White Tunic and a Scarlet Mantle."

And again (p. 92):

"Thou shalt see . . . a God . . . clad in a Robe of Brightness."

The "Scarlet Mantle" is an exact parallel with the "Purple Mantle" of our Poem.

The nature of the Divine Robe, or, Glory, as a Heavenly Dwelling, was understood by Paul when he writes (*I. Cor.* v. 1 ff.):

"For know that if our house on earth of the [fleshly] tabernacle be dissolved, we have a God-made Building, a House not made with hands, eternal [*lit.* æonian] in the Heavens.

"For, indeed, we are groaning in this [habitation on earth], longing to be *clothed* with our Heaven-made Habitation."

Paul was well versed in Gnostic nomenclature; and the extended meaning of the Robe of Glory, as it was understood by the Mystics, may be grasped by the present-day Mystic who reads the following passages from one of the inspired outbursts of the beautiful *Untitled*

11 8

THE HYMN OF THE
ROBE OF GLORY.

Apocalypse of the Coptic Gnostic Codex Brucianus :

" In this City it is that they move and live ; it is the House of the Father, and the Vesture of the Son, and the Power of the Mother, and the Image of the Fulness [Plērōma]." (*F.* p. 547).

And again :

" And they praised the One and Only One, and Conception [or Thought, the Mother], and the Mind-born Logos, praising the Three who are One, for through Him they became supersubstantial.

" And the Father took their whole Likeness and made it into a City or into a Man. He limned the Universe in His [*sci.* the Man's] Likeness—that is all these Powers.

" Each one of them knew Him in this City ; all began to sing myriads of songs of praise to the Man or the City of the Father of the universe.

" And the Father hath taken His Glory and made it into a Vesture without for the Man. . . . He created His Body in the type of the Holy Plērōma." (*F.* p. 566).

And yet again the Ineffable Vesture is sung of as follows :

" The First Monad hath sent Him an Ineffable Vesture, which is all Light and all Life, and all Resurrection, and all Love, and all Hope, and all Faith, and all Wisdom, and all Gnosis, and all Truth, and all Peace. . . .

· " And in it is the universe, and the universe hath found itself in it, and knows itself therein.

" And it [*sci.* the Vesture] gave them all light in its Ineffable Light ; myriads of myriads of powers were given it, in order that it should raise up the universe once for all.

" It gathered its vestures to itself, and made them after the fashion of a Veil which surrounds it on all sides, and poured itself over them, and raised up all, and separated them all according to order and law and forethought." (*F.* p. 557.)

And yet once more from the same high document of deep mystic lore :

" He is the Man begotten of Mind, to whom Reflection gave form.

" Thou hast given all things to the Man. He weareth them like these garments, and putteth them on like these vestures, and wrappeth Himself with creation as with a mantle." (*F.* p. 562.)

If we were to set down all the passages in Gnostic and allied literature connected with the mystery of the Robe of Glory, the Wedding Garment, and the rest of the Light-Vestures of the Soul, we should speedily exhaust the space of this little volume and of several other volumes.

We must, however, find room for a brief notice of the magnificent description of the Descent of the Vesture of Light on the Master, the Gnostic Transfiguration, in the *Pistis Sophia* (*P.S.* 5 ff. ; *F.* pp. 259 ff.). The whole subject is treated more fully in my essay on " The Soul-Vestures," in *The World-Mystery* (2nd ed., pp. 117 ff.) :

" But the Disciples saw not Jesus because of the Great Light in which He was, or which shone on Him ; for their eyes were darkened because of the Great Light in which He was. They saw the Light only, sending forth a host of light-rays.

" And the light-rays were not like to one another. The Light was of various kinds, and it was of various types, from below above, each ray being more admirable than its fellow . . . in a Great Glory of immeasurable Light ; it stretched from below the Earth right up unto Heaven. . . .

" It was of three degrees. The first was more admirable than the rest [? of the rays] ; the second, which was in the midst, was more admirable than the first which was below it ; and the third, which was above them all, was more admirable than the two below *it*."

The Master explains this mystery to His Disciples as follows :

" Lo, I have now put on my Vesture,

119

THE HYMN OF THE
ROBE OF GLORY.

and all authority hath been given me by the First Mystery. . . .

" It came to pass, when the Sun had risen in the East, that a Great Light-power descended, in which was my Vesture, which I had left behind in the Four-and-twentieth Mystery. . . .

" And I found a Mystery in my Vesture, written in Five Words of those from the Height . . . of which the interpretation is this :

" O Mystery that is Without, in the World, because of which All hath come into existence ! This is the whole Out-going and the ₊whole Up-going, which hath emanated all Emanations and all that is therein, because of which all Mysteries exist and all their Regions.

" Come unto us ! For we are Thy Fellow-Members [or Limbs]; we are all one with Thee ; we are one and the same. Thou art the First Mystery which hath existed from the beginning in the Ineffable before it came forth, and the Name thereof is all of us.

" Now, therefore, we all together draw nigh unto Thee at the Last Limit (that is, at the Last Mystery from Within) ; it is itself a portion of us.

" Now, therefore, we have sent Thee Thy Vesture, which indeed hath belonged to Thee from the beginning, which Thou didst leave behind in the Last Limit, which is the Last Mystery from Within, until its time should be fulfilled, according to the Command of the First Mystery.

" Lo, its time is fulfilled ; clothe Thyself therewith !

" Come unto us ! For we all draw nigh unto Thee to clothe Thee with the First Mystery and all His Glory, by Commandment of the same; in that the First Mystery hath given us it, consisting of two Vestures, besides the one that we have sent Thee, for Thou art worthy of them ; for in sooth Thou art prior to us and came into being before us. Wherefore now hath the First Mystery sent Thee through us the Mystery of all His Glory, two Vestures."

The text then goes on to enumerate the Hierarchies of Æons, Powers, and Gods, which compose these Heavenly Garments—corresponding detail for detail with the whole emanative potencies of the Universe whereby the Garment of Deity is woven, and then continues its magnificent exposition ; the Living Powers which form the Vesture speaking as follows on the Great Day " Be with us " —the moment of Supreme Perfection :

" Lo, therefore, have we sent Thee Thy Vesture, which no one from the First Law [or Precept] downwards hath known ; for the Glory of its Light was hidden in it [*sci.* the Law], and all Regions from the First Law downwards have not known it.

" Make haste, therefore, clothe Thyself with this Vesture, and come unto us ! For we draw nigh unto Thee, in order to clothe Thee with thy Two Vestures, which have been for Thee from the beginning with the First Mystery, until the time appointed by the Ineffable should be fulfilled.

" Come, therefore, to us quickly, that we may clothe Thee with them, until Thou hast fulfilled the whole Ministry of the Perfection of the First Mystery, the Ministry appointed by the Ineffable !

" Come, therefore, to us quickly that we may clothe Thee with them according to the Commandment of the First Mystery ! For yet a little while, a very little while, and Thou shalt come to us and leave the world.

" Come, therefore, quickly, that Thou mayest receive Thy whole Glory, the Glory of the First Mystery ! "

This gives us all the light we need to throw on the inner meaning of our Poem ; it is the inner tradition intended for the initiated, whereas our Poem was intended to be circulated among the people. Which was prior ? If the former, then we have found a *terminus* for the dating, if not of the *Pistis Sophia* as a whole, then of one of its " sources," and the date must be pushed back into the second century.

120

THE HYMN OF THE ROBE OF GLORY.

A STORY OF THE INFANCY.

But before we leave the *Pistis Sophia* there is another instructive passage that is reminiscent of the same ideas which underlie the words : " Unto me I took it and kissed it " (50) ; and also : " That we were twain in distinction, And yet again one in one likeness" (78). It is an otherwise unknown Story of the Infancy and runs as follows (*P.S.* pp. 120 ff.) :

" And Mary [the Mother] answered and said :

" My Master, concerning the word which Thy Power prophesied through David, to wit : ' Grace and Truth met together, Righteousness and Peace kissed each other ; Truth sprouted out of the Earth, and Righteousness looked down from Heaven '—Thy Power prophesied this word of old concerning Thee.

" When Thou wert a child, before the Spirit had descended upon Thee, whilst thou wert in a vineyard with Joseph, the Spirit came from the Height, and came to me in my house, like unto Thee ; and I knew Him not, and thought that He was Thou.

" And the Spirit said unto me : Where is Jesus my Brother, that I may go to meet Him ?

" And when He had said this unto me, I was in perplexity and thought it was a phantom [come] to tempt me.

" So I took Him and bound Him to the foot of the bed that was in my house, until I had gone unto you—to Thee and Joseph, in the field—and found you in the vineyard—Joseph propping up the vines.

" It came to pass, therefore, when Thou didst hear me speaking the word unto Joseph, that Thou didst understand the word, and wert joyful and saidest : Where is He that I may see Him ? Otherwise I await Him in this place.

" It came to pass when Joseph heard Thee saying these words, that he was troubled, and we went together, we entered the house, and found the Spirit bound to the bed. And we gazed on Thee and Him, and found Thee like unto Him.

" And He that was bound to the bed was loosed ; He embraced Thee and kissed Thee, and Thou also didst kiss Him ; and ye become one."

I am somewhat persuaded that under the apparently naïve details of this infancy story there is a concealed meaning. Once I gave a lecture in which I endeavoured to suggest what the nature of its under-meaning may have been, but it is too long to set down here.

It is apparently from another " source " of the *P. S.* document, and not due to the compiler.

THE TWO COURIERS.

The Two Couriers also pertain to the mystery hidden under the symbolism of the Twins which meets us everywhere in the ancient myths and legends of initiation ; in reversed reflection they would be the Two Thieves crucified with Him.

In the Transfiguration - scene in the canonical Gospels, when the Master is clothed with Light, the Two are taken by the unknowing Disciples for Moses and Elias.

In *The Gospel of Peter*, in the story of the Mystery of the Resurrection, they are seen as Two Men, of the appearance of Light, whose heads reach unto heaven. This mystic tradition may be compared with the more prosaic " two men in shining garments " of the third Gospel ; while its Gnostic analogue may be seen in the Two Great Beings reaching unto heaven, of whom the precise mystic dimensions are given, in the Nazoræan, or Galilean, scripture, *The Book of Elxai*, that is *The Book of the Hidden Power* (see *Did Jesus live* 100 B.C. ? pp. 365 ff.).

In the *Pistis Sophia*, as Receivers of Light, they are called Gabriel and Michael, who led " the Light-stream over Pistis Sophia "—the repentant faithful soul

THE HYMN OF THE
ROBE OF GLORY.

(*P.S.* 130 ff.), and who elsewhere in the same document take back the souls to the Light. They lead " the Light-stream into Chaos and bring it forth again " (*P.S.* 133).

In the *Book of Enoch* (lxxi. 3) it is Michael who brings Enoch before the most High, and Abraham to the Throne of God.

The Two Angels of opposite sex— allegorizing or substantializing the man's good and evil deeds—who lead the soul through the Middle Distance are native to the Magian and presumably Old Iranian traditions.

In Hellenic mythology and Hellenistic mystagogy it is Hermes who is the psychagogue and psychopomp, and he bears in his hand a Rod twined about with the Serpent Twins.

THE ALLEGORICAL GEOGRAPHY.

The geography of the way down from Hyrcania to Egypt, and back again, is consistent with itself (*p* 125 - 124), but puzzling in some of its details.

Hyrcania was the mountainous region on the southern shores of the Caspian Sea.

The territory of Maishān lay between Mesopotamia and the sea ; Maishān the city (Forāt Maishān = ? Messene) was in all probability the chief emporium of the sea-borne commerce of Babylonia and the West with India, and lay slightly to the south of the present-day Baṣra.

Babylonia was the Tigris-Euphrates valley.

Sarbūg is a puzzle. The best solution seems to be that it stands for the City of Babylon itself. Now, strangely enough, the Greek, in both traditions, renders Sarbūg by the " Labyrinth." This may possibly refer to the labyrinth of the streets of the great city. But it may also preserve for us a hint of how the geography was allegorized by the Gnostic exegetes ; for " The Labyrinth "

was a technical term of the Gnosis, as may be seen from a fine Naassene Hymn, two lines of which, referring to the soul, run as follows :

" Now is born, with no way out for her ;
    in misery
She enters in her wandering the
    Labyrinth of ills." (*H.* i. 191).

Whatever the precise situation of the otherwise unknown Sarbūg may have been, it must be very patent to the Mystic that the Gnostic poet intended it for a certain stage of the descent of the soul, or spiritual mind, into the regions of manifestation.

Hoffmann (pp. 289 ff.) has attempted an interpretation on these lines. The Way of the Soul, he says, leads from (1) Heaven as the God-realm, through (2) the Firmament, to (3) the Earth— corresponding with the three natures of man : spirit, soul, and body.

He further sets forth a diagrammatic representation as follows :

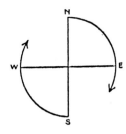

N = The Region of the Ineffable, the Mountain of the Gods, Hyrcania. This is the Over-world or Plērōma.

E = The Heaven of the Fixed Stars, Æther, the Midst, the Virgin of Light (of *P.S.*).
Between this and the Earth comes the Boundary of the Over-world and the World (= S), or Maishān.

THE HYMN OF THE
ROBE OF GLORY.

Next comes the Earth-heaven or Firmament, Babel.

W =Egypt, the Earth and the Underworld.

This seems to me a somewhat too elaborate scheme ; but if it can stand, it strengthens the case for priority of the scheme underlying the *Pistis Sophia* to our Poem.

Maishān is the Mart of the Merchants of the East, and therefore should represent the borders or limit of the material world, or hylic cosmos, its uttermost region upwards.

Babel-land and Sarbūg would thus stand for the state or states lying between the region of direct commerce with the East (or Light-world) — that is, the region of the Heaven-world or Elysium —and the Earth-state.

These are presumably the states of the Middle Distance—that is, Hades ; for in 1. 50 we are told that the Letter is sealed :

" 'Gainst the Children of Babel, the wicked,
The tyrannical Daimons of Sarbūg."

These are presumably under the rule of the Prince of the Powers of the (Lower) Air.

The rest of our space may now be devoted to a few notes of detail, and to an endeavour to suggest some considerations of a mystical nature that may be of interest to those who delight in such studies, on the ground that the whole Poem is concerned with the mystery of the Light-spark, or Spiritual Man, or Sonship, or Christ-nature.

NOTES.

The opening words seem to suggest, from the human point of view, the Birth of the Christ-nature and its state before it descends into manifestation, or drops into personality.

The " little child " may be taken to denote the Light-spark (or Ātmic ray), as it was symbolically termed by the Gnostics ; in itself it is no " spark," but the potentiality of the Fulness (Plērōma) itself. To aid our dim intuition it may be regarded as " born " onto the plane of the spirit from the ever-divine states of the Fatherhood and Motherhood, of Divine Light and Life.

" Little child," or " little one," means also a certain stage in initiation, when the man below, the personal man, is bringing to birth, that is to consciousness, the spiritual or Christ nature in himself. It is characterized by purity, innocence (harmlessness), spiritual instinct (not mind in its ratiocinative mode), childlikeness. In our Poem, however, it is not the man who is speaking, but the Spark or Sonship.

The " Father's Kingdom " is the state of Ātman, and the " House " is spiritual Personality or Individuality, the Home of the Higher Self.

It is a state of Bliss, the activities of the Child are of the nature of Bliss ; and the " Upringers," or Nurturers, are the Arms of the Divine Life in which the Child is cradled. "Wealth" and "Glories" are characteristics of the Kingdom. The Nurturers, as Nurses of the Divine Infant, might be perhaps more appropriately characterized by " fulness " and " richness."

" From the East." " East " often does not so much refer to a particular state or a definite plane ; it indicates rather a

123

THE HYMN OF THE ROBE OF GLORY.

direction, which connotes as it were the power of cutting directly through planes. Birth from the East is not so much a birth *viâ* planes, that is a stirring of matter, as an inner way of immediate arrival. But in the text it does not seem to be used in such a precise sense.

The " Treasure " seems to denote the Jewels, that is, the senses or instincts, of the Spiritual Mind. There was a certain " binding up " of it ; this suggests the first defining of space or limitation of the Spirit.
It was " large " and " light," spacious but as yet not heavy or possessed of gravity, that is tension or relation to personal environment.

The Treasure was carried in the "heart " of the man ; that is, in the innermost substance of his nature.

" Land of Gīlān." The Geli (οἱ Γῆλοι) were a people who inhabited the district now called Gīlān, on the south-west shore of the Caspian. Bevan, however, prefers " land of the upper ones," and the Greek has it also.
Ganzāk, or Gazzāk, was a district in Atropatēnē (Ādharbaijān).
The Greek has : " Gold of the great treasures uncoined."

Kūshān is perhaps Kāshān in Persia, north of Ispahan.

It may be that a precise symbolism, connected with the nature of the perfected " formal mind," may be hidden under the names of the precious stones, some of which are of uncertain translation. They would thus suggest a pure vesture of a formal nature, corresponding with the mineral kingdom, with which the soul or self is equipped or furnished.
The Greek glosses the Robe as " of gold tissue with jewels incrusted."
It is of " Gold " and " Silver "; that is, has " Sun " and " Moon " powers.

" Chalcedonies," or " Agates," are a puzzle ; but the " iris-hued," or iridescent, colouring well represents the shimmer of all colours of the pure " glory," or purified " aura."
The Greek has " pearls " for "iris-hued [stones]."

All this is " bound " to the spiritual man by the power of the hardest of all the precious stones.
He is " armed " with it, according to the Greek. Compare " Armour of Sounding Light " of *The Chaldæan Oracles,* *fr. 134*

Whether or not there is in the term " Adamant " (Diamond) a play on the Adamas (Adam, the Primal Man) of the Mysteries, must be left to the decision of the reader. It is of interest, however, in this connection to set down a passage from the Naassene Document. Referring to the allegorical " Rock " to which the souls cling in the *Odyssey,* the Jewish commentator writes :
" The ' Rock ' means Adamas. This is : ' The Corner stone ' which ' I insert in the Foundation of Zion.'
" By this [Foundation] he [Isaiah] means the plasm of man." (*H.* i. 161.)

" Purple Mantle." Purple is a sign of royalty ; for our Poet is singing of a Royal Soul. (See *The Chaldæan Oracles, p.*219)
Hoffmann makes the Mantle or Toga = *anima naturaliter divina.* Compare l. 26 :

" And my rank did long for its nature."

" Stature " is in its root-sense a " standing upright," and may be compared with the idea of Him " who has stood, stands, and shall stand " of *The Great Announcement.* (See *The Gnostic Crucifixion,* p. 164) It is the Spiritual Mind of man, his inner steadfastness and stability, and his own measurement and monument.

The " Compact," or Covenant or Ordinance, may be compared with the words

THE HYMN OF THE
ROBE OF GLORY.

of one of the Hymns of the Sophia (*P.S.* 64):

"Thy Commandment [or Statute], (O Light,) hath brought me Below, and I am descended like a Power of Chaos; my Power hath grown cold in me."

It was written "in the heart" (*cf.* l. 55). This means, mystically, written in the spiritual "blood" of the man, in the life-substance of him, in the very atoms of his substance. It was not engraved on the mind, but written deep down in the heart, so that it should not be forgotten.

Memory is connected with past, present, and future; but this record could not be really wiped out even when time should be no more.

The "Pearl" is the Living Gnosis, or again the self-realization of the Logos in man, or again the "Kingdom of Heaven," or rather the "Kingship of the Heavens."

But why should these living ideas be symbolized by a "pearl"—a precious thing, yet the product of disease?

If we may be permitted to speculate on the further meaning of a physical fact not known to the ancient Gnostics, we might suggest that Living Gnosis cannot be gained without the help of the Opposing Powers, the mystical Adversary.

Gnosis from one point of view is the union of the spiritual and personal man. When the spiritual self would attain to Divine consummation, there must be a descent into the spheres of personality, where people and things live, so to speak, within "shells." The spiritual man has to "steal" from within the Great Shell, or from within the shell side of things, that most precious gem which is the product of self-will or "disease"—that is of the "Opposer."

This mystery may also be called a "pearl" because, on the substance side of things, the man in whom Gnosis is born, or who is born in Gnosis, is for ever after wrapped in a pearly Glory, or his substance becomes pearl-like to the opened eye of the seer.

The oyster, or "jelly fish" or plasm, is the "shell" of personality, is the man of "flesh," or unevolved buddhic substance. The Impersonal Spirit, or Ātman, at an earlier stage of evolution, descends and stirs this substance to create, broods over it, and it creates a "pearl," which from the personal and selfish point of view is not at first advantageous to the "jelly fish."

This "pearl" again, later on, is a pure substance or ichōr which the buddhic nature creates or secretes when Ātman begins to energize in the man.

The "loud-breathing Serpent" is Typhon, the Opposer; the Lord of the passions or opposing forces of the planes of form.

The Greek has "the Serpent the Swallower," and Hoffmann has "poison-breathed."

The "Sea" is, of course, the Ocean of Genesis, the manifested planes, or states of manifestation; it is the Ocean of life-and-death, or repeated birth, the Ever-becoming, the Saṁsāra of the Brāhmans and Buddhists. The "poison," if "poison-breathed" is the correct translation, reveals Typhon (Apepī); it is the cause of the "disease" operated by the Opposer.

The Pearl is thus again perfected root-form, or the "permanent atom" of experience, so to speak, to which the Robe of Glory and Mantle of Royalty can be attached, and so union be achieved between the upper and lower.

The Robe is the Cosmic Texture of Light and Life, and is stamped and sealed by the Great Name of the Spiritual Individuality.

"Thy Brother," as we have seen in the comments (p. 118), means from one point of view the Demiurgic or Architectural or

THE HYMN OF THE
ROBE OF GLORY.

Building Power, in an inner mystical sense the Obedient Opposer of Life, own Twin to Ātman. In a still more mysterious sense that is not brought out in our Poem, Ātman, the Christ, may be said to go to seek His lost Brother (in the Christianized Gnosis this was generally His lost Sister or Spouse, the Sophia or Wisdom); they unite in the Mystery of the Sacred Marriage or At-one-ment, and become Heir of Infinity and Eternity.

The Christ descends and carries off or saves the Pearl, thus attaching Himself to the Pure Essence, purified by suffering, born of the energy of the Opposer within form, and so wins the way back to the Kingdom. The Opposer is Next-in-rank to God.

It has been suggested that because of this " twin " idea our Poem has been very appropriately inserted into the *Acts of Judas Thomas*, that is, of Judas the Twin of Jesus; and certainly this hidden mysticism of Judas the Twin and Judas the Betrayer was highly elaborated by the Gnostics, so that we even find traces of a *Gospel of Judas*.

The " Couriers," or Messengers (*lit.* Letter-carriers, Per. Parwānḳin), are, in one sense, a Twin-Ray from the Mind of the Master of all masterhood, Boundless Light, the true Father-Mother of the Soul that is striving to bring itself to birth.

The " Way " from the " East," in its more immediate mystical meaning, denotes a direct path through matter by means of a Ray of the True Sun, of the nature of a " lightning-flash," as set forth so graphically in the mystery-poem known as *The Chaldæan Oracles* (*fg.94*); it " blazes " directly through matter, and does not meander through the labyrinth of the planes. In our Poem, however, there is a descent through planes or states.

Maishān perhaps connotes the plane of the Quintessence or One Element (Buddhi), the complement and source of the four.

The Land of Babel suggests presumably the confused sounds (the confusion of tongues) of the personal " astral " or emotional state ; and the walls of Sarbūg may stand for the city of the personal formal mind, the labyrinth of personal-mind-made planes.

Thereon comes the plunge into the physical body (Egypt), when the direct guidance of the Twin-Ray ceases for a time.

In mystical physiology this Serpent may signify something within the "blood," or perhaps the " elemental essence," which must sleep, or be quieted, before the heavenly ichōr can be born, or the " pearl," the real root-purity within form, be detached from the downward current, and attached again to Ātman. Compare *A Mithriac Ritual* (p.91) :

" For that a man—*I, N.N., Son of N.N. (fem)*—born of the mortal womb—*of N.N. (fem.)*—and of spermatic ichōr, yea of this ichōr, which at Thy Hands to-day hath undergone the transmutation of re-birth [or birth from Above] — one, from so many tens of thousands, transformed to immortality in this same hour, by God's good pleasure, of God transcendent Good—, [a man, I say] presumes to worship Thee, and supplicates with whatsoever power a mortal hath."

Compare this with the ancient reading of the Great Utterance at the Mystical Baptism Rite :

" Thou art my Beloved Son ; this day have I begotten thee ! "

The " lodging " is, literally, a " lodging-place for travellers "—that is to say, an inn, or caravanserai. The Greek has simply " den " or " hole." And here we may call to mind the following paragraph

THE HYMN OF THE
ROBE OF GLORY.

from Hippolytus' summary of Valentinian doctrine :

" And this material man is, according to them, as it were, an inn, or dwelling-place, at one time of the soul alone, at another time of the soul and daimonian existences [elemental essences], at another of the soul and words [logoi, or angels or reasonable essences] which are words sown from Above—from the Common Fruit of the Plērōma [the Christ] and Wisdom [the Divine Mother]—into this world, dwelling in the body of clay together with the soul, when daimons ceased to cohabit with her." (F. p. 352).

This is the body in Egypt, or the hylic world or cosmos of gross matter. As the original Jewish writer of the canonical *Apocalypse* tells us (*Rev.* xi. 7, 8):

" ' The Beast that ascendeth out of the Abyss shall make war with ' them, ' and overcome them,' and slay them.

" And their carcase [shall lie] in the street of the Great City, which is spiritually called ' Sodom ' and Egypt."

To which the Christian over-writer adds :

" Where also our Lord was crucified."

Who this noble youth from the East may be mystically, I am unable precisely to conjecture, unless it refers to the " voice of conscience," the spiritual tendencies in the natural man. The reader, however, may be reminded of the supposition in the Preamble (p. 109), that historically it may be autobiographical.

Preuschen interprets it in terms of the Gospel-story ; the Son being the Christ, and the noble youth Jesus. But this does not work out.

I have adopted the reading of Nicetas; the Syriac " I warned him " seems hopelessly confusing.

Before the true reunion can take place, not only must the " evil one " be " saved," but the " saviour " must be " lost," and dealt with " treacherously "; the Christ must be " betrayed." Without this there would not be perfect balance. It is the formal mind that betrays.

The " food " is the " food of the world " of *P.S.* 346; compare also the passage (*ibid.* 282) :

" And the Babe eateth of the Delights [or Food-stuffs] of the World of the Rulers ; and the Power absorbeth from the portion of the Power which is in the Delights ; and the Soul absorbeth from the portion of the Soul that is in the Delights ; and the Counterfeit Spirit absorbeth from the portion of the Evil which is in the Delights and in its desires ; whilst the Body absorbeth from the unperceptive Matter (*Hylē*) which is in the Delights."

With the forgetfulness, or oblivion, induced by the Victuals, or Delights, compare a passage from one of the Hymns of Repentance of the Sophia (*P.S.* 63) :

" They have taken away my Light, and my Power is dried up.
" I have forgotten my Mystery which I performed from the beginning.
" Because of the din [or confusion] of the Fear and Power of Arrogant [the Opposer, the Serpent of self-interest], my Power hath failed me."

The " draught of oblivion," or forgetfulness, is also described at length in the *Pistis Sophia* (see, for instance, pp. 281, 385).

The "weight of their victuals" is paralleled in *P.S.* (281) by the " very heavy weight of forgetfulness."

In a wider and more mystical sense the food that Ātman now eats has to do with the formal mind in the mode of subject and object ; thus is its simplicity

THE HYMN OF THE ROBE OF GLORY.

differentiated, and it becomes food and food-eater, and so is brought down into time and objects ; and then the curse of memory and forgetfulness begins, and the true natural instinctual awareness of the Spirit sleeps.

The spiritual germ has now become embedded in man and is fast asleep in substance ; and a great impulse, an earthquake, is required to arouse it and awake it from the dead.

For " And this is the counsel they came to," Bevan gives : " So they wove a plan on my behalf."

If " plan " is the key-word, then, taking it in conjunction with the idea of the Letter to which every Prince, or Noble, set his Name, we may hazard the conjecture that, in one sense, it may be taken as referring to the mystery of re-incarnation ; it suggests the weaving, out of all previous lives, some sort of a plan or destiny, stamped with the Name of every Prince.

The Princes may be thought of as " facets " of the King ; they represent the " faces " or " personæ " of the Spiritual Mind, or Highest Self. They would thus stand for not all the prior existences of the man, but rather such lives as had been able to manifest some portion of that Spiritual Mind.

The Letter might thus be said to be woven out of the "substance" of previous lives, to which each proper person or facet of the spiritual Wholeness supplies its due share. This immediately attracts the soul in its last incarnation, for it is itself.

This Letter or Plan, woven out of the permanencies of a man's previous incarnations, is sealed by the Father of Ātman, so that it shall not be torn to pieces as it descends through the regions or planes. It would naturally have a tendency to be scattered ; its substance would naturally remain on the plane of substance, its mind-tendencies on the plane of mind ; but that would be to be no more

permanencies from all the planes, the fruitage of experience.

These are now gathered together into one Plan which is sealed by the Father of universals, or wholenesses or monads or æons, and so it continues to be whole even until it reaches the man, " right down " on the physical plane or in his natural body ; and that is how wholeness in consciousness is born. It is a sort of germ of wholeness.

" King of kings." Compare *Rev.* xix. 16 :

" And He hath in His Vesture and on His Thigh a Name written : King of kings and Lord of lords."

" Remember thy glorious Robe," and " The Book of the Heroes." Compare *Rev.* iii. 5 :

" He who thus conquereth [by not defiling his garments] shall be clothed in White Robes, and I will not blot his Name out of the Book of Life."

Every man has his " book " and there is a Great Book. See *Rev.* xx. 12 :

" And I saw the Dead, the great and the little, standing in the Presence of the Throne, and [their] ' books were opened ' [*Dan.* vii., 10]. And another Book was opened, which is ' [The Book] of Life ' [*Dan.* xii., 1]."

The Eagle, or Hawk, was the name of the highest grade of the Mithriaca—the Fathers. See *A Mithriac Ritual* (p. 89), where the Father's prayer ends :

" So that I, Eagle as I am, by my own self may soar to Heaven, and contemplate all things."

The Eagle-letter—which may be paralleled with the Descent of the Dove in the Baptism-Mystery—flew in the air

THE HYMN OF THE ROBE OF GLORY.

the Bright Æther of the Supernal Realms, or the state of Divine Breath (Ātman); as it contacted the inmost or spiritual plasm of the man, his Buddhic nature, or the nature of his Depth, the Depth of his substance, it became "all sound" or "all speech."

The Buddhic nature is the Quintessence or One Element, the Aithēr or Æther, the Shining One; just as in Sanskrit Ā-kāsha is *par excellence* the Very Shining One, and its root-characteristic is "sound."

It was a true Bath-Kol, or Voice from Heaven, as the mystical Rabbis called it. Lit. Bath-Kol = Daughter of the Voice; that is to say, Echo of the Word or Name.

This Voice is the Inner Voice, the Voice Within, the Voice of the Silence. The "sound of its winging," or "the sound of its rustling," suggest another great symbol: the rustling or the activities of the "leaves" (powers and permanencies) on the man's true "Tree of Life," as the Wind or Divine Breath stirs them, thus awaking them to true activity and life.

"I took it and kissed it," etc. Thereby the two united; the "seal" which held it together as a wholeness was "loosed," and there was union. The Plan and Heart united, atom matched atom in "Mind" and "Blood." The Intelligible married the Sensible, and the Christ was born, the Eternal Memory.

"E'en as it stood in my heart writ." It is written by the Scribe of the Gods, Thoth the Divine, the Tongue and Heart of the Eternal. Compare *II. Cor.* iii., 2 :

"Ye are our Letter written in our hearts."

"Filthy and unclean garments"—that is, the man's unrhythmic "bodies" or rather "vehicles." He leaves his personal-plane garments or vehicles behind on each plane, like a butterfly leaving his grub-case; only these do not die, or go into trance, they go on with their "filthy" or "daily" duties. They are the bodies of "dross." (See *The Chaldæan Oracles,* fr. 123).

His Great Plan, or Spiritual Mind-and-Substance, goes on before, precedes and proceeds. Its Voice or Life is its feminine power that awakens and brings to birth; its Light is its masculine potency that guides, controls, orders—the mode that happens after the awakening or resurrection.

The "fabric of silk" and "letters of red" suggest Buddhic substance and Ātmic radiance.

Burkitt translates :

"For it began to make its silken folds to glow."

And so the "Spark" passes "up" or "in" through the planes, though indeed it does not move; the Spark becomes a Flame. It is the life and journey of a Spark and not of any man-neophyte; though of course the life and journey of any initiate would have many things in common.

"The meeting-place of the merchants." This and the next line seem to be a doublet.

Father-Mother, the Supreme Mystery, give the Glory-Robe of Spiritual Life and Light to the Twin-Powers of Spiritual Mind, to bestow it on the returning Victor (or Prodigal) ascending the Sacred Way in Triumph.

The Robe is sent down from Hyrcania, which for the Parthians was the Mount of the Gods, the Height of Heaven, their Meru.

"The Glory looked like my own self."

THE HYMN OF THE
ROBE OF GLORY.

This is the same idea as that which underlies the mirror-play of Iacchos, the Young Bacchus of the Mysteries. Compare also *II. Cor.* iii. 18:

" With unveiled face mirroring the Glory of the Lord, we are transformed into the same Likeness [or Image] from Glory to Glory as by the Breath of the Lord."

Burkitt translates:

" Myself I saw as in a glass before my face."

When the illuminated neophyte first sees the Self in all things, he sees it as himself reflected in all things. This is a great danger for many.

" The King of Kings' Image " suggests that originally the Embroidered Robe had been woven by the Mother only; but now it is stamped all over with the Image or Likeness of the Father.

" With Sapphires." Compare *Ezekiel* i. 26:

" And above the Firmament that was over their heads was the likeness of a Throne as the appearance of a sapphire stone : and upon the likeness of the Throne was the likeness as the appearance of a Man upon it."

And also *Exodus* xxiv. 10:

" And they saw the God of Israel : and there was under His Feet as it were a paved work of sapphire stone, as it were the Body of Heaven in his clearness."

" The Motions of Gnosis." There is a suggestion here of a certain dramatic state of consciousness where, by the man's own activities, he talks to himself. The Robe is as it were the one uniting

substance, or quintessence, which holds all things in its embrace, and with it comes the idea of reflection from oneself onto it ; so that when the illumined seer contemplates it all the activities or motions of any object become knowledges, or everything seems to stir as if to speak, or become vocal, so that by these activities vital knowledge or gnosis is increased. It is the self talking to the self by means of action.

I follow Burkitt's emended version in his review of Preuschen.

" The Glory of Him who had sent it." Compare *Rev.* xxi. 23:

" For the Glory of God did lighten it [the Heavenly City], and the Lamb is the Lamp thereof."

The Greek " sweet-sounding " is rendered by Hoffmann as "water-organs," and he refers to *Rev.* i. 15:
" And His Voice as the sound of many waters."

And also *Rev.* xix. 6:

" And I heard as it were the Voice of a great multitude, and as the Voice of many waters, and as the Voice of mighty thunderings, saying, Alleluia ! "

And again *Jeremiah* li. 16, 55:

" When He uttereth His Voice there is a multitude of waters."

" Because the Lord hath spoiled Babylon, and destroyed out of her the Great Voice ; when her waves do roar like great waters, a noise of their voice is uttered."

Professor Burkitt writes :

" The remains of yet another stanza

THE HYMN OF THE ROBE OF GLORY.

of the Hymn appear in Syriac. Only three lines are preserved; one is untranslateable, the second is utterly unmetrical, and the third—which appears to be the concluding line of the Poem—contains a very doubtful word. Probably the copy used by the editor who inserted the Hymn in *The Acts of Thomas* was badly damaged at the end. The fragments, thus completed, seem to be genuine, for we almost require some mention of the Pearl at the end of the Poem. I cannot attempt to venture the two missing lines, but the general sense appears to be as follows : ”

Now, while with acclamation all His
   courts resound,
I wait until His gracious Promise be
   fulfilled :
That with Him to the Royal Council I
   should go,
And with my Pearl appear before them
   at His side.

Whatever may be its precise interpretation—and the Mystic at any rate knows that in vita things there cannot possibly be one formal interpretation only—there will be few who will not admit that this ancient Poem of the Gnosis is beautiful. For ourselves, we end with the hope that, when it is better known, no few may find it inspiring and illuminating also.

Note.—Journal of Theological Studies (London, April, 1908), vol. ix. No. 35, p. 473, in a review by C. H. W. Johns of Emil Behren's *Assyrisch-babylonische Briefe Kultischen Inhalts aus Sargonidenzeit* (Leipzig, 1906):

“ The mention of Nabū's writing the ‘ Credit on account ’ of the King and his sons in the ‘ Book of life to last for ever ’ is noteworthy. Deeply interesting are the pilgrimages of the King's ‘ double ’ and the royal cloak (or *pallium ?*).”

131

THE . . .
HYMN . .
OF . . . .
JESUS. . .

THE HYMN OF JESUS

CONTENTS

BIBLIOGRAPHY.

LIPSIUS (R. A.), *Die apocryphen Apostelgeschichten* (Braunschweig, 1883).

CORSSEN (P.), *Monarchianische Prologe zu den Vier Evangelien*, *T. u. A.*, xv. i. (Leipzig, 1896).

JAMES (M. R.), *Apocrypha Anecdota*, *T. and S.*, v. i. (Cambridge, 1897).

BONNET (M.), *Acta Apostolorum Apocrypha* (Leipzig, 1898).

HENNECKE (E.), *Neutestamentliche Apokryphen* (Tübingen, 1904).

MEAD (G. R. S.), *Fragments of a Faith Forgotten*, 2nd. ed. (London, 1906).

MEAD (G. R. S.), *Thrice Greatest Hermes* (London, 1906).

THE HYMN OF JESUS.

THE HYMN OF JESUS.

PREAMBLE.

Just as many other settings of the Sayings and Doings of the Lord existed prior to and alongside of the canonical Gospels, so were there, prior to and alongside of the subsequently selected or canonical Acts, many other narratives professing to record the doings and sayings of the Apostles and Disciples of the Lord.

Most of these originated in circles which were subsequently called heretical, and many of them were later on worked over by orthodox editors to suit doctrinal preconceptions, and so preserved for the edification of large numbers in the Catholic or General Church.

As Lipsius says : " Almost every fresh editor of such narratives, using that freedom which all antiquity was wont to allow itself in dealing with literary monuments, would recast the materials which lay before him, excluding whatever might not suit his theological point of view—dogmatic statements, for example, speeches, prayers, etc., for which he would substitute other formulæ of his own composition, and further expanding and abridging after his own pleasure, or as the immediate object which he had in view might dictate."

Some of these edited and re-edited documents, though for the most part they have come down to us in a very fragmentary condition, still preserve distinct traces of their Gnostic origin ; and Lipsius has shown that their Gnosticism is not to be ascribed to third century Manichæism, as had been previously assumed by many, but to the general Gnosis of the second century.

There was a very wide circulation of such religious romances in the second century, for they formed the main means of Gnostic public propaganda.

The technical inner teachings of Gnosticism were assailed by the subsequently orthodox Church Fathers with misrepresentation and overwhelmed with ridicule. To these onslaughts the Gnostics, as far as we are aware, made no reply ; most probably because they were bound by oaths of secrecy on the one hand, and on the other knew well that the mysteries of the inner life could not be decided by vulgar debate.

The mystic teachings of their Gospel were for those who knew the nature of the inner life by direct experience ; for the rest they were foolishness.

Their Acts-romances also appear often to be based on actual occurrences of the inner life and on direct spiritual experience, subsequently worked up into popular forms ; the marvellous complexity and baffling sublimity of apocalyptic ecstasy, and the over-abundant and pregnant technology which delighted the members of the inner circles of the Gnostic Christians, were excluded, and all was reduced to simpler terms.

These marvellous narratives may seem vastly fantastic to the modern mind, but to every shade of Christianity in those days, they were entirely credible. The orthodox did not repudiate the marvellous nature of the narratives ; what they opposed with such bitterness was the doctrinal implications with which they were involved.

These Acts-romances thus formed the intermediate link between the General Church and the inner teachings of Gnosticism, and they were so popular that they could not be disposed of by ridicule simply. Another method had to be used.

To quote from Lipsius again: "Catholic bishops and teachers knew not how better to stem this flood of Gnostic writings and their influence among the faithful, than by boldly adopting the most popular narratives from the heretical books, and,

THE HYMN OF JESUS.

after carefully eliminating the poison of false doctrine, replacing them in this purified form in the hands of the public."

Fortunately for some of us, this " purification " has not been complete, and some of the " poison of false doctrine " has thus been preserved. Among other things of great beauty for which we are grateful, we especially thank a kindly providence for the preservation of the Hymn of Jesus.

The earliest collection of these Gnostic Acts is said to have been made by a certain Leucius, surnamed Charinus. There is a tradition, though of somewhat doubtful authenticity, that this Leucius was a disciple of John. If we accept it at all, this John must be taken for the writer of the Fourth Gospel, and not the John of the original Twelve.

It would be impossible here to enter into any discussion of the baffling Johannine problem ; those of our readers, however, who are interested in the manifest Gnostic implications with which this problem is involved as far as it relates to the Fourth Gospel, should read Kreyenbühl's exhaustive and instructive study *Das Evangelium der Wahrheit* (Berlin ; 1900, 1905). His " new solution of the Johannine question," which Kreyenbühl entitles " The Gospel of the Truth," boldly claims an immediate Gnostic origin for the Fourth Gospel; and this courageous pioneer of a new way even goes so far as to contend that the writer of what is indubitably the most spiritual of all the Gospels, was no other than Mænander, the teacher of Basilides. It is instructive to remark that this voluminous and important work has been passed over with complete silence in this country.

At any rate the Leucian Acts were early ; in the opinion of Zahn this collection was made at a time when the Gnostics were not yet considered heretical, that is to say prior to 150 A.D.—say 130 A.D.

Lipsius on the other hand places them in the second half of the second century, towards the end, and so does Hennecke.

This maximum of date they are compelled to concede, because Clement of Alexandria at the end of the second century quotes from the Gnostic *Acts of John* which indubitably formed part of the Leucian collection.

The controversy between Lipsius and Zahn was conditioned by the fact that they both agreed that the *Acts of John* quote from the Fourth Gospel. Zahn placed this Gospel earlier in date than Lipsius and was anxious to find in the Acts an early witness to that Gospel, indeed the earliest witness.

It has, however, been strongly contested by Corssen whether the Acts quote from the Gospel ; and as far as I can myself see from the passages adduced, there does not seem to be absolute evidence of any *direct* quotation. There is indubitably a close similarity of diction, as is so often the case in similar problems concerning nearly contemporary documents ; but the problem is more easily satisfied by considering the writers as belonging to the same circle, than by seeking to prove direct literary plagiarism.

However this may be, we are not to suppose that Leucius *invented* the Acts ; he collected and adapted and wrote up the material. If he had invented all of it, he would have been a genius of no mean order.

Leucius has a style of his own, and he also moved in a certain sweet atmosphere that is characteristic of the best in the Johannine tradition—the tradition of love, and intimacy, and simplicity ; very different, for instance, from the more formal Pauline atmosphere.

The *Acts of John* are indubitably Leucian, and judging by literary style so are the *Acts of Peter*. As to the rest of the *Acts* of the original Leucian collection, there is at present no certainty, and those assigned to Leucius by later writers must be put on one side as far as their present remains are concerned.

It has been surmised by James that as Luke (Loukas) wrote the Orthodox Acts,

THE HYMN OF JESUS.

the writer who wrote the Gnostic Acts called himself Leucius (Leukios) to suggest he was one and the same person ; but this I consider highly improbable. The Gnostics are in general inventors and not copyists.

It is also of interest to note that Zahn considers that the account of the genesis of the Fourth Gospel given by the writer of the Muratorian Fragment (c. 170 A.D.) was taken from the Leucian Acts. This Gospel is there said to have been written by a certain John, who was " of the Disciples." His " fellow-disciples and bishops " had apparently urged him to write a Gospel, but John hesitated to accept the responsibility, and proposed that they should all fast together for three days, and tell one another if anything was revealed to them. On the same night it is revealed to Andrew, who is " of the Apostles," that while all revised John should write down all things in his own name.

If this information is taken from the Leucian Acts, it follows of course that their writer was acquainted with the Fourth Gospel. If we take this as certain —though from the adduced parallel phrases alone I cannot myself be quite certain—then the question arises how could Leucius have put into the mouth of John doctrines which are opposed to the teaching of the Gospel ? To this question James gives the following answer :

" His notion is that St. John wrote for the multitude certain comparatively plain and easy episodes in the life of the Lord : but that to the inner circle of the faithful his teaching was widely different. In the Gospel and Epistles we have his exoteric teaching : in the Acts his esoteric."

This of course exactly reverses the relation which Corssen supposes to have existed between the Acts and Gospel ; namely that the author of the Acts did not know the Gospel at all.

It is of course the general Gnostic position that all true scripture had an under-meaning. The gospel-narratives were written for the people, but at the same time in such a fashion as to set forth allegorically the mysteries.

If, then, any propaganda of these hidden mysteries was to be attempted in a less veiled form, it follows that a more spiritual standpoint had to be insisted on ; and the popular narrative which was generally taken in a physical and material sense, was replaced by a more plastic and suggestive setting and exposition.

But—we may ask, at any rate in the case of the Fourth Gospel—was it the Gospel-narrative that was prior in date, and the Gnostic re-writing of Gospel-incidents subsequent ; or was it that the Gnostic ideas existed prior to the writing of the Gospel, and the matter incorporated into the Gnostic Acts derived directly from the same body of ideas that inspired the Gospel ?

As it is now proved beyond all question that the Gnosis was pre-Christian, and that in what is generally called Gnosticism we are dealing with a Christianized Gnosis which demonstrably existed in the time of Paul, and which Paul found already existing in the Churches, we must conclude that there is nothing inherently improbable in the latter alternative.

Moreover, the Gnosticism of the *Acts of John* is general and simple and cannot be assigned to this or that particular school of the Christian Gnosis.

The marvellous and beautiful Hymn, which is the subject of this small volume, is found in what are without doubt the Leucian *Acts of John*. That, however, Leucius himself composed the Hymn is by no means to be taken for granted. Leucius was a collector and redactor—he used sources ; and I have myself no doubt that the Hymn existed in Gnostic circles prior to the composition of the *Acts*—indeed, that it was a most precious document.

The first external testimony to our Hymn is found in its use by the Priscillianists, in Spain, in the last third of

1 3 6

THE HYMN OF JESUS.

the fourth century. The great movement known under the name of Priscillianism was a powerful revival of Gnosticism and Oriental mysticism and theosophy which poured over the Peninsula.

The views of the Priscillianists on scripture were those of the rest of the Gnostics in general ; their canon was catholic in the widest meaning of the term. Just as the Jewish scriptures were an imperfect revelation as compared with the general Christian books, so were the popular scriptures of Christianity imperfect in comparison with the revelations of the Gnosis.

As the Old Covenant books were considered to be replete with types and figures, images and shadows of the Gospel-teaching, so were the books of the New Testament, in their turn, held to be figurative and symbolical of the inner teachings of the Gnosis. The former were intended for those of Faith, the latter for those in Gnosis.

Against this view Augustine and Jerome waged remorseless war ; for the country was flooded with an immense number of Gnostic documents. The Priscillianists were persecuted and martyred and the main care of the orthodox bishops was to seize their books and destroy them.

Ceretius, one of the bishops presumably, had sent Augustine some of the books of these Gnostics ; he himself seems to have been inclined to approve them. Augustine, in his answer, picks out for detailed criticism one document only—our Hymn. Concerning this he writes :

" As for the Hymn which they say is that of our Lord Jesus Christ, and which has so greatly aroused your veneration, it is usually found in apocryphal writings, not peculiar to the Priscillianists but used by other heretics."

Augustine adds a quotation, from the introduction of the Gnostic M.S. of the Hymn, which runs :

" The Hymn of the Lord which He sang in secret to the holy Apostles, His disciples, for it is said in the Gospel : ' And after singing a hymn He ascended the mount.' This Hymn is not put in the canon, because of those who think according to themselves, and not according to the Spirit and Truth of God, and that it is written : ' It is good to hide the sacrament of the King ; but it is honourable to reveal the works of God.' "

The Gospel referred to cannot be either Matthew (xxvi. 31) or Mark (xiv. 26), both of which read : " And after singing a hymn *they went out* to the Mount of Olives." The second quotation I am unable to trace.

An important point which will concern us later on is that Ceretius found the Hymn by itself and not in its context in the *Acts* ; it was in all probability extracted for liturgical purposes.

It is, moreover, evident from what Augustine writes in the first passage we have quoted that the Hymn was well-known in Gnostic circles.

It would also seem as though Augustine, who wrote in Latin, was dealing with a Latin translation, rather than that he translated the quotation himself in his answer to Ceretius.

Part only of the Greek text of this famous Hymn was known prior to 1899, when James published a hitherto unknown and very important fragment of the *Acts of John*, found in a fourteenth century M.S., in the Vienna Imperial Library. This contained what seems to be the full text of our Hymn, though, unfortunately, copied by a sometimes very careless scribe. Nearly the whole of this lengthy fragment consists of a monologue put into the mouth of John, and in it we have preserved to us a very remarkable tradition of the Gnostic side of the life of the Master ; or, if it be preferred, of incidents in the "occult" life of Jesus.

The whole setting of the christology is what is called " docetic." Our fragment

THE HYMN OF JESUS.

is thus a most valuable addition to our knowledge of Docetism, and at last gives us a satisfactory reason why this view was held so widely by the Gnostics. Indeed it is now the most important source we possess, and puts the whole question on a different footing. In future our fragment must always be taken first as the *locus classicus* in any discussion of the question.

Docetism was a theory which found its confirmation in narratives and legends of certain psychic or spiritual powers ascribed to the "perfect man."

The christological and soteriological theories of the Gnostic philosophers were not, as many would have us believe, invented altogether *à priori*; they rested, I hold, on the basis of a veritable historical fact, which has for the most part been obscured out of all recognition by the flood of physical objective historicizing narratives of the origins.

After His death, I believe, as many a Gnostic tradition claims, the Christ did return and teach His disciples and true lovers in the inner circles, and this fact which was made known to their consciousness in many marvellous ways, was to a large extent the origin of the protean Gnostic tradition of an inner instruction.

He returned in the only way He could return in *this way* of return—namely, in a subtle or "spiritual" mode or "body." This "body" could be made visible at will, could even be made sensible to touch, but was, compared with the normally objective physical body, an "illusory" body—hence the term "docetic."

But just as the external tradition of those who are considered the original Jewish Christians, the Ebionīm (or Poor), was gradually transmuted and sublimated, so that it, finally, exalted Jesus from the status of a simple prophet in which it originally regarded him, unto the full Power and Glory of Godhead itself; so the internal tradition extended the doubtlessly simple original docetic notion to every department of the huge

soteriological structure raised by Gnostic genius.

The Leucian *Acts of John* pertain to the latter stream of tendencies, and "John" is the personification, so to say, of one of the lines of tradition of that protean Docetism, which had its origin in one of the best-known and most important facts of the spiritual life, or of "occult" experience, and of those marvellous teachings of initiation which became subsequently historicized or woven into historic settings, and which "John" in our fragment, sums up in the words:

"I held firmly this one thing in myself, that the Lord contrived all things symbolically and by a dispensation towards men, for their conversion and salvation."

That is to say, that all truly inspired narratives of the Doings and Sayings of the Christ are typical; or again, that He who is Christ, in all He does and says, as Christ, acts with the Cosmic Order. This is His "economy" and "ministry"— the doing of His "Father's business."

We will now turn to the Hymn itself, and first give a version of it from Bonnet's text. In the newly-recovered fragment it is introduced as follows:

"Now before He was taken by the lawless Jews—by them who are under the law of the lawless Serpent—He gathered us together and said:

" 'Before I am delivered over unto them we will hymn the Father, and so go forth to what lieth before [us].'

"Then bidding us make as it were a ring, by holding each others' hands, with Him in the midst, He said:

" 'Answer "Amen" to Me.'

"Then He began to hymn a hymn and say:

138

THE HYMN OF JESUS.

Another reading has :
I would be dissolved (or consumed for love) ; and I would dissolve.]

Amen !

THE HYMN.

Glory to Thee, Father !

(And we going round in a ring answered to Him :)

Amen !

Glory to Thee, Word (*Logos*) !

Amen !

Glory to Thee, Grace (*Charis*) !

Amen !

Glory to Thee, Spirit !
Glory to Thee, Holy One !
Glory to Thy Glory !

Amen !

We praise Thee, O Father ;
We give Thanks to Thee, O Light ;
In Whom Darkness dwells not !

Amen !

(For what we give thanks to the Logos).

[Or, if we adopt the " emended " text :
For what we give thanks, I say :]

I would be saved ; and I would save.

Amen !

I would be loosed ; and I would loose.

Amen !

I would be wounded ; and I would wound.

[Or, I would be pierced ; and I would pierce.

I would be begotten ; and I would beget.

Amen !

I would eat ; and I would be eaten.

Amen !

I would hear ; and I would be heard.

Amen !

[I would understand ; and] I would be understood ;   being all Understanding (*Nous*).

[The first clause I have supplied ; the last is probably a gloss.]

I would be washed ; and I would wash.

Amen !

(Grace leadeth the dance.)

I would pipe ; dance ye all.

Amen !

I would play a dirge ; lament ye all.

Amen !

The one Eight (Ogdoad) sounds (or plays) with us.

Amen !

The Twelfth Number above leadeth the dance.

Amen !

THE HYMN OF JESUS.

All whose nature is to dance [doth dance].

Amen !

Who danceth not, knows not what is being done.

Amen !

I would flee ; and I would stay.

Amen !

I would be adorned ; and I would adorn.

[The clauses are reversed in the text.]

Amen !

I would be at-oned ; and I would at-one.

Amen !

I have no dwelling ; and I have dwellings.

Amen !

I have no place ; and I have places.

Amen !

I have no temple ; and I have temples.

Amen !

I am a lamp to thee who seest Me.

Amen !

I am a mirror to thee who understandest Me.

Amen !

I am a door to thee who knockest at Me.

Amen !

I am a way to thee a wayfarer.

Amen !

Now answer to My dancing !

See thyself in Me who speak ;
And seeing what I do,
Keep silence on My Mysteries.

Understand, by dancing, what I do ;
For thine is the Passion of Man
That I am to suffer.

Thou couldst not at all be conscious
Of what thou dost suffer,
Were I not sent as thy Word by the Father.
[The last clause may be emended :
I am thy Word ; I was sent by the Father.]

Seeing what I suffer,
Thou sawest Me as suffering ;
And seeing, thou didst not stand,
But wast moved wholly,
Moved to be wise.

Thou hast Me for a couch ; rest thou upon Me.

Who I am thou shalt know when I depart.
What now I am seen to be, that I am not.
[But what I am] thou shalt see when thou comest.

If thou hadst known how to suffer,
Thou wouldst have power not to suffer.
Know [then] how to suffer, and thou hast power not to suffer.

That which thou knowest not, I Myself will teach thee.

I am thy God, not the Betrayer's.

1 4 0

THE HYMN OF JESUS.

I would be kept in time with holy souls.

In Me know thou the Word of Wisdom.

Say thou to Me again :

Glory to Thee, Father !
Glory to Thee, Word !
Glory to Thee, Holy Spirit !

But as for Me, if thou wouldst know what I was :
In a word I am the Word who did play [or dance] all things, and was not shamed at all.
'Twas I who leaped [and danced].

But do thou understand all, and, understanding, say :

Glory to Thee, Father !

Amen !

(And having danced these things with us, Beloved, the Lord went forth. And we, as though beside ourselves, or wakened out of [deep] sleep, fled each our several ways.)

COMMENTS.

To me it seems almost certain, as I argued in the first edition of *Fragments of a Faith Forgotten*, in 1900, that this Hymn is no hymn, but a mystery-ritual, and perhaps the earliest Christian ritual of which we have any trace.

We have a number of such mystery-rituals in the Coptic Gnostic works—in the extract from the " Books of the Saviour " appended to the so-called *Pistis Sophia* document of the Askew Codex, and in the " Two Books of Ieou " of the Bruce Codex.

In a number of passages the Disciples are bidden to " surround " (that is, join hands round) the Master at certain praise-givings and invocations of the Father, who is addressed as : " Father of all Fatherhood, Boundless Light "—just as the Father is hymned as Light in the last three lines of our opening doxology.

The " Second Book of Ieou " ends with a long praise-giving, in the inner spaces ; for these highly mystical treatises deal with the instruction of the Disciples by the Master out of the body. This praise-giving begins as follows (Carl Schmidt, *Gnost. Schrift. . . . aus d. Codex Brucianus*—Leipzig, 1892—pp. 187 ff.) :

" And He spake unto them, the Twelve : Surround Me all of you !
And they all surrounded Him. He said unto them :
Answer to Me [Amen], and sing praise with Me ; and I will praise My Father for the Emanation of all Treasures.
And He began to sing a hymn, praising His Father, and saying :
I praise Thee . . .; for Thou hast drawn Thyself unto Thyself altogether in Truth, till Thou hast set free the space of this Little Idea [? the Cosmos]; yet hast Thou not withdrawn Thyself. For what

THE HYMN OF JESUS.

now is Thy Will, O Unapproachable God ?

Thereon He made His Disciples answer three times : Amen, Amen, Amen ! ''

As far as I can discover from the most recent works of reference, " Amen " is considered by scholars to be a pure Hebrew word. It is said to have been originally an adjective signifying " stability," " firmness," " certainty," which subsequently became an interjection, used first of all in conversation, and then restricted to the most solemn form of asseveration ; as, for instance, in oaths, and, in the temple ritual, in the responses of the congregation to the doxologies and solemn utterances of the priests and readers.

According to the Portuguese reading of the vowels it is pronounced Âmēn (the vowels as in Italian). The Greek transliteration is Amēn.

In *Revelation* (iii. 14), Christ is called the Amen : " These things saith the Amen, the faithful and true Witness."

We are told that in the great synagogue at Alexandria, at the conclusion of the reader's doxology, the attendant signalled with a flag for the congregation to respond Amen.

This use of this sacred utterance was taken over by the Christian churches ; so that we find Jerome writing : " Like unto celestial thunder the Amen re-echoes."

It is well known that Hebrew and Aramaic are exceedingly rich in loan-words from other languages. I have, however, never seen it yet suggested that Amen may be a loan-word. I would now, with all submission to Hebraist specialists, make this suggestion, for Plutarch in his treatise *On Isis and Osiris* writes (ix. 4) :

" Moreover, while the majority think that the proper name of Zeus with the Egyptians is Amoun (which we by a slight change call Ammōn), Manethō, the Sebennyte, considers it His hidden one, and

that His power of hiding is made plain by the very articulation of the sound.

" Hecatæus of Abdera, however, says that the Egyptians use this word to one another also when they call one to them, for that its sound has got the power of 'calling to.'

" Wherefore when they call to the First God—who they think is the same for every man—as unto the Unmanifest and Hidden, invoking Him to make Him manifest and plain to them, they say ' Amoun! ' "

Ammōn or Amoun is usually transliterated directly from the hieroglyphics as Amen. We thus learn that in Egypt Amen was a " word of power," indeed the chief " word of power " in general theurgic use.

We cannot suppose that Hecatæus, in his *History of Egypt*, intended us to understand that the Egyptians shouted it after one another in the street. It was rather used as a word of magic, for evoking the *Ka* of a person, or as the chiefest of all invocations to the Invisible Deity.

The exact parallel is to be found to-day in the use of the " Word of Glory " (the Praṇava), Oṁ or Auṁ, in India.

The sacred dancing was common to all great mystery-ceremonies. Here it will be sufficient to quote from what Philo of Alexandria, in the first quarter of our era, tells us, in his famous treatise *On the Contemplative Life*, about the sacred dances of the Therapeuts or " Servants of God." He writes :

" Then the president rising chants a hymn which has been made in God's honour, either a new one which he has composed, or an old one of the ancient poets.

" For they have left behind them many metres and tunes in trimetric epics, processional hymns, libation-odes, altar-

142

THE HYMN OF JESUS.

chants, stationary choruses, and dance-songs, all admirably measured off in diversified strains.

"And after him the others also, in bands, in proper order, take up the chanting, while the rest listen in deep silence, except when they have to join in the burden and refrains ; for they all, both men and women, join in. . . .

"After the banquet they keep the holy all-night festival. And this is how it is kept :

"They all stand up in a body ; and about the middle of the ceremony they first of all separate into two bands, men in one and women in the other. And a leader is chosen for each, the conductor whose reputation is greatest and the one most suitable for the post.

"They then chant hymns made in God's honour, in many metres and melodies ; sometimes singing in chorus, sometimes one band beating time to the answering chant of the other, now dancing to its music, now inspiring it, at one time in processional hymns, at another in standing songs, turning and returning in the dance.

"Then when each band has feasted [that is, has sung and danced] apart by itself, drinking of God-pleasing nectar, just as in the Bacchic rites men drink the wine unmixed, they join together, and one chorus is formed of the two bands. . .

"So the chorus of men and women Therapeuts . . . , by means of melodies in parts and harmony—the high notes of the women answering to the deep tones of the men—produces a harmonious and most musical symphony. The ideas are of the most beautiful, the expressions of the most beautiful, and the dancers reverent ; while the goal of the ideas, expressions, and dancers is piety.

"Thus drunken unto morning's light with this fair drunkenness, with no head-heaviness or drowsiness, but with eyes and body fresher even than when they came to the banquet, they take their stand at dawn, when, catching sight of the rising sun, they raise their hands to heaven, praying for Sunlight and Truth, and keenness of Spiritual Vision."

And now we will turn to the text of our Hymn, which pertains to a still higher mystery, first of all dealing with the introductory words of the writer of the *Acts*.

The "lawless Jews" refers to those who are "under the law of the lawless Serpent" ; that is to say, those who are under the sway of Generation as contrasted with those who are under the law of Regeneration, of carnal birth as opposed to spiritual birth ; or again, of the Lesser as contrasted with the Greater Mysteries.

As the pre-Christian Greek redactor of the Naassene Document phrases it (*T.G.H.*, i. 162) :

"For He [the Great Man, the Logos, the Serpent of Wisdom] is Ocean—' birth-causing of gods and birth-causing of men ' —flowing and ebbing for ever, now up and now down."

And on this the early Jewish commentator remarks :

"When Ocean flows down, it is the birth-causing of men ; and when He flows up, . . . it is the birth-causing of gods."

And further on he adds :

"This is the Great Jordan, which flowing downwards and preventing the Sons of Israel from going forth out of Egypt, or from the Intercourse Below, was turned back by Jesus [LXX. for Joshua] and made to flow upwards."

This one and the same Serpent was thus either the Agathodaimōn (or Good Spirit) or the Kakodaimōn (or Evil Spirit), according to the will of man. The re-generated or perfected man, the man of

143

THE HYMN OF JESUS.

repentance, he who has turned Homewards, or has his "face" set Above, whose will is being at-oned with the Divine Will, turns the waters of Ocean upwards, and thus gives birth to himself as a god.

The doxology of our Hymn is triadic— Father, Son, Mother.

Charis, Grace or Love, is Wisdom, or God's Good-Will, the Holy Spirit, or Great Breath; that is, the Power and Spouse of Deity.

The order of the triple praise-giving is then reversed: Mother, Son, Father ; for Glory is the Great Presence, the Father.

And finally there is a trinity in unity, Praise being given to the Father as Light ; the same as the oft-recurring invocation in the Coptic Gnostic works : " Father of all Fatherhood, Boundless Light ! "

The doxology being ended, we come to a striking series of double clauses or antitheses. I at once submit that these were not originally intended to be uttered by one and the same person. On the contrary they are evidently amœbæan ; that is, answering as in a dialogue. Nor were they addressed to the Disciples ; there was some single person for whom the whole was intended, and to whom much of it is addressed.

If, then, we have before us not a hymn, but the remains of a mystery-ritual, there must have been two people in the circle. One of them was the Master, the Initiator. Who was the other ? Manifestly, the one to be initiated.

Now the ultimate end of all Gnosis was the at-one-ment or union of the little man with the Great Man, of the human soul with the Divine Soul.

In the great Wisdom-myth, the human soul was regarded as the " lost sheep," the erring and suffering Sophia fallen into generation, from which she was saved by the Christ, her true Lord and Spouse.

On the side of the Great Descent we have the most wonderful attempts made by the Gnostics to pierce the veil of the mysteries of cosmogony—to catch some glimpse of how the Cosmos came into existence, and was fashioned by the creative power of the Logos, the Supernal Christ. This was called the " enformation according to substance "—the " substance " being the Sophia or Wisdom Herself as viewed in Her self-isolation from the Plērōma or Fullness of Divine Being, the Transcendent Presence.

On the way of the Great Ascent or Return, the Gnosis attempted to raise the veil of the mysteries of soteriology, or of the rescue of the separated human soul, and its restoration to the Bosom of the Divine. This was called the " enformation according to gnosis "—that is, Self-consciousness.

The duologue is therefore carried on by those who are acting out the mystery of the Sophia and the Christ ; though we should never forget that they are in reality or essentially one and the same Person, the lower and higher self in the Presence of the Great Self.

The twelve disciples are the representatives of the powers of the Master, sent forth (apostles) into the outer worlds, corresponding with the Great Twelve of the Presence, the Twelve Above ; and they dance to the dancing or cosmic motions of the Twelve, even as the candidate, or neophyte, the Sophia below, dances to the cosmic motion of the Charis or Grace or Sophia Above.

And if this rite be duly consummated, the Presence that enwraps the doers of the mystery is Divine. The Presence is that of the Father Himself, who has no human form, but is as it were a " Heart," or " Head," a " Face," a Shekinah or Glory. How the seers of the Gnosis conceived this marvel of the Godhead may perhaps be seized dimly in the following passages from the " Untitled Apocalypse " of the Bruce Codex (F.F.F., p. 548) :

" The Outline of His Face is beyond all possibility of knowing in the Outer Worlds—those Worlds that ever seek His

THE HYMN OF JESUS.

Face, desiring to know it ; for His Word has gone forth into them, and they long to see Him.

" The Light of His Eyes penetrates the Spaces of the Outer Plērōma ; and the Word that comes forth from His Mouth penetrates the Above and the Below.

" The Hair of His Head is the number of the Hidden Worlds, and the Outline of His Face is the type of the Æons [*i.e.*, Perfect Spheres and Eternities].

" The Hairs of His Face are the number of the Outer Worlds, and the Outspreading of His Hands is the manifestation of the Cross. . . .

" The Source of the Cross is the Man [Logos] whom no man can comprehend.

" He is the Father ; He is the Source from which the Silence [the Mother of the Æons] wells."

And as to the consummation of at-one-ment and the state of him who makes joyful surrender of himself unto the Powers, " and thus becoming Powers he is in God," as Pœmandrēs teaches, some intuition may be gleaned from the same document which tells of the Host of Powers, " having wreaths (or crowns) on their heads "—that is Æons or Christs or Masters crowned with their Twelve Powers, and all the other orderings of spiritual energies (*F.F.F.*, p. 556) :

" Their Crowns send forth Rays. The Brilliancy of Their Bodies is as the Life of the Space into which They are come.

" The Word (Logos) that comes out of Their Mouth is Eternal Life ; and the Light that comes forth from Their Eyes is Rest for Them.

" The Movement of Their Hands is Their Flight to the Space out of which They are come ; and Their Gazing on Their own Faces is Gnosis of Themselves.

" The Going to Themselves is a repeated Return ; and the Stretching forth of Their Hands establishes Them.

" The Hearing of Their Ears is the Perception in Their Heart ; and the Union of Their Limbs is the Ingathering of Israel.

" Their Holding to one another is Their Fortification in the Logos."

All this is doubtless " foolishness " to many but it is Light and Life and Wisdom for some few, who would strive towards becoming the Many in One, and One in Many.

But to the somewhat lesser mysteries of our ritual. All the terms must, I think, be interpreted as mystery-words ; they contained for the Gnostics a wealth of meaning, which differed for each according to his understanding and experience. If, then, I venture on any suggestions of meaning, it should be understood that they are but tentative and ephemeral, and as it were only rough notes in pencil in the margin that may be rubbed out and emended by every one according to his knowledge and preference.

" I would be saved."

The human soul is " wandering in the labyrinth of ills," as the Naassene Hymn has it (*T.G.H.*, i. 191) ; is being swirled about by the " fierce flood " of Ignorance as the Preacher, in one of the Trismegistic sermons, phrases it (*T.G.H.*, ii. 120). The soul is being swirled about in the Ocean of Genesis, in the Spheres of Fate.

She prays for safety, for that state of stability which is attained when the worlds of swirl in the Magna Vorago, or Great Whirlpool, to use a term of the Orphic tradition, are transcended, by means of at-one-ment with the Great Stability, the Logos—" He who stands, has stood and will stand," as the Simonian *Great Announcement* calls Him.

In its beginnings this safety expresses neither motion nor stability, but a ceasing from agitation ; the mind or anxiety is no longer within the movement, the Procession of Fate.

The tempest-tossed self cries out to be drawn apart from the swirl ; while the other self that is not in the swirl would like to enter.

1 4 5

THE HYMN OF JESUS.

The self within, or subject to, the "downward" elements has to unite with the self of the "upward" elements in order to be saved from the swirling of the passions; while the "higher" self has to be drawn into the "lower," so to say, and unite with it, in order to be "saved" from the incapacity of self-expression.

"I would be loosed."

That is, loosed from the bonds of Fate and Genesis. In some of the rites the candidate was bound with a rope. In Egypt the rope symbolized a serpent, the Typhonic "loud-breathing serpent" of the passions, as the "Hymn of the Soul" of Bardaisan calls it (*F.F.F.*, p. 477).

"I would be wounded."

Or "I would be pierced." This suggests the entrance of the ray of the higher self into the heart whereby the "knot in the heart," as the Upaniṣhads phrase it, may be unloosed, or dissolved, or in order that the lower self may receive the divine radiance of the higher. This interpretation is borne out by the alternative reading from a Latin translation, which may have originated in a gloss by one who knew the mystery, for he writes: "I would be dissolved"; that is, "consumed by love."

And so we continue with the mysteries of this truly "Sacred Marriage," or "Spiritual Union," as it was called.

"I would be begotten."

This is the Mystery of the Immaculate Conception, or Self-birth. "I would be begotten" as a Christ, the New Man, or True Man, who is in verity the Alone-begotten—that is, Begotten-from-Himself-alone, or Self-begotten.

"I would eat."

By "eating," food and eater become one. The Logos is called the "Bread of Life"; that is, the Supersubstantial Bread, one of the Elements of the Eucharist. The soul desires to "eat" the Life in everything; this expresses how the soul must become everything before it can enjoy cosmic consciousness, and be nourished by the Life in all.

So is it that men can become part of the Cosmos through right action. But to reach this consummation we must no longer long to live and act our little life, but rather to be, if one may so phrase it, in our turn "eaten"; that is to say, to have our own self-will eaten out of us. And then our fate or life or activity becomes part of the Great Records, and the man becomes a Living Oracle or Drama, a Christ. All Life then becomes a happening with meaning; but this can never be until the man surrenders his self-will and becomes one with the Great Will.

This "eating" signifies a very intimate kind of union, in which the life of a man becomes part of a Great Life.

"I would hear."

It is to be remarked that there is no "I would see." If we can legitimately lay any stress on this, it is presumably because the candidate is already "seeing"; he has already reached the "epopt" stage, and therefore this "hearing" is beyond the probationary stage of "hearing" or of the "mystēs."

Hearing is much more cosmic or "greater" than seeing, as we learn later on from our fragment, in the Vision of the Cross, where John "sees the Lord Himself above the Cross, not having any shape, but only a voice."

In such hearing the hearer draws nigh unto the Root-sound, or Breath (Ātman), which creates all that it is possible to see. To see there must be form, even if the form is only an idea.

Again, hearing may be said to be the verb of action when power is being conveyed to a person; while seeing is the verb of action of that person after receiving the power.

"I would understand."

This recalls the idea of "standing,"

14 6

THE HYMN OF JESUS.

"stability." Plato attributes this understanding to the Sphere of Sameness (the Eighth), in this, I believe, handing on an echo from Egypt. It is by means of this stability of the true mind that consciousness is enabled to link on the happenings in the whirling spheres, or whorls, of Fate to the Great Things or Things-that-are, and so perceive greater soul-records in phenomena. The last clause is evidently a gloss, but by a knowing scribe. The *Logos* is the *true* Understanding or Mind (*Nous*).

"I would be washed."
That is, I would be baptized, or immersed wholly in the Ocean of Living Water, the Great Oneness. It may mean simply "I would be purified." But the full rite of baptism was immersion and not sprinkling; as Thrice-greatest Hermes says in the sermon "The Cup," or "The Monad" (*T.G.H.*, ii. 86):

"He filled a Mighty Cup (Kratēr) with it (Mind), and sent it down, joining a Herald to it, to whom He gave command to make this proclamation to the hearts of men :

"'Baptize thyself with this Cup's baptism, what heart can do so, thou who hast faith thou canst ascend to Him Who hath sent down the Cup, thou who dost know for what thou didst come into being !'

"As many then as understand the Herald's tidings and *dowsed themselves* in Mind, became partakers in the Gnosis ; and when they had 'received the Mind' they were made 'perfect men.'"

The Cup is perchance the Presence substantially.

"Grace leadeth the dance."
In the text this has the next sentence run on to it ; but I am myself inclined to think that it is a note or a rubric rather than an utterance of the Initiator. The ceremony changes. Hitherto there had been the circle-dance, the "going round in a ring," which enclosed the mystery-drama, and the chanting of the sacred word.

Contact is now mystically established with the Great Sphere, Charis or Sophia, the Counterpart or Spouse or Syzygy of the Supernal Christ, or of the Christ Above. She "leads the dance"; that is to say, the actors begin to act according to the great cosmic movements.

"I would pipe."
In the Naassene Document (*T.G.H.*, i. 183), we read :

"The Phrygians also say that that which is generated from Him is Syriktēs."

Syriktēs is the Piper, properly the player on the syrinx, or seven-reeded Pan-pipe, whereby the music of the spheres is created.

And on this the early Jewish commentator remarks :

"For that which is generated is Spirit in harmony."

That is to say, Spirit, or Sophia the Holy Breath, is harmony ; and the Harmony was the name of the Seven Spheres encircled by the Eighth. Curiously enough, later on in our fragment the Logos is called "Wisdom in harmony."

The Greek word for "dance" in the sentence "dance ye all" is different from that in the phrase "leadeth the dance." It reminds us of the "orchēstra" in the Greek theatre.

The Greek drama, I hold, arose from the Mysteries. The general view, however, is that it "sprang from the choral dances round the altar of Dionysus," and so the architectural form of the Greek theatre "was developed from the circular dancing place," the *orchēstra*.

The dance is to represent the dance of

THE HYMN OF JESUS.

the world-mystery, and therefore of the man-mystery—of joy and sorrow, of rejoicing and beating the breast.

It is hardly necessary here to remind the reader of the Gospel-saying taken by the first (*Matth.*, xi. 17) and third (*Lk.*, vii. 27) Evangelist from a common source :

"We have piped unto you, and ye have not danced ;
"We have played a dirge unto you, and ye have not lamented."

Is it possible that there was an inner tradition of a scripture in which this Saying stood in the first person singular ? I think I have made out a presumption in my analysis of the Naassene Document (*T.H.G.*, i. 195) that the Christian commentator, in his parallels with the Fourth Gospel, legitimately opens up for us the question whether or no he was in touch with " sources " of that " Johannine " document.

In any case, I would suggest that for the Gnostic there was an under-meaning, and that it is here in our Hymn expressed for us though still mystically hidden.

The higher quaternion, or tetrad, as the Gnostic Marcus would have phrased it, of joy is to blend with the lower tetrad of sorrow ; and both together are to form an octave, whereby the man is raised from his littleness into the Greatness ; that is to say, he can now respond to cosmic music.

Therefore what was apparently originally a rubric (" The one Eight " etc.), has been put by an unknowing scribe into the mouth of the Initiator, and an Amen added.

The Ogdoad or Eight (in music the full Octave), " sounds with us " ; that is, we are now beginning to dance to the Music of the Spheres.

And this being so, the sense of the initiated soul may be said to become cosmic, for it begins to vibrate with, or answer back to, or become in sympathy with, the ordered motions of the Greatness ; and therefore the Higher Twelve, the Powers that transcend the separated soul, and which crown or surround the Great Sphere, now lead the dance.

Or, to speculate more daringly ; the indications seem to denote a belief that at this stage in the rite there was present the Presence of Masterhood ; and this would mean for the aspirant—as is so nobly set forth in the Trismegistic " Secret Sermon on the Mount," which might very well be called " The Initiation of Tat "—that he passes out of himself to greater things.

And so his " twelve disciples," as it were, begin to dance above him or outside him ; for the real disciples or apostles of a new-born Christ are not the things he has been taught on earth as man, but powers raying forth from the true Person into still greater regions.

Apostles who go forth into the world of men are but reflections of Great Powers who now go forth from the true Person and link him on to the Great Cosmos.

It is not easy to conjecture the meaning of the phrase " all whose nature is to dance doth dance," for the text is so faulty that we cannot be certain of a correct version. If, however, this be the right rendering, then I would suggest that the " all " is the cosmic order ; and that now all is made ready, and spiritual communion has been established between the church, or circle below, and the Church Above, who again is the Supernal Sophia.

" Who danceth not, knows not what is being done."

The soul must dance, or be active in a corresponding way, with the Great Dance, in order to know, or attain true Gnosis. Knowledge of the Great World can only be attained when the man has abandoned his self-will and acts in harmony with the Great Happenings.

148

THE HYMN OF JESUS.

This reminds us of the Saying in the Fourth Gospel (vii. 17) : "If a man will to do His Will, he shall know of the Doctrine" ; and again (ix. 31) : "If a man be a worshipper of God and do His Will, He will hear him." And the Will of God is His Divine Spouse, the Sophia or Wisdom, by Whom and in Whom He has made the worlds.

"I would flee."
It may be that here the new-born is in fear ; the new motions of the Great Passion are too great for him. Or, again, it may signify the necessity of balance, or equilibrium ; the soul feels itself swept away into the infinitudes, and is held back by the greater power of the Master—the that in him which alone is stable ; these two are then the centrifugal and centripetal powers.

"I would be adorned."
The original Greek term suggests the idea of being rightly "ordered" (*kosmein*). It may also mean "clothed in fit garments" ; that is, the soul prays that his little cosmos, which has previously been awry or out of order, may be made like unto the Great Order, and so he may be clad in "glories" or "robes of glory" or "power" like unto the Great Glories of the Heavenly Spheres.

"I would be at-oned."
We now approach the mystery of union, when the soul abandons with joy its separateness, and frees itself from the limitations of its "possessions"—of that which is "mine" as apart from the rest.

And so we have the triple declaration as to the loss of "dwelling," "place" and "temple" (the very "shrine" of the soul), and the assurance of the gain of all "dwellings," "places" and "temples." And in illustration of this sublime idea we may yet again quote from the "Untitled Apocalypse" of the Bruce Codex (*F.F.F.*, p. 554) :

" 'Holy, Holy, Holy is He, the [here come the seven vowels each three times repeated]'
"That is to say :
" 'Thou art the Living One among the living.
" 'Thou art the Holy One among the holy.
" 'Thou art Being among beings.
" 'Thou art Father among fathers.
" 'Thou art God among gods.
" 'Thou art Lord among lords.
" 'Thou art Space among spaces.'
"Thus too do they praise Him :
" 'Thou art the House ;
" 'And Thou art the Dweller in the House.'
"And yet again do they praise the Son hidden in Him :
" 'Thou art ; Thou art the Alone-begotten—Light, Life and Grace.' "

"The Son of Man hath nowhere to lay His head" — for indeed He has all "places" in His possession.

Then follow the comfortable words that the Christ, the Logos, is the Lamp, the Mirror, the Door and the Way for the human soul ; the Divine Soul is all things for the beloved.

In the worlds of darkness and uncertainty Christ is the Lamp, whom we must follow, for He leads us along the Way.

For those who can perceive the Christ-essence in all, this Christ-essence is a Mirror reflecting the great truths of the higher worlds.

There is one means alone of passing through the Wall of Separation between the Higher and the Lower, and that is Christ the Mediator. He is the Door ; even as Thrice-greatest Hermes calls the Mind the "Inner Door" (*T.G.H.*, iii. 274). And Parmenides in his "Truthwards" refers to the same mystery when he describes the Gates, twixt Day and Night, or Light and Darkness.

For him who truly knocks at this Door,

149

that is who turns all his attention and power in this direction, the Great Wall or Limit will be no more, and he shall go in and out at will.

Again, Christ the Logos is the Way. He is our Path to God, both on the Light-side of things and on the Substance-side ; either as a Lamp, or that for which the pure mind looks, or a Way, that on which the feet walk. In either case the Christ is that which leads to God.

The ceremony again changes with the words : " Now answer to My dancing."

All now may be believed to be taking place within the Master-Presence. Union of substance has been attained, but not yet union of consciousness. Before that final mystery can be consummated, the know-ledge of the Passion of Man, that is of the Great Passion or perpetual experience of the Great Act, must be achieved.

The soul is to gaze upon the mystery as upon its own Passion. The perfected soul can gaze upon the mystery in peace ; as yet, however, the soul of the aspirant is not perfected in gnosis, but in substance only, so that it may feel the Great Passion in itself, and yet as apart from itself.

Hereupon in the lower rite, the mystery-drama, the Passion of Man, must have been shown. What it may have been is not easy to conjecture ; it must, however, have been something of a most distressing nature, for the neophyte is moved or shaken completely—that is to say, un-nerved. He had not the strength of perfect faith in the Power of the Master ; for, presumably, he saw that very Master dismembered before his eyes, or becoming many from one, or in some way done to death.

After the Passion-drama or Passion-vision comes the instruction ; for in such rites—such passions or experiences for the sake of knowing—there must be

the actual experience in feeling before there can be gnosis.

This knowledge is given by the Master Himself, the Logos in man : Wherefore it needs must be the lover should first behold the Beloved suffering.

And then follow the comfortable words : " I am a couch ; rest thou upon Me." For the Suffering Christ is but the trans-lation into manifestation in time and space of the Triumphant Eternal Christ, the Æon. It is here that that mystery of Docetism, of what the Vedānta calls Māyā, receives a philosophical meaning. This mystery is suggested in many a *logos ;* but here I will quote only from the Trismegistic sermon called " The Inner Door " (*T.G.H.*, iii. 275) :

" And being so minded and so ordering his life, he shall behold the Son of God becoming all things for holy souls, that he may draw her (the soul) forth from out the region of the Fate into the Incor-poreal.

" For having power in all, He becometh all things, whatsoever He will ; and in obedience to the Father's nod, through the whole Body doth He penetrate, and pouring forth His Light into the mind of every soul, He starts it back into the Blessed Region, where it was before it had become corporeal—following after Him, and led by Him into the Light."

" Who I am thou shalt know when I depart."

This and the two following sentences seem to suggest—that is, if we may venture to believe that there was true vision of an inner mystery accompanying the outer drama—some such idea as this.

The substantial nature of the Presence, the Body, so to speak, of atmosphere, which may have been seen—with some suggestion of an idea of human form as its " pillar " or " support," and at the same time of a sphere or completeness

THE HYMN OF JESUS.

holding it together—this, says the Master, is not my true Self. I am not this Mirror of the World, I am not this Word or Living Symbol which contains the whole world, and also stamps it with meaning and idea. What the nature of the real Christ is thou shalt know when thou comest, or becomest Him.

"If thou hadst known how to suffer."

The sentences so beginning are perhaps the most pregnant in meaning in the whole of this marvellous ritual. It seems in one sense (for there are infinite meanings) to signify : If the substance of your body had really known how to dance, and so been able to respond exactly to My Passion (that is, the manifestation in activity of real life and consciousness), then you would have had the power to have kept stable about the Mystic Centre, and not have been dragged back into your body of suffering, or in-harmony ; you would not have been dragged back onto the dramatic side of things and been swamped by the drama.

"That which thou knowest not, I Myself will teach thee."

That which the soul unaided cannot know, the Master will teach. That is to say, presumably: This Power or Presence is a link between your own "body" or atmosphere and the realities of Great Things.

As soon as the sphere-"body" (the psychic envelope of normal man is said to be an ellipse, egg-shaped, imperfect) is capable of dancing, the Power of the Master will stamp it with meaning. The little self cannot do this. The Power is not connected with little things. It comes from the greater worlds as a natural result of the perfect dancing of the substances of all man's "bodies."

"I am thy God, not the Betrayer's."

Taken in connection with the introductory words before our Hymn, this will probably suggest to most readers the thought of Judas. But the Gnostics moved in a wider circle of ideas.

The Betrayer is rather the lawless Serpent, the Kakodaimōn, that which hands the soul over to the bodies of death—a mystery that is not touched upon in our ritual.

"I would be kept in time with holy souls."

This sentence appears to me to be misplaced. One of its meanings seems to be that as the soul watches the Dance, it prays to be brought into harmony with "Holy Souls" ; that is to have its consciousness and form brought into such perfect relationship as to become one. Then the little soul would become a Great Soul or Master, a Perfect or Balanced Soul.

The concluding sentences are evidently drawn from two different traditions of the original text ; they are two separate endings copied down one after the other. It is thus to be conjectured that there were several variants of this ritual, and that it was, therefore, widely known and used in Gnostic circles.

It must, however, have been at first kept very secret, for later on in the text of our fragment we read the injunction of the Master to John :

"That Passion which I showed unto thee and unto the rest in the Dance, I will that it be called a mystery."

Can it be that in the original form, it was John, the Beloved himself, who was the candidate ?

It may have been so ; but even if so, "John" would not be understood by a Gnostic to be the name of one single historical character. There had been, there were, and there would be many Johns.

From the Twelve Three; and from the Three One.

151

THE HYMN OF JESUS.

For just as we find that there were Three—Peter, James and John—who were nearest the Lord in His Great Moments, so also do we find in the Johannine tradition that of these Three, it was John who was nearest to Him in His Great Acts.

Moreover, just as in the Trismegistic tradition we find that out of the Three— Ammon, Asclepius and Tat—it is Tat, the most spiritual of the disciples, who succeeds his " Father," Thrice-greatest Hermes, when He is taken to the Gods ; so also do we find in the Johannine tradition that it is John who succeeds Jesus when He ascends to the Father of all " Fathers."

" Father " was the technical name of the Master, or Initiator, and the Head of the community.

And so, in a codex of the Fourth Gospel, preserved in the archives of the Templars of St. John of Jerusalem in Paris—that is to say in all probability in a document that belonged to those who came into contact with the Johannine tradition in the East—we find (Thilo, *Cod. Apoc. N.T.*, p. 880) the following additions which are absent from the Textus Receptus.

To *John*, xvii. 26 :
" Amen, I say unto you, I am not of this world ; but John shall be your Father, till he shall go with Me into Paradise. And He anointed them with the Holy Spirit."

And to *John*, xix. 26-30 :
" He saith to His Mother : Weep not ; I go to My Father and to Eternal Life. Behold Thy Son. He will keep My place.
" Then saith He to the Disciple : Behold thy Mother !
" Then bowing His Head He breathed forth His Spirit."

But if it be willed that that which " I showed unto thee . . . in the Dance"

be " called a mystery," it must equally be willed that it be kept a mystery.

I therefore offer my surmises on the altar of the Outer Court, though hardly venturing to think they will be regarded as reasonable oblations to the Great Presence by many of the Many who serve there.

I would, however, venture to hope that I have at least established a strong presumption that the Hymn of Jesus is no hymn, but a very early Christian mystery-ritual, and perhaps the oldest Christian ritual of any kind preserved to us.

152

THE . . .
GNOSTIC
CRUCI- .
FIXION. .

THE GNOSTIC CRUCIFIXION

CONTENTS

TEXTS

Bonnet (M.), *Acta Apostolorum Apocrypha* (Leipzig, 1898).

James (M. R.), *Apocrypha Anecdota, T. & S.*, v. i. (Cambridge, 1897).

F. = *Fragments of a Faith Forgotten*, 2nd. ed. (London, 1906).

H. = *Thrice Greatest Hermes* (London, 1906).

THE GNOSTIC CRUCIFIXION.

THE GNOSTIC CRUCIFIXION.

PREFACE.

The Gnostic Mystery of the Crucifixion is most clearly set forth in the new-found fragments of *The Acts of John*, and follows immediately on the Sacred Dance and Ritual of Initiation which we endeavoured to elucidate in Vol. IV. of these little books, in treating of *The Hymn of Jesus*.

The reader is, therefore, referred to the " Preamble " of that volume for a short introduction concerning the nature of the Gnostic Acts in general and of the Leucian *Acts of John* in particular. I would, however, add a point of interest bearing on the date which was forgotten, though I have frequently remarked upon it when lecturing on the subject.

The strongest proof that we have in our fragment very early material is found in the text itself, when it relates the following simple form of the miracle of the loaves.

" Now if at any time He were invited by one of the Pharisees and went to the bidding, we used to go with Him. And before each was set a single loaf by the host ; and of them He Himself also received one. Then He would give thanks and divide His loaf among us ; and from this little each had enough, and our own loaves were saved whole, so that those who bade Him were amazed."

If the marvellous narratives of the feeding of the five thousand had been already in circulation, it is incredible that this simple story, which we may so easily believe, should have been invented. Of what use, when the minds of the hearers had been strung to the pitch of faith which had already accepted the feeding of the five thousand as an actual physical occurrence, would it have been

to invent comparatively so small a wonder ? On the other hand, it is easy to believe that from similar simple stories of the power of the Master, which were first of all circulated in the inner circles, the popular narratives of the multitude-feeding miracles could be developed. We, therefore, conclude, with every probability, that we have here an indication of material of very early date.

Nevertheless when we come to the Mystery of the Crucifixion as set forth in our fragment, we are not entitled to argue that the popular history was developed from it in a similar fashion. The problem it raises is of another order, and to it we will return when the reader has been put in possession of the narrative, as translated from Bonnet's text. John is supposed to be the narrator.

(The Arabic figures and the Roman figures in square brackets refer respectively to Bonnet's and James' texts. I have added the side figures for convenience of reference in the comments.)

THE VISION OF THE CROSS.

1. [97 (xii.)] And having danced these things with us, Beloved, the Lord went out. And we, as though beside ourselves, or wakened out of sleep, fled each our several ways.

2. I, however, though I saw the beginning of His passion could not stay to the end, but fled unto the Mount of Olives weeping over that which had befallen.

3. And when He was hung on the tree of the cross, at the sixth hour of the day darkness came over the whole earth.

    And my Lord stood in the midst of the Cave, and filled it with light, and said :

4. " John, to the multitude below, in Jerusalem, I am being crucified,

THE GNOSTIC CRUCIFIXION.

and pierced with spears and reeds, and vinegar and gall is being given Me to drink. To thee now I speak, and give ear to what I say. 'Twas I who put it in thy heart to ascend this Mount, that thou mightest hear what disciple should learn from Master, and man from God."

5. [98 (xiii.)] And having thus spoken, He showed me a Cross of Light set up, and round the Cross a vast multitude, and therein one form and a similar appearance, and in the Cross another multitude not having one form.

6. And I beheld the Lord Himself above the Cross. He had, however, no shape, but only as it were a voice—not, however, this voice to which we are accustomed, but one of its own kind and beneficent and truly of God, saying unto me :

7. "John, one there needs must be to hear those things, from Me ; for I long for one who will hear.

8. "This Cross of Light is called by Me for your sakes sometimes Word (Logos), sometimes Mind, sometimes Jesus, sometimes Christ, sometimes Door, sometimes Way, sometimes Bread, sometimes Seed, sometimes Resurrection, sometimes Son, some-times Father, sometimes Spirit, some-times Life, sometimes Truth, some-times Faith, sometimes Grace.

9. "Now those things [it is called] as towards men ; but as to what it is in truth, itself in its own meaning to itself, and declared unto Us, [it is] the defining (or delimitation) of all things, both the firm necessity of things fixed from things unstable, and the 'harmony' of Wisdom.

10. "And as it is Wisdom in 'harmony,' there are those on the Right and those on the Left—powers, authori-ties, principalities, and dæmons, energies, threats, powers of wrath, slanderings—and the Lower. Root from which hath come forth the things in genesis.

11. [99]. "This, then, is the Cross which by the Word (Logos) hath been the means of 'cross-beaming' all things—at the same time separating off the things that proceed from genesis and those below it [from those above], and also compacting them all into one.

12. "But this is not the cross of wood which thou shalt see when thou descendest hence ; nor am I he that is upon the cross—[I] whom now thou seest not, but only hearest a voice.

13. "I was held [to be] what I am not, not being what I was to many others ; nay, they will call Me something else, abject and not worthy of Me. As, then, the Place of Rest is neither seen nor spoken of, much more shall I, the Lord of it, be neither seen [nor spoken of].

14. [100 (xiv.)] "Now the multitude of one appearance round the Cross is the Lower Nature. And as to those whom thou seest in the Cross, if they have not also one form, [it is because] the whole Race (or every Limb) of Him who descended hath not yet been gathered together.

15. "But when the Upper Nature, yea, the Race that is coming unto Me, in obedience to My Voice, is taken up, then thou who now heark-enest to Me, shalt become it, and it shall no longer be what it is now, but above them as I am now.

16. "For so long as thou callest not thyself Mine, I am not what I am. But if thou hearkenest unto Me, hearing, thou, too, shalt be as I [am], and I shall be what I was, when thou [art] as I am with My-self ; for from this thou art.

17. "Pay no attention, then, to the many, and them that are without the mystery think little of ; for know that I am wholly with the Father and the Father with Me.

18. [101 (xv.)] "Nothing, then, of the

1 5 7

things which they will say of Me have I suffered; nay that Passion as well which I showed unto thee and the rest, by dancing [it], I will that it be called a mystery.

19. "What thou art, thou seest; this did I show unto thee. But what I am, this I alone know, [and] none else.

20. "What, then, is Mine suffer Me to keep; but what is thine see thou through Me. To see Me as I really am I said is not possible, but only what thou art able to recognise, as being kin [to Me] (or of the same Race).

21. "Thou hearest that I suffered; yet I did not suffer: that I suffered not; yet I did suffer: that I was pierced; yet was I not smitten: that I was hanged; yet I was not hanged: that blood flowed from me; yet it did not flow: and in a word the things they say about Me I had not, and the things they do not say those I suffered. Now what they are I will riddle for thee; for I know that thou wilt understand.

22. "Understand, therefore, in Me, the slaying of a Word (Logos), the piercing of a Word, the blood of a Word, the wounding of a Word, the hanging of a Word, the passion of a Word, the nailing (or putting together) of a Word, the death of a Word.

23. "And thus I speak separating off the man. First, then, understand the Word, then shalt thou understand the Lord, and in the third place [only] the man and what he suffered."

24. [102 (xvi.)] And having said these things to me, and others which I know not how to say as He Himself would have it, He was taken up, no one of the multitude beholding Him.

25. And when I descended I laughed at them all, when they told Me what they did concerning Him, firmly possessed in myself of this [truth] only, that the Lord contrived all things symbolically, and according to [His] dispensation for the conversion and salvation of man.

COMMENTS.

The translation is frequently a matter of difficulty, for the text has been copied in a most careless and unintelligent fashion, so that the ingenuity of the editors has often been taxed to the utmost and has not infrequently completely broken down. It is of course quite natural that orthodox scribes should blunder when transcribing Gnostic documents, owing to their ignorance of the subject and their strangeness to the ideas; but this particular copyist is at times quite barbarous, and as the subject is deeply mystical and deals with the unexpected, the reconstruction of the original reading is a matter of great difficulty. With a number of passages I am still unsatisfied, though I hope they are somewhat nearer the spirit of the

THE GNOSTIC CRUCIFIXION.

original than other reconstructions which have been attempted.

It is always a matter of difficulty for the rigidly objective mind to understand the point of view of the Gnostic scripture-writers. One thing, however, is certain : they lived in times when the rigid ortho-doxy of the canon was not yet established. They were in the closest touch with the living tradition of scripture-writing, and they knew the manner of it.

The probability is that paragraphs 1—3 are from the pen of the redactor or compiler of the *Acts*, and that the narra-tive, beginning with the words " And my Lord stood in the midst of the Cave," is incorporated from prior material—a mystic vision or apocalypse circulated in the inner circles.

The compiler knows the general Gospel-story, and seems prepared to admit its historical basis ; at the same time he knows well that the story circulated among the people is but the outer veil of the mystery, and so he hands on what we may well believe was but one of many visions of the mystic crucifixion.

The gentle contempt of those who had entered into the mystery, for those un-knowing ones who would fain limit the crucifixion to one brief historic event, is brought out strongly, and savours, though mildly, of the bitterness of the struggle between the two great forces of the inner and spiritualizing and the outer and materializing traditions.

1. The disciples flee after beholding the inner mystery of the Passion and At-one-ment as set forth in the initiating drama of the Mystic Dance which formed the subject of our fourth volume.

2. Yet even John the Beloved, in spite of this initiation, cannot yet bear the thought that his Master did actually suffer historically as a malefactor òn the physical cross. In his distress he flees unto the Mount of Olives, above Jerusalem.

But to the Gnostic the Mount of Olives was no physical hill, though it was a mount in the physical, and Jerusalem no physical city, though a city in the physical. The Mount, however it might be dis-tinguished locally, was the Height of Contemplation, and the bringing into activity of a certain inner consciousness; even as Jerusalem here was the Jerusalem below, the physical consciousness.

3. The sentence " when He was hung on the tree of the Cross" contains a great puzzle. The word for " tree " in the original is *batos* ; this may mean the " bush " or " tree " of the cross. But the Cross for the Gnostics was a living symbol. It was not only the cross of dead wood, or the dead trunk of a tree lopped of its branches—a symbol of Osiris in death ; it was also the Tree of Life, and was equated with the " Fiery Bush " out of which the Angel of God spake to Moses—that is the Tree of Fiery Life, in the Paradise of man's inner nature, whence the Word of God expresses itself to one who is worthy to hear. And this Tree of Life was also, as the Cross, the Tree of Knowledge of Good and Evil ; indeed, both are but one Tree, for the fruit of the Tree of Life is the knowledge of good and evil, the cross of the opposites.

But seeing that the word *batos* in Greek had also another meaning, the Gnostics, by their method of mystical word-play, based on the power of sound, brought this further meaning into use for the expansion of the idea. The difference of accentuation and of gender (though the reading of the Septuagint is masculine and not feminine as is usual with *batos* in the sense of bush or tree) presented no difficulty to the word-alchemy of these allegorists.

Hippolytus, in his *Refutation of all Heretics*, attempts to summarize a sys-tem of the Christianized Gnosis which is assigned to the Docetæ ; and Docetism is precisely the chief characteristic of our *Acts of John*, as we have already pointed out in Vol. IV. In this unsym-pathetic summary there is a passage

THE GNOSTIC CRUCIFIXION.

which throws some light on our puzzle. It would, of course, require a detailed analysis of our hæresiologist's "refutation" of the Docetic system to make the passage to which we refer (*op. cit.*, viii., 9) fully comprehensible; but as this would be too lengthy an undertaking for these short comments, we must content ourselves with a bald statement.

The pure spiritual emanations or ideas or intelligences of the Light descend into the lowest Darkness of matter. For the moulding of vehicles or bodies for them it is necessary to call in the aid of the God of Fire, the creative or rather formative Power, who is "Living Fire begotten of Light."

Hippolytus summarizes, doubtless imperfectly, from the Docetic document that lay before him, as follows : '

"Moses refers to this God as the Fiery God who spake from the *Batos*, that is to say, from the Dark Air ; for *Batos* is all the Air subjected to Darkness."

That is, presumably, the material Air, Air of the Darkness, as compared with the spiritual Air or Air of the Light. The Docetic writer, Hippolytus says, explained the use of the term as follows :

"Moses called it *Batos*, because, in their passing from Above, Below, all the Ideas of the Light [that is, the Light-sparks or spirits of men] used the Air as their means of passage (*batos*)."

In other words *Batos*, as Air, was the link between Light and Darkness, which Darkness was regarded as essentially a flowing or Watery chaos. The Batos was the Way Down and the Way Up of souls.

We are not, however, to suppose that the origin of this idea was the text of *Exodus*. By no means ; the idea came first, indeed was fundamental with the Gnosis ; the mystic exegesis of the "burning bush" passage was an exercise in ingenuity. For the Gnosis, the that which at once separated and united the Light and the Darkness was the Cross.

The Angel of God speaking to Moses out of the Fiery Batos was for the Christian Gnostics one of the most striking apocalypses of ancient Jewish scripture ; and it was primarily one of the chief functions of the Gnosis to throw light on the under-meaning. This the Docetic exegete does in his own fashion, using the reading of the Greek Targum or Translation of the Seventy, in this wise : " *Batos* ? *Batos* does not mean 'bush' really, but 'medium of transmission,' " It is by means of this that the Word of God comes unto us—namely, by the mystery of the uniter-separator in one, which was called by many names.

For instance, in setting forth the Sophia-mythus, or Wisdom-story, or mystery of cosmogenesis, of the Valentinian school, Hippolytus (*op. cit.*, vi. 3), treats of the Cross as the final mystery of all. With original documents before him, he writes :

"Now it is called Boundary, because it bounds off the Deficiency from the Fullness [so as to make it] exterior to it ; it is called Partaker because it partakes of the Deficiency as well ; and it is called Cross (or Stock) because it hath been fixed immovably and unchangeably, so that nothing of the Deficiency should be able to approach the eternities within the Fullness."

Here it is useless to tie oneself to the physical symbol of a cross. The Stauros (Cross) in its true self is a living idea, a reality or root-principle. It is the principle of separation and limit, dividing entity from non-entity, being from non-being, perfection from imperfection, fullness or sufficiency from deficiency or insufficiency—Light from Darkness. It is the that which causes all opposites. At the same time it shares in all opposites, for it is the immediate emanation of the Father Himself, and therefore unites while separating. It is, therefore, the principle of participation or sharing in, sharing in both the Fullness and the

THE GNOSTIC CRUCIFIXION.

Deficiency. Finally, it is the Stock or Pillar as that which " has stood, stands and will stand "—the principle of immobility, as the energy of the Father in His aspect of the supreme Individuality that changes not, because he is Lord of the ever-changing.

That such a master-idea is difficult to grasp goes without saying; it was confessedly the supreme mystery. From it the mind, the formal mind of man, "falls back unable to grasp it "; for it is precisely this personal mind that creates duality, and insinuates itself between cause and effect. The spiritual Mind alone can embrace the opposites.

But to return to our text. " When He was hung on the *batos* of the Cross " —when He had reached the state of balance, was in the mystic centre—then at the sixth hour, that is mid-day, when there was greatest light, there was also greatest darkness.

And then when the Lord, the Higher Self of the man, was balanced and justified, the man, the disciple, became conscious, in the cave of his heart—that is to say, in his inmost substantial nature —of the Presence of Light.

4. Thereon follow the illumination and the explanation of the familiar drama of appearance taught·to those " without the mystery."

" The multitude below in Jerusalem " is the lower nature of the man, his unillumined mind. " Jerusalem Below " is set over against " Jerusalem Above," the City of God. Jerusalem Below is that nature in him that is still unordered and unpurified ; while Jerusalem Above is that ordered and purified portion of his substance that can respond to the immediate shining of the Light, which further orders it according to the Ordering of Heaven.

And yet the drama below is real enough; there are ever crucifixion and piercing and the drinking of vinegar and gall, before the triumphant Christ is born. It is by such means that His Body is conformed ; it is the mystery of the transformation of what we call evil into. good. The Body of the Christ is perfected by the absorption of the impersonal evil of the world, which He transmutes into blessing.

" 'Twas I who put it in thy heart to ascend this Mount." I am thy Self, thy true God ; 'twas I energizing in thee who enabled thee to rise to the height of contemplation, where thou canst "hear what disciple should learn from Master and man from God." The man has now reached the stage of Hearer in the Spiritual Mysteries.

5. There then follows the vision of the great Cross of Light, fixed firm, and stretching from earth to heaven. Round its foot on earth is a vast multitude of all the nations of the world ; they resemble one another in that they are configured according to the Darkness, their "Spark burns low." On the Cross, or in it, for doubtless the seer saw within as well as without, was another multitude of various grades of light, being formed into some marvellous Image like unto the Divine, but not yet completed—as it might be the Rose on the Cross, in the famous symbol of the Rosicrucians.

6. And above the Cross, lost in the dazzling brilliancy of the Fullness, John beheld the Lord ; he *beheld* but could not *see*, because of the Great Light, as we are told in another great vision of the Master in the *Pistis Sophia*. He can hear only a Voice. But this Voice is no voice of man, but one " truly of God " —a Bath-kol or " Heavenly Voice," as the Rabbis called it—a Voice of sweetest reasonableness, using no words, but of a higher order of utterance, that can make the man speak to himself in his own language, using his own terms.

7. The sentence " I long for one who will hear," is instinct with the yearning of the Divine Love, the eagerness to bestow, the longing to speak if only there be one to hear.

8. There then follows a list of synonyms

THE GNOSTIC CRUCIFIXION.

of the Cross, every one of which shows that the Cross, if a symbol, must be taken to denote the master-symbol of all symbols. It is the key to the chief nomenclature of the Gnosis and the greatest terms of the Gospel. These terms, it is stated, are used by the Wisdom " for your sakes," that is, to bring home in many ways to the hearts of men the intuition of the mystery.

As is explained later on in the text, the mystery of the Cross is the mystery of the Word, the Spiritual Man, or Great Man, the Divine Individuality. Therefore is it called Word or Reason, Mind, Jesus and Christ, Son and Father; for Jesus is the Christ, both as human and divine, the two natures uniting in one in the Cross; and the Son is the Father in a still more divine meaning of the mystery; for both Son and Cross are of the Father alone, they are Himself manifesting Himself to Himself. The whole is the mystery of Ātman or the Self.

The Door is the Door of the Two in One, the state of equilibrium of the opposites which opens out into the all-embracing consciousness and understanding of all oppositions.

The Cross is the Way on which there is no travelling, for it perpetually enters into itself; it is the true Meth-od, not so much in the sense of the Way-between or the Medium or Mediator, as in the sense of the Means of Gnosis.

It is also called Seed because it is the mystery of the power of growth and development; it is self-initiative.

And if the Cross be Son and Father in separation and union, or as simultaneously Cause and Result, it is likewise Spirit or Ātman, and therefore Life.

It is also Truth or the Perpetual Paradox, distinguishing and uniting' in itself all pros and cons, and all analysis and synthesis in simultaneous operation.

Therefore also is it called Faith, because it is the that which is stable and unchanging amid perpetual change.

Faith in its true mystic meaning seems to denote the power of withdrawing the personal consciousness from between the pairs of opposites, where these appear external and other than oneself, and embracing the opposites within the greater consciousness, when they are within oneself and appear as natural processes in the great economy.

Faith is of the contemplative mind; it embraces, it includes. It is therefore of the Great Mother, as the life and substance of the Cross; so also is it of Grace, elsewhere called Wisdom.

Finally, the Cross regarded from this point of view is called Bread, the substance of Life.

In a remarkable paper in *The Theosophical Review*, Nov., 1907, E. R. Innes speaks of a vision of a great drama of those Powers beyond the mind-spheres, which in the Indian scriptures are called Food and Eater—that is to say, the mystical union between the Not-self and the Self.

In the *Chhāndogyopaniṣhad*, for instance, we read of one who had passed into the heaven-world possessing a knowledge of the identity of the Self and Not-self. The transformations of his vehicles that thus occur in the inner states or worlds become as it were processes of natural digestion in his Great Body, for we read :

" Having what food he wills, what form he wills, this song he singing sits :

" ' O wonder, wonder, wonder !

Food I ; food I ; food I !

Food-eater I ; food-eater I ; food-eater I !' "

(See my *World-Mystery*, 2nd ed., p. 179.)

Our author in similar fashion writes of a soul watching the processes of its own substance in the heaven-world.

" She watched the interaction of those two great currents of the One Great Life-Force—the Life-Force as Supporter, the Life-Force as Sustainer. She watched the great transfiguration of the crossing over of the surface-forms as life met life

THE GNOSTIC CRUCIFIXION.

in perfect mystic union. As the currents crossed the forms changed, but without loss of life or consciousness. The Powers crossed and recrossed; and with each appearance of that sacred symbol there was further expansion and intensification of the Life-Force. At each piercing or insinuation of the one into the other, that which had been two became one, yet there still remained the two. She watched the great mystery of that Cross on which the Heavenly Man dies in order to live again.

"In heaven you do not demolish forms in order to sustain life, you daily insinuate yourself into all the forms you meet, and thus by supplying them with food, the food of your own greater life, you become each separate object, and gain in power and expansiveness. Thus in heaven by sacrifice do you grow and live, and slowly become the world. Thus in heaven do you give life to others in order to live yourself; thus do the many rebecome the One. The Great Mystery of the Bread of Life which must be partaken of by all before the Day of Triumph was acted out before her eyes."

And it might be added that as heaven is a state and not a place, the mystery can be consummated on earth, and that this is the true sacrifice of the Christ and the Way to become a Christ.

9. Ideas of this or a similar order may be held not rashly to underlie the words of our text. The Cross of Life may well be called the Harmony—or articulation, or joining-together—of Wisdom, for it is by means of Wisdom that all the contraries are joined together, and this Articulation constitutes the "firm necessity" of Fate, which was also called in the Gnostic schools the Harmony. And if it is a Cross of Life, it is also a Cross of Light, for Life and Light are the eternally united twin-natures, female and male, of the Logos, the Good. Life is Passion and Light is Understanding. The Logos divides Himself to experience and know Himself.

10. All opposites unite in Wisdom as a ground; she is the pure substance in which all the powers play. It is only when the Cross is regarded as a separator, that it may be said to have a right and a left, with good forces on the one hand and evil on the other. The forces are in reality in themselves the same forces; it is the personality of the man (represented by the upright of the Cross), which refers all things to its incomplete self, that regards them as good and evil.

This personality is rooted in the Lower Root or lower nature, and stretches upward towards the Above.

But in reality there are roots above and branches below, or roots below and branches above, of the trunk of this Tree of Life and Light. Though the nomenclature is somewhat different, I cannot refrain from quoting a striking passage from a Gnostic scripture to give the reader some idea of the lofty region of thought to which the Gnosis accustomed its disciples.

It is taken from *The Great Announcement*, a document ascribed by Hippolytus to the very beginning of the Christianized Gnosis. Strong efforts have been made to question this ascription, and to prove the document to be of a later date, but I think I have established a high probability that it may be even a pre-Christian writing (see *H.*, i. 184).

The text is to be found in Hippolytus' *Refutation of all Heresies* (vi., 18):

"To you, therefore, I say what I say and write what I write. And the writing is this:

"Of the universal Æons (Eternities) there are two Branchings, without beginning or end, from one Root, which is the Power unseeable, incomprehensible Silence.

"Of these Branchings one is manifested from Above—the Great Power, Mind of the universals, ordering all things, male; and the other from Below—Great Thought, female, generating all things.

" Thence partnering one another they pair (lit. have union—*syzygía*), and bring into manifestation the Middle Distance, incomprehensible Air without beginning or end.

" In this is that Father, who supports and nourishes the things which have beginning and end.

" This is He who has stood, stands and shall stand—a male-female Power in accordance with the transcendent Boundless Power, which hath neither beginning nor end, subsisting in onlyness.

" It was by emanating from this Power (*sci.*, Incomprehensible Silence) that Thought-in-onlyness became two.

" Yet was He, (the Supernal Father) one ; for having her (*sci.* Thought) in Himself He was alone [that is, all-one, or only, that is one-ly]. He was not, however, [in this state] ' first,' although transcendent ; it was only in manifesting Himself from Himself that He became ' second ' [that is to say, as He who stands]. Nay, He was not even called ' Father ' till Thought named Him ' Father.'

" As, therefore, Himself pro-ducing Himself by means of Himself, He manifested to Himself His own Thought ; so also His Thought on manifesting did not make [Him], but beholding Him, she concealed the Father, that is the Power, in Herself, and is [thus] male-female, Power and Thought.

" Thence is it that they partner one another (for Power in no way differs from Thought) and yet are one. From the things Above is discovered Power, and from those Below Thought.

" So is it, too, with that which is manifested from them ; namely, that though it (*sci.* the Middle Distance, Incomprehensible Air) is one, it is found to be two, male-female, having female in itself.

" Thus is Mind in Thought—inseparable from one another, which though one are yet found to be two."

I believe that our Vision of the Cross sets forth in living symbol precisely what is explained above in more " abstract " terms. It would, however, be a mistake to make abstractions of these sublime ideas ; they must be realized as fullnesses, as transcendent realities. The Air, the Batos, the Middle Distance, is the manifestation, or thinking-manifest, of the Divine to Itself, the true meaning of *mā-yā*. (See the Trismegistic Sermon, " Though Unmanifest God is most Manifest," and the commentary, *H.*, ii., 99-109).

11. I have translated the term διαπηξ-άμενος by " cross-beaming," for διαπήγιον is a " cross-beam "; and I would refer the reader to the famous myth of Plato known as " The Vision of Er," where the same idea is set forth when we read :

" There they saw the extremities of the Boundaries of the Heaven, extended in the midst of the Light ; for this Light was the final Boundary of Heaven— *somewhat like the undergirdings of ships*— and thus confined its whole revolution." (See *H.*, i., 440.)

This " cross-beaming " or operation of the Cross is the mode of the energizing of the Logos. It is the simultaneous separating and joining of the generable and the ingenerable, the two modes of the Self-generable ; it is the link between personal and impersonal, bound and free, finite and infinite. It is the instrument of creation, male-female in one.

12. There is little surprise, therefore, in learning that this mystery is not the " cross of wood " which the disciple will see and has seen in the pictures framed by his lower mind, when reading the historicized narrative of the mystery-drama or hearing the great story. Nor is it to be imagined that the Lord could be hung upon such a cross of wood, seeing that He is crucified in all men —He whom even the disciple in contemplation cannot see as He is, but can only hear the Wisdom of His Voice.

13. " I was held to be what I am not." As to what the many say concerning the mystery, they speak as the many vain

THE GNOSTIC CRUCIFIXION.

and contradictory opinions. Nay, even those who believed in Him have not understood; they have been content with a poor and unworthy conception of the mystery.

The teaching seems to be that as the Christ-story was intended to be the setting-forth of an exemplar of what perfected man might be—namely, that the path was fully opened for him all the way up to God—it was spiritual suicide to rest content with a limited and pre-judiced view. Every mould of thought was to be broken, every imperfect conception was to be transcended, if there was to be realization.

For those who cling to the outward forms and symbols the Place of Rest is neither seen nor spoken of. This Place of Rest, this Home of Peace, is in reality the very Cross itself, the Firm Foundation, the that on which the whole creation rests. And if the Place of Rest, where all things cross, and unite, the Mystic Centre of the whole system, which is everywhere, is not seen or spoken of, " much more shall the Lord of it be neither seen nor spoken of "—He who has the power of the Centre, who can adjust His "centre of gravity" at every moment of time, and therewith the attitude of this Great Body or, if it be preferred, of his Mind, and thus be in perpetual balance, as the Justified and the Just One.

14. The interpretation of the Vision that follows in the text may in its turn be interpreted from several standpoints. It may be regarded cosmically according to the *restauratio omnium*, when the whole creation becomes the object of the Great Mercy, as Basilides calls it ; or it may be taken soteriologically as referring to the salvation or the making safe or sure of our humanity, or it may be referred to the perfection of the individual man.

The multitude of one appearance are the Earth-bound, the Hylics as the Gnostics called them ; that is, those who are immersed in things of matter, the

" delights of the world." They are the Dead, because they are under the sway of birth-and-death, the spheres of Fate. They have not yet " risen from the Dead," and consciously ascended the Cross of Light and Life.

Thus in the preface to *The Book of the Gnoses of the Invisible God*, that is to say, " The Book of the Gnosis of Jesus the Living One "—which begins with the beautiful words : " I have loved you and longed to give you Life "—we read the following Saying of the Lord :

" Jesus saith : Blessed is the man who crucifieth the world, and doth not let the world crucify him."

And later on the mystery is set forth in another Saying :

" Jesus saith : Blessed is the man who knoweth this Word, and hath brought down the Heaven, and borne the Earth and raised it heavenwards ; and he becometh the Midst, for it (the Midst) is a ' nothing.' " (*F.*, 518, 519.)

Those who have become spiritual, who have " risen from the Dead," are born into the Race of the Logos, they become kin with Him.

Of this Race much has been written by the mystics of the many different schools of these early days.

Thus the Jewish Gnostic commentator of the Naassene Document writes :

" One is the Nature Below which is subject to Death ; and one is the Race without a king [that is, those who are kings of themselves] which is born Above " (*H.*, i., 164.).

And the Christian Gnostic commentator refers to the " ineffable Race of perfect men " (*H.*, i., 166), who are in the Logos. Such *illuminati* were called by one tradition of the Christianized Gnosis the Race of Elxai, the Hidden Power or Holy Spirit, the Spouse of Iexai, the Hidden Lord or Logos. (*H.*, ii., 242 ; see my *Did Jesus live 100 B.C.?* chap. xviii.)

Philo of Alexandria tells us that " Wisdom, who, after the fashion of a mother, brings forth the self-taught Race,

THE GNOSTIC CRUCIFIXION.

declares that God is the Sower of it" (*H.*, i., 220). This is the term he applies to his beloved Therapeuts, adding that "this Race is rare and found with difficulty."

Elsewhere he tells us that the angels are the "people" of God; but there is a still higher degree of union, whereby a man becomes one of the Race, or Kin, of God. This Race is an intimate union of all them who are "kin to Him"; they become one. For this Race "is one, the highest one; but 'people' is the name of many."

"As many, then, as have advanced in discipline and instruction, and been perfected therein, have their lot among this 'many.'

"But they who have passed beyond these introductory exercises, becoming natural disciples of God, receiving Wisdom free from all toil, migrate to this incorruptible and perfect Race, receiving a lot superior to their former lives in genesis" (*H.*, i., 554.)

And so in one of the Hymns of Thrice Greatest Hermes, after the triple trisagion, the "Hermes" or Illuminated prays:

"And fill me with Thy Power and with this Grace of Thine, that I may give the Light to those in ignorance of the Race—my Brethren and Thy Sons." (*H.*, ii., 20.).

Philo calls it "self-taught," just as the Buddhists speak of the Arhats as *asekha*; and the Trismegistic teacher writes:

"This Race, my sons, is never taught; but when He willeth it, its memory is restored by God." (*H.*, ii., 221.)

The "Elect Race" of Valentinus is the "Sonship" of Basilides that incarnates on earth for the abolition of Death. (*F.*, 303.)

In the *Pistis Sophia* document, the Sophia, or the soul turning towards the Light, first utters seven repentances, or "turnings-of-the-mind," or rather of the whole nature. At the fourth of these, the turning-point of some subcycle of the great Return, she prays that the Image of the Light may not be turned or averted from her, for the time is come when "those who turn in the lowest regions" should be regarded—"the mystery which is made the type of the Race." (*F.*, 471.)

Again in the introduction to *The Book of the Great Logos according to the Mystery*, the disciples beg the Master to explain the Mystery of the Word. Jesus answers that the Life of His Father consists in their purifying their souls from all earthly stain, and making them to become the Race of the Mind, so that they may be filled with understanding and by His teaching perfect themselves. (*F.*, 528.)

Finally in the marvellous *Untitled Apocalypse* of the Bruce Codex we read:

"These words said the Lord of the Universe to them, and disappeared from them, and hid Himself from them.

"And the Births-of-matter rejoiced that they had been remembered, and were glad that they had come out of the narrow and difficult place, and prayed to the Hidden Mystery:

"'Give us authority that we may create for ourselves æons and worlds according to Thy Word, upon which Thou didst agree with Thy servant; for Thou alone art the changeless One, Thou alone the boundless, the uncontainable, self-taught, self-born Self-father; Thou alone ait the unshakeable and unknowable; Thou alone art Silence and Love, and Source of all; Thou alone art virgin of matter, spotless; whose Race no man can tell, whose manifestation no man can comprehend.'" (*F.*, 564.)

To understand, man must pass beyond the stage of man, and self-realize himself as "kin to Him"—the Logos.

It is, however, doubtful whether "Race" is the correct reading in our text; but as it is the clear reading in 15 of the above notes are germane to our study. The MS. apparently reads "every Limb." This again is one of the most general Gnostic mystical terms, and is taken over from the Osiric Mysteries. The Limbs of the God are scattered abroad, and

166

THE GNOSTIC CRUCIFIXION.

collected together again in the resurrection. The inner meaning of this graphic symbolism may be gleaned from the following striking passages.

In a MS. of the Gnostic Marcus there is a description of the method of symbolizing the Great Body of the Heavenly Man, whereby the twenty-four letters of the Greek alphabet were assigned in pairs to the twelve Limbs. This Body was the symbol of the ideal economy, dispensation or ordering of the universe, its planes, regions, hierarchies, and powers. (*F.*, 366.)

This also is the true Body of man, the Source of all his bodies. And so we read the following mystery-saying in *The Gospel of Eve* :

" I stood on a lofty mountain and saw a Great Man, and another, a dwarf, and heard as it were a Voice of thunder, and drew nigh for to hear. And He spake unto me and said : ' I am thou, and thou art I ; and wheresoever thou art, I am there, and in all am I sown (or scattered). And whencesoever thou willest, thou gatherest Me; and gathering Me, thou gatherest Thyself." (*F.*, 439.)

This is a vision of the Great Person and little person, of the Higher Self and lower self. It may also be interpreted in terms of the Logos and humanity ; but it comes nearer home to think of it as the mystery of the individual man—the scattering of the Limbs of the Great Person in the personalities that have been his in many births.

This idea is brought out more clearly in a passage from *The Gospel of Philip*. It is an apology or defence, as it was called, a formula to be used by the soul in its ascent above, as it passed through the space of the Midst ; and for the mystic it is a declaration of the state of a man who is in his last compulsory earth-life.

" I have recognised myself, and gathered myself together from all sides. I have sown no children for the Ruler, but have torn up his roots, and have gathered together my Limbs that were scattered abroad. I know Thee who Thou art ; for I am of those from Above." (*Ibid.*)

He has sown no children to the Ruler, the Lord of Death ; he has not contracted any fresh debt, or created a new form of personality, into which he must again incarnate. But he has torn up the roots of Death, by shattering the form of egoity, and bursting the bonds of Fate. He has gathered together his Limbs, completed the articulation of his Perfect Body.

The Limbs were according to certain orderings, one of which was the configuration of the five-fold Star, the five-limbed Man. Thus in *The Acts of Thomas* we read :

" Come Thou who art more ancient far than the five holy Limbs—Mind, Thought, Reflection, Thinking, Reasoning ! Commune with them of later birth ! " (*F.*, 422.)

These five Limbs are also the five Words of the mystery of the Vesture of Light in the *Pistis Sophia* (p. 16), with which the Christ is clothed in power on the Day of Triumph, the Great Day " Come unto us," when His Limbs are gathered together and the Song of the Powers begins :

" Come unto us, for we are Thy Fellow-Limbs. We are all one with thee. We are one and the same, and Thou art one and the same."

In the whole document much is said of the " sweet mysteries that are in the Limbs of the Ineffable," but it would be too long to repeat it here. It will be perhaps of greater service to append a very striking passage, from *The Books of the Saviour*, which has been copied into the MS. of the *Pistis Sophia* (pp. 253, 254) :

" And they who are worthy of the Mysteries that dwell in the Ineffable, which are those that have not emanated— these are prior to the First Mystery. To use a similitude and correspondence of speech that ye may understand, they are the Limbs of the Ineffable. And each is according to the dignity of its Glory—the Head according to the dignity of the Head, the Eye according to the dignity of the Eye, the Ear according to the dignity of the Ear, and the rest of the Limbs [in like fashion] ; so that the matter is plain : There are many Limbs (Members) but only one Body.

" Of this I have spoken in a plan, a correspondence and similitude, but not in its true form ; nor have I revealed the Word in Truth, but as the Mystery of the Ineffable.

" And all the Limbs that are in Him . . . , that is, they that dwell in the Mystery of the Ineffable, and they that dwell in Him, and also the Three Spaces that follow according to their Mysteries— . of all of these in truth and verity am I the Treasure ; apart from which there is no Treasure peculiar to [this] cosmos. But there are other Words and Mysteries and Regions [of other worlds].

" Now, therefore, Blessed is he who hath found the Words of the Mysteries of the Space towards the exterior. He is a God who hath found the Words of the Mysteries of the second Space, in the midst. He is a Saviour and free of every space who hath found the Words of the Mysteries of the third Space towards the interior. . . .

" But He, on the other hand, who hath found the Words of the Mysteries which I have set forth for you according to a similitude—namely, the Limbs of the Ineffable—Amēn I say unto you, that man who hath found the Words of those Mysteries in the Truth of God, he is the First in Truth, and like unto Him ; for ·it is through these Words and Mysteries that [all things are made] and the universe itself stands through that First Ohe. Therefore is he who hath found the Words of these Mysteries, like unto the First. For it is the gnosis of the Gnosis of the Ineffable in which I have spoken with you this day."

It is thus seen that the means used in revealing the manner of the highest Mysteries of the Ineffable was by the similitude of the Limbs or Members of the Body. It, therefore, follows, as we have already seen, that this symbolism was one of the most, if not the most, fundamental in this Gnosis. The three stages of perfectioning are those of the Saint, God and Saviour. But these are still stages in evolution or process, no matter how sublime they be. The fourth or consummation is other ; it transcends process, it is ever itself with itself, embracing all processes and all powers simultaneously. But we must not be tempted to comment on this instructive passage, for there is quite enough material in it to develop into a small treatise in itself. For an admirable intuition of the Mystery of the Limbs of the Ineffable, and the meaning of the words " the Head is according to the dignity of the Head," etc., the reader is referred to the beautiful passage in *The Untitled Apocalypse* of the Bruce Codex, quoted in the comments on *The Hymn of Jesus* (pp. 145).

The Gnostic seers lost themselves in the contemplation of the simultaneous simplicity and multiplicity of these Mysteries. Thus again in the same *Untitled Apocalypse* we read :

" He it is whose Limbs (Members) make a myriad of myriads of Powers, each one of which comes from Him." (*F.*, 547).

This graphic symbolism of the Limbs is derived from the tradition of the Osiric Mysteries. Many a passage could be quoted in illustration from *The Book of the Coming-forth by Day*, that strange and marvellous collection of Egyptian Rituals commonly known as the *Book of the Dead ;* but perhaps the under-meaning of the mystery is nowhere more clearly shown than in the following magnificent passage from *The Litany of the Sun*, inscribed on the Tombs of the Kings of ancient Thebes :

" The Kingly Osiris is an intelligent

1 6 8

THE GNOSTIC CRUCIFIXION.

Essence. His Limbs conduct Him; His 'Fleshes' open the way for Him. Those who are born from Him create Him. They rest when they have caused the Kingly Osiris to be born.

"It is He who causes them to be born. It is He who engenders them. It is He who causes them to exist. His Birth is the Birth of Rā in Amenti. He causes the Kingly Osiris to be born; He causes the Birth of Himself."

(See my *World-Mystery*, 2nd ed., p. 162.)

It requires no elaboration to show that this is precisely the same mystery as the secret set forth in our Vision of the Cross. The Kingly Osiris is Ātman, the Self, the True Man, the Monad. This is the Kingly Osiris in his male-female nature, self-creative. Ātman is both the producer and product of evolution. In a restricted sense the above may be interpreted from the standpoint of the individuality and its series of personalities in incarnation.

15. And now to return to the text. The Race is the Upper Nature, now scattered abroad in the hearts of men; it is the true Spirit of man, the hidden Divinity within him. It is this which re-turns, and so causes the man to turn or repent. It is obedient, that is audient, to the Voice of the Self, the compelling Utterance of the Logos. He who not only hears, but hearkens to or obeys the sweet counsels of this Great Persuasion, becomes this Upper Nature consciously; and therefore it no longer is what it was, for it is conscious in the man, and so the man is above men of the lower nature.

16. These mysterious sentences all set forth the state of true Self-consciousness. So long as man is not conscious that he is Divine, so long is the Divine in him not what it really is; the "lower" "limits" the "higher." Union is attained by "hearkening," by "attention." Then it is that the man becomes his Higher Self, and that Higher Self be-

comes in its turn the Self, having taken his self in separation into his Self as union.

17. This "attention" is the straining or striving towards the One; and therefore no attention must be paid to the many. The whole strife of warring opinions and doubts must be reconciled, or at-oned, within the Mystery. The thought must be allowed to dwell but little on "those without." A height must be reached from which the whole human drama can be seen as a spectacle below and within; this height is not with regard to space and place, but with respect to consciousness and realization that all is taking place within the man's Great Body as the operations of the Divine economy. They who are "without the mystery" are not arbitrarily excluded, but are those who prefer to go forth without instead of returning within.

18. They who have re-turned, or turned back on themselves, and entered into themselves for the realization of true Self-consciousness, alone can understand the meaning of the Great Passion, as has been so admirably set forth in the Mystery-Ritual of the Dance.

Those who have consciousness of these spiritual verities, nay, even those who have but dimly felt their greatness, will easily understand that the story of the crucifixion as believed in by the masses was for the Gnostics but the shadow of an eternal happening that most intimately concerned every man in his inmost nature.

19. The outer story was centred round a dramatic crisis of death on a stationary cross—a dead symbol, and a symbol of death. But the inner rite was one of movement and "dancing," a living symbol and a symbol of life. This was shown to the disciple—indeed, as we have seen, he was made in the Dance to partake in it—that he might know the mystery of suffering in a moment of Great Experience. He saw it and became it; it was shown him in action. He had seen

sorrow and suffering, and the cause of it had been dimly felt; but its ceasing he did not yet know really, for the ceasing of sorrow could only come when he could realize sorrow and joy, suffering and bliss, simultaneously. And that mystery the Christ alone knows.

20. Let the disciple then first see the suffering of the man through, not his own, but His Master's eyes. He will first only see the mystery, grasp it intellectually; he will not as yet realize it. When he realizes it, there will then be bliss indeed, for he will begin to become the Master Himself. And the Master is the conqueror of woe—not, however, in the sense of the annihilator of it, but as the one who rejoices in it; for he knows that it is the necessary concomitant of bliss, and that the more pain he suffers in one portion of his nature, the more bliss he experiences in another; the deeper the one the deeper the other, and therewith the intenser becomes his whole nature. His Great Body is learning to respond to greater and greater impulses or " vibrations."

The consummation is that he becomes capable of experiencing joy in sorrow and sorrow in joy; and thus reaches to the gnosis that these are inseparables, and that the solution of the mystery is the power of ever experiencing both simultaneously.

21. It may thus to some extent become clear that what is asserted of the Christ in the general Gospel-story is typically true and yet is not true. Those who look at one side only of the living picture see in a glass darkly.

If we could only realize that all the ugliness and misery and confusion of life is but the underside, as it were, of a pattern woven on the Great Loom or embroidered by Divine Fingers! We can in our imperfect consciousness see only the underside, the medley of crossing of threads, the knots and finishings-off; we cannot see the pattern. Nevertheless it exists simultaneously with the under-

side. The Christ sees both sides simultaneously, and understands.

22. But the term that our Gnostic writer chooses with which to depict this grade of being is not Christ, but Word or Reason (Logos). This Reason is not the ratiocinative faculty in man which conditions him as a duality; it is rather more as a Divine Monad, as Pure Reason, or that which can hold all opposites in one. It is called Word because it is the immediate intelligible Utterance of God.

23. This is the first mystery that man must learn to understand; then will he be able to understand God as unity; and only finally will he understand the greatest mystery of all—man, the personal man, the thing we each of us now are, God in multiplicity, and why there is suffering.

24. With this the writer breaks off, knowing fully how difficult it is to express in human speech the living ideas that have come to birth in him, and knowing that there are still more marvellous truths of which he has caught some glimpse or heard some echo, but which he feels he can in no way set forth in proper decency.

And so he tells us the Lord is taken up, unseen by the multitudes. That is to say, presumably, no one in the state of the multiplicity of the lower nature can behold the vision of unity.

25. When he descends from the height of contemplation, however, he remembers enough to enable him to laugh at the echoes of his former doubts and fancies and misconceptions, and to make him realize the marvellous power of the natural living symbolic language that underlies the words of the mystery-narrative that sets forth the story of the Christ.

THE GNOSTIC CRUCIFIXION.

The vision itself is not so marvellous as the instruction; nevertheless it allows us to see that the Cross in its supernal nature is the Heavenly Man with arms outstretched in blessing, showering benefits on all—the perpetual Self-sacrifice (*F.*, 330). And in this connection we should remind ourselves of the following striking sentence from *The Untitled Apocalypse* of the Bruce Codex, an apocalypse which contains perhaps the most sublime visions that have survived to us from the Gnosis :

" The Outspreading of His Hands is the manifestation of the Cross."

And then follows the key of the mystery :
" The Source of the Cross is the Man [Logos] whom no man can comprehend."
(See *Hymn of Jesus*, p. 145)

No man can comprehend Man ; the little cannot contain the Great, except potentially.

It was some echo of this sublime teaching that found its way into the naïve though allegorical narrative of *The Acts of Philip*. When Philip was crucified he cursed his enemies.

" And behold suddenly the abyss was opened, and the whole of the place in which the proconsul was sitting was swallowed up, and the whole of the temple, and the viper which they worshipped, and great crowds, and the priests of the viper, about seven thousand men, besides women and children, except where the apostles were ; they remained unshaken."

This is a cataclysm in which the lower nature of the man is engulfed. The apostles are his higher powers ; the rest the opposing forces. The latter plunge into Hades and experience the punishments of those who crucify the Christ

and his apostles. They are thus converted and sing their repentance. Whereupon a Voice was heard saying : " I shall be merciful to you in the Cross of Light."

Philip is reproved by the Saviour for his unmerciful spirit.

" But I, O Philip, will not endure thee, because thou hast swallowed up the men in the abyss ; but behold My Spirit is in them, and I will bring them up from the dead ; and thus they, seeing thee, shall believe in the Glory of Him that sent thee.

" And the Saviour having turned, stretched up His hand, and marked a Cross in the Air coming down from Above even unto the Abyss, and it was full of Light, and had its form after the likeness of a ladder. And all the multitude that had gone down from the City into the Abyss came up on the Ladder of the Cross of Light ; but there remained below the proconsul and the viper which these worshipped. And when the multitude had come up, having looked upon Philip hanging head downwards, they lamented with great lamentation at the lawless action which they had done."

The doers of the "lawless" deed are the same as the "lawless Jews" in the *Acts of John*—" those who are under the law of the lawless Serpent " ; that is to say, those who are under the sway of Generation, as contrasted with those under the law of Re-generation (see *Hymn of Jesus*, pp. 138, 143).

Philip stands for the man learning the last lesson of divine mercy. The Proconsul and the Viper are the antitypes of the Saviour and the Serpent of Wisdom. The crucifixion of Philip is, however, not the same as the crucifixion of the Christ ; he is hanged reversed, his head to the earth and not towards heaven. It is a lower grade of the mysteries.

Concerning the mystery of the crucifixion of the Christ we learn somewhat of its inner nature from the doctrines of the Docetæ.

His baptism was on this wise : He

171

THE GNOSTIC CRUCIFIXION.

washed Himself in the Jordan, that is the Stream of the Logos, and after His purification in the Life-giving Water, He became possessed of a spiritual or perfect body, the type and signature of which were in accordance with the matter of his virginity, that is of virgin substance ; so that when the World-ruler, or God of generation or death, condemned his own plasm, the physical body, to death, that is to the Cross, the soul nourished in that physical body might strip off the body of flesh, and nail it to the " tree,"[1] and yet triumph over the powers of the Ruler and not be found naked, but clothed in a robe of glory. Hence the saying : " Except a man be born of Water and the Spirit he cannot enter into the King-ship of the Heavens ; that which is born of the flesh is flesh." (*F.*, p. 221).

It was because of these and such like ideas, and in the conviction that the mystery of the crucifixion was to be worked out in every man, that a Gnostic writer, following the Valentinian tradition, explains a famous passage in the Pauline *Letter to the Ephesians* as follows :

" 'For this cause I bow my knees to the God and Father and Lord of our Lord Jesus Christ, that God may vouch-safe to you that Christ may dwell in your inner man '—that is to say, the psychic and not the bodily man—' that ye may be strong to know what is the Depth'— that is, the Father of the universals—' and what is the Breadth '—that is the Cross, the Boundary of the Plērōma [or Fullness]—' and what is the Greatness '—that is, the Plērōma of the æons [the eternities or universals, the Limbs of the Body of the Ineffable]." (*F.*, 532).

To be closely compared with the Vision in *The Acts of John* is the Address of Andrew to the Cross in *The Acts of Andrew*. They both plainly belong to the same tradition, and might indeed have been written by the same hand.

" Rejoicing I come to thee, Thou Cross, the Life-giver, Cross whom I now know to be mine. I know thy mystery ; for thou hast been planted in the world to make-fast things unstable.

" Thy head stretcheth up into heaven, that thou mayest symbol-forth the Heavenly Logos, the Head of all things.

" Thy middle parts are stretched forth, as it were hands to right and left, to put to flight the envious and hostile power of the Evil One, that thou mayest gather together into one them [*sci.*, the Limbs] that are scattered abroad.

" Thy foot is set in the earth, sunk in the deep [*i.e.*, abyss], that thou mayest draw up those that lie beneath the earth and are held fast in the regions beneath it, and mayest join them to those in heaven.

" O Cross, engine, most skilfully de-vised, of Salvation, given unto men by the Highest ; O Cross, invincible trophy of the Conquest of Christ o'er His foes ; O Cross, thou life-giving tree, roots planted on earth, fruit treasured in heaven ; O Cross most venerable, sweet thing and sweet name ; O Cross most worshipful, who bearest as grapes the Master, the true vine, who dost bear, too, the Thief as thy fruit, fruitage of faith through confession ; thou who bringest the worthy to God through the Gnosis and summonest sinners home through repentance ! "

A magnificent address indeed. The identification of the Master and the man with the Cross and in the Cross is hardly disguised. The Cross is the Tree of Life and the tree of death simultaneously. " Give up thy life that thou mayest live," says that inspired mystic treatise, *The Voice of the Silence*, and this is no other than the secret of the Mystery of the Cross. The Master is hanged between two thieves, the one repentant and the other obdurate, the soul turned towards the Light and towards the Darkness, all united in the one Mystery of the Cross—the Mystery of Man.

We have seen above that Philip is hanged head downwards, but he is not

172

THE GNOSTIC CRUCIFIXION.

the most famous instance of this reversal. The best known is associated with the name of Peter in the mystic romances.

Thus in a fragment of the Linus-collection called *The Martyrdom of Peter*, we learn the doctrine as set forth in a speech put into the mouth of Peter thus crucified :

" Fitly wast Thou alone stretched on the Cross with head on high, O Lord, who hast redeemed all of the world from sin.

" I have desired to imitate Thee in Thy Passion too ; yet would I not take on myself to be hanged upright.

" For we, pure men and sinners, are born from Adam, but Thou art God of God, Light of true Light, before all æons and after them ; thought worthy ˙to become for men Man without strain of man, Thou has stood forth man's glorious Saviour—Thou ever upright, ever raised on high, eternally Above !

" We, men according to the flesh, are sons of the First Man (Adam), who sank his being in the earth, whose fall in human generation is shown forth.

" For we are brought to birth in such a way, that we do seem to be poured into earth, so that the right is left, the left doth right become ; in that our state is changed in those who are the authors of this life.

" For this world down below doth think the right what is the left—this world in which Thou, Lord, hast found us like the Ninevites, and by Thy holy preaching hast thou rescued these about to die."

The " authors of this life " of reversal, are the " parents " of the " lower nature "; not our natural parents whom we are to love, but the powers of illusion we are to abandon. The Jonah-myth was used as a type of the Initiate, who after being " three days " in the Belly of the Fish, the Great Life or Animal that dwells in the Ocean or Great Water, is vomited forth re-generate, and so a fit vehicle for preaching with compelling words or acts for the benefit of those in Nineveh or the Jerusalem Below, or this world.

But for those who had ears to hear there was a still further instruction concerning the secret of the Mystic Cross.

" But ye, my brothers, who have the right to hear, lend me the ears of your heart, and understand what now must be revealed to you—the hidden mystery of every nature and secret source of every thing composed.

" For the First Man, whose race I represent by my position, with head reversed, doth symbolize the birth into destruction ; for that his birth was death and lacked the Life-stream.

" But of His own compassion the Power Above came down into the world, by means of corporal substance, to him who by a just decree had been cast down into the earth, and hanged upon the Cross, and by the means of this most holy calling [the Cross] He did restore us, and did make for us these present things (which had till then remained unchanged by men's unrighteous error) into the Left, and those that men had taken for the Left into eternal things.

" In exaltation of the Right He hath changed all the signs into their proper nature, considering as good those thought not good, and those men thought malefic most benign.

" Whence in a mystery the Lord hath said : ' If ye make not the Right like to the Left, the Left like to the Right, Above as the Below, Before as the Behind, ye shall not know God's Kingdom.' "

(This saying is from *The Gospel according to the Egyptians*.)

" This saying have I made manifest in myself, my brothers ; this is the way in which your eyes of flesh behold me hanging. It figures forth the Way of the First Man.

" But ye, beloved, hearing these words, and, by conversion of your nature and changing of your life, perfecting them, even as ye have turned you from that Way of Error where ye trod, unto the most sure state of Faith, so keep ye running, and strive towards the Peace that calls you from Above, living the holy life. For that the Way in which ye travel there is Christ.

" Therefore with Jesus, Christ, true God, ascend the Cross. He hath been made for us the One and Only Word ; whence also doth the Spirit say : ' Christ is the Word and Voice of God.'

" The Word in truth is symbolled forth by that straight stem on which I hang. As for the Voice—since that voice is a thing of flesh, with features not to be ascribed unto God's nature, the cross-piece of the Cross is thought to figure forth that human nature which suffered the fault of change in the First Man, but by the help of God-and-man received again its real Mind.

" Right in the centre, joining twain in one, is set the nail of discipline—conversion and repentance." (*F.F.*, 446-449.)

The interpretation becomes somewhat strained towards the end. The reversed hanging typified the man of sex, or the man still under the sway of generation, separated into male and female. Such hang head-downwards in the Great Womb of Nature, and all is reversed for them. Hanged upright, the re-generate man contains in himself in active operation the twin powers in union, now used for spiritual creation, and self-perfection.

And if it be thought that there is abandonment of any thing in this consummation, then let it be known that it is only a giving up of the part for the whole, the passing from the state of separation to the realization of inexpressible bliss ; for as the inspired writer of *The Untitled Apocalypse* phrases it in an ecstasy of enthusiasm :

" This is the eternal Father ; this the ineffable, unthinkable, incomprehensible, untranscendible Father. He it is in whom the All became joyous ; it rejoiced and was joyful, and brought forth in its joy myriads of myriads of Æons ;

they were called the ' Births of Joy,' because the All had joyed with the Father.

" These are the worlds from which the Cross upsprang ; out of these incorporeal Members did the Man arise." (*F.*, 550).

THE . . .
CHALDÆAN
ORACLES. .
VOL. I. . .

THE CHALDÆAN ORACLES.

VOLUME I.

CONTENTS.

The Seven Firmaments
The True Sun
The Moon
The Elements
The Shells of the Cosmic Egg
The Physiology of the Cosmic Body
The Globular Cosmos
Nature and Necessity
The Principles and Rulers of the Sensible
World

BIBLIOGRAPHY.

K. = Kroll (G.), *De Oraculis Chaldaicis;* in *Breslauer philologische Abhandlungen*, Bd. vii., Hft. i. (Breslau ; 1894).

C. = Cory (I. P.), *Ancient Fragments* (London ; 2nd ed., 1832), pp. 239—280. The first and third editions do not contain the text of our Oracles.

F. = Mead (G. R. S.), *Fragments of a Faith Forgotten* (London ; 2nd. ed., 1906).

H. = Mead (G. R. S.), *Thrice Greatest Hermes* (London ; 1906).

THE CHALDÆAN ORACLES.

INTRODUCTION.

The Chaldæan Oracles (*Lógia, Oracula, Responsa*) are a product of Hellenistic (and more precisely Alexandrian) syncretism.

The Alexandrian religio-philosophy proper was a blend of Orphic, Pythagoræan, Platonic, and Stoic elements, and constituted the theology of the learned in the great city which had gradually, from the third century B.C., made herself the centre of Hellenic culture.

In her intimate contact with the Orient, the mind of Greece freely united with the mysterious and enthusiastic cults and wisdom-traditions of the other nations, and became very industrious in "philosophizing" their mythology, theosophy and gnosis, their oracular utterances, symbolic apocalypses and initiatory lore.

The two nations that made the deepest impression on the Greek thinkers were Egypt and Chaldæa ; these they regarded as the possessors of the most ancient wisdom-traditions.

How Hellenism philosophized the ancient wisdom of Egypt, we have already shown at great length in our volumes on Thrice-greatest Hermes. The Chaldæan Oracles are a parallel endeavour, on a smaller scale, to philosophize the wisdom of Chaldæa. In the Trismegistic writings, moreover, we had to deal with a series of prose treatises, whereas in our Oracles we are to treat of the fragments of a single mystery-poem, which may with advantage be compared with the cycle of Jewish and Christian pseudepigraphic poems known as the Sibylline Oracles.

The Great Library of Alexandria contained a valuable collection of MSS. of what we may term the then "Sacred Books

of the East " in their original tongues. Many of these were translated, and among them the "Books of the Chaldæans." Thus Zosimus, the early alchemist, and a member of one of the later Trismegistic communities, writes, somewhere at the end of the third century A.D. :

"The Chaldæans and Parthians and Medes and Hebrews call him [the First Man] Adam, which is by interpretation virgin Earth, and blood-red Earth, and fiery Earth, and fleshly Earth.

"And these indications were found in the book-collections of the Ptolemies, which they stored away in every temple, and especially in the Serapeum " (*H.*, iii., 277).

The term Chaldæan is, of course, vague, and scientifically inaccurate. Chaldæan is a Greek synonym for Babylonian, and is the way they transliterated the Assyrian name Kaldû. The land of the Kaldû proper lay S.E. of Babylonia proper on what was then the sea-coast. As the *Encyclopædia Biblica* informs us : "The Chaldæans not only furnished an early dynasty of Babylon, but also were incessantly pressing into Babylonia ; and, despite their repeated defeats by Assyria, they gradually gained the upper hand there. The founder of the New Babylonian Kingdom, Nabopolassar (*circa* 626 B.C.), was a Chaldæan, and from that time Chaldæa meant Babylonia. . . .

"We find ' Chaldæans ' used in *Daniel*, as a name for a caste of wise men. As Chaldæan meant Babylonian in the wider sense of a member of the dominant race in the times of the new Babylonian Empire, so after the Persian conquest it seems to have connoted the Babylonian *literati* and became a synonym of soothsayer and astrologer. In this sense it passed into classical writers."

We shall, however, see from the fragments of our poem that some of the Chaldæi were something more than soothsayers and astrologers.

As to our sources ; the *disjecta membra* of this lost mystery-poem are chiefly

179

THE CHALDÆAN ORACLES.

found in the books and commentaries of the Platonici—that is, of the Later Platonic school. In addition to this there are extant five treatises of the Byzantine period, dealing directly with the doctrines of the "Chaldæan philosophy": five chapters of a book of Proclus, three treatises of Psellus (eleventh century), and a letter of a contemporary letter-writer, following on Psellus.

But by far the greatest number of our fragments is found in the books of the Later Platonic philosophers, who from the time of Porphyry (*fl. c.* 250-300)—and, therefore, we may conclude from that of Plotinus, the corypheus of the school—held these Oracles in the highest estimation. Almost without a break, the succession of the Chain praise and comment elaborately on them, from Porphyry onwards—Iamblichus, Julian the Emperor, Synesius, Syrianus, Proclus, Hierocles—till the last group who flourished in the first half of the sixth century, when Simplicius, Damascius and Olympiodorus were still busy with the philosophy of our Oracles.

Some of them—Porphyry, Iamblichus and Proclus—wrote elaborate treatises on the subject ; Syrianus wrote a "symphony" of Orpheus, Pythagoras and Plato with reference to and in explanation of the Oracles ; while Hierocles, in his treatise *On Providence*, endeavoured to bring the doctrine of the Oracles into "symphony" with the dogmas of the Theurgists and the philosophy of Plato. All these books are, unfortunately, lost, and we have to be content with the scattered, though numerous, references, with occasional quotations, in such of their other works as have been preserved to us.

In this brief introduction it would take too long to discuss the "literature" of the Oracles ; and indeed this is all the more unnecessary as until the work of Kroll appeared, the subject had never been treated scientifically. Prior to Kroll it had been, more or less, generally held that the Oracles were a collection of sayings deriving immediately from the Chaldæan wisdom, and even by some as direct translations or paraphrases from a Chaldæan original.

This was the general impression made by the vagueness with which the Later Platonic commentators introduced their authority; as, for instance: The Chaldæan Oracles, the Chaldæans, the Assyrians, the Foreigners (*lit.*, Barbarians or Natives), the God-transmitted. Wisdom, or Mystagogy handed on by the Gods ; and, generally, simply : The Oracles, the Oracle, the Gods, or one of the Gods.

Kroll has been the first to establish that for all this there was but a single authority—namely, a poem in hexameter verse, in the conventional style of Greek Oracular utterances, as is the case with the Sibyllines and Homeric centones.

The fragments of this poem have, for the most part, been preserved to us by being embedded in a refined stratum of elaborate commentary, in which the simple forms of the poetical imagery and the symbolic expressions of the original have been blended with the subtleties of a highly developed and abstract systematization, which is for the most part foreign to the enthusiastic and vital spirit of the mystic utterances of the poem.

To understand the doctrines of the original poem, we must recover the fragments that remain, and piece them together as best we can under general and natural headings ; we must not, as has previously been done, content ourselves with reading them through the eyes of the philosophers of the Later Platonic School, whose one pre-occupation was not only to make a "harmony" or "symphony" between Orpheus, Pythagoras, Plato and the Oracles, but also to wrest the latter into accommodation with their own elaborations of Platonic and Plotinian doctrine.

When we have done this, we shall have before us the remains of a mystery-

1 8 0

THE CHALDÆAN ORACLES.

poem, addressed to "initiates," and evidently forming part of the inner instruction of a School or Community; but even so we shall not have the clear original, for there are several interpolations, which have crept in with the tradition of the text from hand to hand of many scribes.

What is the date of this original poem ? It was known to Porphyry. Now Porphyry (Malek) was a Semite by birth and knew Hebrew; he may also have known "Chaldæan." At any rate we know he was a good scholar and had good critical ability, and that he was at pains to sift out "genuine" from spurious "Oracles," thus showing that there were many Oracles circulating in his day. The genuine ones he collected in his lost work entitled, On the Philosophy of the Oracles, and among them was our poem.

Kroll places this poem at the end of the second century or the beginning of the third, chiefly because it breathes the spirit of a "saving cult," and such cults, he believes, did not come into general prominence till the days of Marcus Aurelius (imp. 161-180). But saving cults had been a common-place of the East and in Alexandria for centuries, and this, therefore, does not seem to me to afford us any indication of date.

The two Julians, father and son, moreover, the former of whom Suidas calls a "Chaldæan philosopher," and the latter "the Theurgist," adding that the son flourished under Marcus Aurelius, will hardly help us in this connection ; for the father wrote a book On Daimones only, and, though the son wrote works on theurgy and also on the oracles of theurgy and the "secrets of this science," Porphyry did not associate him with our Oracles, for he devoted a separate book of commentaries (now lost) to "The Doctrines of Julian the Chaldæan," while Proclus and Damascius dissociate this Julian from our Oracles, by quoting him separately under the title "The Theurgist" (K. 71).

Porphyry evidently considered our Oracles as old, but how old ? To this, we can give no precise answer. The problem is the same as that which confronts us in both the Trismegistic and Sibylline literature, which can be pushed back in an unbroken line to the early years of the Ptolemaic period. We are, therefore, justified in saying that our poem may as easily be placed in the first as in the second century.

It remains only to be remarked that, as might very well be expected with such scattered shreds and fragments of highly poetical imagery and symbolic and mystical poetry, the task of translation is often very arduous, all the more so owing to the absence of truly critical texts of the documents from which they are recovered. Kroll has supplied us with an excellent apparatus and many emendations of the tradition of the printed texts ; but until the extant works of the Later Platonic School are critically edited from the MSS. (as has been done only in a few instances) a truly critical text of our Oracle-fragments is out of the question. Kroll has printed all the texts, both of the fragments and of the contexts, in the ancient authors, where they are found, in his indispensable treatise in Latin on the subject, but, as is usual with the work of specialists, he does not translate a single line. With these brief remarks we now present the reader with a translation and comments on the fragments of what might be called "The Gnosis of the Fire."

THE CHALDÆAN ORACLES.

THE SUPREME PRINCIPLE.

In the extant fragments of our Oracle-poem the Supreme Principle is characterized simply as Father, or Mind, or Mind of the Father, or again as Fire.

Psellus, however, in his commentary, declares that the Oracles hymned the Source of all as the One and Good (K. 10); and there can be little doubt that in the circle of our poet, the Deity was either regarded as the "One and All"—according to the grand formula of Heraclitus (*fl.* 500 B.C.), who had probably to some extent already "philosophized" the intuitions and symbols of a Mago-Chaldæan tradition—or, as with so many Gnostic schools of the time, was conceived of as the Ineffable.

Cory, in his collection of Oracle-fragments, includes (C. 1) a definition of the Supreme which Eusebius attributed to the "Persian Zoroaster." This may very well have been derived from some Hellenistic document influenced by the "Books of the Chaldæans," or "Books of the Medes," and may, therefore, be considered as generally consonant with the basic doctrine of our Oracles. As, however, Kroll rightly omits this, we append it in illustration only:

"He is the First, indestructible, eternal, ingenerable, impartible, entirely unlike aught else, Disposer of all beauty, unbribable, of all the good the Best, of all the wisest the Most Wise; the Father of good-rule and righteousness is He as well, self-taught, and natural, perfect, and wise, the sole Discoverer of sacred nature-lore."

THE END OF UNDERSTANDING.

If, however, we have no excerpt bearing directly on the Summum Mysterium, we have enough, and more than enough, to support us in our conjecture that it was conceived of in our Oracles as being itself beyond all words, in a fragment of eleven lines which sets forth the supreme end of contemplation as follows:

Yea, there is That which is the End-of-understanding, the That which thou must understand with flower of mind. 1

For should'st thou turn thy mind inwards on It, and understand It as understanding " something," thou shalt not understand It.

For that there is a power of [the mind's] prime that shineth forth in all directions, flashing with intellectual rays [lit., sectors].

Yet, in good sooth, thou should'st not [strive] with vehemence [to] understand that End-of-understanding, nor even with the wide-extended flame of wide-extended mind that measures all things—except that End-of-understanding [only].

Indeed there is no need of strain in understanding This; but thou should'st have the vision of thy soul in purity, turned from aught else, so as to make thy mind empty [of all things else], attentive to that End, in order that thou mayest learn that End-of-understanding; for It subsists beyond the mind.

The "That which is the End-of-understanding" is generally rendered the Intelligible. But *to noëtón*, for the Gnostic of this tradition, in this connection signifies the Self-creative Mind, that is, the Mind that creates its own understanding.

It is both the simultaneous beginning and end, or cause and result of itself; and thus is the end or goal of all understanding. It has, therefore, to be distinguished from all formal modes of intellection; the normal mind that is conditioned by the opposites, subject and object, cannot grasp it. So long as we conceive it as object, as other than ourselves, as though we are "understanding 'something,'" so long are we

182

THE CHALDÆAN ORACLES.

without it. It must be contemplated with the "flower of mind," by mind in its "prime," that is, at the moment of blossoming of the growing mind, which rays within and without in intellectual brilliance, both penetrating its own depths and becoming one with them.

"Flower of mind," however, is not the fruit or jewels of mind, though it is a power of fiery mind, for flowers are on the sun-side of things. To understand "with flower of mind" thus seems to suggest to catch, like petals, in a cup-like way, with the *kratēres* or deeps of mind, the true fiery intelligence of the Great Mind, as flowers catch the sun-rays, and by means of them to bring to birth within oneself the fruit or jewels of the Mind, which are of the nature of immediate or spiritual understanding, that is to say, the greater mind-senses, or powers of understanding.

The fragment seems to be an instruction in a method of initiating the mind in understanding or true gnosis—a very subtle process. It is not to be expected that the normal, formal, partial mind can seize a complete idea, a fullness, as it erroneously imagines it does in the region of form; in the living intelligible "spheres" there are no such limited ideas defined by form or outline; they are measureless.

In this symbolism flame and flower are much the same; flame of mind and flower of mind suggest the same happening in the "mineral" and "vegetable" kingdoms of the mind-realms. The mind has to grow of itself towards its sun. Most men's minds are at best smouldering fire; they require a "breath" of the Great Breath to make them burst into flame, and so extend themselves, or possess themselves of new re-generative power. Most men's minds, or persons, are unripe plants; we have not yet brought ourselves to the blossoming point. This is achieved only by Heat from the Sun. A blossoming person may be said to be one who is beginning to know how to form fruit and re-generate himself.

In this vital exercise of inner growth there must be no formal thinking. The personal mind must be made empty or void of all preconceptions, but at the same time become keenly attentive, transformed into pure sense, or capacity for greater sensations. The soul must be in a searching frame of mind, searching not enquiring, that is to say synthetic not analytic. Enquiry suggests penetrating into a thing with the personal mind; while searching denotes embracing and seizing ideas, "eating" or "digesting" or "absorbing" them, so to say; getting all round them and making them one's own, surrounding them—it is no longer a question of separated subject and object as with the personal and analyzing mind.

MYSTIC UNION.

The whole instruction might be termed a method of *yoga* or mystic union (*unio mystica*) of the spiritual or kingly mind, the mind that rules itself—*rāja-yoga*, the royal art proper. But there must be no "vehemence" (no "fierce impetuosity," to use a phrase of Patañjali's in his *Yoga-sūtra*) in one direction only; there must be expansion in every direction within and without in stillness.

The "vision" of the soul is, literally, the "eye" of the soul. The mind must be emptied of every object, so that it may receive the fullness. It becomes the "pure eye," the æon, all-eye; not, however, to perceive anything other than itself, but to understand the nature of understanding—namely, that it transcends all distinctions of subject and object.

And yet though the Reality may be said to be "beyond the mind," or "without it," it is really not so. It may very well be said to be beyond or transcend the personal or formal mind, or mind in separation, for that is the mind that separates; but the Intelligible and

1 8 3

THE CHALDÆAN ORACLES.

the Mind-in-itself are really one. As one of the fragments says:

2   *For Mind is not without the That-which-makes-it-Mind ; and That-which-is-the-End-of-Mind doth not subsist apart from Mind.*

Both these hyphened terms represent the same word in Greek, usually rendered the Intelligible. The Oracle might thus be made to run : " For Intellect is not without the Intelligible, and the Intelgible subsists not apart from Intellect." But this makes *to noētón* the object only of understanding ; whereas it is neither subject nor object, but both.

THE ONE DESIRABLE.

The Father is the Source of all sources and the End of all ends ; He is the One Desirable, Perfect and Benignant, the Good, the Summum Bonum, as we learn from the following three disconnected fragments.

3   *For from the Paternal Source naught that's imperfect spins [or wheels].*

The soul must have measure, rhythm, and perfection, to spin, circulate or throb with this Divine Principle.

4   *The Father doth not sow fear, but pours forth persuasion.*

The Father controls from within and not from without ; controls by *being*, by living within, and not by constraining.

5   *Not knowing that God is wholly Good. O wretched slaves, be sober !*

Compare with this the address of the preacher inserted in the Trismegistic " Man-Shepherd " treatise (*H.*, ii. 17) :
" O ye people, earth-born folk, ye who have given yourselves to drunkenness and sleep and ignorance of God, be sober now ! "
And also the Oracle quoted as follows :

6   *The soul of men shall press God closely to itself, with naught subject to death in it ; [but now] it is all drunk, for it doth glory in the Harmony [that is, the Sublunary or Fate Spheres] beneath whose sway the mortal frame exists.*

THE DIVINE TRIAD.

How the Divine Simplicity conditions its self-revelation no fragment tells us. But in spite of Kroll's scepticism I believe the Later Platonic commentators were not wrong when they sought for it in the riddle of the triad or trinity.

The doctrine of the Oracles as to the Self-conditioning of the Supreme Monad may, however, perhaps, be recovered from the passage of the Simonian *Great Announcement* quoted in our last little volume (p 163 ff). This striking exposition of the Gnosis was " philosophized " upon a Mago-Chaldæan background, and that, too, at a date at least contemporaneous with the very origins of Christianity, as is now, I think, demonstrated with high probability (*H.*, i. 184). The passage is so important that it deserves re-quotation ; but as it is so easily accessible, it may be sufficient simply to refer the interested reader to it.

Centuries before Proclus this tripartite or triadic dogma was known to the Greeks as pre-eminently Assyrian, that is Syrian or Chaldæan. Thus Hippolytus, commenting on the Naassene Document, in which the references to the Initiatory Rites are pre-Christian, writes :
" And first of all, in considering the triple division of Man [the Monad or Logos], they [the Naassenes] fly for help to the Initiations of the Assyrians ; for the Assyrians were the first to consider the Soul triple and yet one." (*H.*, i. 151).

In the same Document the early Jewish commentator, who was in all probability a contemporary of Philo's in the earliest years of the Christian era, gives the first words of a mystery-hymn which run : " *From Thee* is Father and *Through Thee* Mother " (*ibid.*, 146) ; and,

THE CHALDÆAN ORACLES.

it might be added: "*To Thee* is Son."
This represents the values of the three
" Great Names " on the Path of Return ;
but in the Way of Descent, that is of
cosmogenesis, or world-shaping, their
values would differ. Curiously enough
one of our Oracles reads :

7   *For Power is With Him, but Mind*
From Him.

Power always represents the Mother-
side (the Many), the Spouse of Deity
(the Mind, the One), and Son is the Result,
the " From Him "—the Mind in manifestation. Hence we read of the Father,
or Mind Proper, as becoming unmani-
fested or withdrawn, or hidden, after
giving the First Impulse to Himself.

8   *The Father withdrew Himself, yet shut*
not up His own peculiar Fire within His
Gnostic Power.

" His own peculiar Fire " seems to mean
that which characterizes the One Mystery
as Father, or creative. He withdrew
Himself into Silence and Darkness, but
left His Fire, or Fiery Mind, to operate
the whole creation. May not this throw
some light on the meaning of the obscure
mystery-hymn at the end of the Christian
Gnostic *Second Book of Ieou* (Carl
Schmidt, *Gnost. Schrift.*, p. 187) ?
" I praise Thee . . .; for Thou hast
drawn Thyself into Thyself altogether
in Truth, till Thou hast set free the space
of this Little Idea [? the manifested
cosmos] ; yet hast Thou not withdrawn
Thyself."

GOD-NURTURING SILENCE.

In the first passage from the Simonian
Great Announcement, to which we have
referred above (p.184), the Great Power
of the Father is called Incomprehensible
Silence, and, as is well known, Silence
(Sigē) was, in a number of systems of
the Christianized Gnosis, the Syzygy,
or Co-partner, or Complement, of the

Ineffable. Among the Pythagoræans and
Trismegistic Gnostics also Silence was
the condition of Wisdom.
Though there is no verse of our Oracle-
poem preserved which sets this forth,
there are phrases quoted by Proclus
(K. 16) which speak of the Paternal
Silence. It is the Divine " *Calm*," the
" *Silence, Nurturer of the Divine* "; it is
the unsurpassable unity of the Father,
the that concerning which words fail ;
the mind must be silenced to know it— 9
that is, to " *accord with* " it (K. 16,
C. 12, 5).
Proclus in all probability had our
Oracles in mind when he wrote (C. 12) :
" For such is the Mind in that state,
energizing prior to energizing [in the
sensible world], in that it had in no way
emanated, but rested in the Father's
Depth [*i.e.*, its own Depth], and in the
Sacred Shrine, held in the Arms of
Silence, ' *Nurturer of the Divine.*' "
Silence is known through mind alone.
While things are objective to one, while
we are taught or told *about* things, they
cannot be real. The Great Silence on
the mind-side of things corresponds with
the Great Sea on the matter-side of things ;
the latter is active, the former inactive ;
and the only way to attain wisdom,
which is other than knowledge, is to
" re-create " or re-generate oneself. Man
only " knows " God by getting to this
Silence, in which naught but the creative
words of true Power are heard. He then
no longer conceives formal ideas in his
mind, but utters living ideas in all his
acts—thoughts, words and deeds.

The Fatherhood is equated by Proclus
(K. 13) with Essence (*ousía*), or Subsis- 10
tence (*hyparxis*) ; the Motherhood with
Life (*zōḗ*) or Power (*dynamis*) ; and the
Sonship with Operation or Actuality
(*enérgeia*). These philosophical terms are,
of course, not the names used in the
Oracles, which preferred more graphic,
symbolic and poetical expressions.

THE CHALDÆAN ORACLES.

THE HOLY FIRE.

Thus Mind "in potentiality" is the "Hidden Fire" of Simon the Magian (who doubtless knew of the "Books of the Chaldæans"), and the "Manifested Fire" was the Mind "in operation" or Formative Mind. As *The Great Announcement* of the Simonian tradition has it (Hipp., *Ref.*, vi. 9-11) :

"The hidden aspects of the Fire are concealed in the manifest, and the manifest produced in the hidden. . . .

"And the manifested side of the Fire has all things in itself which a man can perceive of things visible, or which he unconsciously fails to perceive ; whereas the hidden side is every thing which one can conceive as intelligible, or which a man fails to conceive."

And so in our Oracles, as with Simon, and with Heraclitus, who called it "Ever-living Fire," the greatest symbol of the Power of Deity was called "*Holy Fire*," as Proclus tells us (K. 13). This Fire was both intelligible and immaterial and sensible and material, according to the point of view from which it was regarded.

MIND OF MIND.

The fiery self-creative Energy of the Father is regarded as intelligible ; that is, as determined by the vital potencies of Mind alone. Here all is "in potentiality" or hidden from the senses ; it is the truly "occult world." The sensible, or manifested, universe comes into existence by the demiurgic, or formative, or shaping Energy of the Mind, which now, as Architect of matter, is called Mind of Mind, or Mind Son of Mind, as we have Man Son of Man in the Christianized Chaldæan Gnosis. This is set forth in the following lines :

For He [the Father] doth not in-lock His Fire transcendent, the Primal Fire, His Power, into Matter by means of works, but by energy of Mind. For it is Mind of Mind who is the Architect of this [the manifested] fiery world.

"Works" seem here to mean activities, objects, creatures — separation. This Father, who is wholly beyond the Sea of Matter, does not shut up His Power into Matter by in-locking it in bodies, or works, or separate objects, but energizes by means of some mysterious abstract and infinite penetration—thus laying down as it were the foundations of root-form, the ground-plan so to speak, the nexus of the first Limit ; this makes Matter to assume the first beginnings of Mass. As soon as the Father, or Mind of all minds, has made this frame-work or net-work of Fire, Mind of Mind is born ; and this Mind is the Fiery Cosmic Mind, which by contacting Matter in its first essential nature generates the beginnings of the World-Body and of all bodies. This is the work of Mind of Mind.

So also we find the Supreme addressing Hermes in "The Virgin of the World" treatise as :

"Soul of My Soul, and Holy Mind of My own Mind" (*H.*, iii. 104).

And again in another Trismegistic fragment we read :

"There was One Gnostic Light alone—nay, Light transcending Gnostic Light. He is for ever Mind of Mind who makes that Light to shine" (*H.*, iii. 257).

For as our Oracles have it :

The Father out-perfected all, and gave them over to His second Mind, whom ye, all nations of mankind, sing of as first.

Intelligible Fire has the essence of all things for its "sparks" or "atoms." "Out-perfected" seems to mean that the Father of Himself is the Complement or Fulfilment of each separate thing. In a certain mystic sense, there are never more than two things in the universe—namely, any one thing which one may choose to think of, and its complement, the rest of the All ; and that completion of every imperfection is God.

The contention of the Gnostics was that the nations worshipped the Demiurgic

186

THE CHALDÆAN ORACLES.

or Fabricative Power of the Deity as His most transcendent mystery; this, they contended, was really a secondary mode of the Divine Power as compared with the mystery of the ineffable Self-determination of the Supreme.

A volume might be written on the subject, with innumerable quotations from Jewish and Christian Gnostics, from Philo and the Trismegistic writers, and from early Orientalist Platonists such as Numenius. The Father, as Absolute Mind, or Paramātman, perfects all things; but when we distinguish Spirit and Matter, when we regard the mystery from our state of duality, and imagine Matter as set over against Spirit, then the administration of Matter is said to be entrusted to Mind in operation in space and time; and this was called Mind of Mind, Mind Son of Mind, or Man Son of Man.

THE MONAD AND DYAD.

This Mind of Mind is conceived as dual, as containing the idea of the Dyad, in contrast with the Paternal Mind which is the Monad—both terms of the Pythagoræan *mathēsis* or *gnōsis*. His duality consists in His having power over both the intelligible and sensible universe. This is set forth in our Oracles as follows:

14 *The Dyad hath His seat with Him [the Father]; for He hath both—[both power] to master things intelligible [or ideal], and also to induce the sense of feeling in the world [of form].*

Nevertheless, there are not two Gods, but one; not two Minds, but one; not two Fires, but one; for:

15 *All things have for their Father the One Fire.*

The Father is thus called the Paternal Monad.

16 *He is the all-embracing [lit., widestretching] Monad who begets the Two.*

THE ONE BODY OF ALL THINGS.

In connection with this verse we may take the following two verses of very obscure reading:

From both of these [the Monad and Dyad] there flows the Body of the Three, 17 *first yet not first; for it is not by it that things intelligible are measured.*

This appears to mean that, for the sensible universe, the Body of the Triad —that is, the Mother-substance—comes first as being the container of all things sensible; it is not, however, the measurer of things intelligible or ideal. It is first as Body, or the First or Primal Body, but Mind is prior to it.

ONCE BEYOND AND TWICE BEYOND.

The Three Persons of the Supernal Triad were also called in the Oracles by the names Once Beyond, Twice Beyond and Hecatē; when so called they seem to have been regarded by the commentators as either simply synonyms of the three Great Names, or else as in some way the self-reflection of the Primal Triad, or as the Primal Triad mirrored in itself, that is in the One Body of all things.

It is difficult to say what is the precise meaning of the mystery-names Once Beyond and Twice Beyond. If we take them as designations of the self-reflected Triad, it may be that Once Beyond was so called because it was regarded as Beyond, not in the sense of transcending, but as beyond the threshold, so to say, of the pure spiritual state, or, in other words, as raying forth into manifestation; and so also with Twice Beyond. They paralleled the first and second Minds of the Primal Unity.

Hecatē seems to have been the best equivalent our Greek mystics could find in the Hellenic pantheon for the mysterious and awe-inspiring Primal Mother or Great Mother of Oriental mystagogy.

187

THE CHALDÆAN ORACLES.

This reflected Trinity seems to have been regarded as the Three-in-one of the Second Mind. The Later Platonist commentators seem to have in general equated these names with their Kronos, Zeus and Rhea ; while an anonymous commentator earlier than Proclus tells us that Once Beyond is the Paternal Mind of all cosmic intellection ; Hecatē is the ineffable Power of this Mind and fills all things with intellectual light, but apparently does not enter them ; whereas Twice Beyond gives of himself into the worlds, and sows into them "*agile splen-*
18 *dours,*" as the Oracles phrase it (K., 16, 17). All this is a refinement of intellectual subtlety that need not detain us ; it is foreign to the simpler mysticism of the Oracles.

THE GREAT MOTHER.

Hecatē is the Great Mother or Life of the universe, the Magna Mater, or Mother of the Gods and all creatures.

She is the Spouse of Mind, and simultaneously Mother and Spouse of Mind of Mind ; she is, therefore, said to be centered between them.

19 *'Mid the Fathers the Centre of Hecatē circles.*

She is the Mother of souls, the In-breather of life. Concerning this cosmic "vitalizing," or "quickening," or "ensouling" (*psychōsis*), as Proclus calls it, three obscure verses are preserved :

20 *About the hollows beneath the ribs of her right side there spouts, full-bursting, forth the Fountain of the Primal Soul, all at once ensouling Light, Fire, Æther, Worlds.*

If the "hollows beneath the ribs " is the correct translation (for the Greek seems very faulty, no matter what license we give to poetic imagery), it would appear that Hecatē, the Great Mother, or World-Soul, was figured in woman's form. Hecatē is, of course, as

we have already remarked, not her native name (*nomen barbarum*), but the best equivalent the Greeks could find in their humanized pantheon, a *bourgeois* company as compared with the majestic, awesome and mysterious divinities of the Orient.

This was the cosmic *psychōsis* ; the mixture of individual souls was—according to the Trismegistic " Virgin of the World " treatise, and as we might naturally expect—of a somewhat more substantial, or plastic, nature. In this treatise we read :

" And since it neither thawed when fire was set to it (for it was made of Fire), nor yet did freeze when it had once been properly produced (for it was made of Breath), but kept its mixture's composition a certain special kind, peculiar to itself, of special type and special blend—(which composition you must know, God called *psychōsis* . . .)—it was from this coagulate He fashioned souls enough in myriads " (*H.,* iii. 99).

It was probably in the mouth of the Great Mother that our poet placed the following lines :

After the Father's Thinkings, you must 21
know, I, the Soul, dwell, making all things to live by Heat.

In the mystery of re-generation also, as soon as the conception from the Father takes place—the implanting of the Light-spark, or germ of the spiritual man—the soul of the man becomes sensible to the passion of the Great Soul, the One and Only Soul, and he feels himself pulsing in the fiery net-work of lives.

But why, it may be asked, does the great Life-stream come forth from the Mother's right side ? The fragments we possess do not tell us ; but the original presumably contained some description of the Mother-Body, for we are told :

THE CHALDÆAN ORACLES.

22 *On the left side of Hecatē is a Fountain of Virtue, remaining entirely within, not sending forth its pure virginity.*

We have thus to think out the symbolism in a far more vital mode than the figurative expressions naturally suggest. And again:

23 *And from her back, on either side the Goddess, boundless Nature hangs.*

This suggests that Nature is the Garment or Mantle of the Goddess-Mother. The Byzantine commentators ascribe to every Limb of the Mother the power of life-giving; every Limb and Organ was a fountain of life. Her hair, her temples, the top of her head, her sides or flanks, were all so regarded; and even her dress, the coverings or veilings of her head, and her girdle. Whether they had full authority for this in the original text we do not know. Kroll considers this "*fraus aperta*" (K. 29); but the Mother of Life must be All-Life, one would have naturally thought, and one verse still preserved to us reads:

24 *Her hair seems like a Mane of Light a-bristle piercingly.*

Damascius speaks of her crown; this may possibly have been figured as the wall-crown or turreted diadem of Cybelē (Rhea), in which case it might have typified the "Walls of Fire" of Stoic tradition.
Her girdle seems to have been figured as a serpent of fire.
The Great Mother is also called Rhea in the Oracles, as the following three verses inform us:

25 *Rhea, in sooth, is both the Fountain and the Flood of the blest Knowing Ones; for she it is who first receives the Father's Powers into her countless Bosoms, and poureth forth on every thing birth [-and-death] that spins like to a wheel.*

The "Knowing Ones" are the Intelligences or Gnostic Thoughts of the Father. She is the Mother of Genesis, the Wheel or Sphere of Re-becoming. In one of her aspects she is called in the Oracles the "*wondrous and awe-inspiring Goddess*," as Proclus tells us. **26** With the above verses may be compared K. 36, C. 140, 125 below.

ALL THINGS ARE TRIPLE.

The statement of Hippolytus that the Assyrians (*i.e.*, the Chaldæans) "were the first to consider the soul triple and yet one," is borne out by several quotations from our Oracle-poem.

27 *The Mind of the Father uttered [the Word] that all should be divided [or cut] into three. His Will nodded assent, and at once all things were so divided.*

The Father-Mind thought "Three," acted "Three." Thought and action agreed, and it immediately happened.
An apparent continuation of this is found in the lines which characterize the Forth-thinker as:

28 *He who governs all things with the Mind of the Eternal.*

This fundamental Triplicity of all things is "intelligible," that is to say, determined by the Mind. The Mind is the Great Measurer, Divider and Separator. Thus Philo of Alexandria writes concerning the Logos, or Mind or Reason of God:
"So God, having sharpened His Reason (Logos), the Divider of all things, cut off both the formless and undifferentiated essence of all things, and the four elements of cosmos which had been separated out of it [*sci.*, the essence, or quintessence], and the animals and plants which had been compacted by means of these" (H., i. 236).
We learn from Damascius also that, according to our Oracles, the "ideal division" (? of all things into three) was

THE CHALDÆAN ORACLES.

29 the " *root (or source) of every division* " in the sensible universe (K. 18, C. 58). This law was summed up as follows :

30 *In every cosmos there shineth [or is manifested] a Triad, of which a Monad is source.*

31 It is this Triad that "*measures and delimits all things*" (K. 18, C. 8) from highest to lowest. And again :

32 *All things are served in the Gulphs of the Triad.*

This is very obscure ; but perhaps the following verse may throw some light on the imagery :

33 *From this Triad the Father mixed every spirit.*

In the first verse " Gulphs " are generally translated by " Bosoms," and " are served " by " are governed "; but the latter expression is a technical Homeric term for serving the wine for libation purposes from the great mixing-bowl (*kratēr*) into the cups, and the mixing, or mingling or blending, of souls is operated, in Plato, in the great Mixing-bowl of the Creator. These gulphs are thus mother-vortices in primal space.

The " Three " is the number of determination, and therefore stands for the root-conditioning of form, and of all classification. But if the " Three " from one point of view is formative, and therefore determining and limiting, from another point of view, it endows with power ; and so one of our Oracles runs :

34 *Arming both mind and soul with triple Might.*

In the original, "triple" is a poetical term that might be rendered "three-barbed "; if, however, it is to be connected with Pythagoræan nomenclature, it would denote a triple angle—that is

to say, presumably, the solid angle of a tetrahedron or regular four-faced pyramid.

THE MOTHER-DEPTHS.

The Bosoms or Gulphs (? Vortices, Voragines, Whirl-swirls, Æons, Atoms) are also called Depths—a technical term of very frequent occurrence in all the Gnostic schools of the time. The Great Depth of all depths was that of the Father, the Paternal Depth. Thus one of our Oracles reads

35 *Ye who, understanding, know the Paternal Depth cosmos-transcending.*

This Paternal Depth is the ultimate mystery ; but from another point of view it may be regarded as the Intelligible Ordering of all things. It is called super-cosmic or cosmos-transcending, when cosmos is regarded as the sensible or manifested order; it is the Occult, or Hidden, Eternal Type of universals, or wholes, simultaneously interpenetrating one another, undivided (sensibly) yet divided (intelligibly). We are told, therefore, concerning this super-cosmic or trans-mundane Depth, that

36 *It is all things, but intelligibly [all].*

That is to say, in it things are not divided in time and space ; there is no sensible separation. It is not the specific state, or state of species ; but the state of wholes or genera. It is neither Father nor Mother, yet both. It is the state of " At Once "; and perhaps this may explain the strange term " Once Beyond " —that is, the At-Once in the state of the Beyond, beyond the sensible divided cosmos. Proclus and Damascius speak of it as " of the form of oneness " and " indivisible "; and an Oracle characterizes it as :

37 *That which cannot be cut up ; the Holder-together of all sources.*

THE CHALDÆAN ORACLES.

As such it may be regarded as the Mother-side of things, and thus is called:

38   *Source of [all] sources, Womb that holds all things together.*

The Later Platonic commentators compared this with Plato's *Auto-zōon*, the Living Thing-in-itself, the Source of life to all; and thus the That-which-gives-life-to-itself; and, therefore, the Womb of all living creatures. The Oracles, however, regard it as the Womb of Life, the Divine Mother.

39   *She is the Energizer [lit., Work-woman] and Forth-giver of Life-bringing Fire.*

"She fills the Life-giving Bosom [or Womb] of Hecatē." — the Supernal Mother's self-reflection in the sensible universe—says Proclus, basing himself on an Oracle, and:

40   *Flows fresh and fresh [or on and on] into the wombs of things.*

The "wombs of things" are, literally, the "holders-together of things." They are reflections of the Great "Holder-together of all sources" of the fourth fragment back. This poetical expression for the Mother-Depth and her infinite reflections in her own nature of manifoldness, was developed by the Later Platonic commentators into the formal designation of a hierarchy—the Synoches. That which she imparts is called:

41   *The Life-giving Might of Fire possessed of mighty power.*

This is all on the Mother-side of things; but this should never be divorced from the Father-side, as may be seen from the nature of the mysterious Æon.

THE ÆON.

On the æon-doctrine (*cf. H.*, i. 387-412), which probably occupied a prominent position in the mysticism of our Oracle-poem (though, of course, in a simple form and not as in the over-developed æonology of the Christianized Gnosis), we unfortunately possess only four verses.

One of the names given to the Æon was "*Father-begotten*" Light, because "He makes to shine His unifying light on all," as Proclus tells us.

For He [the Æon] alone, culling unto its full the Flower of Mind [the Son] from 42 *out the Father's Might [the Mother], possesseth [both] the power to understand the Father's Mind, and to bestow that Mind both on all sources and upon all principles,—both power to understand [al., whirl], and ever bide upon His never-tiring pivot.*

The nature of this Æonic Principle (or Ātmic Mystery), according to the belief of the Theurgists, is described by Proclus. But whether this description was based upon our poem or not, we cannot be certain. We, therefore, append what Proclus says, in illustration only (C. 2):

"Theurgists declare that He [Duration, Time without bounds, the Æon] is God, 43 and hymn His divinity as both older [than old], and younger [than young], as ever-circling into itself [the Egg] and æon-wise; both as conceiving the sum total of all numbered things that move within the cosmos of His Mind, yet, over and beyond them all, as infinite by reason of His Power, and yet [again, when] viewed with them, as spirally convolved [the Serpent]."

The "ever-circling" is the principle of self-motivity. On the spiral-side of things there is procession to infinity; while on the sphere-side beginning and end are immediate and "at once."

With this passage must be taken two others quoted by Taylor, but without giving the references (C. 3 and 4):

"God [energizing] in the cosmos, æonian, boundless, young and old, in spiral mode convolved."

THE CHALDÆAN ORACLES.

44 " For Eternity [the Æon], according to the Oracles, is Cause of Life that never falleth short, and of untiring Power, and restless Energy."

THE UTTERANCE OF THE FIRE.

In connection with the idea of the Living Intellectual Fire as the Perfect Intelligible, Father and Mother in one (both creating Matter and impregnating it), conceived of sensibly as the " Descent into Matter," we may, perhaps, take the following verses :

45 *Thence there leaps forth the Genesis of Matter manifoldly wrought in varied colours. Thence the Fire-flash down-streaming dims its [fair] Flower of Fire, as it leaps forth into the wombs of worlds. For thence all things begin downwards to shoot their admirable rays.*

The origin of matter and the genesis of matter is thus to be sought for in the Intelligible itself. The doctrine of the Pythagoræans and Platonists was that the origin of matter was to be traced to the Monad. The Flower of Fire is here the quintessence of it.

LIMIT THE SEPARATOR.

To the same part of the poem we must also refer the following :

46 *For from Him leap forth both Thunderings inexorable, and the Fireflash-receiving Bosoms of the All-fiery Radiance of Father-begotten Hecatē, and that by which the Flower of Fire and mighty Breath beyond the fiery poles is girt.*

Those who have studied attentively the *Mithriac Ritual* (Vol. VI.), will feel themselves in a familiar atmosphere when reading these lines. The " Thunderings " are the Creative Utterances of the Father ; the " Bosoms " of Hecatē are the receptive vortices on the Mother-side of things. Yet Father and Mother

and also Son are all three the Monad. She is " Father-begotten," and He the Son is Mother-begotten—the Monad perpetually giving birth to itself. The Son is the that which " girds " or limits or separates, the Gnostic Horos or Limit, the Form-side of things, which shuts out the Below from the Above, and determines all opposites. It is the Cross, the " Undergirding " of the universe, as we have seen in *The Gnostic Crucifixion* (Vol. VII., pp. 157, 164 ff.).

The commentators, however, with their rage for intellectual precision, have turned this into a technical term, making it a special name ; but in the Oracles *Hypezōkós* is used more simply and generally as the separator.

Proclus characterizes this Hypezōkós as the prototype of division, the " separation of the things-that-are from matter," basing himself apparently on the verse :

Just as a diaphragm [hypezōkós], a knowing membrane, He divides. **47**

The nature of this separation is that of " knowing " or " gnostic " Fire. The Epicuræans called the separation between the visible and invisible the " Flaming Walls " of the universe. Compare the Angel with the flaming sword who guards the Gates of Paradise.

So also with the epithet " inexorable " (*ameíliktoi*) applied to the " Thunderings "; these have been transformed by the over-elaboration of the commentators into a hierarchy of Inexorables or Implacables, just as is the gorgeous imagery of the Coptic Gnostic treatises of the Askew and Bruce codices.

The simpler use may be seen in the following two verses :

The Mind of the Father, vehicled in rare Drawers-of-straight-lines, flashing inflexibly in furrows of implacable Fire. **48**

This seems to refer to the Rays of the Divine Intelligence vehicled in creative

THE CHALDÆAN ORACLES.

Fire. It is the Divine Ploughing of primal substance. Straight lines are characteristic of the Mind.

It is the first furrowing, so to speak, of the Sea of Matter in a universal pattern that impresses upon the surface a network of Light (as may be seen in protoplasm under a strong microscope) from the Ruler of the Sea above. It is the first Descent of the Father, and the first Ascent or Arising of the Son ; it suggests the idea of riding and controlling . The epithet "rare" or "attenuated" suggests drawn out to the finest thread ; these threads or lines govern and map out the Sea ; they are the Lines on the Surface ; they glitter and look like furrows of the essence of Fire.

THE EMANATION OF IDEAS.

In close connection with the lines beginning "For from Him leap forth," we may take the longest fragment (16 lines) preserved to us :

49

The Father's Mind forth-bubbled, conceiving, with His Will in all its prime, Ideas that can take upon themselves all forms ; and from One Source they, taking flight, sprang forth. For from the Father was both Will and End.

These were made differentiate by Gnostic Fire, allotted into different knowing modes.

For, for the world of many forms, the King laid out an intellectual Plan [or Type] not subject unto change. Kept to the tracing of this Plan, that no world can express, the World, made glad with the Ideas that take all shapes, grew manifest with form.

Of these Ideas there is One only Source, from which there bubble-forth in differentiation other [ones] that no one can approach—forth-bursting round the bodies of the World—which circle round its awe-inspiring Depths [or Bosoms], like unto swarms of bees, flashing around them and about, incuriously, some hither and some thither,—the Gnostic Thoughts from the Paternal Source that cull unto their full

the Flower of Fire at height of sleepless Time.

It was the Father's first self-perfect Source that welled-forth these original Ideas.

With this "culling" or "plucking" of the Flower of Fire compare the ancient gnomic couplet preserved by Hesiod (*O. et D.*, 741 f.) :

"Nor from Five-branched at Gods' Fire-looming
Cut Dry from Green with flashing Blade."

As has been previously stated (*H.*, i. 265, n. 5), I believe that Hesiod has preserved this scrap of ancient wisdom from the "Orphic" fragments in circulation in his day among the people in Bœotia, who had them from an older Greece than that of Homer's heroes ; in other words, that we have in it a trace of the contact of pre-Homeric Greece with "Chaldæa."

These living Ideas or creative Thoughts are emanations (or forth-flowings) of the Divine Mind, and constitute the Plan of that Mind, the Divine Economy. They are more transcendent even than the Fire, for they are said to be able to gather for themselves the subtlest essence or Flower of Fire. "At height of sleepless Time " is a beautiful phrase, though it is difficult to assign to it a very precise meaning. The "height of Time " is, perhaps, the supreme moment, and thus may mean momentarily—not, however, in the sense of lasting only the smallest fraction of time, but referring to Time at its limit where it touches Eternity. The Thoughts of the Father-Mind are on the Borderland of Time. They are living Intelligences of Light and Life, of the nature of Logoi.

Thoughts of the Father ! Brightness a-flame, pure Fire !

50

THE BOND OF LOVE DIVINE.

Next we may take the verses referring to the Birth of Love (Erōs), the Bond-of-union between all things.

THE CHALDÆAN ORACLES.

51 *For the Self-begotten One, the Father-Mind, perceiving His [own] Works, sowed into all Love's Bond, that with his Fire o'ermasters all ; so that all might continue loving on for endless time, and that these Weavings of the Father's Gnostic Light might never fail, With this Love, too, it is the Elements of Cosmos keep on running.*

The Works of the Father are the Operations of the Divine Mind—the Souls. The same idea, though on a lower scale, so to say, may be seen in the Announcement of the Monarch of the Worlds, sitting on the Throne of Truth, to the Souls, in the Trismegistic " Virgin of the World " treatise :

" O Souls, Love and Necessity shall be your Lords, they who are Lords and Marshals after Me of all " (*H.*, ii. 110).

The Marriage of the Elements and their perpetual transmutation was one of the leading doctrines of Heraclitus. The Elements married and transformed themselves into one another, as may also be seen from the Magian myth quoted in Vol. V. of these little books, *The Mysteries of Mithra* (p. 73). The idea is summed up in the following fine lines from a Hymn of Praise to the Æon or Eternity, in the Magic Papyri :

" Hail unto Thee, O Thou Beginning and Thou End of Nature naught can move ! Hail unto Thee, Thou Vortex of the Liturgy [or Service] unweariable of Nature's Elements ! "

In close connection with the above verses of our poem we must plainly take the following :

52 *With the Bond of admirable Love, who leaped forth first, clothed round with Fire, his fellow bound to him, that he might mix the Mixing-bowls original by pouring in the Flower of his own Fire.*

In the last line I read ἐπιχῶν (" pouring in ") for ἐπισχών. The Mixing-bowls, or Kratēres, are the Fiery Crucibles in which the elements and souls of things are mixed. The Mixer is not Love as apart from the Father, but the Mind of the Father as Love, as we learn from the following verses :

Having mingled the Spark of Soul with two in unanimity—with Mind and Breath Divine—to them He added, as a third, pure Love, the august Master binding all. 53

· Compare with this the Mixing of Souls in " The Virgin of the World " treatise :
" For taking breath from His own Breath and blending with it Knowing Fire, He mingled them with other substances which have no power to know ; and having made the two—either with other—one, with certain hidden Words of Power, He thus set all the mixture going thoroughly " (*H.*, iii. 98).

This Chaste and Holy and Divine Love is invoked as follows in the Paris Papyrus (1748) :

" Thee I invoke, Thou Primal Author of all generation, who dost out-stretch Thy wings o'er all the universe ; Thee the unapproachable, Thee the immeasurable, who dost inspire into all souls the generative sense [*lit.*, reason], who dost conjoin all things by power of Thine own Self " (K. 26).

Elsewhere in the same Papyrus (1762), Love is called :

" The Hidden One who secretly doth cause to spread among all souls the Fire that cannot be attained by contemplation."

What men think of as love, is, as contrasted with this Divine Love, called in our Oracles, the " *stifling of True Love.*" 54 True Love is also called " *Deep Love,*" 55 with which we are to fill our souls, as Proclus tells us (K. 26). Elsewhere in the Oracles this Love was united with Faith and Truth into a triad, which may be compared with another triad in the following verse quoted by Damascius :

Virtue and Wisdom and deliberate Certainty. 56

THE CHALDÆAN ORACLES.

So far we have been dealing with the Divine Powers when conceived as transcending the manifested universe ; we now come to the world-shaping, or economy of the material cosmos, and to the Powers concerned with it.

THE SEVEN FIRMAMENTS.

As we have seen above, in treating of the Great Mother (p.188), it is she who, as the Primal Soul, " all at once ensouls Light, Fire, Æther, Worlds " (K. 28, C. 38).

The Later Platonist commentators regard this Light as a monad embracing a triad of states—empyrean, ætherial, and hylic (that is, of gross matter). They further assert that the last state only is visible to normal physical sight (K. 31).

These four thus constituted the quaternary or tetrad of the whole sensible universe. This would, of course, be somewhat of a daring " philosophizing " of the simple statement of the original poem, if the verse we have quoted were the only authority for the precise statement of the commentators. But we are hardly justified in assuming, as Kroll appears to do throughout, that if no verse is quoted, therefore no verse existed. The Platonic commentators had the full poem before them, and (like the systematizers of the Upanishads) tried to evolve a consistent system out of its mystic utterances. There were also, in the highest probability, other Hellenistic documents of a similar character, giving back some reflections from the " Books of the Chaldæans " ; and also in the air a kind of general tradition of a " Chaldæan philosophy."

The Sensible Universe was thus divided by them, basing themselves on the pregnant imagery of the Oracles, into three states or " planes " — the empyrean, ætherial, and hylic. To these planes or states they referred the mysterious septenary of spheres mentioned in the verse :

The Father caused to swell forth seven firmaments of worlds. 58

This Father is, of course, Mind of Mind, and the " causing to swell forth " gives the idea of the swelling from a centre to the limit of a surround.

The most interesting point is that those who knew the Oracles, and were in the direct line of their tradition, did not regard these seven firmaments or zones as the " planetary orbits." One of the seven they assigned to the empyrean, three to the ætherial, and three to the gross-material or sublunary. There was thus a chain or coil of seven depending from the eighth, the octave, of Light, the Borderland between the intelligible and the sensible worlds. All the seven, however, were " corporeal " worlds (K. 32). The three hylic (those of gross matter) may be compared with the solid, liquid and gaseous states of physical matter ; the three ætherial with similar states of æther or subtle matter ; and the seventh corresponds with the atomic or empyrean or true fiery or fire-mist state.

Moreover, as to the hylic world or world of gross matter, which had three spheres or states, we learn :

The centres of the hylic world are fixed in the æther above it. 59

That is to say, presumably, the æther was supposed to surround and interpenetrate the cosmos of gross matter.

THE TRUE SUN.

As to the Sun, the tradition handed on a mysterious doctrine that cannot now be completely recovered in the absence of the original text. Proclus, however,

THE CHALDÆAN ORACLES.

tells us that the real Sun, as distinguished from the visible disk, was trans-mundane or super-cosmic—that is, beyond the worlds visible to the senses. In other words, it belonged to the Light-world proper, the monadic cosmos, and poured forth thence its "fountains of Light." The tradition of the most arcane or mystic of the Oracles, he tells us, was that the Sun's "wholeness"—*i.e.*, monad —was to be sought on the trans-mundane plane (K. 32, C. 130); "for there," he says, "is the 'Solar Cosmos' and the
60 'Whole Light,' as the Oracles of the Chaldæans say, and I believe" (K 33).

Elsewhere he speaks of "what appears to be the circuit of the Sun," and contrasts this with its true circulation, "which, proceeding from above somewhence, from out the hidden and super-celestial ordering of things beyond the heavens, sows into all the [suns] in cosmos the proper portion of their light for each." This also seems to have been based on the doctrine of the Oracles.

As the Enforming Mind was called
61 Mind of Mind, so was the "truer Sun" called in the Oracles "*Time of Time*," because it measures all things with Time, as Proclus tells us ; and this Time is, of course, the Æon. It was also called
62 "*Fire, Sluice of Fire*," and also "*Fire-disposer*" (K. 33, C. 133), and, we may add, by many another name connected with Fire, as we learn from the *Mithriac Ritual*.

THE MOON.

If the visible sun, as we have seen, was not the true Sun, equally so must we suppose the visible moon to be an image of the true Moon reflected in the atmosphere of gross matter. Concerning the Moon we have these five scattered shreds of fragments.

63 *Both the ætherial course and the measureless rush and the aërial floods [or fluxes] of the Moon.*

O Æther, Sun, Moon's Breath, Leaders of Air ! 64

Both of the solar circles and lunar pulsings and aërial bosoms. 65

The melody of Æther and of Sun, and of the streams of Moon and Air. 66

And wide Air, and lunar course, and the ætherial vault of Sun. 67

These scraps are too fragmentary to comment on with much profit.

THE ELEMENTS.

From what remains we learn, as Proclus tells us, that the Sun-space came first, then the Moon-space, and then the Air-space. The Elements of cosmos, however, were not simply our Earthy fire, air, water, and earth, but of a greater order. Thus Olympiodorus tells us that the elements at the highest points of the earth, that is on the tops of the highest mountains, were also thought of as elements of cosmic Water—as it were Watery air ; and this air in its turn was (? moist) Æther, while Æther itself was the uttermost Æther ; it was in that state that were to be sought the "*Æthers of the Elements*" proper, as the Oracles 68 call them (K. 34, C. 112).

THE SHELLS OF THE COSMIC EGG.

The diagrammatic representation of cosmic limit was a curve ; whether hyperbolic, parabolic or elliptical we do not know. Damascius, quoting from the Oracles, speaks of it as a single line— "*drawn out in a curved (or convex) outline*," or figure ; and adds that this figure 69 was frequently used in the Oracles (K. 34). It signified the periphery of heaven.

In the Orphic mythology (doubtless based on "Chaldæan" sources) the dome of heaven is fabled to have been formed out of the upper shell of the Great Egg, when it broke in twain. The Egg in its upper half was sphere-like, in its lower "conical" or elliptical.

Proclus tells us that the Oracles taught that there were seven circuits or rounds of the irregular or imperfect "spheres," and in addition the single motion of the eighth or perfect sphere which carried the whole heaven round in the contrary direction towards the west.

THE PHYSIOLOGY OF THE COSMIC BODY.

To this eighth sphere we must refer the "progression," spoken of in the verses :

70   *Both lunar course and star-progression. [This] star-progression was not delivered from the womb of things because of thee.*

Man, the normal mind of man, was subject to the irregular spheres ; he is egg-shaped and not spherical. And if there were spheres there were also certain mysterious "centres," and "channels" —pipes, canals, conduits, or ducts ; but what and how many these were, we can no longer discover owing to the loss of the original text. One obscure fragment alone remains :

71   *And fifth, [and] in the midst, another fiery sluice, whence the life-bringing Fire descendeth to the hylic channels.*

This apparently concerns the anatomy and physiology of the Great Body. Proclus introduces this quotation with the statement : "The conduit of the Power-of-generating-lives descends into the centre [of the cosmos], as also the Oracles say, when discoursing on the middle one of the five centres that extends right through to the opposite [side], through the centre of the earth."

How a centre can enter and go through another centre is not clear. These channels or centres, however, were clearly ways of conveying the nourishing and sustaining Fire to the world and all the lives in it.

The Primal Centre of the universe is presumably referred to in the following verse :

The Centre, from which all [? rays]   72 to the periphery are equal.

THE GLOBULAR COSMOS.

In any case the root-plan of the universe was globular. Proclus tells us that God as the Demiurge, or World-shaper, made the whole cosmos :

From Fire, from Water, Earth, and all-   73 nourishing Æther.

Where Æther is presumably the "Watery Æther" or Air, as we have seen above (p. 80). He tells us further that the Maker, working by Himself, or on Himself, or with His own Hands, framed, or shaped (*lit.*, "carpentered") the cosmos, as follows :

Yea, for there was a Second Mass of   74 Fire working of its own self all things below (lit., *there*), *in order that the Cosmic Body might be wound into a ball, in order that Cosmos might be made plainly manifest, and not appear as membrane-like.*

It is, of course, very difficult to guess the meaning of these scraps without their context. The appearance of cosmos as membranous, however, suggests the idea of the thinnest skin or surface, that is the lines, or threads, or initial markings, on the surface of things ; that is to say, that the action of the Enforming Fire rolls up the surfaces of things into three-dimensional things or solids (even as the threads of wool are wound into a ball). The underlying idea may be seen in another Oracle, which, referring to the Path of Return, where the mode of Outgoing, or Involving, has to be reversed or unwound, warns us :

Do not soil the spirit, nor turn the   75 plane into the solid.

THE CHALDÆAN ORACLES.

To this we shall return later on at the end of our comments. (*Cf. H.*, iii. 174).

The " Second Mass of Fire " is, presumably, the Sensible Fire, or rather the Fire that brings into manifestation the sensible world, as contrasted with the Pure Hidden Fire—the Unmanifest, Intelligible or Ideal Mind of the Father. The Second is of course Mind of Mind, poetically figured, as contrasted with Mind in itself; it is Mind going forth from itself.

The word translated " Mass " (ὄγκος) has a variety of refined meanings in Greek philosophical language; it can mean space, dimension, atom, etc., and gives the idea of the simplest determination of Body.

The World or Cosmos is, so to say, the " Outline " of the Mind turned to the thought of Body :

76 *For it is a Copy of Mind ; but that which is brought forth* [or *engendered*] *has something of Body.*

NATURE AND NECESSITY.

The whole of Nature, of growth and evolution, depends, or derives its origin, from the Great Mother, the Spouse of Deity, as we have seen from the verse quoted above (189 ., K. 29, C. 141). In some way Nature is identified with Fate and Custom, as the following three verses show :

77 *For Nature that doth never tire, rules over worlds and works ; in order that the Heaven may run its course for aye, downdrawn, and the swift Sun, around its Centre, that custom-wise he may return.*

If by Apollo Proclus means the Sun, and if " one of the Theurgists " is a reference to the writer of our poem, then **78** the words " *exulting in the Harmony of Light* " may be compared with the familiar " rejoicing as a giant to run his course." The Oracles speak of the Sun **79** as possessing " *three-powered* (lit., three-

winged) *rule* "—that is, presumably, above, on, and beneath the earth.

THE PRINCIPLES OR RULERS OF THE SENSIBLE WORLD.

In the fragments that remain it is very rare to find the Powers that administer the government of the universe, given Greek names. Though Proclus refers the following verse to Athēna, there is nothing to show that her name was mentioned in the Oracles. It is more probable (as we may see from K. 51, C. 170, below) that the phrase refers to the soul, or rather the new-born man of gnostic power, who leaps forth from his lower nature. Proclus may have seen in this an analogy with the birth of Athēna full-armed from the head of Zeus, and so the confusion has arisen. The phrase runs :

Yea, verily, full-armed within and armed **80** *without, like to a goddess.*

The first epithet is used of the Trojan Horse with the armed warriors within it. In the mystery of re-generation this may refer to the re-making of all man's " bodies " according to the cut and pattern of the Great or Cosmic Body. This would be all on the Mother-side of things— the gestation of the true Body of Resurrection.

It is the Later Platonic commentators, most probably, who have added names from the Hellenic pantheon in elaborating the simple, and for the most part nameless, statements of the original poem.

It is, however, clear that corresponding with what are called Fountains (πηγαί) when considered as Sources of Light and Life, in the Intelligible, there were Principles, Rulerships or Sovereignties (ἀρχαί), which ruled and ordered the Sensible Cosmos.

That these were divided into a hierarchy of four triads, twelve in all, as our commentators would have it, matches,

THE CHALDÆAN ORACLES.

it is true, with the Twelve of the traditional Chaldæan star-lore; but this was probably not so definitely set forth in the original text. Concerning these Principles the following lines are preserved:

81   *Principles which, perceiving in their minds the Works thought in the Father's Mind, clothed them about with works and bodies that the sense can apprehend.*

The chief ruling Principles of the sensible world were three in number. Damascius calls them "the three Fathers"—*sci.*, of the manifested cosmos; but this seems to be an echo of the nomenclature of the Theurgic or Magical school and not of the Oracles proper. He, however, quotes the following three verses with regard to the threefold division of the sensible world.

82   *Among them the first Course is the Sacred one; and in the midst the Aëry; third is another [one] which warms the Earth in Fire. For all things are the slaves of these three mighty Principles.*

This seems to mean, according to Damascius, that corresponding with the Heaven, Earth, and the Interspace, Air, there are three Principles; or rather, there is One Principle in three modes—heavenly (or empyrean), middle (aëry or ætherial), and terrene (or hylic). The heavenly course is, presumably, the revolution of the Great Sphere of fixed stars; the terrene is connected with the Central Fire; and the middle with the motions of the irregular spheres.

It may also be that the last "course," connected with the Air simply, has to do with the mysterious "Winds" or currents of the Great Breath, as we saw in the symbolism of the *Mithriac Ritual.* This conjecture is confirmed by certain obscure references in Damascius, when, using the language of the Oracles, he speaks of a "*Pipe*" or "*Conduit*" connected with the Principles of the sensible world, and says that this is subordinate to a Pipe connected with the Fountains of the intelligible world.

The difference between Fountain and Principle is clear enough; one wells out from itself, the other rules something not itself. The terms seem to be somewhat of a *hysteron proteron* if we insist on a precise meaning; we should remember, however, that we are dealing largely with symbolism and poetical imagery.

Proclus endeavours to draw up a precise scale of terms in connection with this imagery of Fountains or Sources, when he tells us that the highest point of every chain (or series) is called a Fountain (or Source); next came Springs; after these Channels; and then Streams. But this is probably a refinement of Proclus' and not native to the Logia.

THE . . .
CHALDÆAN
ORACLES. .
VOL. II. . .

THE CHALDÆAN ORACLES.

VOLUME II.

CONTENTS.

The Purifying Mysteries
The Fire-Gnosis
The Manifestations of the Gods
The Theurgic Art
The Royal Souls
The Light-Spark
The Unregenerate
The Perfecting of the Body
Reincarnation
The Darkness
The Infernal Stairs
On Conduct
The Gnosis of Piety

BIBLIOGRAPHY.

K. = Kroll (G.), *De Oraculis Chaldaicis;* in *Breslauer philologische Abhandlungen,* Bd. vii., Hft. i. (Breslau ; 1894).

C. = Cory (I. P.), *Ancient Fragments* (London ; 2nd ed., 1832), pp. 239—280. The first and third editions do not contain the text of our Oracles.

F. = Mead (G. R. S.), *Fragments of a Faith Forgotten* (London ; 2nd. ed., 1906).

H. = Mead (G. R. S.), *Thrice Greatest Hermes* (London ; 1906).

THE CHALDÆAN ORACLES.

FRAGMENTS AND COMMENTS.

(Continued.)

THE STARTERS.

On the borderland between the intelligible and sensible worlds were the Iynges—mysterious beings whose name may perhaps be translated as Wheels or Whirls, or even as Shriekers. As, however, I seem to detect in these three ruling Principles a correspondence with the creators, preservers and destroyers, or rather regenerators (perfecters or enders) of Indian theosophy, I will call these Iynges Starters, in the sense of Initiators or Setters-up of the initial impulse.

We will first set down the "wisdom" of the lexicon on this puzzling subject, warning the reader that he is having his attention turned to the wrong side of the thing—the littleness and superstition of what in the Oracles was clearly intended to be a revelation of some greatness.

Iynx is said to be the bird which we call the wryneck; it was called *iynx* in Greek from its cry, as it is called wryneck in English from the movement of its head. *Iygē* and *iygmós* are used of howling, shrieking, yelling, both for shouts of joy and cries of pain, and also of the hissing of snakes.

The ancient wizards, it is said, used to bind the wryneck to a wheel, which they made to revolve, in the belief that they thus drew men's hearts along with it and chained them to obedience ; hence this magic wheel was frequently used in the belief that it was a means of recovering unfaithful lovers. This operation was called setting the magic bird or magic wheel agoing. The unfortunate bird seems to have been attached to the wheel with its wings and legs pegged out crosswise so as to form four spokes, spread-eagle fashion. The word *iynx* thus came to mean a charm, and a spell, and also a passionate yearning.

The root-idea accordingly seems to have been that of a " winged wheel " that emitted sound, and we are reminded of the winged creatures or wheels in the famous Vision of Ezekiel, who saw the mystic sight in Babylon, and thus probably caught some reflection of the symbolism of the Chaldæan mysteries.

How the wryneck was first brought in, and finally assumed the chief place, is a puzzle. It reminds one of the story of the calf in the Vaidik rite, which so interfered with the sacred service of the sage that he had to tie it up to a post before he could continue the rite. This casual incident became finally sterotyped into the chief feature of the rite !

Certain it is that the Iynges of our Oracles have nothing to do with wrynecks ; we shall, therefore, make bold to translate them as Wheels or Starters. They were presumably thought of as Living Spheres, whirling out in every direction from the centre, and wirling in again to that same centre, once they had reached the limit of their periphery or surround. They were also, in all probability, conceived of as Winged Globes—a familiar figure in Babylonian and Egyptian art—thus symbolizing that they were powers of the Air, midway between Heaven, the Great Surround, and Earth, the fixed Centre. In other words, they were the Children of the Æon.

An anonymous ancient writer tells us (K. 39) that it is the blending of the intellectual (or gnostic) and intelligible (or ideal) orders—that is, the union of the prototypes of what we distinguish as subject and object in the sense-world of diversity, or what we might call the self-reflective energy of the Mind on the plane of reality—that first " spirts forth " the One Iynx, and after this the three Iynges that are called "paternal"

THE CHALDÆAN ORACLES.

and also "unspeakables." This writer also characterizes the Iynx as the "One in the three Depths after it" (it is, therefore, of an æonic nature), and says that it is this three-in-one hierarchy that divides the worlds into three—namely, empyrean, ætherial, and terrene.

The information of Damascius refines and complicates the idea, when he tells us that "the Mind of the Father is said to bring forward [on to the stage of manifestation] the triadic ordering—Iynges, Synoches, Teletarchæ"—which we may render tentatively as Whirlings, Holdings-together and Perfectings.

The Synoches we have come across before (fr.41). Teletarchía is used by ecclesiastical writers as a synonym of the Trinity; while Orpheus is called *teletárchēs* as the founder of mysteries or perfectionings.

The root-meanings underlying the names of the members of this triad seem to suggest, as we have already said, the ideas of creating (or preferably starting), preserving (or maintaining), and completing (or perfecting or finishing).

Damascius thinks that the last words of the following two verses refer to the triad of the One Iynx.

85 *Many are these who leaping mount upon the shining worlds ; among them are three excellencies* [or *heights*].

The meaning of the first clause is doubtful. Who the many (fem. pl.) are, is not clear ; it may mean that there are hosts of subordinate Iynges. On the contrary, it may have nothing to do with these Nature-Iynges on the Path of Descent, that is the bringing into manifestation, but may refer to souls who in the Ascent win their way to the "shining worlds" or Worlds of Light, and become Iynges consciously

According to both Damascius and Proclus, the Order of Iynges is characterized as having the power both of

proceeding or going-forth and of drawing-together or contracting—that is, both of expansion and contraction, of out-breathing and in-breathing. They are, moreover, free Intelligences.

The Whirls [*Iynges*] *created by the* 84 *Father's Thought are themselves, too, intelligent* [or *gnostic*], *being moved by Wills ineffable to understand.*

They are created by Divine Thought, as Sons of Will and Yoga, and procreate by thought ; they are Mind-born and give birth to minds. Their epithet is the "*Ineffables*" or "*Unspeakables*"; they 85 are further called in the Oracles "*swift*," 86 and are said to proceed from and to "*rush to*" or "*desire eagerly*" the Father (C. 52) ; they are the "*Father's Powers.*" 87 Indeed, as Proclus declares :

"For not only do these three divinities [or divine natures] of themselves bring into manifestation and contract them [*sci.*, out of manifestation], but they are also '*Guardians*' [or Watchers or Pre-88 servers] of the '*works*' of the Father, according to the Oracle—yea, of the One Mind that doth create itself" (K. 40, C. 41).

Iynx in its root-meaning, according to Proclus, signifies the "power of transmission," which is said, in the Oracles, "*to sustain the fountains.*" The same 89 idea seems to be latent in the following verse :

For all cosmos has inflexible intelligent 90 *sustainers.*

The meaning is quite clearly brought out when Proclus, elsewhere, affirms that the Order of the Iynges "has a transmissive [that is, intermediary or ferrying] power, as the Theologers call it, of all things from the Intelligible [or Typal] Order into Matter, and again of all things into it [*sci.*, the Intelligible]."

In other words, they are the direct link between the Divine and physical,

204

THE CHALDÆAN ORACLES.

and to some extent also suggest the idea of Angels or Messengers ; yet are they like to Wheels and Whirls, or Vortices—on the one hand to vortical atoms, and on the other to individualities. They are, of course, in essence, quite unbound by ideas of extension in space, and sequence in time ; though they manifest in space and time.

Porphyry preserves a curious Oracle which reads :

91 *With secret rites drawing the* iynx *from the æther.*

This Oracle, however, may have been taken from some Theurgist or Hellenized Magian source and not from our poem ; and so also may the following quoted by Proclus :

92 *Be active* [or *operate*] *round the Hecatic spinning thing.*

It is doubtful what *strôphalus* means exactly. It may sometimes mean a top ; and in the Mysteries tops were included among the mystic play-things of the young Bacchus, or Iacchus. They represented, among other things, the "fixed" stars (humming tops) and planets (whipping tops).

The Iynx was said to be active, or to energize, on the three—empyrean, ætherial and terrene—planes.

THE MAINTAINERS.

Though the Later Platonic commentators make two other allied hierarchies out of the Synoches and Teletarchæ, both these, as we have seen, should rather be taken as modes of this same mysterious Iynx. In manifestation, from one it passed to three, and so became many. Thus a scrap of our Oracles reads :

93 *Nay, and as many as are subject to the hylic* [or *terrene*] *Synoches.*

This would seem to mean simply the Powers that hold together, or con-tract, or mass, material things ; and these Powers are again the Iynges, or simultaneously creative, preservative, and destructive or perfective Intelligences of the Father-Mind, which are in the Oracles symbolically called His "*Lightnings*" when thought of as Rays or Intelligences. The word *Prēstēres* (Lightnings), however, is more graphically and literally rendered as Fiery Whirlwinds—like waterspouts. These are again our Iynges or Whirls or Swirls or Wheels, spinning in and out. Thus two verses read :

94 *But to the Knowing Fire-whirls of the Knowing Fire* [i.e., *the Father*] *all things do yield, subject unto the Father's Will which makes them to obey.*

As we have seen above (p.204) these Whirls, as Synoches—that is, in their power of holding together—were called "Guardians," and this is borne out by two verses :

95 *He gave to His own Fire-whirls the power to guard the summits, commingling with the Synoches the proper power of His own Might.*

The "summits" suggest these selfsame Iynges in their creative mode ; the series of which they were the "summits" being creative (or inceptive), preservative (or guardian), and perfective (consummative or regenerative).

Thus Damascius tells us that the whole Demiurgic Order—that is to say, the order of things in genesis—was surrounded by what the Oracles call the "*Fire-whirling Guard.*" In brief it is the power of holding together (? gravitation on the life-side of things).

This is fundamentally the great power of the Mother-side of things ; for, as we have seen (p.191), the Great Mother is :

96 *Source of all sources, Womb that holds all things together.*

THE CHALDÆAN ORACLES.

It follows, therefore, that the Iynges, as creative, are on the Father-side; as preservative (or Synoches) on the Mother-side; and as result or consummating or perfecting (or Teletarchæ) on the Son-side.

Damascius bears this out when he tells us that the Oracles call the Synoches

97 the "*Whole-makers*" (*holopoioi*)—that is to say, they are connected with the idea of wholeness or oneness or the root-substance side of things, and again with the idea of the Æon.

Of course, the symbolic categories of Father, Mother, and Son are really all aspects of One and the same Mystery— the That which understands itself alone and yet is beyond understanding. To this Proclus refers when he writes (K. 42, C. 7): " Including [containing, preserving] all things in the one excellency [or summit] of His own subsistence,

98 ' *Himself subsists wholly beyond*,' according to the Oracle."

THE ENDERS.

So also with the Teletarchæ or Perfecting Powers ; as Proclus tells us, they have the same divisions as the Synoches (and Iynges); that is to say, it is again all the same thing looked at from the Son-side of things. There was thus, in the elaboration of the Later Platonic commentators, a triple, and even a seven-fold, division of this order or hierarchy. Considering the Teletarchic energy, or activity, as triadic, Proclus tells us that in its first mode it has to do with the finest or ultimate substance, the Empyrean, and says that it plays the part

99 of Driver or Guide to the "*foot* [?—tarsón] *of Fire* "—which may be simply a poetical phrase for the Fire in its first contact with substance. Its middle mode, embracing beginnings and ends and middles, perfects the Æther ; while its third mode is concerned with Gross Matter (*Hylē*), still confused and unshaped, which it also perfects.

From these and other elaborations of a like nature, we learn that the Teletarchs

were regarded as three, and were intimately bound up with the Synoches, **100** and therefore with the Iynges (C. 58). The unifying or holding-together of the Synochic power is de-fined and delimited by the perfecting nature of the Teletarchic power—

Into beginning and end and middle **101** *things by Order of Necessity.*

In this connection it is of interest to cite a sentence from Proclus that is almost certainly quoted from the Oracles. It relates to the Ascent of the individual soul and not to cosmogenesis, to perfection in the Mysteries and not to the Mysteries that perfect the world :

The Soul-lord, he who doth set his feet **102** *upon the realms ætherial, is the Perfectioner* [*Teletarch*].

Finally, Proclus refers the following two verses to the Teletarchs :

Nay, a Name of august majesty, and, **103** *with sleepless whirling, leaping into the worlds, by reason of the Father's swift Announcement.*

In another passage Proclus refers to the " *Transmissive* " Name that leaps **104** into activity in the " *boundless worlds* " **105** (K. 44); and in yet another passage (K. 40), which we have already quoted (*p.204*), he gives this " Name " to the Iynges. This plainly refers to the " *Intermediaries who stand* " between the **106** Father and Matter, as Damascius says (K. 44), who further affirms that in their aspect of Teletarchs they are perfecting, and rule over all perfections, or the perfecting rites of the Mysteries.

So much, then, for the highest Principles or Ruling Powers of the Sensible World. The commentators further speak of a division among the Gods into Gods within the Zones and Gods beyond the Zones ; but no verse from the Oracles is extant by which we can control this statement. It seems to mean simply that they were classified according as to whether their operations were concerned with the Seven Spheres, or were beyond them.

THE DAIMONES.

The lesser powers were, according to Olympiodorus, divided into Angels, Daimones and Heroes. Concerning the Heroes, however, we have no fragment remaining; while Angels and Daimones are at times somewhat confused. On the Daimones we have the following two verses :

107 *Nature persuades us that the Daimones are pure, and things that grow from evil matter useful and good.*

Kroll thinks that this means that Nature deceives us into thinking that the evil Daimones are good; it may, however, mean that whereas from Man's standpoint Daimones are good or evil, according to Nature they are pure, or indifferent, or non-moral. Their operations are conditioned by man's nature. They are in themselves non-human entities, and there is a scale of them from lowest to highest.

THE DOGS.

Certain classes of them the Oracles call " Dogs "; and here we may quote an interesting passage from Lydus (K. 30) : " Whence the tradition of the Mystic Discourse [? the Oracles] that Hecatē [the World-Mother] is four-headed because of the four elements. And the fire-breathing head of the Horse evidently refers as it were to the sphere of fire ; the bellowing head of the Bull has reference to a certain bellowing power connected with the sphere af air ; the bitter and unstable nature of the Hydra [or Water-serpent] is connected with the sphere of water ; and the chastening and avenging nature of the Dog with that of earth."

The last clause throws some light on the allied figure of Anubis in Egyptian psychopompy, and also on the following fragment of the Oracles :

Out of the Womb of Earth leap Dogs 108 *terrestrial that unto mortal never show true sign.*

It is impossible to say what this means precisely without the context. " Dogs " are the intelligent guardians of the secrets of various mystery-traditions ; they are ever watchful. The Outer Guards of the Adyta in which the mystic rites were celebrated, were sometimes called Dogs. Much could be written on this symbolism, beginning with Anubis and the Dog-ape of Thoth (see " Dog " in the Index of *H.*). Dog was a name of honour in the Mysteries. The Pythagoræans called the Planets the " Dogs of Persephonē"; sparks were poetically called the " Dogs of Hephæstus." The Eumenides, were called " Dogs," and the Harpies " Dogs of Great Zeus." Perhaps this may throw some light on our particular Oracle ; in the Oracles generally, however, they seem to have been a generic name of apparently wider meaning than in the symbolism which Lydus uses ; unless we assume that for him the earth-sphere extended to the moon, when it would have three " planes "—terrene, watery and aëry—each of which had its appropriate Dogs.

Thus Olympiodorus writes : " From the aëry spaces begin to come into existence the irrational Daimones. Wherefore also the Oracle says : "

She [? *Hecatē*] *is the Driver of the aëry* 109 *and the earthy and the watery Dogs.*

Kroll refers to the last of these Dogs the epithet " *Water-walkers*," which Proclus quotes from the Oracles in the following passage :

" ' Watery ' as applied to divine natures signifies the undivided domain over

THE CHALDÆAN ORACLES.

water; for which cause, too, the Oracle
110 calls these Gods 'Water-walkers'" (K.
45, C. 76).

It is clear, however, that this refers
to a far higher " dominion " than that
of the Dogs. These inferior Daimones
had their existence as far as the Moon
only, in what was regarded as the realm
of the impure nature or gross matter.
Beyond the Moon the Daimones were
held to be of a higher and purer order;
these were also called Angels—a term
that in all probability came into our
Hellenized Oracles along the line of the
Mago-Chaldæan tradition.

111   Psellus speaks of "the manifoldly-
flowing tribes" (the group-soul idea) of
the Daimones, and this phrase was in
all probability taken from the Oracles.
(K. 46). It would seem to indicate that
the nature of the Daimones was unstable
and Protean, or rather that they could
assume any form at will.

THE HUMAN SOUL.

We now come to the important subject
of the doctrine of the Oracles concerning
the human soul.

The soul, as we have already seen
(fr. 53), was brought into being by the
union of three; it is a triad, or rather
a monad united with a triad.

53   Having mingled the Spark of soul with
two in unanimity—with Mind and Breath
Divine—to them He added, as a third,
Pure Love, the august Master binding all.

We must, then, suppose that the
individual souls, as lives, flow forth from
the World-Soul, the Great Mother; it
is, however, the Father who conditions
them by His Creative Thought.

112   These things the Father thought, and [so]
made mortal [man] to be ensouled.

"Mortal man" here seems to mean
man as conditioned by body. The Soul
is, as it were, a middle term between
Mind and Body—both for the Great
World and for the little world, or man;
for two verses run:

The Father of men and gods placed Mind 113
in Soul, and Soul in inert Body.

The fundamental distinction, however,
between the Mind and Soul is not easy to
draw with any great clearness. They
may be thought of as Light and Life,
the eternally united complements of the
One Mystery, the masculine and feminine
powers of the sexless Supreme. So also
with the individual soul in man; the
soul-spark is a light-spark which is also
a life-spark, or rather life-flood; it is
centre and sphere in perpetual embrace
—for mind and soul are not to be separated, no man can put them asunder.
The nature of this " soul " (ātma-buddhi)
is immortal and divine.

For Soul being shining Fire, by reason 114
of the Father's Power, both keeps immune
from Death, and body is of Life, and hath
the fulnesses [plērōmata] of many wombs.

In the cosmic process (and also in the
case of the individual) when the Sea of
Substance has been impregnated by the
Beams of Light, the whole Sea changes
from dull and sluggish Matter (tamas) to
bright Soul (sattva). It has become one
now instead of indeterminate, cosmic and
no longer chaotic. It is now the Sea of
Life, the complement of all imperfection.

It is in all probability to the individual
Soul that Psellus refers, when he writes:
"For if, according to the Oracles, it is
'a portion of the Fire Divine,' and ' shining 115
Fire," and ' a creation of the Father's
Thought,' its form is immaterial and
self-subsistent " (K. 47, n. 2).

THE VEHICLES OF MAN.

The original text of our Oracle-poem
had, probably, something to tell us of

THE CHALDÆAN ORACLES.

other "vehicles" or "garments" of the Soul besides the gross body; but no verses on this interesting subject are extant.

Proclus, however, tells us that the disciples of Porphyry "seem to follow the Oracles, in saying that in its Descent the Soul 'collects a portion of Æther and of Sun and Moon, and all the elements contained in Air.'" Compare with this the Oracle quoted above :

65   *O Æther, Sun, Moon's Breath, Leaders of Air.*

And also a fragment of Porphyry preserved by Stobæus :

"For when the soul goes forth from the solid body, there follows along with it the spirit which it collected from the spheres" (K. 47, n. 3).

And with this compare the following passage from the Trismegistic tractate "The Key":

"Now the principles of man are this wise vehicled : mind in the reason, the reason in the soul, soul in the spirit, and spirit in the body.

"Spirit pervading body, by means of veins and arteries and blood, bestows upon the living creature motion, and, as it were, doth bear it in a way. . . .

"It is the same for those who go out from the body.

"For when the soul withdraws into itself, the spirit doth contract within the blood, and soul within the spirit. And then the mind, stripped of its wrappings, and naturally divine, takes to itself a fiery body" (*H.*, ii. 149, 151).

And so also Proclus, treating of the Ascent or Return, and plainly referring to the Oracles, writes :

"In order that both the visible vehicle may, through the visible action of them [*sci.*, the Rays], obtain its proper treatment [or care], and that the vehicle that's more divine than this, may secretly be purified, and [so] return to its own
116 proper lot, '*drawn upward by the lunar*

and the solar Rays,' as says somewhere one of the Gods [*i.e.*, the Oracles]."

Compare with this the Pitṛi-yăna and Deva-yăna, or Way of the Fathers and Way of the Gods, in the Upanishads. This "more divine vehicle" was generally called by the Later Platonic school the "ray-like" (*augo-eidés*), or "star-like" (*astro-eidés*), or "spirituous" (*pneumatik-ón*) body; and its purification and enlivening by means of the Rays are admirably set forth in the rubrics of the *Mithriac Ritual* (Vol. VI.).

SOUL-SLAVERY.

In itself, the Soul is possessed of a divine nature, and is naturally free; in the earth-state, however, it is now in slavery owing to its being drunk with the things of gross matter (*hylē*). This at any rate seems to be the meaning of the following three lines that have, unfortunately, been considerably mangled by the copyists :

The Soul of man shall press God closely 117
*to itself, with naught subject to death in
it; [but now] it is all drunk, for it doth
glory in the Harmony beneath whose sway
the mortal frame exists*

With these lines are probably to be taken the verse quoted above :

*Not knowing God is wholly God. O
wretched slaves, be sober !*

The Harmony is the system of the Seven Formative Spheres of Genesis, or Fate. And so Proclus, speaking of Souls, writes :

"Which also the Gods [*i.e.*, the Oracles] say are slaves when they turn to generation (*genesis*); but '*if they serve their* 118 *slavery with neck unbent,*' they are brought home again from out this state, leaving the state of birth-and-death (*genesis*) behind."

THE CHALDÆAN ORACLES.

THE BODY.

As to body, the doctrine of the Oracles was, as with nearly all the mystic schools of the time, that of naïve ascetic dualism in general, that is if we can trust the commentators. Body seems more or less to have been identified with matter. It is said to be " in a state of flux," " spread out," and " scattered." It was apparently called, in the Oracles, the " *tumultuous vessel* " or " *vessel of tumult* "—the epithet being derived from rushing, roaring and dashing waves, and the idea being connected with the flowing nature of material things, presumably, as contrasted with the quiet of the contemplative mind.

Proclus speaks of " the earth from which one must ' *lighten the heart* ' " (K. 48), and this " heart " must be associated with what he calls, after the Oracles, " the ' *inner heart* ' in the essence of the soul " (K. 47, n. 1).

The unfortunate body is thus regarded as the " *root of evil*," or " *naughtiness*," and is said to be even the " *purgation of matter* " (K. 48), one of our extant fragments characterizing it plainly as the " *dung* " or " *dross of matter* " (K. 61, C. 147).

It may here be noted that in the *Pistis Sophia*, matter is called the "superfluity of naughtiness," and men (that is men's bodies) are said to be the " purgation of the matter (*hylē*) of the Rulers " (*P.S.*, 249, 251, 337) ; and it is very credible that this was one of the doctrines of the " Books of the Chaldæans."

Matter (*hylē*) is here not regarded as the fruitful substance of the universe, the " Land flowing with milk and honey," but as the dry and squalid element beneath the Moon, which, Proclus tells us, is called, in the Oracles, the " *unwatered*," that is' in itself unfruitful, the Desert as compared with the Land of true living substance (K. 48).

NATURE.

In this gross matter dwells the body which is subject to Nature, that is Fate.

The physical body, then, appears to have been regarded as an excretion within the domain of Nature or the Fate-sphere. Psellus, accordingly, writes concerning the Soul, or rather the Light-spark :

" But the Gnostic Fire comes from Above, and is in need of its native Source alone [presumably, the true spiritual life-substance] ; but if it be affected by the feelings of the body, Necessity compels that it should serve it [the body] and [so] be set beneath the sway of Fate, and led about by Nature " (K. 48).

This suggests the putting on the " form of a servant," of the Pauline Letters (*Phil.*, ii. 7), and the Trismegistic " becoming a slave within the Harmony [*i.e.*, Fate-sphere] " (*H.*, ii. 10).

This gross matter, or hylic substance, extended as far as the Moon ; it constituted, therefore, practically the atmosphere, or surround, of the earth, generally spoken of as the sublunary region. The Moon was its " Ruler," being the " image " of the Great Mother, Nature, who conditions all genesis—that is, becoming or birth-and-death. Speaking of this Lunar Sphere, which surrounds the hylic regions, Proclus tells us that in it were " the causes of all genesis " or generation; and quotes a sacred *logos* in confirmation :

The self-revealed glory [or *image*] *of Nature shines forth.*

Whether these words are quoted directly from our poem, is not quite certain ; it is, however, highly probable, for an isolated verse runs :

Do not invoke the self-revealed image of Nature.

Here Mother Nature is what the Greeks called Hecatē, and her " image " or nature-symbol, or glory, is the Moon. Very similar to this is the fragment :

Turn not thy face Naturewards ; [*for*] *her Name is identical with Fate.*

THE CHALDÆAN ORACLES.

Perhaps the second clause has been defaced in the tradition; it is difficult to make out the precise sense from the present text, unless it means simply, as Iamblichus tells us, that : "The whole being [or essence] of Fate is in Nature"—that is to say, that Nature and Fate are identical.

In close connection with this we must take the Oracular prohibition :

129 *Do not increase thy Fate !*

Fate may here be said to be the result of contact with many people and objects. Everything that we have intercourse with on earth enlarges our destiny, for destiny in this sense is the result of earthly happenings. We should, accordingly, seek within everything for further ideas, and not simply rush about and spread ourselves all over space. This seeking within by means of true mind is not stirring up the secret powers of Great Nature; it is rather the understanding of Fate. The prohibition thus seems to mean : Do not increase the dominion of the body of the lower nature, or rather the Moon-ruled plasm.

Within the same range of ideas also, we may, perhaps, bring the isolated apostrophe from the Oracles :

130 *O man, thou subtle handiwork of daring Nature !*

This refers to the body of man that is wrought by the Nature-powers, the elemental intelligences of the Mother.

THE DIVINE SPARK.

The "soul" is thus thought of, in this doctrine, as struggling against the "body"; in this great Struggle, or Passion, it is helped by the Father, who has bestowed upon it a particle, or rather portion, of His own Mind, the living "symbol," or pledge, or token, of Himself. This struggle, or passion, is in reality the travail, or birth-throes, of the

self-born Son. It is because of this Light-spark, by reason of this pledge, that souls fallen into generation, and therefore forgetful in time of their Divine origin, can recover the memory of the Father.

For the Mind of the Father hath sown 131 *symbols through the world—[the Mind] that understands things understandable, and that thinks-forth ineffable beauties.*

Psellus has a variant of the first verse, namely :

The Mind of the Father has sown 131 *symbols in the souls.*

These "symbols" are the seeds of Divinity (the *logoi* or "words" of Philo and the Christian Gnosis), but they are not operative until the soul converts its will from the things of Fate to those of Freedom, from self-will to spiritual free-will. On this we have, fortunately, three verses preserved :

But the Mind of the Father doth not 132 *receive her will, until she hath departed from Oblivion, and uttereth the word, by putting in its [Oblivion's] place the Memory of the Fatherhood's pure token.*

On this Psellus comments : "Each, therefore, diving into the ineffable depths of his own nature, findeth the symbol of the All-Father." "Uttering the word" is, mystically, bringing this *logos*, or light-spark, into activity.

THE WAY OF RETURN.

The Path of Return to the Father was set forth at length in the Oracles, and on it we have, fortunately, a number of fragments :

Seek out the channel of the Soul-stream, 133 *—whence and from what order is it that the soul in slavery to body [did descend, and] to what order thou again shalt rise, at-one-ing work with holy word.*

211

THE CHALDÆAN ORACLES.

The meaning of "word" in this and the preceding fragment is doubtful. We may either take it mystically, as we have suggested above, or it may be taken magically, as the utterance of compelling speech—in the lower sense, the theurgic use of invocations, and in the higher the utterance of true "words of power," that is the "speech of the gods" which is uttered by right action, or "work." This reminds us of the "Great Work" of the Alchemists, and of Karma-yoga, or the "union by works," of Vaidik theosophy, taken in the mystic sense and not the usual meaning of ceremonial acts. Kroll thinks that the "holy word" means the knowledge of the intelligible world of the Father, but I do not quite follow him.

THE ARMOUR OF SOUNDING LIGHT.

The nature of the Quest is set forth mysteriously as follows :

134   *Armed at all points, clad in the bloom of Sounding Light, arming both mind and soul with three-barbed Might, he must set in his heart the Triad's every symbol, and not move scatteredly along the empyrean ways [or channels], but [move] collectedly.*

Compare with this:

135   *Yea, verily, full-armed without and armed within like to a goddess.*

This refers to the Re-generate, as described in the *Mithriac Ritual*. The "three-barbed Might" is taken probably from the symbol of the trident, and represents the triple-power of the Monad. As the *Ritual* says (page 91), he must hold himself steady and not allow himself to be "scattered abroad"; all his "limbs" must be collected, or gathered together, as the Osiris in resurrection. Compare with this *The Gnostic Crucifixion* (pp. 157, 166), and also the remarkable description of a somewhat similar experience in a story, by E. R. Innes, in *The Theosophical Review* (vol. xli., p. 343., Dec., 1907).

Especially to be noticed is the graphic phrase "Sounding Light," showing that the close connection between colour and sound was known to the initiates of these mysteries. This Sounding Light, however, in its mystical sense, was probably the Uttered Word, or, to use another figure, the putting-on of the "Robe of Glory." Compare with this the Descent of the Eagle in the Hymn of the Soul of Bardaisan :

" It flew in the form of the Eagle,
    Of all the winged tribes the king-bird;
It flew and alighted beside me,
    And turned into speech altogether."
                            (*F.*, p. 410).

This Sounding Light is thus the true "symbol" of the Paternal or Spiritual or Intelligible Monad. Proclus speaks of the intelligence as being "well-wheeled," by which he means smoothly spinning round a centre ; this centre being the Intelligible (K. 51). But, to our taste, this is by no means a good simile, for the Intelligible or Spiritual Mind embraces all things and is not a centre. Proclus, however, seems to base himself upon this verse :

Urging himself to the centre of Sounding 136 *Light.*

But when we remember the "three-barbed Might" of our first fragment above (K. 51, C. 170), we may, perhaps, be permitted to translate *kéntron* as "goad" :

Urging himself on with the goad of Sounding Light.

We thus bring the main idea into relation with the contemporaneous Trismegistic doctrine of the Master-Mind (*i.e.*, the Spiritual Mind) being the Charioteer, and driving the soul-chariot, with gnostic rays (or reins) that sound forth its true counsels. In any case the mystic should find no difficulty in transmuting the symbols, passing from centre to periphery or from periphery to centre as the thought requires.

Finally, with regard to the first quotation under this heading, it may be said that in re-generation man begins to re-clothe himself; only when he makes these new clothes, they no longer bind but clothe him with power. The "bloom" (or vigour) of Sounding (or Resounding) Light is an armour that rays forth. "Might" (or Strength) suggests inner stability, that which is planted within and is the root of stability, the foundation. The ātmic, or spiritual, "spark," in the virgin soil, or womb, of the man's spiritual nature, is the Strength of the Father. It is the Power to stop chaos swirling, and so start the enforming or ordering of itself. Thus it is that the man starts making the symbols and sounds whereby his Name or Word is actualized.

THE WAY ABOVE.

Such a man should begin to know the nature of the regions unto which he is being brought, and so understand the mystic precept :

137 *Let the immortal depths of thy soul be opened, and open all thy eyes at once to the Above.*

It is proper to follow the "great" passions and desires of the soul, provided the "eye," or true centre of the mind, be fixed Above; for then the passions are sure to be pure, and not personal attractions, not little bonds of feeling and sentiment.

This "opening of all the eyes" concerns the mystery of the Æon. In the Depths of the New Dawn every atom of the man must become an eye; he must be "all eye." As vehicle of Sounding Light he must become an Æon—"a Star in the world of men, an Eye in the regions of the gods."

But to be clothed with this Royal Vesture, this Robe of Glory, he must strip off the "garb of the servant," the bonds of slavery, the "earthy carapace" :

The mortal once endowed with Mind 138 *must on his soul put bridle, in order that it may not plunge into the ill-starred Earth but win to freedom.*

"Endowed with Mind" is the Trismegistic "Mind-led." This Spiritual Mind, or Great Mind, is the Promethean, or Foreseeing, Mind in man (as Proclus tells us), who plays the part of Providence over the life of reason in us—that is, the rational man or animal—that this life may not be destroyed by being—

Dowsed in the frenzies of the Earth and 139 *the necessities of Nature.*

This is quoted by Proclus from our poem, for he adds : "As one of the Oracles says." This "dowsing," or baptism, of the soul in the waves of the Ocean of Genesis, or Generation, the Watery Spheres, is referred to several times in the Trismegistic fragments (K. 52, n. 1), and is the converse of the Spiritual Baptism or "Dowsing in the Mind," as we read in the Divine Herald's Proclamation, in the treatise called "The Cup" or "Mixing-bowl"—the Monad.

"Baptize thyself with this Cup's Baptism, what heart can do so, thou that hast faith thou canst ascend to Him who hath sent down the Cup, thou that dost know for what thou did'st come into being" (*H.*, li. 87).

Of similar purport are the verses :

Unto the Light and to the Father's Rays 140 *thou ought'st to hasten, whence hath been sent to thee a soul richly with Mind arrayed.*

"Hasten" is a mystery-word, suggesting activity without motion. The soul must be lightened and stripped of its gross garments of matter (*hylē*).

THE CHALDÆAN ORACLES.

141 *For things Divine are not accessible to mortals who fix their minds on body; 'tis they who strip them naked [of this thing], that speed aloft unto the Height.*

These are the true Naked, the real Gymnosophists, as Apollonius of Tyana would have called them, who strip off the "form of the servant," the rags of the lower nature. Compare with this the early Jewish commentator in the Naassene Document, who was evidently well versed in the "Books of the Chaldæans":

"For this Mystery is the Gate of Heaven, and this is the House of God, where the Good God dwells alone; into which House no impure man shall come. But it is kept under watch for the Spiritual alone; where, when they come, they must cast away their garments, and all become bridegrooms, obtaining their true manhood through the Virginal Spirit" (*H.*, i. 181).

If this transmutation be effected, and the "rags" changed into the shining garments of the pure elements, the "wedding garments" of the Gospel parables, the soul by its own power wins its freedom. Such a man is characterized by Proclus as "having a soul that looks down upon body, and is capable of **142** looking Above, 'by its own might,' according to the Oracle, divorced from the hylic organs of sense" (K. 52).

PURIFICATION BY FIRE.

The Path of Return, or Way Above, was conceived as a purification of the soul from the hylic elements, and therewith an entry into the purifying mystery of the Baptism of Fire, which in its highest sense is the "Dowsing" in the Divine Mind of the Trismegistic teaching.

143 *For if the mortal draw nigh to the Fire, he shall have Light from God.*

Speaking of the "perfecting purification," Proclus tells us that it was operated by means of the "*Divine Fire*," and that **144** it was the highest degree of purification, which caused all the "*stains*" that dimmed the pure nature of the soul, through her converse with generation, to disappear. This he takes directly from the Oracles.

THE ANGELIC POWERS OF PURIFICATION.

In this purification certain Divine Powers, or Intelligences, take part; they are called Angels (Messengers or Mediators). They are the higher correspondence of the infernal Daimones in *The Vision of Aridæus* (p 49 ff.), in which the "stains" of the souls are graphically depicted.

The part played by these Intelligences, however, is not external to the soul, but an integral part of the transmutation; it is the Angelic portion of the man that leads the soul Above.

It is this, as Proclus tells us, from the Oracles, that "*makes*" the soul "*to* **145** *shine with Fire*"—that is, which itself shines round the man on all sides; it rays-forth, becomes truly "astral" (*augo-eidés* or *astro-eidés*), rays-forth with intelligence.

It is this Angelic power that purifies the soul of gross matter (*hylē*), and "*lightens it with warm spirit*"—that is, **146** endows it with a true impersonal or "cosmic" subtle vehicle, tempered by means of that "temperature" or "blend" which the *Mithriac Ritual* (p.89) tells us depends entirely on the Fire.

The original poem seems, from Proclus' comments, further to have contained verses which referred to certain Angelic Powers who, as it were, made to indraw the external protrusions of the soul which it sympathetically projects in conformity with the configuration of the limbs of its earthy prison-house; their function, therefore, was to restore it to its pure spherical shape. To this may refer the very corrupt and obscure verse:

214

THE CHALDÆAN ORACLES.

147 *The projections of the soul are easy to unloose by being inbreathed.*

THE SACRED FIRES.

Breath (Spirit) is said mystically to be the Spouse of Fire (Mind) ; and so we find Proclus speaking of " perfecting the 148 travail of souls and ' *lighting up the Fire* ' in them," and also of "lighting up the fires that lead them Home " ; all of which, for the mystic, can refer to nothing else than the starting of what are called the "sacred fires " of spiritual transformation. These " fires " are intelligent transforming currents that re-form the soul-plasm into the " perfect body," that is, the " body of resurrection," as the *Mithriac Ritual* (p. 89) informs us. And so we read :

149 *Extend on every side the reins of Fire to [guide] the unformed soul.*

That is, constrain the flowing watery nature of the soul by the fiery breath or spirit of the true Mind. And this seems also to be the meaning of the difficult fragment :

150 *If thou extendest fiery Mind to flowing work of piety, thou shalt preserve thy body too.*

This seems to mean that, when by means of purification, and by dint of pious practices, the soul is made fluid—that is to say, is no longer bound to any configuration of external things, when it is freed from prejudice, or opinion, and personal passion, or sentiment, and is " with pure purities now purified," as the *Mithriac Ritual* (p. 89) has it—then this re-generated soul-plasm, the germ of the " perfect body," can be configured afresh according to the plans or symbols of the true Mind.
Then shall the re-generate souls have Gnosis of the Divine Mind, be free from Fate, and breathe the Intelligible Fire, thus understanding the Works of the Father.

151 *They flee the reckless fated wing of Fate, and stay themselves in God, drawing unto themselves the Fires in all their prime, as they descend from out the Father, from which, as they descend, the soul doth cull the Flower of Empyrean Fruit that nourisheth the soul.*

It is hazardous to say what this may mean with any great precision, for in all probability the text is corrupt in several places. Taking it as it stands, however, we may conjecture that the first line refers to the state of the souls in subjection to Fate ; they are figured elsewhere as leaving the state of sameness and rest, and flying forth down into the hylic realms of Genesis, or repeated birth and death. This is winging the " shameless " (or reckless) " wing of Fate ;" and yet this too is " fated." They who return to the memory of their spiritual state, once more rest in God, and breathe in the " Gnostic Fires " of the Holy Spirit—the true Ambrosia, that which bestows immortality (*athanasía*).

THE FRUIT OF THE FIRE-TREE.

This Fruit of Life—that is, the Gnosis, or Gnostic Son of God—as may be seen from *The Great Announcement*, of the Simonian tradition, based on Mago-Chaldæan mystic doctrines (see *The Gnostic Crucifixion*, pp. 163 ff.), was figured as the Fruit of the Fire-Tree. The Church Father Hippolytus (*Ref.*, vi. 9) summarizes the original text as follows :
" And, generally, we may say, of all things that are, both sensible and intelligible, which he [the writer of the *Announcement*] calls Manifested and Hidden, the Fire which is above the Heavens, is the Treasure, as it were a Great Tree, like that seen by Nebuchadonosor in vision, from which all flesh is nourished. And he considers the manifested side of the Fire to be the trunk, branches, leaves, and the bark surrounding it on the outside. All the parts of the Great Tree, he says, are set on fire by the devouring flame of the Fire and destroyed. But the Fruit of the Tree,

215

THE CHALDÆAN ORACLES.

if its imaging hath been perfected, and it takes the shape of itself, is placed in the Storehouse, and not cast into the Fire. For the Fruit, he says, is produced to be placed in the Storehouse, but the husk to be committed to the Fire ; that is to say, the trunk which is generated not for its own sake but for that of the Fruit."

See further my *Simon Magus* (p. 14). The original form of this *Great Announcement* is in all probability a pre-Christian document (see *H.*, 184, n. 4), for the early Jewish commentator in the Naassene Document is acquainted with it. Now in this Document the pre-Christian Hellenistic initiate writes :

"Moreover, also, the Phrygians say that the Father of Wholes is Amygdalos [*lit.*, the Almond-Tree]."

And this is glossed by the same Jewish commentator, who knew *The Great Announcement,* as follows :

"No ordinary tree ; but that He is that Amygdalos the Pre-existing, who, having in Himself the Perfect Fruit, as it were, throbbing and moving in His Depth, tore asunder His Womb, and gave birth to His own Son " (*H.*, i. 182).

THE PÆAN OF THE SOUL.

But to return to the Oracles ; Proclus evidently bases himself upon a very similar passage to the last-quoted verses of our poem, when he writes :

152 "Let us then offer this praise-giving to God—the becoming - like - unto - Him. Let us leave the Flowing Essence [the River of Genesis] and draw nigh to the true End ; let us get to know the Master, let all our love be poured forth to the Father. When He calls us, let us be obedient ; let us haste to the Hot, and flee the Cold ; let us be Fire ; let us 'fare on our *Way through Fire.*' We have an '*agile Way*' for our Return. '*Our Father is our Guide,*' who '*openeth the Ways of Fire,*' lest in forgetfulness we let ourselves flow in a '*downward stream*'" (K. 54).

The lust of generation is said to "moisten" the soul and make it watery ; the Fire dries it and lightens it. The Hymn, or Praise-giving, which the souls sing on their Way Above is called by Olympiodorus, quoting most probably from the text of our poem, the "*Pæan,*" 153 or Song of Joy (C. 85) ; it is a continual praise-giving of the man who tunes himself into harmony with the Music of the Spheres. (See *The Hymns of Hermes,* pp. 23 , and 33).

THE MYSTERY-CULTUS.

The cultus of the Oracles is, before all else, the cult of Fire, and that, too, for the most part, in a high mystical sense rather than in the cruder form of external fire-worship. The Sacred Living Fire was to be adored in the shrine of the silence of the inner nature. These inner mysteries were in themselves inexpressible, and even the very method of approach, it seems, was handed on under the vow of silence.

Our poem was thus originally intended to be an apocryphon (in the original sense of the term), or esoteric document ; for Proclus tells us that its mystagogy was prefaced by the words :

Keep silence, thou who art admitted to 154 *the secret rites* [mýsta].

And elsewhere he says that the Oracles were handed on to the Mystæ alone. As a way of approach to the innermost form of the rites, which was indubitably a solitary sacrament like the *dynamis* of the *Mithriac Ritual,* there was an inner ceremonial cultus. Thus from one fragment we recover the following instruction to the officiating priest :

But, first of all, the priest who doth direct 155 *the Works of Fire, must sprinkle with cold wave of the deep-sounding brine.*

There was, therefore, a ceremonial ritual. The consummation of the innermost rite, however, was solitary, and of the nature of a Mystic Union or Sacred Marriage.

THE MYSTIC MARRIAGE.

Thus Proclus speaks of the soul, " according to a certain ineffable at-one-ment, leading that-which-is-filled into sameness with that-which-fills, making one portion of itself, in an immaterial and impalpable fashion, a receptacle for the in-shining, and provoking the other to the imparting of its Light." This, he says, is the meaning of the verse :

156   *When the currents mingle in consummation of the Works of Deathless Fire.*

THE PURIFYING MYSTERIES.

But this can be accomplished only in the perfected body, or rather " perfect body "; therefore, with regard to visions of the lower powers, operated by the daimones, Proclus tells us :

" The Gods admonish us not to look upon them before we are fenced round with the powers brought to birth by the Mystery-rites : "

157   *Thou should'st not look on them before the body is perfected ; [for] ever do they fascinate men's souls and draw them from the Mysteries.*

The lower visions were to be turned from in order that the higher theophanies, or manifestations of the Gods, might be seen. But this could be accomplished only by an orderly discipline. And so Proclus writes :

" For in contemplation and the art of perfectioning, that which makes the Way Above safe and free from stumbling-blocks for us, is orderly progress. At any rate, as the Oracles say : "

158   *Never so much is God estranged from man, and, with Living Power, sends him on fruitless quests—*

" As when, in disorder and in discord, we [try to] make the Ascent to the most divine heights of contemplation or the most sacred acts of Works—as it is said, ' *with lips unhallowed and un-* 159 *washen feet.*' "

THE FIRE - GNOSIS.

Proclus further tells us that the first preliminary of this truly sacred cultus is that we should have a right intuition of the nature of the Divine, or, in the graphic words of the Oracles, a " *Fire-* 160 *warmed intuition* " (K. 56) :

For if the mortal draw nigh to the Fire, 143 *he shall have Light from God.*

There must, however, be no rush or hurry, but calm steadfast perseverance, for it is all a natural growth. Therefore is it said that :

For the mortal man who takes due time 161 *the Blessed Ones are swift to come into being.*

This, however, does not mean to say that the man should be slow; for :

A mortal sluggish in these things spells 162 *the dismissal of the Gods.*

This is explained by an interesting passage of Damascius, who, speaking of the mysterious " instrument " the *iynx*, writes : " When it turns inwards, it invokes the Gods ; and when outwards, it dismisses those it has invoked." Mystically this seems to mean that when the " whirl "—or vortex " instrument " of consciousness, or the one-sense "perfect body "—turns inwards, theophanies, or manifestations of the Gods, appear ; and when it turns outward, to the physical, they disappear.

THE MANIFESTATIONS OF THE GODS.

In themselves the Gods have no forms, they are incorporeal ; they, however, assume forms for the sake of mortals,

THE CHALDÆAN ORACLES.

as Proclus writes : "For though we [the Gods] are incorporeal : "

163 *Bodies are allowed to our self-revealed manifestations for your sakes.*

This self-revelation, which in one mode signifies the selection of some image in the seer's own mind, and in another, connotes the seeing by one's own light, pertains to the mystery of that monadic Light which transcends the three lower (empyrean, ætherial and hylic) planes or states (K. 31). And Simplicius further informs us (K. 57), quoting from Proclus : "This, he says, is the Light which first receives the invisible allotments of the Gods, and for those worthy makes manifest in itself the self-revealed spectacles. For in it, he says, according to the Oracle : "

164 *The things that have no shape, take shape.*

This seems to be the Astral Light proper, "cosmic" and not personal. To this interpretation of Proclus', however, Simplicius objects that, according to the Oracles, the impressions of typical forms, or root-symbols, and of the other divine visions, do not occur in the Light, but are rather made on the æther (C. 113). We, however, need not labour the point further than to remark that Proclus had wider personal experience of those things than Simplicius. The things seen in the Great Light were true, for this Light constituted the Plane of Truth, whereas the ætherial was a reflection, and was further conditioned by the personality of the seer. Proclus, therefore, tells us that :

166 "The Gods [*i.e.*, presumably the Oracles] warn us to have understanding of '*the form of light that they display*'" (K. 57, C. 159).

In another passage Proclus refers to the mystic experience of these theophanies on the empyrean plane, where shapes of fire are assumed : "The

tradition of these [visions] is handed on by the mystagogy of the tradition of the Gods ; for it says : "

When thou hast uttered these [? words of 167 power], thou shalt behold either a fire [? flame] resembling a boy, dancing upon the surface of the waves of air [? æther] ; or even a flame that hath no shape, from which a voice proceeds ; or [yet] a wealth of light around the area [of sight], strident, a-whirl. Nay, thou shalt see a horse as well, all made of fire, a-flash with light ; or yet again a boy, on a swift horse's back astride,—a boy clad all in flame, or all bedecked with gold, or else with nothing on ; or even shooting with a bow, and standing on horse-back.

With the above may be compared the symbolic visions in *A Mithriac Ritual* (pp. 91, 92) ; we have here evidently to do with the same order of experiences, and so also in the following four verses :

If thou should'st oft address Me, thou 168 shalt behold all things grow dark ; for at that hour no Heaven's curved dome is seen ; there shine no Stars ; Moon's light is veiled ; Earth is no longer firm ; with Lightning-flash all is a-flame.

In connection with the idea underlying the phrase "a flame that hath no shape, from which a voice proceeds," of the last fragment but one, we must take the lines :

But when thou dost behold the very 169 sacred Fire with dancing radiance flashing formless through the depths of the whole world, then hearken to the Voice of Fire.

THE THEURGIC ART.

But to reach this pure and formless vision was very difficult ; for all kinds of false appearances and changing shapes could intervene. These had to be cleaned from the field of vision, for they were held to be due to impure presences, or,

THE CHALDÆAN ORACLES.

as we should prefer it, to the impurities of the man's own lower nature. On this subject our Oracles (though more probably it is an interpolation from a Theurgic tradition) had instruction, as we learn from the curious fragment:

170 *But when thou dost perceive an earthward daimon drawing nigh, make offering with the stone* mnouziris, *uttering [the proper chant].*

What this stone may have been, we have no knowledge. To "make offering" with a stone can mean nothing else than to put it into the fire, and this should connect with alchemy. *Mnouziris is a barbarum nomen.*

The chant, or *mantra*, would also consist of *barbara nomina* (native names), concerning which Psellus quotes the famous lines that are generally referred to our Oracles, but which, for reasons of metre, could not have stood as part of the poem (C. 155):

171 "See that thou never change the native names; for there are names in every nation, given by the Gods, possessed of power, in mystic rites, no language can express."

In this Theurgy, or "Divine Work," moreover, certain symbols, or symbolic figures, were employed, for Proclus says (K. 58) that the Oracles "call the angular 172 points of the figures '*the compactors.*'"

THE ROYAL SOULS.

But Theurgy was not for all; it was the Royal Art, and could be practised with spiritual success only by those whom the Trismegistic writers (*H.*, iii. 125) would have called Royal Souls. Their nature is set forth in the following verses, preserved by Synesius:

173 *Yea, verily, indeed, do they at least, most happy far of all the souls, pour down to Earth from Heaven; most blest are they with fates* [lit., *threads*] *no tongue can tell, as many as are born from out*

Thy Radiant Self, O King, and from the Seed of Zeus Himself, through strong Necessity.

This is evidently a reference to the Race, the Sons of God. (See *The Gnostic Crucifixion*, pp 165 ff). So also does the Orphic initiate declares : " My Race is from Heaven."

There may be some slight doubt as to whether the above fragment is from our poem, for Synesius does not say from what source he takes his quotation ; but short of the precise statement everything is in favour of its authenticity, and especially the following from the same philosophic and mystical Bishop :

THE LIGHT-SPARK.

"Let him hear the sacred Oracles which tell about the different ways. After the full list of inducements [or promptings] that come from Home to cause us to return, according to which it is within our power to cause the inplanted Seed to grow, they continue :"

To some He gave it to receive the Token 174 *of the Light, to others, even when asleep, He gave the power of bearing Fruit from His own Might.*

The "Token of Light" is evidently the "Symbol" that the Father implants in souls. It is the Seed of Divinity, the Light-spark, that gradually flames forth into the Fire. This Light-spark was conceived of as a seed sown in good soil that could bear fruit, thirty, or sixty or a hundred fold, as the Christianized Gnosis has it.

And so in the Excerpts from the lost work of the Christian Gnostic Theodotus, made by the Church Father Clement of Alexandria, we read (K. 59) : "The followers of the Valentinian doctrine declare that when the Psychic Body hath been enformed, into the Elect Soul in sleep the Masculine Seed is implanted by the Logos."

219

THE CHALDÆAN ORACLES.

If the soul can pronounce its own true Word (Logos), utter its Sound, and so create by itself symbols, then may the man hope really to understand what his consciousness may catch from the highest spheres. But even if his soul cannot do this, even while it is unaware of its surroundings, and without this creative power, it is still possible that it may be able to catch some of the Strength and Might (not Light) of the Father-Mind, and thus be inspired to conceive some true ideas.

The re-generated soul is said to become a " Five-fold Star," as we learn from the *Mithriac Ritual* (p. 90), and also from Lydus (*De Mens.*, 23.6), who tells us that : " The Oracle declares that souls, when restored to their former nature by means of this Pentad, transcend Fate."

175   *For Theurgists are not counted in the herd subject to Fate.*

And so also Proclus tells us that : " We should avoid the multitude of men that go ' *in herds*,' as says the Oracle."

The " herd " has, so to speak, got only one " over-soul " between them,— they do not yet stand alone; or, rather, they have a soul each, and only one " over-mind " between them.

Those of the " herd " are the " processions of Fate " of the Trismegistic writings (*H.*, iii. 273) ; while those who have perfected themselves, are freed from the Wheel of Fate, and become Angels or Gods. Speaking of the man who is truly devoted to sacred things, Proclus quotes an Oracle which says :

176   *Alive in power he runs, an Angel.*

THE UNREGENERATE.

On the contrary, the unregenerate is characterized as :

177   *Hard to turn, with burden on the back, who has no share in Light.*

While concerning those who " lead an evil life," Proclus tells us that the Oracles declared :

For as for them they are no great way 178 *off from Dogs irrational.*   .

Of such a one it is said :

My vessel the Beasts of the Earth shall 179 *inhabit.*

Compare with this the Gnostic Valentinian doctrine, as summarized by Hippolytus :
" And this material man is, according to them, as it were an inn, or dwelling-place, at one time of the soul alone, at another of the soul and daimonian existences, at another of the soul and words (*logoi*), which are words sown from Above —from the Common Fruit of the Plērōma (Fulness) and Wisdom—into this world, dwelling in the body of clay together with the soul, when daimons cease to cohabit with her " (*F.*, p. 352).

And also the Basilidian doctrine, as summarized by Clement of Alexandria :
" The Basilidians are accustomed to give the name of appendages [or accretions] to the passions. These essences, they say, have a certain substantial existence, and are attached to the rational soul, owing to a certain turmoil and primitive confusion.

" Onto this nucleus other bastard and alien natures of the essence grow, such as those of the wolf, ape, lion, goat, etc. And when the peculiar qualities of such natures appear round the soul, they cause the desires of the soul to become like to the special natures of these animals, for they imitate the actions of those whose characteristics they bear " (*F.*, pp. 276, 277).

THE PERFECTING OF THE BODY.

The physical body was called in the Oracles the " dung of matter," as we have

THE CHALDÆAN ORACLES.

seen above (p. 210), and as we may see from the obscure couplet :

180 *Thou shalt not leave behind the dung of matter on the height; the image* [eidōlon] *also hath its portion in the space that shines on every side.*

This seems to mean either that the higher states of consciousness were not to be contaminated and befouled with the passions of the body, or that in the highest theurgy the body was not to be left behind in trance, but, on the contrary, that conscious contact was to be kept with it throughout the whole of the sacred operation, as we learn from the *Mithriac Ritual*. The " image " also—presumably the image - man, or subtle vehicle of the soul, the *augoeidēs* or *astroeidēs*—had an important part to play in linking the consciousness up with the Light-world.

In this connection we may also take the lines already quoted above :

150 *If thou dost stretch thy fiery mind unto the flowing work of piety, thou shalt pre-serve thy body too.*

What the " flowing work of piety " may be, it is hazardous to say. It is probably a poetical expression for the pure plastic substance out of which the " perfect body " was to be formed, as set forth in the *Mithriac Ritual*. The work of the " fiery mind " is thus described in the Trismegistic sermon " The Key " :

" For when the soul withdraws into itself, the spirit doth contract itself within the blood, and soul within the spirit. And then the mind, stript of its wrappings, and naturally divine, taking unto itself a fiery body, doth traverse every space " (*H.*, ii. 151).

And again :

" When mind becomes a daimon, the law requires that it should take a fiery body to execute the services of God " (*H.*, ii. 154).

And here we may append a passage

from Julian the Emperor-Philosopher, who loved our Oracles :

" To this the Oracles of the Gods bear witness ; and [therefore] I say that, by means of the holy life of purity, not only our souls but also our bodies are made worthy to receive much help and saving [or soundness] ; for they declare : "

Save ye as well the mortal thing of 181 *bitter matter that surrounds you.*

For the mystery-term " bitter matter " see the note in the *Mithriac Ritual* (pp. 95 ff.). Kroll thinks that all this refers to the dogma of the resurrection of the physical body, but the Ritual makes it plain that the only " body of resurrection " with which the Mystics and Gnostics were acquainted, was the " perfect body"; the resurrection of the gross physical body was a superstition of the ignorant.

The " dung of matter " referred to above may be rendered as " dross " or " scum," and a somewhat more mystical interpretation might be suggested. " Dross " as a mystery-word is essentially the same as " scum," but from an analytical point of view suggests the reverse of " scum." Certain states of the soul may be spoken of as scum ; in spiritual alchemy when the soul-plasm is thought of as the " watery " sphere being gradually dried, so as to be eventually built up, or enformed, by the " fire " of the spiritual mind, then the scum rises to the top and is handed over to Fate. Scum would then mean men under the bondage of Fate. Dross, however, suggests the earth or metal side of things, and here the refuse falls and does not rise, and is again handed over to further schooling and discipline, and not allowed freedom from the law, like jewels and pure earth are.

Scum and dross are on the matter-side of things ; images may be said to correspond to them on the mind-side. As scum is to the soul, as dross to pure matter, so is image to pure mind. Both

THE CHALDÆAN ORACLES.

scum and image have to do with the surface of things and not with the depth.

RE-INCARNATION.

As we might expect, the Oracles taught the doctrine of the repeated descents and returnings of the soul, by whatever name we may call it, whether transmigration, re-incarnation, palingenesis, metempsychosis, metensomatosis, or transcorporation. And so Proclus tells us that :

182   "They make the soul descend many times into the world for many causes, either through the shedding of its feathers [or wings], or by the Will of the Father" (K. 62).

The soul of a man, however, as also in the Trismegistic doctrine (*H.*, ii. 153, 166), could not be reborn into the body of a brute ; as to this Proclus is quite clear when he writes :

"And that the passing into irrational natures is contrary to nature for human souls, not only do the Oracles teach us, when they declare that '*this is the law from the Blessed Ones that naught can break*': the human soul : "

183   *Completes its life again in men and not in beasts.*

THE DARKNESS.

There was also in our Oracles a doctrine of punishment in the Invisible (Hadēs) ; for Proclus speaks of "the Avenging

184   Powers (*Poinai*), '*Throttlers of mortals*,'" and of a state of gloom and pain, below which stretched a still more awful gulf of Darkness, as the following verses tell us :

185   *See that thou verge not down unto the world of the Dark Rays, 'neath which is ever spread the Deep [or Abyss] devoid of form, where is no light to see, wrapped in black gloom befouling, that joys in shades [eidōla], void of all understanding, precipitous and sinuous, for ever winding*

round its own blind depth, eternally in marriage with a body that cannot be seen, inert [and] lifeless.

With this description of the Serpent of Darkness, ever in congress with his infernal counterpart of blind Matter and Ignorance, may be compared the vision of the Trismegistic "Man-Shepherd" treatise :

"But in a little while Darkness came settling down on part of it, awesome and gloomy, coiling in sinuous folds, so that methought it like unto a snake" (*H.*, ii. 4.).

This is a vision of the other side, or antipodes, of the Light ; and so we find Proclus writing : "For this region is '*Hater of the Light*,' as the Oracle also 186 saith" (K. 63). Also with regard to the system thought to underlie the Oracles, Psellus informs us that below. the Æther come three hylic worlds or planes of gross matter—the sublunary, terrene, and sub-terrene—" the uttermost of which is called chthonian and '*Light-hater*,' and is not only sublunary, but also contains within it that matter (*hylē*) which they call the '*Deep*.'"

THE INFERNAL STAIRS.

In connection with the above fragment we must also take the following corrupt lines, which evidently form part of the directions given to the soul for its journey through Hades :

But verge not downwards ! Beneath 187 thee lies a Precipice, sheer from the earth, that draws one down a Stair of seven steps, beneath which lies the Throne of Dire Necessity.

The topography of the Throne of Necessity corresponds somewhat with that in Plato's famous Vision of Er—which was probably derived from an Orphic mystery-myth ; and the old Orphic tradition was in contact with "Chaldæan" sources. So also in the Vision

222

THE CHALDÆAN ORACLES.

of Aridæus, which again is perhaps connected with Orphic initiation, it is Adrasteia, Daughter of Necessity, who presides over the punishments in Tartarus, and her dominion extends to the uttermost parts of the hylic cosmos, as we learn from a fragment of a theogony preserved by Jerome (K. 63).

Proclus also speaks of the whole generative or genesiurgic Nature—that is, Nature under the sway of Necessity— 188 in which, he says, is " both the ' *turbulence of matter* ' and the ' *light-hating world*,' as the Gods [*i.e.*, the Oracles] say, 189 and the ' *sinuous streams*,' by which the many are drawn down, as the Oracles tell us."

Moreover, there must have been mention of some roaring or bellowing sound that struck the evil soul with terror, as in the Vision of Er ; for Psellus quotes a mutilated fragment, which runs :

190 " *Ah ! Ah !* " *the Earth doth roar at them, until* [*they turn*] *to children* (*?*).

We may, however, venture to suggest another point of view from which the above symbolic imagery (K. 62) can be regarded, and take it not as a warning to ordinary fate-full people, but as an admonition to those who are being initiated or re-generated, and who can thus begin to stand aside from the Fate-spheres.

The " Precipice," or Gulph, could thus be regarded as the way of descent from the Light and the Fulness into the Fate-spheres, and so the organ or instrument of creation of darkness and " flat " things (shades). The soul descends by means of a " flat " ladder of planes, the way of the formal mind.

The admonition thus seems to say : Do not let the mind travel down into the Fate-spheres by means of " planes " and formal ideas, and the ordinary surface view of things ; because if so, it is apt to leave some of itself behind. There is a way of descending direct and straight into, or rather fathoming, the uttermost

Depths quite safely, but it is by way of living creatures, and not by way of mind-made ladders.

In mystical language " Throne " is the point of stability ; it suggests contact with the Stable One. This plan of seven, the ladder or root of form, is essentially stable and not vital ; and for an initiate who is on the return journey, active in the mystery of re-generation, it is to be avoided, as it leads back into imprisonment ; it is the proper way down, but not the right way back. It leads to states dominated by Fate, to a prison or school where the soul is bound all round with rules ; it does not lead to Freedom.

ON CONDUCT.

We may now conclude with some fragments concerning right living ; in the first place with the famous riddle :

Soil not the spirit, and deepen not 75 *the plane !*

The first clause is generally thought to refer to the spiritual, or rather spirituous, body, while the second is supposed to mean : " Turn not the plane into the solid "—that is to say, if we follow Pythagoræan tradition : Do not make the subtle body dense or gross.

From a more mystical point of view it might be suggested that normal Nature is but as a superficies. Until a man is initiated properly, that is to say, naturally re-generated, it is better for him not to delve into her magical powers too soon, but rather keep within the plane-side of things till his own substance is made pure. When pure there is nothing in him to which these magical powers can attach themselves. As soon as his nature is purified then Spiritual Mind begins to enter his " perfect body," and so he can control the inner forces, or forces within, or sexual powers of Nature — those creative powers and passions which make her double herself. The superficial side of Nature is complete in its own way,

THE CHALDÆAN ORACLES.

and normal man should be content with this ; he should not attempt to stir the secret powers of her Depth, or Womb, till he is guided by the wisdom of the Spiritual Mind.

In the Latin translation of Proclus' lost treatise *On Providence*, the following three sayings are ascribed to the Oracles (*Responsa*). Kroll, however, thinks that the second only is authentic :

191 *When thou dost look upon thyself, let fear come on thee.*

192 *Believe thyself to be out of body, and thou art.*

193 *The spawning of illnesses in us is in our own control, for they are born out of the life we lead.*

If the man regards his own lower self, he fears because of his imperfection ; if he gazes on his higher self, he feels awe.

With the second aphorism compare the instruction of the Trismegistic treatise " The Mind to Hermes " (§ 19) :

" And, thus, think from thyself, and bid thy soul go unto any land, and there more quickly than thy bidding will it be " (*H.*, ii. 186).

THE GNOSIS OF PIETY.

That the spirit of the doctrine of the Oracles was far removed from the practice of the arts of astrology, earth-measurement, divination, augury, and the rest, and turned the mind to the contemplation of spiritual verities alone, may be seen from the following fine fragment :

194 *Submit not to thy mind the earth's vast measures, for that the Tree of Truth grows not on earth ; and measure not the measure of the sun by adding rod to rod, for that his course is in accordance with the Will eternal of the Father, and not for sake of thee. Let thou the moon's rush go ; she ever runs by operation of*

Necessity. The stars' procession was not brought forth for sake of thee.

The birds' wide-winging high in air is never true, nor yet the slicings of the victims' entrails. These are all toys, lending support to mercenary fraud.

Flee thou these things, if thou would'st enter in True Worship's Paradise, where Virtue, Wisdom, and Good-rule are met together.

There is somewhat of a Jewish Sibylline flavour about this which might seem to indicate contact with Jewish Gnostic circles. As, however, there is nothing else in our fragments which shows signs of Jewish influence, we may fairly conclude that the ethic of our Oracles was similar, and that similarity does not spell plagiarism.

Moreover the phaseology is identical with that of other fragments which can lie under no suspicion of a " Judaizing " influence ; for instance :

Both lunar course and star-progression. 70 *This star-progression was not delivered from the womb of things because of thee.*

Bodies are allowed our self-revealed 163 *manifestations for your sakes.*

And so we bring these two small volumes to a close in the hope that a few at least of the many riddles connected with these famous Oracles may have been made somewhat less puzzling.

THE . . .
WEDDING-
SONG OF .
WISDOM. .

THE WEDDING-SONG OF WISDOM.

CONTENTS.

BIBLIOGRAPHY.

Thilo (J. C.), *Acta S. Thomæ Apostoli* (Leipzig, 1823).

Wright (W.), *Apocryphal Acts of the Apostles* (London, 1871), ii. 150-152.

Nöldecke (T.), Rev. of Wright, *Zeitschrift der deutschen morgenländischen Gesellschaft* (1871), pp. 670 ff.

Macke (K.), "Syrische Lieder gnostischen Ursprungs. Eine Studie über die apocryphen syrischen Thomasacten," *Theologische Quartalschrift* (Tübingen, 1874), pp. 1 ff.

Lipsius (R. A.), *Die apocryphen Apostelgeschichten u. Apostellegenden* (Brunswick, 1883, 1884), i. pp. 301 ff.

Bonnet (M.), *Acta Apostolorum Apocrypha* (edd. Lipsius et Bonnet), vol. ii., pt. ii. (Leipzig, 1903).

Hoffmann (G.), "Zwei Hymnen der Thomasakten," *Zeitschrift für die neutestamentliche Wissenschaft* (Giessen, 1903), vol. iv. pp. 295—309.

Preuschen (E.), *Zwei gnostische Hymnen* (Giessen, 1904).

Burkitt (F. C.), Review of Preuschen, *Theologisch Tijdschrift* (Amsterdam), May, 1905, pp. 270—282.

F. = Mead (G. R. S.), *Fragments of a Faith Forgotten* (2nd. ed., London, 1906).

H. = Mead (G. R. S.), *Thrice Greatest Hermes* (London, 1906).

THE WEDDING-SONG OF WISDOM.

THE WEDDING-SONG OF WISDOM.

PREAMBLE.

The Hymn which forms the subject of this little volume has no traditional title. Like *The Hymn of the Robe of Glory*, which formed the last of these *Echoes*, it is found in the Syriac *Acts of Judas Thomas*, where it is put in the mouth of the Apostle who is said, on his travels, to have been guest of honour at a bridal feast.

In addition to the Syriac we have a Greek text which is plainly a translation. The Greek is in prose, but the Syriac for the most part in verses of twelve syllables, in couplets, just like *The Hymn of the Robe of Glory*. As Macke tells us (p. 17), where the Greek and Syriac agree the verses are of six syllables; or more correctly, as Burkitt has pointed out (p. 277), normally 6+6, but sometimes 5+7. Moreover, the Greek can be translated back into metred Syriac where the present Syriac departs from the metre.

An Armenian version also existed, of which, unfortunately, we now possess only the opening and closing lines.

All scholars agree that the original Hymn was composed in Syriac; but is our Syriac text as it stands the original? It plainly is not; it has been " overworked," as the Germans call it, by an editor, and that too, to serve certain theological interests, while the scraps of the Armenian version show that it in its turn had been still further over-worked.

The first thing that strikes the careful reader is that where the Greek differs most widely from the Syriac, there the Syriac has been " over-worked," for it is precisely in such places that the metre is broken. It is again precisely in these passages that the Greek is strongly Gnostic, while the Syriac is as strongly Catholic.

It is therefore to be concluded, with all reasonable certainty, that the Greek preserves the original Syriac more closely, and that this original Syriac was the composition of a Gnostic poet. As to this, there has been an unbroken *consensus* of opinion from Thilo (*Acta Thomæ*, p. 121 ff.) onwards; but lately (1905), Professor Burkitt has put forward another view. He first of all remarks (p. 270), that the contents and styles of the two Hymns, the Bridal Song and the Hymn of the Robe, are so different that they must be treated entirely apart from one another; and with this I am quite disposed to agree. Dr. Burkitt, however, goes on to say (p. 278): " I venture to think that the Bridal Ode is an integral part of the Acts of Thomas, and that it was composed for the very position which it now occupies," and further to contend that it is not a Gnostic Hymn, but quite in keeping with the early " orthodoxy " of the Syriac Church.

Professor Burkitt would himself admit that his belief (p. 282), that the " theology of the Hymn would pass as orthodox when judged by the standard of the early Syriac-speaking Church," is difficult of proof, unless we allow that that " orthodoxy " is referable to a time when " Gnostic " and " Catholic " were still intermingled.

His main contention is that " Gnosticism " is " intellectual " and not " moral," and that the whole atmosphere of the Thomas-Acts is the latter and not the former. Preuschen strongly argues the contrary, and shows that the main preoccupation of the Gnostics was the scheme of moral salvation and not an intellectual science, and with this I fully agree; for the whole of the Gnosis appears to me to have been of the nature of a vital realization mystically conceived, operated chiefly by a moral conversion or regeneration, and not a rational system

THE WEDDING-SONG OF WISDOM.

of knowledge of the nature of a science; and I do not see how the Gnosis can possibly be understood on any but the former hypothesis.

Among the apocryphal religious romances *The Acts of Thomas* have hitherto been regarded as strongly tinctured with Gnosticism. *The Acts of Thomas* were, I hold, originally Gnostic; but have since passed through the hands of Catholic editors. The general state of affairs concerning the Gnostic Acts-romances may be seen in the Preamble to Vol. IV. of these little books, *The Hymn of Jesus*; and I will here requote what Lipsius, whose authority on the subject is great, has said:

"Almost every fresh editor of such narratives, using that freedom which all antiquity was wont to allow itself in dealing with literary monuments, would recast the materials which lay before him, excluding whatever might not suit his theological point of view—dogmatic statements, for example, speeches, prayers [hymns we might add], etc., for which he would substitute other formulæ of his own composition, and further expanding and abridging after his own pleasure, or as the immediate object which he had in view might dictate. . .

"Catholic bishops and teachers knew not how better to stem this flood of Gnostic writings and their influence among the faithful, than by boldly adopting the most popular narratives from the heretical books, and, *after carefully eliminating the poison of false doctrine,* replacing them in this purified form in the hands of the public."

With the general criticism of the extant forms of the text of *The Acts of Thomas* we cannot concern ourselves in this little treatise, but as against Professor Burkitt's view of our Hymn—which he himself has characterised as "rather extreme"—I venture to associate myself with the otherwise unanimous body of learned opinion, that the Hymn was originally from the pen of a Gnostic poet. Not

only so, but it may be contended that the whole of the *Acta Thomæ* were originally Gnostic. Did the original compiler, then, write the Hymn, or did he incorporate it from some other source? I am inclined to adopt the latter hypothesis, though I grant it is open to objection. But in any case, according to what has been said above, it was originally Gnostic rather than what subsequently became Catholic, and some later Catholic hand has "carefully eliminated" from the original Syriac "the poison of false doctrine,"—to quote the phrase of Lipsius which I have italicized—while the Greek translator has more or less faithfully followed his original. When, for instance, we find such a phrase as "the Son's Twelve Apostles" (p. 14), we agree with Macke (p. 9), that: "*Der alte gnostische Text ist katholisch überarbeitet*" (The original Gnostic text has been worked over in a Catholic sense).

In brief, the later Syrian redactor has "cooked" the text to suit his orthodoxy; whereas the Greek translator, though not very skilful, is trustworthy (see Preuschen, p. 8). The Greek form is nearest the original; still it is not pure, for it has additions and exclusions, while in places it is somewhat paraphrastic (*ibid.* p. 28).

If then the Hymn was incorporated by the Syrian compiler of the Acts from some other source, was it taken over just as it stood? That is to say, Was it originally composed as a Gnostic Hymn? I think it was; and if it be suggested, as it has been by early critical opinion, that it was originally a profane Syrian Bridal Ode, and that it was subsequently Gnosticized, this two-stage hypothesis seems unnecessary if we admit, with Preuschen (pp. 7 and 29), the simpler probability that it was built on the model of similar Syrian wedding-songs and customs, even as they obtain to-day, during the seven days festivities, when the bride and bridegroom are represented as a royal couple.

230

THE WEDDING-SONG OF WISDOM.

And now what shall we call our Ode, for it has no title ? On the whole I think that " The Wedding-Song of Wisdom " is a good description, if we take " of Wisdom " to signify " in praise of Wisdom," where Wisdom stands for the Gnostic Sophia, the purified human soul, awaiting the coming of her Divine Spouse and Complement the Christ. That this is a legitimate title may be seen from the Hymn itself, which in the Greek ends with the couplet :

" So with the Living Spirit they sang praise and hymn unto Truth's Father and to Wisdom's Mother."

This plainly stood in the lost Syriac original, for which in the present text the redactor or over-worker has substituted an orthodox doxology from some liturgy, beginning :

" Praise ye the Father, the Lord."

As to the contents and style of this Song, it must be confessed that we have to do with a poem of far less originality than the Hymn of the Robe of Glory, and I have taken it as a subject not so much for its intrinsic merits, as because it affords an opportunity to set forth some information on that great mystery which was in antiquity generally known as the Sacred Marriage.

With these brief introductory remarks the reader may perhaps approach the perusal of the translation of the Greek, Syriac and Armenian with greater understanding. For the Syriac I have compared all the existing versions, and for the Armenian fragments I have translated from the German the version printed by Preuschen.

TRANSLATIONS.

FROM THE GREEK VERSION.

The Maiden is Light's Daughter ;
On her the Kings' Radiance resteth.

Stately her Look and delightsome,
With radiant beauty forth-shining.

Like unto spring-flowers are her Garments,
From them streameth scent of sweet odour.

On the Crown of her Head the King throneth,
[With Living Food] feeding those 'neath Him.

Truth on her Head doth repose,
She sendeth forth Joy from her Feet.

Her Mouth is opened, and meetly ;
Two-and-thirty are they who sing praises.

* * * * *
* * * * *

Her Tongue is like the Door-hanging
Set in motion by those who enter.

Step-wise her Neck riseth—a Stairway
The first of all Builders hath builded.

The Two Palms of her Hands
Suggest the Choir of the Æons.

Her Fingers are secretly setting
The Gates of the City ajar.

Her Bridechamber shineth with Light,
Forth-pouring scent of balsam and sweet-
herbs,

Exhaling the sweet perfume both of myrrh
and savoury plants,
And crowds of scented flowers.

231

THE WEDDING-SONG OF WISDOM.

Inside 'tis strewn with myrtle-boughs ;
Its Folding-doors are beautified with reeds.

Her Bridesmen are grouped round her,
Seven in number, whom she hath invited.

Her Bridesmaids, too, are Seven,
Who lead the Dance before her.

And Twelve are her Servants before her,
Their gaze looking out for the Bridegroom ;
That at His sight they may be filled with
    Light.

And then for ever more shall they be with Him
In that eternal everlasting Joy ;

And share in that eternal Wedding-feast,
At which the Great Ones [all] assemble ;

And so abide in that Delight
Of which the Ever-living are deemed worthy.

With Kingly Clothes shall they be clad,
And put on Robes of Light.

And both shall be in Joy and Exultation
    and praise the Father of the Wholes,
Whose Light magnificent they have received.

For at their Master's sight they were now
filled with Light ;

They tasted of His Living Food
That hath no waste at all,

And drank of that [eternal] Wine
That causes thirst and longing never more.

[So] with the Living Spirit they sang
    praise and hymn
Unto Truth's Father and to Wisdom's
    Mother

FROM THE CATHOLICIZED
SYRIAC TEXT.
My Bride is a Daughter of Light ;
Of the Kings' she possesseth the Splendour.

Stately and charming her Aspect,
Fair, with pure beauty adorned.

Her Robes are like unto blossoms,
Whose scent is fragrant and pleasant.

On the Crown of her Head the King throneth,
Giving Food to her Pillars beneath Him.

She setteth Truth on her Head,
Joy eddieth forth from her Feet.

Her Mouth is open—and well doth it suit
    her—
For she singeth with it loud praises.

In her the Son's Twelve Apostles
And the Seventy-two are all-thunderous.

Her Tongue's the Hanging of the Door,
The Priest uplifts and enters.

A Stairway is her Neck
That the first Builder hath builded.

The Palms of her Hands, furthermore,
Predict the Land of the Living.

And of her fingers the Decad
Set for her open the Heaven's Door.

Her Bridal Chamber's a-light,
And filled with the scent of Salvation.

Incense is set in her Midst, of Love,
    and of Faith,
And of Hope, and making all scented.

Within is Truth strewn ;
Its Doors with Verity are decked.

Her Bridesmen surround her,
All, whom she hath invited.

And her Bridesmaids, grouped with them,
Are singing the Praise-hymn before her.

Before her there serve Living Ones,
And watch for the Bridegroom's coming.

That by His Radiance they may be filled
    with Light,

232

THE WEDDING-SONG OF WISDOM.

And with him enter in His Kingdom,
That never more shall pass away,

And go unto that Feast
Where all the Righteous shall assemble ;

And so attain to that Delight
Wherein they each and all shall enter.

Thereon they clothe themselves in Robes of
Light,
And are wrapped in the Radiance of their
Lord,

And to the Living Father praises sing,
In that they have received the Light mag-
nificent,

And by their Lord's Resplendence are made
Light,

And they have tasted of His Living Food
That never more hath waste,

And of the Living [Water] they have drunk,
That suffers them to pant and thirst no more.

Praise ye the Father, the Lord,
And [praise ye] the Son Sole-begotten,
And thanks give unto the Spirit
As [thanks giving] unto His Wisdom.

FROM THE LATER ARMENIAN VERSION. TWO FRAGMENTS.

Great is the Light's Daughter, the Church ;
She is the Desire of thy Kings, longed for
and happy.

* * * * *
* * * * *

We shall go to the Heavenly Marriage
And drink the Wine that makes gladsome ;

We shall [then] be with Him for ever,
From the Bounds of the East bearing
witness.

The Scribe has unfortunately copied only the first and last lines, and omitted the whole body of the Hymn.

COMMENTS.

SYRIAN WEDDING-FESTIVITIES.

The picture that the Hymn conjures up before our eyes is entirely in keeping with the Syrian marriage customs observed among the peasants even to the present day. Cheyne, in his article on "Canticles," in the *Encyclopædia Biblica*, summarizes from Wetzstein's instructive account (" D. syr. Dreschtafel," in Bastian's *Zt. für Ethnologie* (1873), pp. 287-294) of the customs of the Syrian peasants in the month of weddings (March).

" During the seven days after a wedding high festivity, with scarcely interrupted singing and dancing, prevails. The bridegroom and the bride play the parts of king and queen (hence the week is called the 'king's week '), and receive the homage of their neighbours ; the crown, however, is . . . . confined to the bride. The bridegroom has his train of ' companions.' . . . . The bride, too, has her friends, the maidens of the place, who take an important part in the reception of the bridegroom."

Before the wedding a song called *waṣf* (*i.e.*, "laudatory description ") is sung in honour of the bride. Other songs are also sung before and after the wedding.

THE SONG OF SONGS.

The most famous ancient collection of such songs is *The Song of Songs (Shir ha-Shirim*), which the most recent research (see Cheyne, *ibid.*), characterizes as " an anthology of songs used at marriage festivals in or near Jerusalem, revised and loosely connected by an editor without regard to temporal sequence." Hirsch and Toy's article " Song of Songs," in the *Jewish Encyclopædia*, gives the date of compilation as probably in the

THE WEDDING-SONG OF WISDOM.

period 200-100 B.C., but it of course contains more ancient material.

The following lines from a *wasf* in this collection, in their Revised Version, may with advantage be compared with our Ode :

" How beautiful are thy feet in sandals,
  O prince's daughter !
Thy rounded thighs are like jewels,
The work of the hands of a cunning
  workman.

* * * * *

* * * * *

Thy neck is like the tower of ivory ;

* * * * *

Thine head upon thee is like Carmel,
And the hair of thine head like purple ;
The king is held captive in the tresses
  thereof."

We might almost be persuaded that these very lines were in the mind of our Gnostic poet when he wrote his Ode ; but as the *wasf* was invariably in praise of the personal attractions of the bride, describing her charms with the intimacy of unabashed realism, such songs must have been very similar to one another, and must have become in time quite conventionalized. We need not, therefore, in seeking for the prototype of our Ode, be sure we have found it in this particular *wasf* of the *Song of Songs* collection.

Though these songs were originally secular, once they were collected as "scripture," and doubtlessly " over-written " in the interests of religion, they were regarded as portraying the phases of spiritual and not earthly love. They were thus made susceptible of an allegorical interpretation, and perhaps such interpretations were attempted almost as soon as they were thus collected, indeed the very collection of them may have been for this very

purpose. They were then regarded as setting forth the Love of Yahweh and His people, Israel. Of any such interpretations prior to the Christian era we have no definite knowledge, but similar interpretations were general enough among the Jewish mystics in the days of Philo (B.C. 30—A.D. 40), and must have been attempted long before his time, as we are justified in concluding from his statements about the allegorizing art of the Therapeuts. Both Midrash and Targum prove conclusively that the oldest interpretation of *The Song of Songs* was allegorical. It, therefore, follows that the allied schools of the Christianized Gnosis must have as fully delighted in allegorizing *Canticles*, and not only so, but have created new songs the better to express the innermost meaning of the great mystery of the Sacred Marriage, which was one of their chiefest sacraments. Later on this allegorizing passed into the Catholic Church. As *The Jewish Encyclopædia* article says : " The allegorical conception of it passed over into the Christian Church, and has been elaborated by a long line of workers from Origen down to the present time, the deeper meaning being assumed to be the relation between God or Jesus [the Christ rather] and the Church or the individual soul."

Whether or not *The Song of Songs* collection was originally intended to be allegorized, it is quite evident that our Ode was composed chiefly for this purpose; indeed, for the most part it interprets itself in technical Gnostic terms.

THE SACRED MARRIAGE IN THE KABALAH.

From the Talmud we know that R. Shimeon, son of Gamaliel, the teacher of Paul, interpreted *The Song of Songs* allegorically. R. Shimeon was one of the Tannaim of the " first generation," and flourished about the first quarter of the second century A.D. (See H. L. Strack, *Einleitung in den Thalmud*—Leipzig, 1900—p. 78).

234

THE WEDDING-SONG OF WISDOM.

It is not possible here to discuss the date and sources of the Zoharic documents which form the main *corpus* of the extant Kabalah (*The* Tradition *par excellence*, according to the Jewish mystics); it is enough to say that these documents contain ancient material and traditions, which find their nearest relatives in the remains of the Jewish and Christian Gnosis. It will be sufficient for our present purpose to set down a passage from Jean de Pauly's recent French translation of the *Sepher-ha-Zohar* or *Book of Splendour*, the first complete translation which has ever appeared, and is now being published by the devotion of M. Émile Lafuma-Giraud (Paris, 1906, in progress). This passage purports to preserve the tradition of R. Shimeon's views on the Sacred Marriage, and runs as follows (i. 43 ff., *Zohar*, i. 8a):

"Rabbi Shimeon consecrated to the study of the mystic doctrine the whole night on which the Heavenly Bride is united with her Heavenly Spouse."

This is said to have been the eve of the Feast of Pentecost, the day when the Law (Torah) was revealed to the Israelites, and the Covenant (regarded as a marriage contract) contracted between Yahweh and His people.

"For, as it has been taught, all the Members of the Palace of the Heavenly Bride should spend the whole night with her, and on the morrow lead her beneath the wedding canopy, beside her Spouse, and rejoice with her. They should consecrate the eve of the Heavenly Marriage to the study of the Law, the Prophets and the Sacred Writings, to the interpretation of the verses and to the mysteries; for the esoteric science [*i.e.*, gnosis] is as it were the jewels of the Heavenly Bride.

"She and her young maidens, who surround her, rejoice the whole night; and on the morrow she goes beneath the wedding canopy surrounded by them, who are rightly called the 'guests' [*lit.* the invited] of the marriage.'

"The moment the Bride steps under the canopy, the Holy One (Blessed be He !) salutes the companions of the Bride, blesses them, and adorns them with crowns [or wreaths] woven by the Bride; happy the lot of the Brides-maids !

"During the night when the Heavenly Marriage was being consummated, Rabbi Shimeon and his companions chanted hymns and uttered sayings containing new ideas about the mystic doctrine [the gnosis].

"Therefore, addressing his companions, Rabbi Shimeon exclaimed : 'My sons, happy is your lot, for to-morrow will Heavenly Spouse will go beneath the canopy accompanied by you only, because you have rejoiced with her on the eve of the Marriage [or Union]. Ye all shall have your names written in the Heavenly Book ; and the Holy One (Blessed be He !) will overwhelm, you with sixty and six blessings, and adorn you with crowns of the world above."

On this there follows a further interpretation ; but enough has been said to indicate to the reader the striking similarities between the tradition of R. Shimeon b. Gamaliel and the matter of our Ode. With the writing of the name in the Book of Life may be compared *The Hymn of the Robe of Glory* (**א**): "When thy Name is read in the Book of the Heroes," and the note upon it (p. 128). The number 66, is the double of 33, the full number of æons in the Christian Gnostic Plērōma or Fulness. The number of the Kabalistic Ways in the *Sepher Yetzira*, the oldest extant Kabalistic treatise (? VIIth—XIth centuries), is 32. This *Book of Perfecting* (see E. Bischoff, *Die Kabbalah : Einführung in die jüdische Mystik and Geheimwissenschaft*— Leipzig, 1903—pp. 8 and 10) is based upon the 22 letters of the Hebrew alphabet as the 22 " elements " of all things, and the 10 numbers of the decad (Sephiroth), as categories of all Being. These are all summed up in one absolute Unity, 33 in

THE WEDDING-SONG OF WISDOM.

all. Perhaps this may throw light on l. 12 of our Ode (Greek text) :

"Two-and-thirty are they who sing praises."

IN THE WRITINGS OF PHILO JUDÆUS.

But already a century before Rabbi Shimeon, Philo of Alexandria was filled with the idea of the Mystic Union or Sacred Marriage ; it was the favourite doctrine of his circle and of similar circles of allied mystics of the time. I have already at length (*H*. i. 216-224) set forth his doctrines on the subject, with full references to his works, and must here be content with a few quotations only, which embody the doctrine, apart from the scriptural references which he would have us take as the foundation on which the doctrine is built ; whereas it is quite evident that the doctrines were shared in by many who had no knowledge of the Covenant-documents, and that it is Philo himself who accommodates the scripture of his race to the doctrines.

Philo writes :

"But it is not lawful for Virtues, in giving birth to their many perfections, to have part or lot in a mortal husband. And yet they will never bring forth of themselves without conceiving their off-spring of another."

"Who, then, is He who soweth in them their glorious progeny, if not the Father of Wholes—the God beyond all genesis, who yet is Sire of everything that is ? For, for Himself, God doth create no single thing, in that He stands in need of naught ; but for the man who prays to have them He creates all things."

And again :

"God is both Home, the incorporeal Land of incorporeal ideas, and Father of all things, in that He did create them, and Husband of Wisdom, sowing for the race of mankind the seed of blessedness into good virgin soil.

"For it is fitting God should converse with an undefiled, an untouched and pure nature, with her who is in very truth *the* Virgin, in fashion very different from ours.

"For the congress of men for the procreation of children makes virgins wives. But when God begins to associate with the soul, He brings it to pass that she who was formerly woman becomes virgin again. For banishing the foreign and degenerate and non-virile desires, by which it was made womanish, He substitutes for them native and noble and pure virtues. . . .

"Wherefore is it not fitting that God, who is beyond all genesis and all change, should sow in us the ideal seeds of the immortal virgin virtues, and not those of the woman who changes the form of her virginity ? "

Thus, speaking of the impure soul, Philo writes :

. "For when she is a multitude of passions and filled with vices, her children swarming over her—pleasures, appetites, folly, intemperance, unright-eousness, injustice—she is weak and sick, and lies at death's door, dying ; but when she becomes sterile, and ceases to bring them forth, or even casts them from her, forthwith, from the change, she becometh a chaste virgin, and receiving the Divine Seeds she fashions and engenders marvellous excellencies that nature prizeth highly—prudence, courage, temperance, justice, holiness, piety, and the rest of the virtues and good dispositions."

So also speaking of the Therapeutrides, · the women-disciples of the Therapeut communities, he writes :

"Their longing is not for mortal children, but for a deathless progeny, which the soul that is in love with God can alone bring forth, when the Father

THE WEDDING-SONG OF WISDOM.

hath sown into it the spiritual Light-beams, by means of which it shall be able to contemplate the laws of Wisdom."

And a little later he adds :

"And Wisdom, who, after the fashion of a mother, brings forth the self-taught Race, declares that God is the Sower of it."

And yet again, speaking of this spiritual progeny, he writes :

"But all the Servants of God (Thera-peuts) who are lawfully begotten, shall fulfil the law of their nature, which commands them to be parents. For the men shall be fathers of many sons, and the women mothers of many children."

They shall be true Godfathers and Godmothers.

Still contemplating the mystery, though from another standpoint, he writes :

"For some Wisdom judges entirely worthy of living with her, while others seem as yet too young to support such admirable and wise house-sharing ; these latter she hath permitted to solemnize the preliminary initiatory rites of Mar-riage, holding out hopes of its future consummation."

But, indeed, Philo is never weary of descanting on what he evidently regarded as the highest consummation of the holy life, the *raison d'être* of which he sets forth as follows :

"We should, accordingly, understand that the True Reason [*Logos = Âtman* in Sanskrit] of nature has the potency of both father and husband for different purposes—of a husband, when He casts the seed of virtues into the soul as into a good field ; of a father, in that it is His nature to beget good counsels, and fair and virtuous deeds, and when He hath begotten them, He nourisheth them with

those refreshing doctrines which Dis-cipline and Wisdom furnish.

"And the Intelligence [*Buddhi* in Sanskrit] is likened at one time to a virgin, at another to a wife, or a widow, or one who has not yet a husband.

"It is likened to a virgin, when the Intelligence keeps itself chaste and un-corrupted from pleasures and appetites, and griefs and fears, the passions which assault it ; and then the Father who begot it, assumes the leadership thereof.

"And when she (Intelligence) lives as a comely wife with comely Reason (*Logos*), that is with virtuous Reason, this self-same Reason Himself undertakes the care of her, sowing, like a husband, the most excellent concepts in her.

"But whenever the soul is bereft of her children of prudence, and her Marriage with Right Reason, widowed of her most fair possessions, and left desolate of wisdom, through choosing a blame-worthy life—then, let her suffer the pains she hath decreed against herself, with no Wise Reason to play physician to her transgressions, either as husband and consort, or as father and begetter."

As examples of Philo's allegorizing art we may append two instances. Refer-ring to Jacob's dream of the white and spotted and otherwise marked kine, Philo insists that it must be taken allegorically. The first class of souls, he says, are "white."

"The meaning is that when the Soul receives the Divine Seed, the first-born births are spotlessly white, like unto light of utmost purity, to radiance of the greatest brilliance, as though it were the shadowless ray of the sun's beams from a cloudless sky at noon."

Even the realistic primitive-culture story of Tamar does not dismay him, for he writes :

"For being a widow she was com-manded to sit in the House of the Father,

THE WEDDING-SONG OF WISDOM.

the Saviour; for whose sake for ever abandoning the congress and association with mortal things, she is bereft and widowed of all human pleasures, and receives the Divine quickening, and, full-filled with the Seeds of Virtue, conceives and is in travail with fair deeds. And when she brings them forth, she carries off the trophies from her adversaries, and is inscribed as Victor, receiving as a symbol the palm of victory."

Every stage of this Divine conception or self-regeneration is but a shadow of the mystery of cosmic creation, which Philo sums up as follows :

"We shall . . . . be quite correct in saying that the Maker who made all this universe, is also at the same time Father of what has been brought into existence ; while its Mother is the Wisdom of Him who hath made it—with whom God united, though not as man with woman, and implanted the power of Genesis. And she, receiving the Seed of God, brought forth with perfect labour His only beloved Son whom all may perceive—this cosmos."

Did Philo in all this write all he knew ; or is he raising one veil of the mystery only ? Virtue is most admirable, the very foundation of the whole building, but virtues are also powers, and regenera-tion spells actual re-birth and per-fectioning on all planes, and in all states.

IN THE NEW TESTAMENT.

Before giving some indications of how the Gnostics regarded the mystery of the Sacred Marriage, we may set down a summary of what Paterson has to say from an orthodox Biblical standpoint, on "Marriage as a Symbol of Spiritual Truths," in his article in Hastings' *Diction-ary of the Bible* (Edinburgh, 1900), whence all the references can be obtained.

The germ of the idea has been traced by Robertson Smith to Semitic "heathen-ism" where the God was regarded as the husband of the motherland.

After Hosea it became a commonplace of prophecy that Yahweh was to Israel as a Bridegroom and Israel to Yahweh as a Bride. This conception passed over into Christianity with modifications — the Bridegroom being now God in Christ, and the Bride the Church, the spiritual Israel chosen out of every nation.

"How large a portion of the body of Christian doctrine may be set forth, and with the sanction of Scripture, under the category of the marriage relation, may be briefly indicated :

"(1) Under *the doctrine of God* this representation . . . . lays special stress on the attributes of clemency and long - suffering, while it safeguards the holiness of God by showing Him grieved and provoked to anger by contumacy and unfaithfulness. [This is a very human point of view.—G.R.S.M.]. As husband God also provides for his people.

"(2) *The doctrine of sin* is, from this point of view, characterized as adultery— a designation which, as regards (a) *the nature of sin*, indicates that its essence consists in indifference or even hatred towards God, and the giving of the affec-tions towards other objects ; (b) *the heinousness of sin* draws attention to its aggravation as unfaithfulness to solemn obligations and ingratitude for high fa-vours ; and (c) *the punishment of sin* teaches that persistance in it entails a casting-off, of which human divorce is a pale emblem."

The Jewish mystics had manifestly reached a higher ideal in Philo's time, and the Christian Gnostics followed on them.

"(3) In the Christological doctrine the points which are chiefly emphasized by the conception are the love of Christ, His kingly office as exercised in His head-ship over the Church, and His intimate union with it through the indwelling spirit."

THE WEDDING-SONG OF WISDOM.

The key-passages are *I. Cor.* xi. 2:

"For I am jealous over you with a jealousy of God : for I espoused you to one husband, that I might present you .as a pure virgin to Christ."

And the *Letter to the Ephesians,* v. 23-32 :

"For the husband is the head of the wife, as Christ also is the Head of the Church, being Himself the Saviour of the Body. . . . Even as Christ also loved the Church, and gave Himself up for it; that he might sanctify it, having cleansed it with the Laver of Water by the Word, that He might present the Church to Himself a glorious [Bride] not having spot or wrinkle or any such thing; but that she should be holy and without blemish. . . . . This mystery is great : but I speak in regard of Christ and the Church."

The last words seem to mean that Paul, or (if it be preferred) whoever wrote the Letter, knew that the above was one interpretation only, and that there was another and more intimate revelation of the mystery, when the individual Soul gathered together the Church, or Assembly, of its scattered Members or Powers, as in the Osiric Mystery.

But to return to Paterson's by no means inspiring and clumsily worded exposition :

"(4) In close relation to the last, the doctrine of the Church is elucidated and enriched by the assertion of its mystical union with and dependence upon Christ, and of its essential note of sanctity— the latter, which includes all the graces included in sanctification, being beautifully portrayed as the bridal adornment.

"(5) Finally, as regards eschatology, the figure concentrates attention on the momentous event of the Second Coming, which is sudden as the coming of the bridegroom, and places in a clear light the bliss, the security, and unutterable glory of the everlasting kingdom."

It can hardly be said that the writer has made it clear that he regards the mystery, which Paul calls "great," as veiling an intense and immediate meaning independent of the Church as orthodoxly understood. The terms "symbol" and "figure" are clearly used rhetorically and not mystically, as it were things we have now outgrown. But to the mystic it is all far otherwise ; the Second Coming is an eternal fact, perpetually happening ; the Union is of like nature.

But before we can understand the Gnostic point of view some indications of the nature of Wisdom as the World-Soul and individual soul must be attempted.

WISDOM.

In all the ancient great religions the Power whereby the God brought Himself into manifestation was regarded as His Divine Spouse ; and so it is even to-day in Indian theosophy, every God has his Shakti or Power, every Deva his Devī. This was apparently (apart from Judaism) a common feature in all the ancient Semitic traditions, as may be seen in the Phœnician cosmogony preserved in the *Histories* of Philo Byblius (*H.* i. 122 ff.).

In Babylonian cosmogony the Spouse of the Supreme was Wisdom. Wisdom dwelt in the Depths of the Great Sea with Ea the Creative Deity. Ea is the Bēl-nimequi, the Lord of Unfathomable Wisdom ; *emēqu=* to be deep, and to be wise. The Deep or Depth is, therefore, symbol of Unfathomable Wisdom ; compare Apsū=Waterdeep and House of Wisdom. (See Hehn, p. 2, in the work referred to later on, p.248).

The post-exilic scriptures of the Hebrews (and pre-exilic for a matter of that) were strongly tinctured with Babylonian ideas, and a Wisdom-literature was gradually developed which later on became strongly

THE WEDDING-SONG OF WISDOM.

influenced by the "philosophizing" of Hellas. This Ḥokmah-literature (for references see Kohler's art. "Wisdom" in *The Jewish Encyclopædia*) was partly included in the later canon, but the major part of it, of which large portions have been lost, was apocryphal.

In the now canonical literature Wisdom was regarded as "the all-encompassing Intelligence of God, the Helper of the Creator, the Foundation of the World.

"In exact proportion as Israel's God was believed to be the God of the universe, Wisdom was regarded as the Cosmic Power, God's Master-Workman [lit. Master-Workwoman] and His Designer, while at the same time Wisdom became the law of life and the Divine guide and ruler of man. . . .

"Under the influence of Greek philosophy Wisdom became a divine agency of a personal character, so that Philo terms it . . . the Mother of the Creative Word. . . .

"In Christian and Gentile Gnosticism Wisdom became the centre of speculation."

In the last sentence we would reverse the order, the doctrines were Gentile first of all and were later Christianized.

The orthodox Jews, with their fanaticism for the exclusive masculine, regarded Wisdom as a Constructive Formative Energy. The Gnostics regarded Her as a Conceptive, all-encompassing Power, that received and brought forth the Ideas of the Divine Mind, and manifested the Divine Laws.

In brief, Wisdom was the World-Soul for cosmos, and the individual soul for man; and what specially interested the Gnostics, what indeed is the special interest of all mystics, was that the myth of the one was the myth of the other. To use Sanskrit terms, she is Mahā-buddhi, Great Buddhi, the World-Soul or Divine Instinct, and individual Buddhi in man. We will, therefore, turn to the doctrines of the Christianized Gnosis on this mystery.

Wisdom (Ḥokmah in Hebrew, Sophia in Greek, both feminine) dwelt with God before the Creation of the World, and sported continually before Him (*Proverbs*, viii.). Wisdom is the *Lĭlā* or Sport of Deity, His *Māyā* in Sanskrit, which does not mean Illusion, but rather Creative Power, from *mā*, to measure.

In the "Syrian Gnosis," perhaps the oldest form of the Christianized Gnosis, to Wisdom is assigned both the conception of the manifested worlds and the production of its Seven Ruling Powers (the Hebdomad). She herself was throned above them all, in the Place of the Midst (the Ogdoad), between the Spiritual World proper, that is the Divine Mind (the Plērōma or Fulness) and the Sensible World (the Kenōma or Emptiness, or Hysterēma or Insufficiency). The same idea is seen in *Proverbs*, ix. 1 (LXX.) :

"Wisdom hath built for herself a House and underpropped it with Seven Pillars."

What these Seven may be we will enquire later on. They are referred to in "her Pillars beneath" of our Syriac Ode (l. 8).

That there was already a fully developed Gnosis among the Jewish Mystics when the Proverbs-collection was compiled, may be seen from the graphic description (viii. 2, LXX.) :

"Wisdom is on the lofty Heights ; she standeth in the Midst of the Paths ; for she sitteth by the Gates of the Mighty, and singeth Hymns at the Entrances."

The Gnostics knew that this referred to Sophia sitting in the Place of the Midst, above the Seven Fate-spheres, in the Eighth or Ogdoad, at the Gates of the Mighty, that is the Entrances of the Plērōma or Fulness, the Shekinah, to which the Paths of Return lead.

She is thus the Mediatrix between the Upper and the Lower, and brings forth the mundane appearances after the spiritual

THE WEDDING-SONG OF WISDOM.

prototypes. She is thus called Mother, and Mother of the Living. (All the references may be obtained from Lipsius' art. "Sophia," in Smith and Wace's *Dict. of Christ. Biog.*). She is also called Light-Mother or Shining Mother, and the Power Above, and from her all spiritual souls draw their origin.

But how is it that the Divine Spouse, in bringing the universe into manifestation, had herself apparently fallen from the Perfection, and stood between it and the Imperfection ? There were many myths which speculated concerning this mystery, but as it would take several small volumes to set them forth in detail, we must content ourselves with a few brief indications only.

To quote from Lipsius (*loc. cit.*) :

"The fate of the 'Mother' was regarded as the prototype of what is repeated in the history of all individual souls, which being of heavenly pneumatic [spiritual] origin, have fallen from the upper World of Light, their Home, and come under the sway of evil powers, from whom they must endure a long series of sufferings in transmigration till a Return to the Upper World be vouchsaded them. . .

"It was . . . . taught that the souls of the Pneumatici [Spiritual], having lost the remembrance of their heavenly derivation, required to become once more partakers of Gnosis, or knowledge of their own pneumatic essence [not intellectual but spiritual knowledge therefore], in order to make a Return to the Realm of Light. In the impartation of this Gnosis consists, according to the doctrine common to all Gnostics, the Redemption brought and vouchsaded by Christ to all pneumatic souls. But the various fortunes of all such souls were wont to be contemplated in those of this mythical personage Sophia, and so it was taught that the Sophia also needed Redemption wrought by Christ, by whom she is delivered from her [spiritual] ignorance and her passions, and will at the end

of the World's development [in the case of individual souls at the end of *their* development or evolution, that is when perfected] be brought back to her long-lost Home, the Upper Plērōma, into which this Mother will find an entrance along with all pneumatic souls, her children [in the case of the individual soul, her powers, that is the powers of her past lives which are worthy of immortality], and there, in the Heavenly Bridal Chamber, celebrate the Marriage Feast of Eternity."

In the Gnostic systems mangled by Irenæus, "the cosmogonies of Syrian paganism have a preponderating influence."

In one of these we are told of the creation of man, whom the Sophia uses as a means to deprive the Opposing Powers of the Light they have stolen, "of the perpetual conflict on his Mother's part with the self-exalting efforts of the Archontes [the Rulers or Opposing Powers, without whom, however, there would be no manifestation], and of her continuous striving to recover again and again the Light-spark [Ātmic or Spiritual energy] hidden in human nature, till, at length, Christ [the Logos] comes to her assistance and, in answer to her prayers, proceeds to draw all the Sparks of Light to Himself, unites himself with Sophia as the Bridegroom with the Bride, descends on Jesus [purified man] who has been prepared, as a pure vessel for His reception, by Sophia [Jesus as the purified soul is also Sophia from another point of view], and leaves him again before the crucifixion [here meaning the death of the body], ascending with Sophia into the Æon that will never pass away."

One of the names given to Wisdom by the Gnostics was Prunicus (Προύνικος) which is generally rendered the Lustful or Lewd, but which mystically refers to "her attempts to entice away again from the Cosmic Powers [the Powers

THE WEDDING-SONG OF WISDOM.

forth to procreation] the Seeds of Divine Light."

She is called the Harlot, because she unites with the Light-sparks. Thus in the Simonian legend, Helen (Sophia), the consort of Simon (Shamash, the Sun, the Christ), is fabled to have been a harlot whom he picked up in a brothel at Tyre. This betrays a Phœnician background, and Tyre probably equates with the Jerusalem Below, and Egypt, the manifested world of physical nature.

The Sophia was further regarded as the World-Womb, and the symbolism worked out instructively for the mystic. This is the Jagad-yoni of the Hindus.

All these theories are ancient, and certainly did not derive from the "Wisdom" of the Old Testament; it was rather the latter that was accommodated to them. We, therefore, agree with Lipsius when he writes :

" It is obvious that all these cosmogonic theories have their source or archetype *not* in the Sophia of the Old Testament, but in the Thalatth or Moledet of Syrian paganism, the Life-Mother of whom Berossus has so much to relate, or in the World-Egg out of which when cloven asunder Heaven and Earth and all things proceed."

It is true that some very ancient wisdom was at the back of it all, whether originating with Thalatth or not, and modern science entirely corroborates this ancient wide-spread mysticism ; indeed it is difficult to find a symbolism that works out more naturally and satisfactorily.

Another name for Sophia used by the Greek-writing Gnostics was Achamōth, the transliteration of the Aramaic Ḥachmūth (= Hebrew Ḥokmah). Another of her names, of which, however, the derivation is very uncertain, is Barbēlō, or Barbērō. In the *Pistis Sophia* (p. 361), Barbēlō is the Mother of the repentant or returning Sophia, the human soul.

If in one of her aspects she was called the Harlot, equally so was she called the Virgin and Virgin of Light.

In the system of Bardaiṣān, Ḥachmūth gives birth to two daughters, probably typifying the twin soul of man, who are poetically called "Shame of the Dry Land" and "Image of the Waters," earthy and watery. We also hear of "the Maiden who, having sunk down from the upper Paradise, offers up prayers . . . for help from above, and being heard, returns to the joys of the Upper Paradise."

As the Mother of the twin daughters, Ḥachmūth is elsewhere called by Bardaiṣān the Holy Dove, that is the Divine Mother Bird, who lays and hatches both cosmic and human "Eggs." The two poetical names given to the daughters of Ḥachmūth, Wisdom (Buddhi), have hitherto proved an insoluble puzzle. The Mother, however, is always on the substance side of things, and therefore her daughters, as all daughters must be, are equally on the substance side. Now the "Image of the Waters," is also referred to as the "type of the watery body." The names may thus designate the cosmic prototypes of what in the individual are the subtle or watery vehicle, and the gross or physical vehicle.

That this is not so wild a speculation may be seen from the Hellenistic mystery-poem known as the *Chaldæan Oracles*, consisting of Chaldæan (that is, Syrian) stuff elaborately "philosophized." In them (*frgs.* 124,180,181), the physical body is characterized as the "dung" (? = "shame") of gross matter (*hylē*). This Hylē or Gross Matter is not regarded as the Fruitful Substance of the Universe, the "Land flowing with Milk and Honey" (the Jerusalem Above, or Sophia, Mother of all living), but as the dry and squalid element beneath the Moon, which, Proclus tells us, is called in the Oracles, the "Unwatered," that is, which is in itself Unfruitful, the Desert as compared with the Promised Land.

Equally so as to " Image of the Waters "

THE WEDDING-SONG OF WISDOM.

we have information (*fr.* 149). For we read :

" Extend on every side the reins of Fire [Mind] to guide the unformed soul."

That is to say, constrain the flowing watery nature of the soul by means of the Fire of the Spirit ; and this seems also to be the meaning of the difficult fragment :

" If thou extendest Fiery Mind to flowing work of piety, thou shalt preserve thy body too."

This seems to mean that, when by means of purification the soul is made fluid—that is to say, is no longer bound to any configuration of external things, when it is freed from prejudice, or opinion, and personal passion and sentiment, and is " with pure purities now purified," as the *Mithriac Ritual* (p. 69) has it—then is this regenerated soul and plasm, the germ of the " perfect body," ready for union with the true Mind of the Father.

Speaking of the *Acts of Thomas*, Lipsius writes, after mentioning *The Hymn of the Soul* :

" Of the other hymns which are preserved in the Greek version more faithfully than in the Syriac text which has undergone Catholic revision, the first deserving of notice is the *Ode to the Sophia*, which describes the marriage of the ' Maiden ' with her Heavenly Bridegroom and her introduction into the Upper Realm of Light. This ' Maiden,' called ' Daughter of Light,' is not, as the Catholic reviser supposes, the Church, but Hachmūth (Sophia), over whose head the ' King,' *i.e.* the Father of the Living Ones [Light-sparks] sits enthroned ; her Bridegroom is, according to the most probable interpretation, the Son of the Living One, *i.e.* Christ. With her the Living Ones, *i.e.* pneumatic souls, enter into the

Plērōma, and receive the glorious Light of the Living Father, and praise along with the ' Living Spirit,' the ' Father of Truth ' and the ' Mother of Wisdom.' "

Much more could be written on this fascinating subject, but enough has now been given for our immediate purpose.

THE SACRED MARRIAGE IN CHRISTIAN GNOSTICISM.

Sufficient has already been said to show that among the Christian Gnostics the mystery of the Sacred Marriage or Mystic Union formed the chiefest of their innermost sacraments. It would be too long to pursue the subject in detail and bring together all the passages from the " Fragments of a Forgotten Faith "—which we are pleased to see Preuschen (p. 7) refers to as " *Denkmäler eines verschollenen Glaubens* " (the title of the German translation of *Fragments* being *Fragmente eines verschollenen Glaubens*, Berlin, 1902)—but two of the most striking may be set down. The first has already been referred to in the above quotations from Lipsius, but it is worth while to give a full translation from the Old Latin version of Irenæus' lost Greek (I. xxx. 12). Irenæus ascribes the doctrine to those whom he calls Ophites, but who called themselves simply Gnostics, and whom Theodoret calls Sethians. This important passage comes at the end of the Church Father's exposition of what in its cosmogony is evidently a pre-Christian system—probably an ancient and very generally held belief outside Jewry, the main outlines of which have already been given in the comments on *The Hymn of the Robe of Glory*, under the heading " The Dual Sonship " (pp. 116 f.). It runs as follows :

" And since she herself [Wisdom Below or in manifestation] had no rest either in heaven or on earth, in her distress she invoked the Mother [Wisdom Above] to her aid. Accordingly her Mother, the First Woman, had pity on the repentance

THE WEDDING-SONG OF WISDOM.

of her Daughter, and asked the First Man [the Father] that Christ [the Son] should be sent to help her. " So He emanated and descended to His own Sister, the Moistening of Light." That is, to the Light that had become watery or descended into the Watery Realms of Generation.

" And she, the Downward Sophia [that is the Wisdom tending downwards to matter], becoming conscious that her Brother was descending to her, both proclaimed His Coming through John, and made ready the Baptism of repentance, and adopted Jesus beforehand [that is, chose him as her Son]; so that the Christ descending might find a pure vessel. [The present reading of the rest of the sentence is hopeless.]

" He descended through the Seven Heavens, making Himself like to their Sons [that is, taking on the forms of their Rulers], and stage by stage emptied them of their Power [that is, the Light-sparks or Pneumatic souls that they had imprisoned]; for the whole Moistening of Light ran-together to Him.

" And the Christ descending into this World [of gross matter] first clothed Himself with His own Sister Sophia, and both were in bliss in mutual refreshment, the one with the other ; this is the Bridegroom and the Bride.

" Now Jesus being [re-] generated from the Virgin by the energizing of God, was wiser and purer and more righteous than all men ; [so] the Christ-blended-with-Sophia [two-in-one, male-female] descended on him, and he became Jesus-Christ."

To this we may append the following section (§13) to give the reader some idea of one of the great Gnostic traditions concerning Jesus. Irenæus continues :

" They say that many of his Disciples were not conscious of the Descent of the Christ upon him ; it was only when the Christ descended upon Jesus that he began to manifest powers and heal and announce the [hitherto] unknown Father and confess openly that he was Son of the First Man.

" At these things the Rulers and the Father of Jesus [that is, the Father of his body, the Demiurge or Former of the physical world, which they equated with the Jewish idea of God] grew angry and set to work to have him killed. The moment this was brought about the Christ - together-with - Wisdom departed into the Incorruptible Æon [Eternity], while it was the Jesus who suffered the death of crucifixion.

" Yet the Christ did not forget his [Beloved], but sent down from above a certain Power unto him, which raised him up in the body, in that body which they call both vital and spiritual ; for he sent the mundane elements [of his physical body] back again into the world.

" The Disciples, however, though they saw he had risen did not know him [after death], nay, [they did not really know] even Jesus himself [in life], whose Grace [that is, the ' certain Power '] rose from the dead. They say that this very great error prevailed among the Disciples, that they believed he had risen in a mundane body."

All previous translations have missed the meaning of *Gratia* (Grace) in the last sentence but one, taking " *cujus gratia* " to mean " for whose sake " or " through whom." It is sufficient to refer the reader to *The Hymn of Jesus* (pp. 139, 144, 147.), to show that the lost Greek original of Irenæus must have read *Charis*, one of the synonyms of Sophia in one of her aspects. That which rose from the " dead " was the Power or incorruptible " Body " of Light, the " Perfect Body," or " Robe of Glory "—or of " Power."

Our Ode sets forth the perfections of the Bride adorned for the Bridegroom ; but the mystery could be set forth from the complementary point of view as we

THE WEDDING-SONG OF WISDOM.

have already (p. 237) seen from Philo of Alexandria. In the Naassene Document, which so strikingly reveals to us the main moments in the evolution of one line of "Ophite" Gnostic tradition—(see *H.* i. pp. 139-198, "The Myth of Man in the Mysteries")—the early Hellenistic writer tell us :

"And the law is that after they have been initiated into the Little Mysteries [those of Generation], they should be further initiated into the Great [those of Regeneration]."

After describing the nature of the Lesser Mysteries, he adds :

"These are the Little Mysteries, and after men have been initiated into them, they should cease for a little, and become initiated in the Great."

Whereupon the early Jewish Gnostic comments :

"For this Mystery is the Gate of Heaven, and this is the House of God, where the Good God dwells alone ; into which House no impure man shall come—but it is kept under watch for the Spiritual alone ;—where, when they come, they must cast away their garments, and all become Bridegrooms, obtaining their true Manhood through the Virginal Spirit." (*H.* i. 180, 181.)

The Virginal Spirit is the Great Mother, the Sophia Above. This reminds us strongly of the primitive-culture initiatory rite of "young-man-making" as it is called ; but that belongs to the most grossly realistic form of the Lesser Mysteries. What a marvellous transformation is wrought in passing from the Below to the Above, into the Greater Mysteries, which the later Christian Gnostic commentator rightly characterizes as Heavenly !

The Rite of the Sacred Marriage must have been dramatically set forth in some of the inner rituals of the Christianized Gnosis. At any rate we definitely know that this was the case among the Marcosians, for Irenæus (I. xxi. 3), tells us :

"Some of them prepare a Bridal Chamber and celebrate a mystery-rite with certain invocations on those who are being perfected ; and they declare that what is being solemnized by them is a Sacred Marriage, in likeness with the Unions Above."

It has already been pointed out, in treating of that marvellously interesting early Christian Gnostic Ritual of Initiation known as *The Hymn of Jesus*, (p. 144), that "the ultimate end of the Gnosis was the at-one-ment or union of the little man with the Great Man, of the human soul with the Divine Soul " ; indeed, one of the chief keys to the interpretation of some of the most striking formulæ of this Ritual is that of the Sacred Marriage. It will not be out of place here to repeat one or two of these sentences. The neophyte impersonates the purified human soul or Sophia, and the Initiator or Master is the Christ.

"I would be wounded."

Or "I would be pierced." This suggests the entrance of the Ray, the Higher Self, into the Heart, whereby the "Knot in the Heart," as the Upanishads phrase it, may be unloosed, or dissolved, or in order that the purified Lower Self may receive the Divine Radiance of the Higher. This interpretation is borne out by the alternative reading from an old Latin translation, which may have originated in a gloss by one who knew the mystery, for he writes : "I would be dissolved " ; that is, "consumed by love."

And so we continue with the mysteries of this truly Sacred Marriage or Spiritual Union.

"I would be begotten."

THE WEDDING-SONG OF
WISDOM.

This is the Mystery of the Immaculate Conception or Self-birth (p. *146.*)

" I would be adorned.'

The original Greek term suggests the idea of " rightly ordered " (*kosmein*). It may also mean " clothed in fit garments " ; that is, the soul prays that her little cosmos which has been previously out of order may be made like unto the Great Order, and so she may be clad in " Glories" or " Robes of Glory," or " Power," like unto the Great Glories of the Heavenly Spheres.

" I would be at-oned."

We now approach the Mystery of Union, when the soul abandons with joy its separateness, and frees itself from the limitations of its " possessions "—of that which is " mine " as apart from the rest (p. *149.*)

Enough has now been given to assure the reader that the Sacred Marriage was a fundamental mystery with the Christian Gnostics. We may next turn to the Trismegistic Gnosis.

IN THE TRISMEGISTIC GNOSIS.

Thus in the Sacred Sermon called " The Key," we read (§22) :

" Further there is an intercourse, or communion (*koinōía*), of souls ; those of the gods have intercourse with those of men, and those of men with souls of creatures which possess no reason.

" The higher, further, have in charge the lower ; the gods look after men, men after animals irrational, while God hath charge of all ; for He is higher than them all and all are less than He." (*H.* ii. 155, 173.)

Again in the Discourse called " The Secret Sermon on the Mountain," we read (§§1,2) :

" *Tat.* Wherefore I got me ready, and made the thought in me a stranger to the world-illusion.

" And now do thou fill up [suggesting the Plērōma] the things that fall short [suggesting the Hysterēma or Kenōma (*cf.* p. *55*)] in me with what thou saidst would give one the tradition of Re-birth [or Regeneration], setting it forth in speech or as the secret way.

" I know not, O Thrice-greatest one, from out what matter and what womb Man [the Spiritual Man] comes to birth, or of what seed.

" *Hermes.* Wisdom that understands in Silence [such is the Matter and the Womb from out which Man is born], and the True Good the Seed.

" *Tat.* Who is the sower, father ? For I am altogether at a loss.

" *Her.* It is the Will of God, my son.

" *Tat.* And of what kind is he who is begotten, father ? For I have no share of that essence in me that doth transcend the senses. The one that is begot will be another one from God, God's Son ?

" *Her.* All in all, out of all Powers composed. [*Cf.* the Christ as the Common Fruit of the Plērōma.]

" *Tat.* Thou tellest me a riddle, father, and dost not speak as father unto son.

" *Her.* This Race, my son, is never taught ; but when He willeth it, its memory is restored by God." (*H.* ii. 220, 221, 240 f.)

This is the Mystery of the Virgin Birth.

IN THE CHALDÆAN ORACLES.

This Mystic Union was also the supreme mystery of the Hellenized Mago-Chaldæanism to which the first century mystery-poem known as the *Chaldæan Oracles* belonged, as we have shown in two of these little volumes. Thus speaking of the fragment which set forth " The End of Understanding " we wrote :

THE WEDDING-SONG OF WISDOM.

"The whole instruction might be termed a method of *yoga* or mystic union (*unio mystica*) of the spiritual or kingly mind, the mind that rules itself—*Rāja-yoga*, the Royal Art proper" (p. 183.).

And again (p. 217): "Thus Proclus speaks of the soul, 'according to a certain ineffable At-one-ment, leading that-which-is-filled [or the Kenōma] into sameness with that-which-fills [or the Plērōma], making one portion of itself, in an immaterial and impalpable fashion, a receptacle for the In-shining, and provoking the other to the Imparting of its Light.' This, he says, is the meaning of the verse :
"'When the currents mingle in consummation of the Works of Deathless Fire.'"

Indeed the Pagan Mystics interpreted the Loves of the Gods in the only way it was possible to do so, namely, as Sacred Marriages, the Unions Above of the Marcosians (see p. 245 above). Thus Proclus, in his Commentary on Plato's *Parmenides* (ii. 214 ; Stallbaum—Leipzig, 1841—p. 602), writes :

"The Theologers riddle these [Divine operations] by means of the Sacred Marriages ; for without exception they call the like-natured combination and communion of the Divine Causes 'Marriage' in a mystic sense. Sometimes they see it in the co-ordinate [elements] and call it the Marriage of Hēra and Zeus, of Ouranos (Heaven) and Gē (Earth), of Kronos and Rhea ; sometimes in the inferior (or deficient) with the superior, and call it the Marriage of Zeus and Dēmētēr ; and again sometimes in the superior with the lower, and call it the Marriage of Zeus and Korē ; since of the Gods some are communions with the co-ordinate [elements], others with those prior to these, and again others with those subsequent to them ; and it is necessary to have a thorough understanding of the special character of each

[such union] and transfer such intertwining from the Gods [or Wholes or Genera] to the species [individuals or partial existences]."

The elements were considered as co-ordinates (σύστοιχα), that is, standing in the same row or order, or opposite (ἀντίστοιχα), that is, standing in opposite order or facing one another. Thus Air and Fire, Water and Earth, were regarded as co-ordinates, while Water and Fire, and Air and Earth, were considered opposites.

Indeed, we hear of a book entitled *What is Male and Female with the Gods, and what Marriage*, by Hipparchus the Stagirite (Lobeck, *Aglaophamus*—Königsberg, 1829—p. 608).

Many passages could be cited (Lobeck, *ibid.*, pp. 648 ff), but we may be content with two only.

Dio Chrysostom (xxxvi. 453), speaking of certain most sacred rites, says that :

"The Sons of the Sages in the Perfecting Rites that must not be disclosed, sing of the Blessed Marriage of Hēra and Zeus."

And Proclus again, in his Commentary on Plato's *Timæus* (i. 16), writes :

"That the same [Goddess] has union with different [Gods], and the same [God] with more [Goddesses], you may learn from the Mystic Discourses and what are called in the Mysteries the Sacred Marriages."

IN THE MITHRIAC MYSTERIES.

In the mystery-traditions the stages of inner development which the human soul passes through in its transmutation from mortality to immortality, from man to God, were set forth as births (and deaths also, and risings from the dead), and marriages. It is, moreover, not difficult for the experienced mystic to

THE WEDDING-SONG OF WISDOM.

assure himself by the knowledge of his own "passion" that there must be marriage or union before birth. Therefore, though in dealing with the highly instructive Ritual which preserves for us perhaps the innermost rite or mystic sacrament of the Mithriaca (*A Mithriac Ritual*, Vol. VI.), we treated it as a whole from the standpoint of Rebirth or Regeneration, there is in each stage implicitly a union before the birth of new consciousness. This is implicit and not declared in this particular Ritual; the consummation, however, is declared. The Coming of the God is the descent of his Higher Self into the man and the taking up of the man into Him. The Higher and the Lower Self are at length united. And so the last invocation prays:

"Oh Lord of me, abide with me within my Soul! Oh! leave me not!"

Then comes the end; even as on the Cross, the bitter cry: "My God, my God, why hast Thou forsaken me?"—and then, Death . . . and Triumph, Joy and Rebirth.

"O Lord, being born again (or from Above), I pass away in-being-made-Great, and, having-been-made-Great, I die.
"Being born from out the state of birth-and-death [Gk. *Genesis*, Sk. *Saṁsāra*], that giveth birth to mortal lives, I now, set free, pass to the state transcending birth, as Thou hast stablished it, according as Thou hast ordained and made the Mystery" (p. 93).

This is achieved after the "Doors" of the Heavens are thrown open for the third time, Doors within and within, to the without and without, three stages of extended consciousness, or deeper realization.
Now it is to be remarked that just as in our Ode the Bride stands waiting for the Coming of the Bridegroom surrounded by Seven Bridesmaids and Seven Brides-

men, so in the Mithriac Ritual the rubric declares that the symbolic vision preceding the Coming of the God shall be characterized as follows:

"Thou shalt behold the Doors thrown open, and issuing from the Depth, Seven Virgins. . . . . These are they who are the so-called Heaven's Fortunes. . .
"There come forth others, too—Seven Gods. . . . These are the so-called Heaven's Pole-lords" (p. 92).

It is enough to say that, mystically, the Ritual suggests the bringing into activity of seven twin-powers or sense-faculties in the new-born Perfect or Æonic Body, the Body of Wholeness, in which every sense is of the nature of wholeness, that is, this Body becomes all ear when it hears, all eye when it sees, and so forth.
But why Seven? The reader will of course reply: Because of the Seven Planets.

THE SEVEN.

But both mysticism and the most recent scholarship forbid this facile answer. The so-called Planets, the Five and the Sun and Moon, were at a comparatively late date accommodated to the Seven, and were not its origin. The instructive treatise of Dr. Johannes Hehn, *Siebenzahl und Sabbat bei den Babyloniern und im Alten Testament: Eine religionsgeschichtliche Studie*, in the *Leipziger semitische Studien*, Bd. ii., Hft. v. (Leipzig, 1907), leaves no doubt on the subject. VII., when translated by the Babylonians from the Sumerian, appears as: whole, totality, all=universum (pp. 4, 6, 52). This is Hehn's main contention, and he proves it in many ways. On p. 14 there is a hint that it means the Seven Directions [? of Space], but this suggestion he does not follow up. We will take up this point later on, for we know that *Dik* (in Sanskrit), the Directions of Space, is one of the chief categories of Indian philosophy.

THE WEDDING-SONG OF WISDOM.

VII., he says, is the expression of the highest Elevation, or Climax (compare the Stairway of the Neck of Wisdom in our Ode), of the highest Completion or Fulness (that is, Plērōma) and Power (p. 16).

Quoting from a text (p. 19), which speaks of "the Seven Limbs of the Father-house," he says, these naturally mean "all the Limbs" or Members. Compare this with the Pillars of our Ode, and the Pillars of the House of Wisdom in *Proverbs*.

Excellently, too, does he point out (p. 20), that in the Babylonian religion, "Nature, according to this view of the world, is not ruled over by dead Laws, but it is the out-working of living Personalities"—that is, Living Powers or Intelligences.

The VII., then, regarded as a Divine Power, "is not a Group of Gods, but is equivalent to the All-Godhead, and thus implies a comprehension of the whole pantheon" (p. 20).

Moreover, it is of interest to remark that 2×7 often occurs, as in the phrase "the Seven Gods, the Twin-Gods," who are the Great Gods of Heaven and Earth (pp. 20, 23).

Also again in the invocations, both in high magic and in sorcery, the Twice-Seven occur : "Seven are they, Seven are they, Twice-Seven are they!" (pp. 28, 30, 34).

But what is the origin of this "sacred" number ? The old theory of the planets, which has done service, without explaining anything, for so many centuries, must be abandoned, as Zimmern, Roscher, Schiarparelli and Wellhausen, among others, have pointed out in different lines of research (p. 44).

One thing is certain that the sacred character of the VII. goes back to very ancient times, to demonstrably pre-Babylonian days, for it is found as a commonplace in Sumerian culture (p. 46).

Moreover in Babylonian literature there are frequent groupings of stars (not planets), according to the principle of the hebdomad (p. 47).

Hehn, therefore, boldly declares that the cult of the planets was not *old* Babylonian, and reached its full development only in the Alexandrian period (p. 50).

It is true that the Planet-Gods were regarded in *later* Babylonian times as Patrons of the days of the week, but so also were other groups of Star-Gods, and the Planets were never specialized for this purpose. There was something more at the back of it all. What was it ?

Hehn adopts Roscher's theory (p. 50), that the Seven has its origin in the quartering of the days of the month.

Just as the Sun-number was 6 or 60, factors of the 360 days of the year, not counting the odd days, so was the Moon-number 7, a fourth of 28, the 1½ days, to make the proper total 29½, not counting. They dealt only with round numbers. The Moon was for the Babylonians the great time-measurer, the root of their calendar.

With this conclusion I would, with all due deference, venture to disagree. In this way *a* seven was found in natural phenomena, but was it the origin of *the* VII. If VII. was the Perfect Number in very ancient culture, as I think Hehn has proved, and as we shall see it can be shown along many other lines of research, then it is far more probable, in my opinion, that there was once a numbering by sevens, a system of notation where seven was the radix, just as we have in Babylon itself a duodecimal as well as a decimal system. But what lay at the back of this ? Why was it that VII. completed the series ; six, then seven, and then begin again ?

Is it so wild a partial hypothesis (for I believe still far more was at the back of it), that VII. completed or perfected the physical or visible, that is, brought it into manifestation, that there must be 6 before there was any appearance here ; that there must be the 6 directions complete, before anything could be seen ;

THE WEDDING-SONG OF WISDOM.

take away one, and our space is not. A three-dimensional thing that has no top, or bottom, etc., is unthinkable in our space. As to "directions," therefore, there must be first a Within and a Without, and either of these must be measured by 3 dimensions, 3 pairs, making 6 directions in all (up, down, right, left, front, back), *plus* a monad or unity of the 3 or 6. Further, there was a 7 Within and a 7 Without, making in all 7 Twins, male and female, positive and negative, etc. True we have not yet got at the root of the matter, but it is not so difficult to see that here we have a 1 (monad), a 2 (dyad, twins), and a 3 (triad); and again the permutations and combinations of 3 things taken 1 at a time, 2 at a time, and 3 at a time, or all together, are 7,— *e.g., a, b, c ; ab, ac, bc*; *abc*—according to the formula, 2^n-1.

How enormously wide-spread was this category of VII. may be seen by turning to the index of Gerald Massey's two massive volumes, *Ancient Egypt : The Light of the World* (London, 1907), where the references to "seven" occupy two columns. The germ of his theory (p. 25) is that :

"The Ancient Genetrix [the World-Mother] was the Mother who brought forth Seven Children at a birth, or as a companionship, according to the category of phenomena. Her Seven Children were the Nature-Powers of all mythology. They are visibly represented under divers types because the Powers were reborn in different phenomena."

This theory he develops with endless illustrations, it is the vital side and complement of the directions-hypothesis that I have indicated ; it is the feminine completion of the masculine directions— the Virgins and the Pole-lords of the Mithriac Ritual.

THE CHOIR OF THE ÆONS.

But indeed every God, or Divine Power, in the Babylonian religion had a special number, and the Number was the God ; and there is little doubt that Pythagoras derived his *mathesis* in the first place from initiation into the Babylonian mysteries.

The Gods were Æons, or Eternities, and it is interesting to remark that one of the names for a God in the Babylonian language is Igig ; this is probably the origin of the term Iynx (Gk. Iygx, pl. Iygges) which was discussed at length in *The Chaldæan Oracles* (p. 203).

The whole of the Christian Gnostic æonology is based on such Numbers, as may be seen from the study " Some Outlines of Æonology," in *Fragments* (2nd. ed., pp. 311 ff.). But we have already over-run our space, and cannot treat of the 10 and 12, and total, 32 or 33, of the whole Plērōma or Dynamic Pantheon, the Modes of the Divine Mind, Powers of the Divine Soul. The rest of our space must be given to a few necessary Notes.

NOTES.

The Radiance, Splendour or Resplendence (Syr. *ziwā*, Gk. *apaúgasma*), is the Avestan *hvarenō*, or Presence. (Cf. *A Mithriac Ritual*, p.   ). It is the Light of the Kings, the Royal Pair, God and the Spirit, or the Sophia Above.

She, the Sophia Below, or in manifestation, is now pure Nature decked with spring flowers, Buddhi, the Ground of Enlightenment, or Spiritual Soul.

The "sweet-odour" is the "sweet savour" of the Holy Spirit, as Basilides calls it (*F.* p. 264).

The King is Ātman, the Highest Self ; His Home is the Highest Heights, and He pours forth His Power into all the

THE WEDDING-SONG OF WISDOM.

Members of the Pure or Perfected Body. The Pillars are the totality of the Limbs, and not the vertebral column only (Hoffmann).

The Divine Ichōr from the Cup of Ātman (or Chrism) pours throughout her whole economy, and out at her feet, into the outer world.

The Two-and-thirty are a puzzle. Thilo suggested that they stand for the teeth. This may be so, for in the Naassene Document, the Jewish mystic commenting on the term " Rock " in a verse of Homer, writes :

" The ' Rock ' means Adamas. This is the ' Corner-stone ' which ' I insert in the foundation of Zion.'
" By this he (Isaiah) means, allegorically, the plasm of man. For the Adamas who is ' inserted ' is the [inner man, and the ' foundations of Zion ' are] the ' teeth ' —the ' fence of teeth,' as Homer says— the Wall and Palisade in which is the inner man, fallen into it from the Primal Man the Adamas Above, or [the Stone] ' cut without hands' cutting it, and brought down into the plasm of forgetfulness, the earthy, clayey [plasm]." (H. i. 162).

This shows that the " teeth " were regarded as symbols of the Palisade, a term used of the Limit of the Æon-World in Gnostic tradition. For this symbolism, however, the number 30 (which is found as a variant reading), would perhaps be more appropriate, for the Emanation of the Limit that shut off the Æonic Immensities from the imperfect manifested world, in one of the most famous variants of the Sophia-mythus known to us, comes as a 31st, after the completion of 30 (F. pp. 342 ff.).

Perhaps instead of " those (τοῖς) who enter " we should rather read " priests (ἱεροῖς) who enter."

The Head represents the Holy City, the Jerusalem Above, and also the Temple, or Shrine of the God, that was on top of the "Stairway" in the ancient Babylonian truncated pyramids (the Mexican teocallis). They were pyramid-like buildings of six stages, of diminishing area, on the top of which was the shrine of the God. Here again we have our 6 and the monad ruling them.

The Æons were all paired, male-female in one, wholenesses ; they were sometimes figured as set over against one another in rows, like the choirs or choruses of men and women singers and dancers in the Therapeut communities (F. pp. 80 f.). But in reality they were all Wholenesses, Two-in-one, called by twin names, such as Mind-and-Truth, Word-and-Life, Man-and-Church ; they were self-complementary and self-sufficient. The manifested worlds of separation and opposition arose, according to one of the most striking Wisdom-myths (F. pp. 335 ff.), through Wisdom, the last of the Æons, separating herself from her Divine Complement, and so falling into the realm of the opposites.

The Decad of Fingers are the twice Five Great Limbs. Thus in yet another Hymn to Wisdom, in The Acts of Thomas, we read :

" Thou Mother of Compassion, come ; come Spouse of Him, the Man ; come Thou Revealer of the Mysteries concealed ; Thou Mother of the Seven Mansions come, who in the Eighth hath found Thy Rest !
" Come Thou who art the Messenger of the Five Holy Limbs — Mind, Thought, Reflection, Thinking, Reasoning; commune with those of later birth ! "

The City and the Bride-chamber are the same—the most secret place.
In the Pistis Sophia the City is a synonym of the Inheritance, it is in the

THE WEDDING-SONG OF WISDOM.

Midst of the highest Plērōma (*P.S.* pp. 52, 198), to it leads the Gate of Life (p. 292).

From it, the Supernal Mouth, was born the Word of Prophecy, when the Secret Place was regarded as the within of the Head ; and it must be remembered that the Gods were all regarded as Heads, Spheres, as for instance among the Trismegistic Mystics.

See the Sacred Sermon called " The Key " (§11) :

" Since Cosmos is a sphere—that is to say, a head. . . .

" And head itself moved in a sphere-like way—that is to say, as head should move—is mind " (*H.* ii. 148).

The following Marcosian Ritual of the Sacrament of the Illumination of Prophecy (Iren. I. xiii. 3) is highly instructive in this connection. The Christ as Master addresses the Disciple :

" I would have thee share in My Grace [Glory, Power], since the Father of Wholes seeth thy Angel continually before His Face [that is, in His Presence].

" Now the Place of thy Greatness [that is Angel] is in Us. We must be at-oned.

" First receive from Me and through Me My Grace.

" Make thyself ready as a Bride receiving her Bridegroom, in order that thou mayest be what I am, and I what thou art.

" Dedicate in thy Bridal Chamber the Seed of Light.

" Take from Me thy Bridegroom, and make way for Him, and be made way for in Him.

" Lo ! Grace hath descended upon thee !

" Open thy mouth and prophesy ! "

The individual consummation of at-onement was of the same nature as the final consummation of the whole scheme of salvation. Concerning this we may again turn to Irenæus (I. vii. 1), who sums up the Valentinian doctrine on this point as follows :

" Now when the whole [Spiritual] Seed [the Sons of God] has been perfected, they say that Achamōth [Ḥachmûth, Sophia], their Mother, passes from the Place of the Midst and enters within the Plērōma, and receives the Saviour as her Bridegroom, Him who is the Forthbringing of all [the Æons, *viz.*, the Common Fruit of the Plērōma], so that there is Union of the Saviour and Sophia, who is Achamōth.

" And this is the Bridegroom and Bride, while the Bride-chamber is the whole Plērōma.

" The Spiritual [Pneumatici, that is the Redeemed or Regenerate], moreover, stripping off their [animal or irrational] souls [*cf.* the ' stripping off of the garments ' of the Naassene Document (p. above)], and becoming gnostic spirits [or intelligences], entering the Plērōma, without the Opposing Powers being able to detain or see them, are restored back again as Brides to the Angels who surround the Saviour."

And again (*ibid.* 5) :

" The Spiritual [Seeds] after they have been deemed worthy of perfection are restored as Brides to the Angels of the Saviour . . . to enjoy bliss for ever."

The " Great Ones " (μεγιστᾶνες) might perhaps be translated " Grandees," or " Satraps."

It is not quite clear what " both " refers to, unless to the company [Eg. *paut*] of the Bride, both male and female.

" Waste " mystically stands for " deficiency." Their food will henceforth be " Ambrosia," the " Food of Immortality," the Heavenly Manna, the Substance

THE WEDDING-SONG OF
WISDOM.

of the Plērōma, or Fulness, as set over against the food of earth, the delights of the world, the deficiency. But the Gnostics were also ascetics and yogins, and knew of the mysteries of the body. Thus the Valentinians taught that the "free utterance," or perfect expression, of the Alone Good can only be manifested by the man made perfect. Such an one was Jesus. And so we find Valentinus writing to Agathopus (Clem. Alex. *Strom.* III. vii. 59):

"It was by his unremitting self-denial in all things that Jesus digested divinity; he ate and drank in a peculiar manner without any waste. The power of continence was so great in him, that his food did not decay in him, for he himself was without decay" (*F.* p. 302).

The "power" referred to by Valentinus is one of the *siddhis* (powers) mentioned in every treatise on *yoga* (mystic union) in India, and in the Upaniṣhads we read that "very little waste" is one of the first signs of "success" in *haṭha-yoga*, the physical discipline of the art.

As to the Living Food—in reference to the Miracle of the Loaves, the writer of the Fourth Gospel puts the following *logos* into the mouth of the Master (*Joh.* vi. 27):

"Digest not the food that perisheth, but the food that abideth unto æonian life, which the Son of the Man shall give unto you, for on this hath the Father set His seal."

Burkitt, in his review of Preuschen, translates this line:

"Which is longed for and thirsted for by them who drink it."

We have already overstepped our space, and so must conclude with the hope that what has been written may help some of our readers towards a better understanding of the "great" Mystery of the Sacred Marriage, and therewith to a more vital interpretation of "The Wedding-Song of Wisdom."

A CONCORDANCE TO
THE CHALDEAN ORACLES

Introduction

As an aid to the study of the Chaldean Oracles, Mead's translations of the fragments have been re-presented here in a numbered format, and his referen--ces to the editions of Kroll and Cory have been corrected and expanded. Also included are the fragment numbers according to the standard modern edition of des Places.

It is unfortunate that the best known version of the Oracles in English is still that of W.Wynn Westcott. This work is distinctly misleading and is not to be recommended as an introduction to the subject. Westcott was happy to follow Cory's numeration and translation word for word, except for occasionally intoducing his own arbitrary alterations.

The starting point for modern investigation of the Oracles should be Lewy's work, now available in Michel Tardieu's splendid new edition. A concordance to the Oracles in Lewy, Kroll, des Places and works by P.Hadot and W.Theiler can be found there on pages 679 - 691.

Bibliography

KROLL = Wilhelm (Guilelmus) Kroll De Oraculis Chaldaicis, Breslau 1894.
[Reprint : Hildesheim (Georg Olms) 1962]

CORY = Isaac Cory Ancient Fragments, London 1832. [Reprint : Minneapolis (Wizard's Bookshelf) 1975]
cf W.Wynn Westcott (Sapere Aude) The Chaldean Oracles [Recommended edition Gillette (Heptangle) 1978].

DES PLACES = Édouard des Places Oracles Chaldaïques, Paris (Les Belles Lettres) 1971.
cf R.D.Majercik Chaldean Oracles (PhD thesis 1982, Univ. of California, Santa Barbara). Published on demand by University Microfilms.
Majercik is based on des Places.There is an extensive bibliog. on pps 452-465

Hans Lewy Chaldean Oracles and Theurgy 2nd ed. Paris (Études Aug.) 1978.

MEAD, CORY and DES PLACES (Maj.) are arranged by fragment number. KROLL is by page number.

CONCORDANCE

MEAD	KROLL	CORY	DES PLACES
1	11	61,162-3,166-7	1
2	11	43,44	20,20 bis
3	15	9	13
4	15	10	14
5	15	184	15
6	48	83	97
7	13	16	4
8	12	11	3
9	16	5,12	16
10	13	--	--
11	13	--	--
12	13	22	5
13	14	13	7
14	14	27,46	8
15	15	13	10
16	15	26	12
17	15	34	31
18	17	--	125
19	27	65	50
20	28	38	51
21	28	18	53
22	28	187	52
23	29	141	54
24	29	128	55
25	30	59	56
26	31	--	--
27	18	28	22
28	18	29	22
29	18	49	179
30	18	36	27
31	18	8	cf 23

CONCORDANCE

MEAD	KROLL	CORY	DES PLACES
32	18	31	28
33	18	30	29
34	51	170	2
35	18	168	18
36	19	--	21
37	19	--	152,207
38	19	99	30
39	19	55	32
40	19	55	32
41	19	55	32
42	27	71,72	49
43	--	2,3	cf 199
44	--	4	cf 199
45	20	24,101	34
46	20	66	35
47	22	--	6
48	21	17	36
49	23	39	37
50	24	--	38
51	25	107	39
52	25	23	42
53	26	81	44
54	26	--	45
55	26	82	43
56	27	35	182
57	28	38	51
58	31	120	57
59	33	--	--
60	33	130	59
61	33	131	185
62	33	133	60

CONCORDANCE

MEAD	KROLL	CORY	DES PLACES
63	33	135	61a
64	33	136	61b
65	33	129,139	61c
66	33-34	129,139	61d
67	34	137	61f
68	34	112	62
69	34	--	63
70	34	144	64, cf 107
71	35	92	65
72	65	124	167
73	35	117	67
74	35	108	68
75	64	152	104
76	35	110	69
77	36	125,140	70
78	36	--	71
79	36	--	168
80	36	171	72
81	37	73	40
82	37	37	73
83	40	40	76
84	40	54	77
85	40	--	191
86	40	52	--
87	40	--	--
88	40	41	--
89	40	--	--
90	40	33,64	79
91	41n2	--	223
92	41n2	194	206, cf. Maj.
93	41	57	80

CONCORDANCE

MEAD	KROLL	CORY	DES PLACES
94	42	63	81
95	42	56	82
96	19	99	30
97	42	--	83
98	42	7	84
99	42	--	85
100	43	58	177
101	43	--	24
102	43	--	86
103	43	111	87
104	44	--	78
105	44	--	cf 87
106	44 n1	--	78
107	44	191	88
108	45	197	90
109	45	75	91
110	45	76	92
111	46	--	93
112	46	78	25
113	47	18,79	94
114	47	20	96
115	47 n2	--	--
116	47	--	--
117	48	83	97
118	48	--	99
119	48	--	186
120	48	--	--
121	47 n1	--	95
122	48,64	--	cf Maj.105
123	48	--	cf Maj.105
124	61	147	158
125	48	--	100
126	49	--	101
127	49	148	101
128	49	149	102
129	50	153	103
130	50	94	106
131	50	47,80	108
132	50	164	109
133	51	172	110
134	51	170	2
135	(= Mead frag. 80)		
136	51	126	111
137	51	174	112
138	52	175	113
139	52	190	114(partial)
140	52	160	115
141	52	169	116
142	52	84	117
143	53	158	121
144	53	--	196 (partial)
145	53	--	122

CONCORDANCE

MEAD	KROLL	CORY	DES PLACES
146	53	--	123
147	53	88	124
148	53	--	126
149	53	173	127
150	54,61	176	128
151	54	90	130
152	54	--	171 (partial)
153	54	85	131
154	55	51	132
155	55	193	133
156	55	21	66
157	55,44	150	135
158	56	183	136
159	56	183	--
160	56	--	139
161	56	158	140
162	56	--	141
163	56	106	142
164	57	114	144
165	--	113	--
166	57	159	145
167	57	198	146
168	57	196	147
169	58	199	148
170	58	195	149
171	58	155	150
172	58	--	151
173	58	86	218
174	59	165	118
175	59	185	153
176	60	--	137
177	60	--	155
178	60	--	156
179	60	95	157
180	61	147	158
181	61	178	129
182	62	--	--
183	62	--	160
184	62	189	161
185	62	145	163
186	63	--	181
187	63	146	164
188	63	--	180
189	63	116	172
190	63	188	162
191	64	181	cf Maj. notes to fr.105
192	64	181	.. ,, ..
193	64	181	.. ,, ..
194	64	144	107